大使讲中国故事

Tell China's Story

让世界认识真实的中国

大使讲
中国故事

让世界认识真实的中国

刘晓明——著

Tell
China's
Story

中信出版集团 | 北京

图书在版编目（CIP）数据

大使讲中国故事 / 刘晓明著 . -- 北京 : 中信出版社 , 2022.12（2025.4 重印）
ISBN 978-7-5217-4938-0

Ⅰ . ①大… Ⅱ . ①刘… Ⅲ . ①对外政策－宣传工作－中国－学习参考资料 Ⅳ . ① D820

中国版本图书馆 CIP 数据核字（2022）第 211725 号

大使讲中国故事
著者：刘晓明
出版发行：中信出版集团股份有限公司
（北京市朝阳区东三环北路 27 号嘉铭中心　邮编　100020）
承印者：　河北鹏润印刷有限公司

开本：787mm×1092mm 1/16　正文印张：33.25　彩插印张：1　字数：535 千字
版次：2022 年 12 月第 1 版　印次：2025 年 4 月第 8 次印刷
书号：ISBN 978-7-5217-4938-0
定价：98.00 元

重磅推荐

新时代各级领导干部要带头做好国际传播工作，讲好中国故事，传播好中国声音，展示真实、立体、全面的中国。刘晓明大使持节英伦 11 载，其间发表 700 余场公开演讲，与英国各界深入坦率对话，为促进英国社会深化对华了解发挥了重要和积极的作用。这本书收录了刘晓明大使在英国期间具有代表性的演讲，话题不同、受众各异，但对中国发展观、文明观、安全观、人权观、生态观、国际秩序观和全球治理观的娓娓道来始终如一，是推进中国故事和中国声音全球化、区域化、分众化表达的良好范例，对我们全面把握“两个大局”，做好新时代国际传播工作有积极的借鉴意义。

——马建堂

国务院发展研究中心原党组书记

刘晓明大使是我的老朋友，他出使英国 11 年，其间正是中国政治、经济、社会、外交等各领域发展变化最快最好的时期。作为大使如何让驻在国社会各界人士了解中国的变化，推动中英关系不断扩大共识、促进对话、探索合作、互谅互让非常重要。刘大使在 11 年间面对全英各地各界各种各样的听众，发表了 700 多场演讲，用西方人听得到、听得懂、听得进的国际语言，讲述了中国故事，诠释中国政策和行动，发挥了很好的作用。我参加气候变化多边谈判 13 年，深知做到这一点非常不容易，也很不简单。刘晓明大使在让世界了解中国、讲好中国故事方面，进行了积极有效的探索和实践，值得我们学习和借鉴。在此，向《大使讲中国故事》出版表示衷心的祝贺！

——解振华

中国气候变化事务特使　原国家环境保护总局局长

国家发展和改革委员会原副主任

刘晓明大使自 2010 年起出任中国驻英国大使，栉风沐雨，耕耘不辍，历经 11 载春秋，为促进中英友好交往付出良多。在这 11 年中，他是中英关系跌宕起伏最直接的见证者和参与者，也是中英两国交流中最坚实的桥梁。这期间恰是中国政治、经济、社会、文化、外交等各个领域发展变化最快最好的时期，中国整体面貌堪称日新月异。同时，随着我国综合国力和国际地位不断提升，越来越多的国家和国际人士渴望了解中国。所以，如何将这不断发展的新中国讲给世界听，是中国驻外大使工作的重中之重。

刘晓明大使持节英伦期间，在政、商、文化各界发表了 700 余场公开演讲，在主流报刊撰文 170 多篇，接受主流媒体采访 170 多次，被称为“上镜率最高”“被媒体引用次数最多”的外国驻英使节。他讲的中国故事，让英国各界的听众“听得到、听得懂、听得进、听而信”，为促进英国社会深化对中国的了解发挥了举足轻重的作用，堪称公共外交的典范。

这本书选取了刘晓明大使驻英期间发表的 35 篇演讲，围绕“讲好中国故事”这个主题，从中国国情、治国理政、和平发展、外交、国防、改革开放、机遇等多个方面介绍中国，推动世界认识一个真实、立体、全面的中国。同时，每篇演讲均以中英双语的形式展现，读者在欣赏刘大使精彩演讲的同时，也能见识到大国外交家的英语思维和行文智慧，了解如何用西方的语言讲中国的故事。这的确是一本难得的讲中国故事的教科书。

放眼 21 世纪，“读懂中国”已成为当今中外各界人士的迫切需求，讲好中国故事已成为当代显学，并贯穿于中华民族伟大复兴的全过程。真诚希望更多人能加入“讲好中国故事”的伟大事业中，为促进中国与世界的交流和合作，为构建人类命运共同体，建立和平发展、开放合作、多彩和谐的世界贡献一份力量。

——郑永年

香港中文大学（深圳）教授　前海国际事务研究院院长

刘晓明是迄今为止中华人民共和国驻联合王国任期最长的大使。他的任期正值中国发挥越来越重要的经济和战略大国作用，同时也跨越了中英关系的重大高潮和低谷。这本书反映了他任期内中英关系的演变，同时也使我们看到中国希望怎样向西方公众展示它日益增长的实力。在出使英国的 11 年里，刘晓明在运筹中英关系中扮演了一个主要角色。这本书就是一部重要的历史记录。

——菲利普·哈蒙德勋爵

英国议会上院议员　英国前外交大臣　英国前财政大臣

Liu Xiaoming was the longest-serving Ambassador to date of the People's Republic of China to the United Kingdom and his tenure covered a period in which China's importance as an economic and a strategic power increased enormously. It also coincided with significant high points and low points in the UK-China relationship. This collection of essays by Ambassador Liu reflects that evolution of the UK-China relationship over the period of his tenure and also throws important light on how China wished to present its growing power to a Western audience. Over the eleven years he was in London, Liu Xiaoming became a major player in the conduct of UK-China relations and this collection represents an important historic record.

—Rt Hon the Lord Hammond of Runnymede

Former Foreign Secretary of State

Former Chancellor of the Exchequer

1949年中国共产党建立新中国后，“破冰者”踏上克服根本性政治对立的艰难旅途，重新打开一条中英之间互联互通道路，重建贸易自由流动，随之而来的是人员自由流动。

2012年后，中国恢复了其经济透明度，重新发挥全球作用。与此同时，中国经济实力增强，世界政治中心日益向亚洲转移，中国在世界上发挥了越来越大的作用。亚洲崛起首先是基于低劳动力成本，然后是创新。中国也走上了类似的道路。

1971年，中国重返联合国，逐渐成为参与全球问题讨论的重要成员。2012年之后，“破冰者”以及其他中国的朋友建议应当让世界更加容易听到中国的声音，并且更多地使用西方国家的语言讲中国的故事。

刘晓明大使是中国向西方思想开放的先驱，他擅长利用媒体和电视平台，但最能引起共鸣的还是他的演讲。他是一位善用西方的语言、熟悉西方媒体主持人游戏规则的中国高级外交官。他的演讲更加重要，因为他用易于理解的语言讲述了更大的故事。他对英语的熟练运用，以及他对西方人处事方式的了解，都是非常宝贵的能力。他从不害怕面对必要的事实并坚持自己的立场，他还帮助年轻外交官学会如何与西方受众沟通、宣介。他助力改变了中国外交在世界舞台上的作用，这将对未来几十年产生深远影响。

他是一个真正的“破冰者”。

——斯蒂芬·佩里

英国四十八家集团俱乐部主席 “中国改革友谊奖章”获得者

The Icebreakers helped reopen an old road of connectivity between China and the UK following the 1949 assumption of national leadership in China by the CPC. it was not a simple road because of fundamental political opposition but the natural flow of trade was rebuilt, and then the flow of people to people.

Later after 2012 China had returned to its economic clarity and global role. At the same time China played an increasing role in the world due to its rediscovered economic strength, and due to the emergence of Asia as a political centre of the world. Asia emerged based on low labour costs and then on innovation. China trod a similar path.

China from attending the United Nations from 1971 grew to be an important part of world discussions about global issues. In this period after 2012 friends like the Icebreakers suggested China's voice needed to be more easily heard and more in the language of our nations (in the West).

Ambassador Liu Xiaoming was a pioneer in this opening of China to Western minds and learnt to attend media conferences and TV shows. But it was his speeches which resonated the most. Here was a senior Chinese diplomat who could play the Western presenters at their own game in their own language.

And so his speeches became more important as they told the bigger story in words that were easily understood. His grasp of English was very valuable, as was his grasp of the ways of Western peoples.

He was not afraid to confront necessary truths and stand his ground. He would have helped younger diplomats to learn how to speak and present to Western audiences. He helped transform the role of Chinese diplomacy to the global stage, and that impact will be felt for many decades ahead.

He is a true Icebreaker.

—Stephen Perry

Chairman, The 48 Group Club

Awardee of China Reform Friendship Medal

作为中国驻英国大使，刘晓明是成功的、了不起的，他的书说明了一切。大使的工作是确保其政府的政策和观点尽可能广为人知并得到充分阐释。刘大使通过犀利的演讲以及在报纸发表文章和在电视台接受采访，以饱满的热情履行这一使命。从著名的伊顿公学到高级军校，从大学到马克思主义研讨会，他面向全英各地各种各样的听众发表演讲。他发表的公开演讲数量超过任何其他国家驻英国大使。他出色的英语表达和长达 11 年创纪录的使英经历，使得他的演讲更加有力。他担任大使的时间跨越了中英关系的高潮和低谷，包括中英关系的“黄金时代”。有一点是毫无疑问的，那就是无论赞同与否，我们对中国政府的主张都有所了解，这要归功于刘大使的勤奋和他的演讲。

——查尔斯·鲍威尔勋爵

英国议会上院议员　英国首相撒切尔夫人外事顾问

Liu Xiaoming was a formidable and successful Ambassador for China to the United Kingdom and this collection of his speeches shows why. An Ambassador's job is to make sure that his government's policies and views are as widely known and as well explained as possible. Ambassador Liu undertook that task with enthusiasm, not just through his trenchant speeches but also in newspaper articles and television interviews. He spoke in every part of the United Kingdom and to a wide variety of audiences from the seat of privilege at Eton College, to senior military officers, universities and seminars on Marxism. And he spoke more often in public than any other foreign Ambassador. The speeches were the more effective because of his remarkable command of the English language and his long experience of the United Kingdom, serving as Ambassador for a record-breaking eleven years. His time as Ambassador spanned both high points and low points in the relations between Britain and China, including the period he proclaimed as the Golden Era. But of one thing we could always be sure: whether welcome or unwelcome, we all knew what China's government thought, thanks to his diligence and his speeches.

—Lord Powell of Bayswater

Foreign Policy Adviser to Prime Minister Margaret Thatcher

刘晓明大使2010年开始出使英国，11年间，他发表了700多场演讲。他将自己的使命概括为英文缩写“IDEA”，即扩大共同利益（interests），促进对话（dialogue），探索合作（exploration），互谅互让（accommodation）。《大使讲中国故事》从非凡的“IDEA”宝库中精选了35颗宝石，是他在全英各地面向军队、青年、商界发表的演讲，反映了他所称的中英关系“黄金时代”最积极的方面。

他的演讲一方面不断强调中国为国际秩序贡献的核心理念，即合作、开放、和谐、基于规则的治理；另一方面充分展示了中国文化的特点，提供了其独特的吸引人之处：中国特色的马克思主义、孔子和孙子的智慧、百年共产党。他这两方面的思想对英国以及世界共同的未来做出了贡献，值得全世界读者关注。

他的演讲中有许多观点值得读者重视和深思。中国的陆地邻国比其他国家都多，中国派出的联合国维和人员比其他国家都多。让我们思考一下这两件事之间有什么联系，然后更加深入地阅读这本书中非凡的见解。

——马丁·阿尔布劳博士

英国社会科学院院士　英国社会学学会前会长

During Ambassador Liu Xiaoming's 11 year tour of duty in the UK that began in 2010 he delivered over 700 speeches. For his mission he coined the acronym IDEA to summarise its purposes: expanding common interests; promoting dialogue; exploring co-operation; accommodation in bilateral relations.

Tell China's Story contains just 35 gems from that extraordinary IDEA treasure trove. They were offered to the military, to young leaders, to business people, and many more, and delivered in all the corners of the UK. They reflect the most positive aspects of China-UK relations in what he called its Golden Era.

Two aspects of his thinking contribute much more widely to our shared future than just to the UK and make his speeches worthy of attention by a world-wide readership. One is a continuing emphasis on the core ideas that China brings to international order, co-operation, openness, harmony, rule-based governance. The other exposes fully the special features of China's culture that provides its unique selling points: Marxism with Chinese characteristics, the wisdom of Confucius and Sun Tzu, the century old Communist Party.

Throughout, incidental remarks make the reader sit up and think. China has more neighbouring countries on its borders than any other state. China provides more UN peacekeepers than any other nation. Let us reflect on how those two facts might be connected. Then go back and read more of this remarkable collection of insights.

—Martin Albrow

Fellow of the UK Academy of Social Sciences

Former President of the British Sociological Association

刘晓明大使长期担任中国驻英国大使，在伦敦任职期间，他用精湛的英语向广大听众发表了许多演讲。《大使讲中国故事》是他即将出版的演讲集中的第一本，主要聚焦中国的近期发展。刘晓明极具演讲口才，他对中国及其在世界上的地位了如指掌。在这本演讲集中，他对现代中国及其人民进行了大量阐释。他的演讲生动、具有挑战性，有时还会引起争议，但总是耐人寻味且内容丰富。中国和世界需要更好地相互了解，这一点十分重要。这本书正是通往更好地相互了解的道路上非常有益的一步。

——保罗·纳斯爵士

英国弗朗西斯·克里克研究所所长

英国皇家学会前会长　诺贝尔生理学或医学奖获得者

Ambassador Liu Xiaoming was China's long serving Ambassador to the UK, who gave many speeches in accomplished English to a wide range of audiences during his time of service at the London Embassy. These are being published in a number of volumes of which *Tell China's Story* is the first, which focuses on China's recent development. Liu Xiaoming is an articulate speaker knowledgeable about China and its place in the world, who in these texts explains much about modern China and its people. The prose is lively, challenging, sometimes controversial, but always interesting and informative. It is important that China and the world understand each other better, and this book is a very useful step on the path leading to better mutual understanding.

—Sir Paul Nurse

Chief Executive of the Francis Crick Institute

Former President of the Royal Society

Nobel Prize Laureate in Physiology or Medicine

出使伦敦超过十年的大使实属罕见，而像刘晓明大使这样在公众活动中大放异彩者更是凤毛麟角。刘大使通过自己的演讲和文章，为英国公众提供了丰富的中国政策解读，他还经常就中英关系发表敏锐深刻的评论。如果你有兴趣了解中国在 21 世纪第二个 10 年如何向世界讲述自己的故事，以及中国如何看待中英关系的跌宕起伏，刘大使的演讲和文章是重要的资源。

——詹姆斯·沙逊男爵

英国议会上院议员　英中贸易协会名誉主席　英国财政部前首席商业大臣

It is rare for any Ambassador to be in London for over a decade but even rarer for an Ambassador to develop such a public profile as Ambassador Liu Xiaoming. In his speeches and articles Ambassador Liu was a prolific interpreter of Chinese policies to a British audience and a regular and pointed commentator on the China-UK relationship. Ambassador Liu's speeches and articles are an important resource for anyone interested in how China presented itself to the world in the second decade of the twentieth century and on how it saw the twists and turns in the UK-China relationship.

—Lord Sassoon

Honorary President of the China-Britain Business Council

Former First Commercial Secretary to the Treasury

不论是谁，如果希望加深对中国的了解，包括中国如何看待自身、如何看待自身在世界上的作用以及如何在发展和开放方面取得巨大进步，最好读一下刘晓明担任中国驻英大使期间发表的演讲。刘大使是一位讲故事的高手，他不惧公开、清晰地讨论复杂的问题，他将读者带入一个对他们来说可能感到陌生，或者令人困惑，甚至具有挑战性的世界，从而使他们认识到，只要通过相互尊重、把握共同利益的机遇、共建共享繁荣的世界，就可以成就大事。

——范智廉爵士

英国政府“一带一路”特使　英国汇丰集团前主席

For anyone wishing to gain a better understanding of China, how it sees itself, how it envisages its role in the world and how it has achieved the enormous strides it has in terms of its development and opening-up, would do well to read the speeches of Ambassador Liu Xiaoming, delivered while he was Ambassador to the UK. The Ambassador is a consummate storyteller, unafraid to tackle complex issues openly and clearly and draws the reader into a world that may be unfamiliar or confusing, even challenging to them, leaving them with a greater understanding of what can be achieved through mutual respect and a willingness to grasp opportunities of mutual interest to build a world of shared prosperity.

—Sir Douglas Flint

UK Special Envoy to Belt and Road Initiative

Former Group Chairman of HSBC Holdings

刘晓明在他破纪录的11年大使生涯中展现出高超的才智、理解力，有时还带有辛辣的幽默感，同时也有力地捍卫了中国的利益。在政治、经济、教育、文化和社会等各个方面，他希望英国在复杂的多边世界中，能作为中国的伙伴发挥重要作用，他的这一愿望从未让公众质疑。他的这本演讲集集中反映了这一点——这也是中英关系一段非同寻常时期的有力见证。

——大卫·马什博士

国际货币金融机构官方论坛主席

Liu Xiaoming brought to his record-breaking decade as Ambassador a high level of intellect, understanding and sometimes pungent humour, mixed with a forceful defense of Chinese interests. Across many fields of politics, economics, education, culture and social affairs, he never left his audiences in any doubt of his wish for Britain to play a strong role as partners to China in a complex multilateral world. The collected work of his speeches epitomises this approach — a rich testament to an extraordinary period in UK-Chinese relations.

—Dr David Marsh

Chairman of the Official Monetary and

Financial Institutions Forum

刘晓明是中英两国更紧密经济联系的坚定捍卫者，他是一个真正的改革者，既着眼未来，又对过去有着深刻理解。2019 年，他在牛津剑桥俱乐部的一次演讲中指出，中国仍然是一个发展中国家，而且是世界上最大的发展中国家。阅读这些演讲，是为了更深入地了解刘晓明所说的这个“持续扩大开放并深化改革”的国家。

——里士满公爵

全英赛车俱乐部主席

A staunch defender of closer economic ties between China and the UK, Liu Xiaoming is, at heart, a reformer, a man with one eye on the future as well as a deep understanding of the past.

In a speech to the Oxford and Cambridge Club in 2019 he makes the point that China is still a developing country, albeit the biggest one in the world.

To read these speeches is to gain a deeper understanding of a country that, he says, is determined to "keep its doors open to the world and to deepen its reform."

—Lord March

The Duke of Richmond and Gordon

President of the British Automobile Racing Club

这本珍贵的演讲集收录了刘晓明从 2010 年至 2021 年担任中国驻英国大使期间的演讲。它记录了一个非常时期和一个特殊任期。刘大使的演讲涵盖深刻而广泛的主题，他的听众很有代表性，他阐释中国改革开放别具技巧和风格，所有这些都给人留下了深刻的印象。这部演讲集将成为刘大使出使英国、致力于促进外部世界更好地了解中国的最佳见证。

——古沛勤爵士

英中贸易协会主席

This is a very valuable collection of Liu Xiaoming's speeches to mark his extraordinary time and tenure as Ambassador of the People's Republic of China to the Court of St James's — the United Kingdom — from 2010 to 2021. The breadth and depth of the subjects covered, the key audiences addressed, and the skill and style with which Ambassador Liu seeks to explain China's reform and opening-up are all truly impressive. This collection of speeches will stand as a remarkable testimony to his time of service in the UK, and to his commitment to promoting better understanding of China.

—Sir Sherard Cowper-Coles

Chair of the China-Britain Business Council

Former British Ambassador to Israel, Saudi Arabia and Afghanistan

目　录

序　言 *005*

第一章　如何认识中国

如何认识中国　003

中国——一个古老而常青的国家　015

道路坚定，前途光明　031

“中国梦”：国家、民族和人民之梦　045

引领中国发展新时代，开启中英合作新征程　055

读懂新时代中国，构建人类命运共同体　071

认识真实的中国，共建友谊的桥梁　079

把握新机遇，注入新信心，开启新征程　093

第二章　治国理政

读懂当代中国，领略领袖风范　107

领悟中国智慧，感知世界情怀　115

感知东方智慧，读懂中国未来　123

中国为什么选择马克思主义　137
法治照耀中国　151

第三章　和平发展
和平、发展、合作——中国外交的主题　161
从全面、纵深的角度认识和平发展的中国　173
从“十二五”规划看中国的科学发展与和平发展　187
中国让世界更安全　201
中国是亚洲的和平稳定力量　209
和平发展与共享共赢　225
中国将坚定不移走和平发展道路　245
坚持和平发展，推进合作共赢　263

第四章　中国外交
新时期的中国外交　281
使命与梦想　295
共答“时代之问”，同创美好未来　309
同舟共济，共克时艰，构建人类命运共同体　325

第五章　中国国防
《孙子兵法》与中国的外交国防政策　343
“中国梦”引领中国安全观与国防建设　357

第六章　改革开放
成功的道路，全面的发展　377
创新是中国发展的关键　389

全面深化改革是中国发展的强大动力　403
改革促进中国发展，开放推动世界进步　415
纪念改革开放伟业，共谱合作共赢新篇　433

第七章　中国机遇
中国发展给世界带来的机遇　449
坚持开放、合作、协商，为世界增添“中国信心”　475
共享中国机遇，共创美好未来　487

后　记　501

序 言

我于 2009 年 12 月被任命为新中国第 11 任驻英国大使，2010 年 2 月 28 日抵英履职，2021 年 1 月 31 日离英回国，成为任期最长的中国驻英使节。

11 年栉风沐雨，11 年耕耘不辍。我亲眼见证了中国与世界关系的历史性变化，亲身经历了中英关系的起伏跌宕。许多同事和朋友问我：11 年最令我难忘的是什么？最令我高兴的是什么？最令我遗憾的是什么？

最令我难忘的是，英国人民对中国人民的友好情谊，英国各界渴望了解中国的迫切愿望。最令我高兴的是，11 年里我遍访英伦各地，与各界人士广泛交流，增进了了解，收获了友谊。最令我遗憾的是，中英之间仍存在很大的“了解赤字”和“认知赤字”。

中英交往源远流长，英国是最早与中国交往的西方大国。时至今日，两国交流覆盖各个方面，涉及各个领域，其广度和深度今非昔比。然而，英国报纸、电视、电台、网络中关于中国的报道，仍有不少偏见、误导，甚至假消息。这真是印证了英国的一句谚语——“没有消息就是好消息”。在这样的舆论环境里，人们了解不到一个真正的中国。在这样的国度工作，中国外交官的一个重要使命就是“讲好中国故事”，让驻在国民众认识一个真实的中国。

11 年里，我在中国驻英国大使的岗位上，恪尽职守，不辱使命，积极开展公共外交，努力讲好中国故事。有人把我比作中国公共外交的一面旗帜，西方一些媒体称我是中国“战狼鼻祖”（Original Wolf Warrior）。我不敢当旗帜，更不接受西方媒体贴给我的标签，我只是做了我应该做的事情。我将“讲好中国故事”总结为12个字：“听得到、听得懂、听得进、听而信。”

“听得到”，就是多发声、广发声，全覆盖，让中国声音传到每一个角落，让更多的外国民众听到中国故事。英国是国际舆论中心，拥有一批世界级媒体。英国广播公司覆盖全球200多个国家和地区，受众4亿；《金融时报》在全球140个国家和地区发行；《卫报》网站在全球拥有3 200多万读者。我充分利用英国媒体优势，积极投书撰文、接受采访、发表演讲。11年里，我共发表700多场演讲，在主流报刊撰文170多篇，接受主流媒体采访170多次，几乎所有英国大报都刊登过我的文章，所有主流电视台和电台都采访过我。我被英国舆论界和外交界称为“上镜率最高”“被媒体引用次数最多”的外国驻英使节。

“听得懂”，就是使用当地民众的话语体系，让人听得懂，听得明白，进而找到“精神的共通点、思想的共享点、情感的共鸣点”。比如，英国民众对我们批判日本政要在历史问题上的错误言行往往不理解。他们认为，英国和法国已经同德国实现了和解，为什么中国对日本总是揪住不放，不依不饶。我说，如果德国总理去参拜安放纳粹战犯的神社，英国民众会原谅吗？不是我们不依不饶，而是日本领导人拒不反省。如果日本首相能像德国总理跪在华沙犹太人纪念碑前忏悔那样，跪在卢沟桥或者南京大屠杀遇难同胞纪念馆前忏悔反省，中国人民也会原谅日本。针对日本领导人参拜靖国神社，我在英国主流大报《每日电讯报》发表文章写道：“如果把军国主义比作日本的伏地魔，靖国神社无疑是藏着这个国家灵魂最黑暗部分的魂器。”由于小说《哈利·波特》的反面人物“伏地魔”在英国家喻户晓，读者很容易对“军国主义”和“靖国神社”有生动的认识。一些英国媒体评论说，这个比喻通俗易懂，既鲜明地表达了中国的立场，也易于被西方民众接受，在传播上有很强的穿透力。

“听得进”，就是要转变传播思维，从“宣传思维”向“故事思维”转变，而且不能只讲自己的故事，还要讲人家的故事。我称之为“三加一”故事，即中国的故事、中国共产党的故事、中国人民的故事，加中英合作的故事。比如，对“一带一路”倡议，英国人开始并不积极。有一些人认为，英国不是“一带一路”沿线国家，没必要参与；还有人觉得，“一带一路”是搞基础设施建设，这并非英国的长项，英国没办法参与；更有甚者，认为“一带一路”是中国与美国争夺势力范围的工具，英国不应参与。针对这些问题，我带领使馆同志们制定了讲述“一带一路”故事的方案，让英国各界看到“一带一路”在英国蕴藏的巨大机遇。一旦英方听进了“一带一路”故事，态度就发生了很大的变化，并在西方大国中创下多个“第一”：第一个申请加入亚洲基础设施投资银行并向亚投行特别基金注资；第一个签署《“一带一路”融资指导原则》；第一个任命“一带一路”特使；第一个设立“一带一路”专家理事会；第一个宣布支持250亿英镑“一带一路”亚洲项目；两次派财政大臣作为首相特使来华出席“一带一路”高峰论坛。

“听而信”，这是公共外交的最高境界，是一个不断实践、持续参悟、逐步实现的过程。要通过讲中国故事，让世界理解和认可中国的发展观、文明观、安全观、人权观、生态观、国际秩序观和全球治理观，相信中国是一个“可信、可爱、可敬”的国家。

本书收录了我担任驻英国大使期间发表的35篇演讲，围绕一个主题，就是向英国各界“讲好中国故事”。如果说，过去我在英国讲中国故事，为的是不断缩小中英之间的“了解赤字”和“认知赤字”；那么今天，出版这本《大使讲中国故事》，则是希望有更多的人加入讲中国故事的行列。希望这本书对大家讲好中国故事有所帮助。

刘晓明

2021年立冬

第一章

如何认识中国

西方民众对中国存在许多误解，这既是由于他们对中国缺少了解，也是由于一些西方政客极力抹黑、污蔑中国，西方媒体片面、歪曲报道中国。他们诋毁中国的社会制度，歪曲中国的内外政策，丑化中国的国家形象。因此西方民众难以了解一个真实的中国，特别是对中国共产党存在很大误解。一些人听到“共产党”和“共产主义”就产生心理障碍，因而难以客观地看待共产党领导下的中国。针对这种现象，我在讲中国故事时，重点讲了中国共产党的故事，讲中国共产党带领中国人民实现中华民族伟大复兴的故事。我在中英青年领导者圆桌会上，在培养了13位英国首相、素有英国“政治家的摇篮”之称的伊顿公学和丘吉尔的母校哈罗公学，向英国青年讲述中国共产党对内致力于实现民族复兴，对外致力于实现和平发展的故事。一个成功领导本民族走向复兴的政党是一个应当赢得尊敬的政党，一个内求发展、外求和平的国家是一个应当值得信任的国家。

我在英国议会宣讲中共十九大精神，在英国工商界举行的报告会上介绍党的十八大和十九届五中全会，讲解习近平新时代中国特色社会主义思想，解读中国特色社会主义进入新时代。在“新时代中国”国际研讨会上，我强调要读懂中国，就先要读懂中国共产党，指出中国共产党是一个坚持为中国发展谋长远、为中国人民谋幸福、为人类进步事业而奋斗的政党。

如何认识中国 *

尊敬的影阁就业与养老金大臣伯恩阁下，

女士们、先生们：

欢迎大家出席今天的午餐会。不久前，你们赴中国出席第二届中英青年领导者圆桌会。圆桌会取得了圆满成功，我谨向你们表示祝贺，并感谢活动的英方组织者——英中协会的辛勤工作及与中方的默契协调，同时也感谢此次会议的赞助商渣打银行。

此行，你们访问了两个地方——北京和内蒙古，了解、感受了中国的现代化大都市和草原牧区；你们在研讨中回顾了两位著名历史人物——孙中山和凯恩斯，借此比较分析中英历史文化特点，展望两国发展前景；你们在活动中进行了两场模拟游戏——“达·芬奇密码”和“贸易战”，通过这种生动活泼的方式，充分证明跨文化交流的必要性和中英合作的重要性。

英语谚语说：“出行拓宽思想。”作为一名职业外交官，我对此深有体会，也相信你们此行有不少体会和收获。趁你们的印象还很深刻、记忆还很鲜活，我愿与大家一起探讨三个值得深思的问题。

第一个问题是：如何认识、解读共产党领导下的中国？

我这个问题比较直接，但这个问题是当前西方尚未解开的心结。这一心结不解，西方对中国心里总有一块疙瘩，中西方关系总蒙有一层阴影。

---

* 在中英青年领导者圆桌会英方代表举行的午餐会上的讲话。2011 年 6 月 16 日，中国驻英国大使馆。

再过两个星期就是中国共产党成立90周年。中国共产党执政已有62年，中西方打开交往大门也有40年，冷战也早已结束20年。但西方看待共产党领导下的中国时，并没有完全摆脱冷战思维和零和思维，总是戴着有色眼镜看中国，时常给中国戴上各种帽子。这种旧思维和偏见有百害而无一利。

在西方，很多人听到“共产主义”就会产生心理障碍，因而也就难以客观地看待共产党领导下的中国，看不到正是中国共产党领导中国成为世界第二大经济体和第一大出口国。我认为，认识一个国家，最基本的就是看它的内外政策，认识共产党领导下的中国亦是如此。

共产党领导的中国对内致力于实现民族复兴。20世纪前半叶，中国在共产党领导下获得了民族独立和人民解放，完成了中华民族面对的第一大历史任务；今天，共产党正在带领中国完成第二大历史任务，即实现国家繁荣富强和人民共同富裕。30多年来，中国坚持改革开放，坚持走适合中国国情的发展道路，成就举世瞩目，进步前所未有。

共产党领导的中国对外致力于实现和平发展。中国不是苏联，中国不当头争霸，不搞军备竞赛，不拉帮结盟，不输出意识形态。中国始终不渝走和平发展道路，坚持独立自主的和平外交政策，奉行互利共赢的开放战略，全方位开展对外交往合作，倡导建设持久和平、共同繁荣的和谐世界。中国的发展对世界不是威胁，而是机遇。中国不是国际体系的旁观者、搅局者和破坏者，而是参与者、建设者和贡献者。

一个成功领导本民族走向复兴的政党是一个应当赢得尊敬的政党，一个内求发展、外求和平的国家是一个应当值得信任的国家。

孔子曰：“君子和而不同。”中国与西方政治体制、意识形态不同，但这本不应当成为我们合作的障碍。只要我们互相包容、和而不同，放弃遏制与同化，我们完全能够在同一片天空下共同发展。

第二个问题是：英国媒体是否在客观反映一个真实的中国？

我每次与英国朋友谈到英国媒体，他们总是告诉我，对它不要太认真。

但有时英国媒体实在让人难以捉摸。当中国社会和国际舆论热议“十二五”规划——这一今后五年中国的发展目标时，英国媒体却在集中关注一个所谓中国的“行为艺术家”；当英国政府欢迎中国的企业将英作为投资欧洲首选地时，英国媒体却刊登文章，提出要警惕中国企业的所谓“共产党阴影”论调，鼓吹限制中国企业对英投资；当中国大力发展互联网产业、加强网络问政、增强网络安全时，英国媒体却在捕风捉影地将中国政府和军方视为全球范围内网络黑客的背后“主谋”。

为什么在英国媒体眼中的中国，与中国人民正在努力构建的中国如此不同？当然，中国在前进发展的道路上会遇到各种挑战，但中国正在努力跨越各种障碍，消解各种矛盾。无疑，中国不指望世界上所有人对中国的进步满堂喝彩，但也不希望外界总是将中国视作“异类”，并且拿着显微镜从鸡蛋里挑骨头。

我到任一年多来，先后在英主流报刊上发表了一些文章，介绍中国的发展、中国的外交和中英双边关系。但区区一人之力，显然是不够的。不久前，英国一个高级退役将军代表团访问了中国，之后代表团团长拉姆陆军中将有感而发，在《泰晤士报》上写了一篇文章，明确指出西方媒体不应“妖魔化”中国，不应制造一个新敌人，并认为中国致力于发展经济，中国近些年在国际舞台上的举动大都是正面的，中国愿与世界开展对话，西方也应当与中国加强对话。可惜，这样的声音在英国媒体上是少而又少。

在座的各位朋友，你们也刚从中国归来，我希望你们也能不虚此行，将访华的体会和观察凝练成文字，见诸报端，介绍一个你们看到的、感受到的中国。这算是我今天的一个“不情之请”。

第三个问题是：如何不断推进中英关系的发展？

英国联合政府成立一年多来，中英关系总体保持稳定发展势头。双方高层互访不断，合作亮点频现，交流沟通顺畅。但也要看到，中英关系中还有一些问题要得到妥善处理。中英双方应继续齐心协力，共同抓住机遇，克服挑战，深化合作。

我认为，进一步发展中英关系，就如同驾驶一辆汽车，要想跑得又快又舒适，必须牢牢抓住三个关键。

一是方向要稳。中英两国是合作伙伴，不是竞争对手。双方要坚持发展中英全面战略伙伴关系这一大方向不动摇，保持领导人的密切沟通与协调，努力实现 2015 年贸易额达到 1 000 亿美元的目标，增强在国际事务中的对话与合作，扩大两国人文交流，增进民众的相互了解。

二是动力要足。当前，中英各领域合作的意愿强、潜力大，双方应加大“油门”，推动合作取得更多实质性成果。比如，中英当前都将调整经济结构、促进经济增长作为第一要务，都希望扩大出口和双向投资。我们应争取在今后几年使经贸关系有质的提升，打造更多像 MG6（上南合作下生产的首款重量级车型）这样的标志性合作项目，推动更多像华为公司这样的中国企业在英建立欧洲总部，促进更多像生态城市、低碳建筑这样的技术和创新合作。

三是路况要好。一辆汽车开得平稳顺畅，光靠车辆本身性能还不够，还取决于路面状况。因此，加强中英合作需要良好的环境。具体来说，双方要深化政治互信，发挥政府的主动引导作用；重视合理关切，为合作扫清障碍，创造条件；坚持以平等和相互尊重的原则开展对话，处理分歧；积极营造舆论氛围，使合作成为两国社会的共识。

令人高兴的是，温家宝总理即将访英。这是联合政府成立以来最高级别中国领导人访英，对中英关系来说，这无疑将是一次难得的契机、一大有力的推动。我们愿与英方共同努力，确保访问取得圆满成功，使中英关系迈上新的台阶。

最后，祝愿中英青年领导者圆桌会越办越好，为不断增进中英理解和友谊做出贡献。

谢谢！

How to Understand China*

The Rt Hon Liam Byrne,

Ladies and Gentlemen,

It is a great pleasure to welcome you to the Chinese Embassy.

I am reminded of an English proverb following your visit to China and participation in the second China-UK Young Leaders Roundtable.

That well-known proverb is that "travel broadens the mind."

In my career as a diplomat, I really know the value of that proverb. I have had the privilege of working outside China in the USA, Egypt, DPRK, now Britain, and of travelling to more than 60 countries.

Most of you gathered here are at an earlier stage in your careers. You have not had so much time for travel.

I do hope all of you gained valuable experience from this visit to China. In turn I sincerely wish that you share the knowledge to build understanding of China. As China rises it becomes ever more critical that China and the world understand each other. That is the path to a peaceful, sustainable and harmonious world.

I am told that the second China-UK Young Leaders Roundtable was a great success. I must congratulate you on the achievements of the event!

Also, I must say how much I appreciate the hard work of our British organiser—the Great Britain-China Centre. Along with their Chinese colleagues at the All-China Youth Federation, they have displayed tremendous teamwork. Warm thanks should also go to

---

* Remarks at the Lunch in Honour of British Delegates Attending the China-UK Young Leaders Roundtable. Chinese Embassy in the UK, 16 June 2011.

the businesses, such as Standard Chartered Bank, who helped sponsor the Roundtable.

For many of you I gather this may not have been the first visit to China. But I am sure it must be a very interesting and special one.

I was told that you went to Beijing and Inner Mongolia. After that you gained first-hand experience about China's modern cities and its pastoral areas.

In addition, I learned how you studied two great men in our respective histories—Dr. Sun Yat-sen and John Maynard Keynes.

I was briefed that through studying their lives you analysed the historical and cultural traits of our countries. You then used these as a foundation to explore where our countries may be heading.

I gather that you ran two interesting simulations based on *The Da Vinci Code* and *The Trade War*. These exercises were designed to impress why intercultural exchanges are so necessary. In turn that highlights why the China-UK partnership is so crucial.

Today I wish to build upon your experiences in China. I propose to do this by raising three questions. In turn, these questions may help renew your memory about China, and hopefully provoke some thoughts.

This is the first question. How do we perceive China under the leadership of the Communist Party?

For Chinese people this is a straightforward question.

But I recognise that the question has been a puzzle that has been bothering China-West relations over the years.

In just two weeks' time, the Communist Party of China will celebrate its 90th birthday. It has been a ruling party in China for 62 years.

Also, it has been 40 years since China and the West reestablished relations.

And the Cold War ended over 20 years ago.

But regrettably, the Cold War mentality is still casting its shadow as the West looks at China under the leadership of the Communist Party.

This Cold War mentality hampers the building of trust and respect, which underpins all global collaboration. This mentality makes it a serious challenge to achieve progress on trade and investment and on global issues such as climate change, global financial systems and nuclear safety. It results in prejudice and unfair accusations against China.

I believe to understand a country, it is important to keep an open mind and study the country's actual domestic and foreign policies. This is especially true when it comes to understanding China.

For too many people in the western world the mere mention of the word "Communism" induces an immediate mental block. That prevents an open examination of the impact of "Communism" as it has been applied in China.

An open mind would immediately grasp the benefits that the Communist Party in China has brought. Over the past three decades the Communist Party in China has brought unprecedented economic advances in the history of the world.

That Chinese economic strength has had profound consequences in the wake of the most recent financial crisis to hit the western world. The global economy could have been plunged into a far deeper crisis if China had not acted. Those actions manifested themselves as China emerged to rank as the world's second biggest economy and the largest exporter.

Domestically, China led by the Communist Party is committed to revitalising the country.

The first half of the 20th century saw the Communist Party lead the Chinese nation to secure its first historical mission — national independence and liberation. The Communist Party founded in 1949 a New China and ended decades of chaos and extreme deprivation for the Chinese people.

Today the Party is leading the nation and its people towards prosperity — a second historical mission China has to accomplish. No government in the history of the world has taken so many hundreds of millions out of poverty. And that has been achieved in only a few decades.

Over the past three decades and more, China has been committed to reform and opening-up. This has set China on a path to the development suited to China's realities. The result has been remarkable achievements and progress in China.

Internationally, China is committed to peaceful development. China will be totally misunderstood by those who choose to compare it to the former Soviet Union and its interpretation of "Communism."

China has no intention to seek hegemony in the world.

China does not favour any arms race.

China has no ambition to export any ideologies.

China pursues peaceful development unswervingly. That means an independent and peaceful foreign policy.

China is engaged in extensive international cooperation. The Chinese government advocates a harmonious world of lasting peace and common prosperity.

China's development presents opportunities to the world—certainly not threats.

China is a player and contributor in the international system—not an outsider. The last thing China can be accused of is being a saboteur of global peace and harmony.

A political party that has managed to lead its nation to such historically unprecedented revitalisation deserves respect. A country so committed to national development and international peace has earned the right to be trusted.

Confucius is quoted as saying that "harmony can be won without uniformity." In other words, we do not all have to be identical in government systems in order to secure global peace and harmony.

China's differences with the West in political system and ideology should not stand in the way of cooperation. All we need to do to advance together is to be inclusive and accommodating. We must abandon attempts to contain or convert.

Turning to the second of my three questions for you today. That is about how media in this country presents China to the public.

I talk about the British media with some of my friends in this country. They always say: "Don't take British media too seriously!"

Let me give you an example of my confusion about the priorities of the British media. The example is the analysis and coverage of the publication of China's 12th Five-Year Plan.

As you might know, this very important Plan was published a few months ago. In Chinese and the international media, there were very extensive discussions about China's 12th Five-Year Plan.

However, the British media seemed indifferent. Instead, the British media became incredibly obsessed with a so-called Chinese "protest artist."

The British government repeatedly stresses its welcome for Chinese businesses in the UK. That welcome has been successful, as the UK has become the top EU destination for Chinese investment. From my observations, that welcome message from the British government is not reflected in the UK media. Instead, a news story warned the British business community of the so-called "Communist spies" within Chinese investors. The British media even suggested restrictions over Chinese investment in the UK.

In your travels in China, you will have been aware of the scale of the growth of the Internet industry in China. One leading British analyst in China is predicting the next Internet innovations worldwide will come from China. But the UK media in this country runs stories that the Chinese government and military are the masterminds behind web hacking worldwide.

Why in the reports of the British media does China attract such negative coverage?

Why do the stories not reflect the reality of what is happening in China today? According to a top economist of the British Standard Chartered bank, China is experiencing an "industrial revolution" with many years to run and this revolution offers British businesses tremendous opportunities. It is my sincere wish that they could learn more about this in the British media.

There is much to be positive about in my country. Certainly, China is indeed confronted with challenges of one kind or another in its way forward.

But China is also doing all it can to overcome these challenges and bridge the differences.

China does not expect everybody in the world to applaud its progress. But China certainly does not wish to be treated as if it were a "different species."

I arrived in London as the Ambassador of China 16 months ago. Since then, I have written several articles in major newspapers. Through these I wanted to tell the British public more about China's development, its foreign policy and its relations with the UK.

But a better understanding about China requires much more than what I can do.

That is why I am heartened by *the Times* article of retired Lieutenant-General Sir Graeme Lamb. He has recently led a senior delegation of British veteran generals to China. After that trip, he wrote: "We should talk to China, not demonise it. ... The danger lies in making a new enemy. ... China's absolute priority remains economic growth...and China's most recent move on the international stage was a positive one. ... When it comes to relations with the Chinese, ... it's good to talk. That applies to both sides."

I do hope that voices like this will get louder in the British media.

All of you present today are just back from China. My hope is that you will translate what you saw and felt about China into newspaper and web comments. That will help people in this country know more about what China is really like.

My third and last question is how we take China-UK relations forward.

The coalition government has been in place for over one year now. I am glad to say that China-UK relations are in good shape.

We have seen regular exchange of high-level visits, fruitful cooperation and smooth dialogue and communication. But we are also aware of the issues in our relations that need to be tackled properly. I believe that all we need is to continue to work closely, grasp opportunities, overcome challenges and deepen cooperation.

I will use this analogy to describe how I believe we can further China-UK relations. If you want to be a good driver, here are three tips to bear in mind.

The first tip: keep to the right direction.

China and the UK are partners, not rivals. The comprehensive strategic partnership is the one thing we need to strengthen. This ensures close dialogue and coordination at the top level.

In turn that leads to:

- Enhanced dialogue and cooperation in international affairs.
- Expanded cultural exchanges.
- And increased mutual understanding between our people.

By working together, we will strive to double China-UK trade by 2015 to reach 100 billion US dollars.

The second tip: make sure there is enough horsepower.

Various sectors of both China and the UK have shown a keen interest and potential to cooperate. We need to hit the accelerator and facilitate more substantive results.

For instance, China and the UK take economic restructuring and growth as their top priority. Both hope to increase exports and mutual investment.

We should work for significant improvement in the quality of our business ties through more flagship projects. For example, like the MG6, and more businesses like

Huawei that has set up its European headquarters in the UK.

Cooperation in technology and innovation is also key, such as with eco-cities and low-carbon buildings.

The third tip: check the road condition.

A smooth road trip does not just depend on how good the car is, but also the road.

China-UK relations also need a smooth road to run fast, or an environment conducive to cooperation.

To be specific, it means deepening political mutual trust:

- That means bringing into full play the primary role of the government.
- It requires taking seriously the other's legitimate concerns.
- We need to remove obstacles to cooperation.
- We must create the right conditions.
- Dialogue must be conducted based on equality and mutual respect to handle differences.

Also, popular support for cooperation in both countries needs to be strengthened.

Reflecting on our high-level dialogue, I am pleased that Premier Wen Jiabao is coming for an official visit very soon.

Premier Wen Jiabao will be the most senior Chinese leader to visit the UK since the coalition government was formed.

This is no doubt a rare opportunity and a strong boost for our relations. We in China are ready to work with our British partners to make the visit a success and bring the relationship to a new level.

Before I conclude, I wish the China-UK Young Leaders Roundtable ever greater success in the future, fostering deeper friendship and understanding between China and the UK!

Thank you.

中国——一个古老而常青的国家*

尊敬的托尼·里特尔校长，

老师们、同学们：

我和夫人胡平华非常高兴访问伊顿公学。感谢伊顿公学“前沿社”社长弗雷德·金刚才热情的介绍。

你们来到伊顿求学，风华正茂，令人羡慕。在今天这个迅速发展的时代，我个人的体会是，学习是终身的。最近我就学习了两个英文单词。一个是 Oxonian（牛津校友），因为就在上周，我刚访问了牛津大学，在牛津学联发表了一个演讲，在演讲中提到了不少曾为中英关系发展做出贡献的牛津校友。今天，我来到了伊顿，又学习了一个新词：Etonian（伊顿校友）。我要祝贺伊顿校友约翰·格登荣获 2012 年的诺贝尔生理学或医学奖，尽管他在校时曾被时任校长评价为“生物学得糟糕透顶”。伊顿和牛津同样具有数百年历史，同样坐落在泰晤士河畔，同样是《哈利·波特》的拍摄地，同样是英才辈出，我不知道英语中是否有这么一个词：Oxtonian，用来指先后就读于伊顿和牛津的学子。因为，“伊顿 + 牛津”，这是一个最富英国特色的黄金教育组合，培养了许多杰出人才。一个最为人津津乐道的例子是，伊顿和牛津共同造就了 13 位英国首相，包括现任首相，名副其实地成为英国政治家的摇篮。还有一个不为人知的例子是，詹姆斯·邦德据说也是伊顿和牛津校友，不过听说因为他惹了麻烦，伊顿开除了他。

---

* 在英国伊顿公学的演讲。2012 年 10 月 17 日，英国伊顿公学。

今天在座的不少是伊顿公学"前沿社"的成员。刚开始看到"前沿"这个词，我一下子想到了我曾经两次工作过的美国。在美国历史上，"前沿"一词有着特殊含义，指19世纪后半期美国开发的西部边疆。20世纪60年代，美国总统肯尼迪又提出了开发"新边疆"，也就是探索太空。当然，你们社名中的"前沿"被赋予了新的后现代含义——新兴经济体或在未来有重要影响的世界大国，其中包括中国。今天，也有一些来自"东方社"和"凯恩斯社"的成员，你们三个社团共同感兴趣的话题无疑是中国。

今天，我演讲的主题就是中国，一个古老而常青的国家。

中国历史悠久，有一句话最能说明中国历史的特点：在世界四大文明古国中，中国文明是唯一未曾间断、延续至今的。我曾经担任中国驻埃及大使，埃及同样是一个文明古国，有文字记载的历史比中国还要早，但是古埃及文明由于外敌的持续入侵而湮没了。今天埃及使用的文字与古埃及象形文字已经完全不是一个体系。19世纪初，人们幸运地借助现存于英国博物馆的罗塞塔石碑，才解开了失传1 400年古埃及文字的谜团。而中国虽然也曾遭受外敌入侵，但是中华文明因其强大的生命力和包容性得以传承，并不断发展。

古代中国取得了非凡成就，曾经鼎盛辉煌。在过去的两千年里，大多数时间中国是世界上最大的经济体。英国《经济学人》杂志的数据表明，中国的GDP（国内生产总值）曾占全球总量的1/3左右。中国的丝绸、瓷器和茶叶曾是世界上最畅销的产品，那时"Made in China"（中国制造）代表着豪华、昂贵，属于"奢侈品"。中国人形成了博大精深的哲学思想和治世之道——儒家和道家，既富有进取心和使命感，又崇尚人与自然和谐共处。

中国创造的四大发明：造纸术、指南针、火药和活字印刷术，对世界文明和人类进步产生了重大影响。弗朗西斯·培根曾经写道："印刷术、火药和指南针分别改变了文学、战争和航海，进而彻底改变了整个世界。"剑桥大学学者李约瑟博士为此悉心研究整理，花费近50年时间编写出皇皇巨著《中国科学技术史》。

但是，近代中国落后了。18世纪产生于英国的工业革命改变了世界，中国传统的农业文明迅速被时代甩在了后面。中国经历了一百多年的内忧外患，甚至一度处于民族危亡的关头。新中国成立后，中国在建设发展过程中也走了一些弯路。逆境中的人们都熟悉这样一句诗：“如果冬天来了，春天还会远吗？”这句诗的作者就是一位伊顿校友——英国诗人雪莱。

到了 20 世纪 70 年代末，中国终于迎来了改革开放的春天，开始了民族复兴。中国连续 30 年保持了 GDP 年均 10% 的增速，6 亿多人摆脱了贫困，创造了世界经济增长的奇迹。今天的中国已成为全球第二大经济体和第二大贸易体，是世界经济增长的发动机和稳定器。中国不仅经济发展了，文化、政治、社会等各领域也取得了全面进步。就在上周，中国作家莫言获得了诺贝尔文学奖，这是中国籍作家首次获此殊荣。

世界非常关注当代的中国。英国的报纸、电视新闻里，几乎每天都有关于中国的报道。走进英国最大的连锁书店 WATERSTONES（水石书店），书架上关于中国的书籍也是琳琅满目。面对海量信息和各种解读，如何清晰地认识当代中国？我认为，可以从三方面去把握。

一是中国正在走一条适合中国国情的发展道路。一个 13 亿人口的大国，该如何谋发展，历史上没有先例，教科书上没有答案，照搬国外不行，闭门造车也不行。中国人牢牢把握自己的国情，借鉴吸取世界各国有益经验，不断摸索实践和改革创新，获得了成功。这条发展道路的特点是以经济建设为中心，以人为本，全面协调和可持续发展，同时坚持社会公平正义，保障人民的民主权利。这条发展道路的政治制度保障是人民代表大会制度及中国共产党领导的多党合作和政治协商制度，经济制度保障是以公有制为主体、多种所有制经济共同发展，包括私营经济、个体经济和外资经济。这既与世界各国有共同点，又有着鲜明的中国特色。

二是中国仍然是一个发展中国家。中国经济总量很大，但 2011 年人均 GDP 仅约 5 432 美元，根据 IMF（国际货币基金组织）的排名，居世界第 89 位，仅为英国人均 GDP 的 1/7。中国的贫困人口仍有 1.28 亿（按中国的贫困标准相当于每人每天 1 美元），若按联合国制定的每人每天 1.25 美元的新标准，则这个数字还要大。中国单位 GDP 的能耗是国际水平的 3~4 倍，是英国的 8 倍。我曾经在中国最贫穷的西部省份之一甘肃省工作，走访了甘肃 86

个县区市中的60多个，深刻体会到中国西部地区与东部沿海省份相比、农村与城市相比还有很大差距。在甘肃农村的一些地区，基本生活用水都存在困难，脱贫还有很长的路要走。

三是中国致力于和平发展。今天的中国坚持独立自主的和平外交政策，将维护世界和平、促进共同发展作为中国外交政策的宗旨。中国倡导“互信、互利、平等、协作”的新安全观，秉持积极有为的国际责任观，奉行睦邻友好的地区合作观，主张世界各国一道建立持久和平、共同繁荣的和谐世界。中国绝不搞侵略扩张，永远不争霸、不称霸，绝不走历史上“国强必霸”的老路。中国致力于和平解决国际争端和热点问题。中国累计向联合国30项维和行动派出各类人员2万多人次，是派出维和人员最多的联合国安理会常任理事国。中国同12个陆地邻国解决了历史遗留的边界问题，主张通过和平谈判处理同邻国的领土和海洋权益争端，尽最大努力维护南海、东海及周边和平稳定。

最近，日本宣布对中国的领土钓鱼岛实施“国有化”，这是对中国领土主权的严重侵犯，引起中国人民的坚决反对和强烈抗议。我们敦促日本立即停止一切损害中国领土主权的行为，回到和平谈判解决争议的轨道上来。

我在英国工作两年多，经常看到西方媒体上对中国未来的各种“担心”，甚至“唱衰”。而事实上，中国民众对自己的国家抱有信心。根据美国著名民调机构皮尤研究中心2012年7月公布的调查报告，83%的中国民众对中国经济感到乐观，而在美国和英国，认为本国经济形势良好的分别只有31%和15%。作为一个中国外交官，我对中国未来发展更充满信心。

首先，中国经济发展潜力巨大，动力充沛。中国2011年城镇化率历史上首次超过了50%，而英国在1851年就达到了这一水平，发达国家目前的城镇化率普遍在80%左右。中国城镇化发展还将持续几十年，将创造出巨大的城市住宅、基础设施建设的需求。中国地区发展不平衡，而今后的平衡进程可以有效带动投资和内需的增长，提供更大的市场规模。中国的整体消费结构正从吃、穿等生存性消费向住、行、教育等发展性消费升级，提振空间很大。中国劳动力总量巨大的优势还会持续一段时间，并且随着政府加大教育投入，人力资本提升空间很大，这将形成新的“人口红利”。

其次，中国的发展将更加全面和谐，人民将更加幸福。中国将继续致力于民主法治建设，维护社会公平正义，实现人的自由和全面发展。中国将更好地保障和改善民生，使发展成果更好地惠及全体人民。中国将努力建设资源节约型、环境友好型社会，走可持续发展之路。中国人均 GDP 要向发达国家看齐，但人均能源消费、温室气体排放强度绝不能赶超发达国家。

最后，中国将在世界上发挥更加积极的作用。中国需要争取和平的环境来发展自己，也会以自身的发展来维护世界和平，促进共同发展。中国将积极参与国际体系和国际事务，努力发挥建设性促进作用。中国将继续奉行互利共赢的开放战略，积极扩大进口，增加对外投资，为各国创造更多的就业和财富，促进世界经济增长。

中国过去 30 多年的发展道路深刻地改变了中国，沿着这条道路走下去，我们完全有理由相信，中国的未来只会更加光明，更加美好！

同学们，

我曾经去过英国几十所大学，也去过多所中小学。每当我访问一所学校，我都很想知道这个学校是否教授中文。因为，我一直坚持这么一种观点：“了解中国，自中文始。”语言是构成一个国家和民族的基本要素，掌握了一门外语，也就是掌握了开启另一个世界的钥匙。学习汉语将让你们了解中国，了解中国丰富灿烂的文化、日新月异的发展和勤劳智慧的人民；学习汉语将让你们更加自豪，因为你们不仅掌握了世界上使用最广泛的语言——英语，也学会了世界上使用人口最多的语言——汉语。

我很高兴地获知伊顿是英国最早开设中文课程的中学之一，将中文课程列入学校 A-Level 课程（英国高中课程）。在此基础上，伊顿还开设了“短期中国游学”“中国学生伊顿夏令营”等项目，增强学生学习中文的兴趣。我也期待着孔子课堂早日在贵校开办，为你们学习中文、了解中国提供新的渠道。

为使你们更好地学习中文、了解中国，我此次也特意带来了一些关于中国文学艺术、风土人情的书籍和光盘，既有英文的，也有中英文对照的，希望你们喜欢。

老师们、同学们，

中国和英国都是伟大的国家，都曾为人类文明发展做出重大贡献。在新的世纪，中英应当携手合作，促进共同发展，同时为世界的和平与繁荣做出新的更大贡献。伊顿校友惠灵顿公爵曾有一句名言：“滑铁卢的胜利，是在伊顿公学的操场上决定的。”或许，中英关系的未来，很大程度上也还在这里，因为你们将成为中英关系的参与者、建设者。我衷心希望你们与中国的年青一代共同努力，缔造中英关系的美好未来。

谢谢。

下面，我愿回答你们的提问。

China: Ever Old, Ever Young*

Headmaster Anthony Little,

Teachers and students,

It is a real pleasure for me and my wife Pinghua to visit Eton College.

Thank you for the warm welcome. I also want to thank Secretary of the Frontier Society Fred Kim for the kind introduction.

You have come to Eton College to learn. I hope I may also encourage you that, in such a fast-changing world, the habit of learning will be a life-time occupation. Certainly, that is my experience!

Recently I have learned two English words.

One is *Oxonian*. I just visited Oxford University last week and gave a speech at the Oxford Union. In my speech I mentioned several *Oxonians* who made huge contributions to China-UK relations.

Today at Eton I have learned the other word—*Etonian*.

Many *Old Etonians* have made a profound impact on the world. The most recent is Sir John Gurdon who shared this year's Nobel Prize in Physiology or Medicine. I warmly congratulate him especially as he overcame the burden of former Eton Headmaster's comment that he was "too stupid for biology!"

Eton and Oxford have a lot in common:

- They both have a history of hundreds of years.
- They are both located by the river Thames.

---

* Speech at Eton College. Election Hall, Eton College, 17 October 2012.

- They were both chosen to be the settings for the film *Harry Potter*.
- And they have both produced a wealth of talents.

I wonder whether you have a word *Oxtonian* for those attending both Eton and Oxford!

Eton plus Oxford is an optimal combination of education. This combination is distinctively British. Together they have cultivated a galaxy of great people. Thirteen Prime Ministers have come from Eton and Oxford, including the incumbent one. As a traditional description explains, Eton is truly "the chief nurse of England's statesmen."

James Bond is in the news again with the latest movie called *Skyfall*. You may be interested to know Bond films are very popular in China! A less known story is James Bond also went to Eton and Oxford. I gather the story goes that he was expelled by Eton for his talent in trouble making!

Many of you are members of the Frontier Society. The word "frontier" reminds me of the United States where I was posted twice.

In the US history, "frontier" was a term with special meaning. It referred to the "wild west" of the US in the second half of the 19th century.

In the 1960s President Kennedy made an initiative to explore the "New Frontier," which meant space. I have been told that the word "frontier" in the name of your society has taken on a new post-modernist meaning—emerging economies or powers that will assume major influences in the future. These include China.

In today's audience there are also members from the Oriental Society and Keynes Society. Obviously, a common subject of interest to all the three societies is China. So, my topic today is China, a country that is ever old, ever young.

China has a long history. Among the world's four great ancient civilisations, China is the only one that has continued to this day without any break.

I was Chinese Ambassador to Egypt. Egypt is also a very old civilisation. Its recorded history started even earlier than that of China.

But due to many years of foreign occupation and rule, the Egyptian civilisation died out. The writing system currently used in Egypt is entirely different from the hieroglyph in ancient Egypt.

Luckily in early 19th century, archeologists deciphered ancient Egyptian characters that had been lost for 1,400 years. This was done with the help of the Rosetta Stone which is now kept in the British Museum.

China also suffered foreign invasion and aggression. However, unlike other civilisations, the Chinese culture and civilisation has had the strength and resilience to survive. As I will explain, it has survived well.

China was the biggest economy in the world for almost all of the past 2,000 years. Data from *The Economist* also points to China having about a third of global GDP for most of that period. So, it should not be a surprise that products from China were in high demand. For centuries, China's silk, porcelain and tea were the most sought-after products around the world. In those times, "Made in China" was synonymous with the most expensive luxury goods.

Apart from its vast economy and wealth, China fostered a highly developed and sophisticated culture.

Two major native Chinese philosophies were Confucianism and Taoism. They encouraged the pursuit of success and stressed a sense of mission. At the same time, they aimed at harmony between man and nature.

The four major inventions by China—paper making, compass, gun powder and movable printing—contributed greatly to world civilisation and human progress.

This was partly recognised by Sir Francis Bacon. He wrote:

"Printing, gunpowder and the compass—these three have changed the whole face and state of things throughout the world; the first in literature, the second in warfare, the third in navigation."

The monumental impact on world civilisation and progress of humanity by Chinese inventions was fully recognised by a British scholar in the past century.

Ancient Chinese civilisation was so rich and advanced that it took that famous scholar from Cambridge University, Joseph Needham, 50 years to create almost 30 volumes called "Science and Civilisation in China."

China fell behind in modern times. The industrialisation that started in Britain changed the world. The traditional agricultural civilisation of China struggled to find its place in the rapidly industrialised world.

In addition, in the 20th century, China was caught between the millstones of foreign invaders and civil war. The poverty, misery and humiliation that the Chinese people suffered are indescribable.

Even after the founding of The People's Republic in 1949, China also made some mistakes in its development cause. People in hard times were inspired by one line of poem:

"If winter comes, can spring be far behind?"

The author of this poem was an *Old Etonian*—Shelley.

China finally ushered in the spring in the late 1970s when it embarked on reform and opening-up. In the more than 30 years that followed, the Chinese economy has grown at an annual rate of 10%. No country in human history has industrialised so fast and on such a scale. In addition, more than 600 million people were lifted out of poverty.

Today, China ranks number two in world economy and is the world's second largest trading nation.

Since the financial crisis hit the world five years ago, China has become the powerhouse and ballast of global economic growth.

Besides economic prosperity, China has made across-the-broad progress in cultural, political and social fields. Last week, Chinese writer Mo Yan was awarded Nobel Prize in Literature. This is the first time that a Chinese writer has had this honour.

Now the whole world is watching China. China makes headlines in British newspapers and TV media. Walking into any Waterstone's bookshop, you will find a full shelf on China.

So, how to get a clear picture of today's China when there is a flood of information and so many perspectives? I would like to offer you three observations.

First, China is following a development path suitable to its national realities.

So, how should a large country with 1.3 billion people achieve its development goals?

- There is no precedent in history.
- There is no ready answer in the textbook.
- Copying others won't work.
- Wishful thinking in isolation of the world is a dead end.

So, the Chinese people have based their efforts on China's national conditions while drawing on useful experience of other countries.

It has been a process of exploration, experiment, reform and innovation. With hard efforts China has succeeded in finding the right path. This path has the following features:

- It focuses on economic development.
- It puts people first.
- It promotes comprehensive, coordinated and sustainable development.
- It upholds social equity and justice and protects people's democratic rights.

The political institutional guarantee of this development path is built on:

- The system of people's congresses.
- And the system of multi-party cooperation and political consultation under the leadership of the Communist Party of China.

The economic institutional guarantee for this development path is a multi-ownership economy. Public ownership is the mainstay of the economy. At the same time, it allows development of private ownership and foreign investment side by side.

This development path has similarities with other countries. It also has characteristics only found in China.

My second observation to get a clear focus is that China is still a developing country:

- China is a large economy in total size.
- But per capita GDP of China was only 5,432 US dollars last year. According to IMF statistics, this figure was only one seventh of that of Britain.
- That ranks China at 89th place in the world.
- In China, 128 million people still live in poverty.

That means 128 million Chinese live on one dollar per day. If measured against the UN criteria of poverty, i.e., 1.25 dollars per day, then the Chinese poor population will be even higher.

Let me draw on my own experience to give a sense of this poverty. I once worked in one of China's poorest western provinces—Gansu as Assistant Governor. I visited more than 60 of its 86 counties. Here I felt very strongly the wide gap between China's western region and its eastern coastal areas. This is the divide between rural and urban areas. In some villages of Gansu even clean water was difficult to access. These people have a long way to go before they get out of poverty.

My third observation to help you focus is that China is committed to peaceful development:

- Today's China pursues an independent foreign policy of peace. The goal of Chinese foreign policy is to maintain world peace and promote common development.
- China embraces a new security concept that stresses mutual trust, mutual benefit, equality and cooperation.
- China proactively fulfills its international responsibility.
- It insists on good neighbourliness and regional cooperation.
- It calls on all other countries to work together for a harmonious world of lasting peace and common prosperity.
- China will never seek expansion or hegemony.
- The theory that "a strong country must seek hegemony" will never apply to China.

China is committed to peaceful settlement of international disputes and crisis issues.

As evidence of this, China has sent a total of more than 20 thousand personnel of various types to 30 UN peacekeeping missions. This makes China the permanent member of the UN Security Council that has contributed the largest number of peacekeeping personnel.

China has resolved boundary issues with its 12 neighbouring countries on land. China believes disputes over territory and maritime rights with neighbouring countries should be resolved through peaceful negotiations. China will do its best to maintain peace and stability in South China Sea, East China Sea and its surrounding areas.

Recently, Japan has announced its so-called "nationalisation" of Chinese territory Diaoyu Islands. This move has grossly violated China's sovereignty and territorial integrity. It has sparked firm opposition and strong protest from the Chinese people.

We urge Japan to immediately stop all its actions that violate China's sovereignty and territorial integrity and return to the track of resolving disputes through peaceful negotiations.

It has been over two years since I arrived in the UK as Chinese Ambassador. Since my arrival, I have often read in Western media worries about China's future—sometimes even prophecies about China's doom.

The reality is that we Chinese people are confident about our own country. This is backed up even by an American research company.

The Pew Research Centre's survey last July showed that 83% of Chinese people were optimistic about Chinese economy. While in the US and the UK, the figures were only 31% and 15% respectively. As a Chinese diplomat, I have every confidence in China's future!

So, what is the basis of my confidence?

First, the Chinese economy has great potential and a strong drive. Last year, urbanisation rate in China for the first time passed 50%. Britain already reached this level in 1851. The average urbanisation rate in developed countries now stands at around 80%. Urbanisation in China will continue for several more decades. This will create immense demand in housing and infrastructure.

As I said earlier, China's development is not balanced between different regions. The regional balancing process will boost investment and domestic demand and provide a bigger marketplace.

China's consumption mix is upgrading from living necessities like food and clothing to houses, cars and education. China's strength in its large labour force will continue for a long period. With more government input in education, China's human capital will be strengthened. This will bring new population dividends.

The second reason for my confidence is that China's development will be more comprehensive and inclusive.

The Chinese people will be better off in these ways:

- China will continue to advance democracy and rule of law.
- China will uphold social equity and justice.
- China will realise free and all-round development of the people.

- China will ensure and improve people's welfare so that all Chinese people will benefit more from development.
- China will build a resource-conserving and environment-friendly society.
- China will focus on sustainable development.

We will try to catch up with developed countries' per capita GDP figures. But, most important, China must not overtake developed countries in energy intensity and greenhouse gas emissions.

My third point about my confidence is that China will play an even more active role in world affairs:

- China needs a peaceful environment for its development.
- It will also safeguard world peace and promote common development with its own development.
- China will actively participate in international system and global affairs and play a constructive role in it.
- China will adhere to its win-win opening-up strategy.
- This will be done by expanding imports, increasing outbound investment and creating more jobs.

In turn, China's actions will create wealth for all other countries and promote world economic growth.

The development path that China has followed for more than three decades has profoundly changed China.

We have every reason to believe that staying on this path will lead China to a brighter and better future.

Teachers and Students,

I have been to dozens of British universities and many middle and primary schools. Every time I visit a school, I want to know about language teaching, in particular, whether Chinese is being taught. The reason is that I always believe that understanding China starts from learning its language.

Language is one of the essentials that form the culture and character of a country and a nation. Mastery of a foreign language gives you a key to the wider world.

So, learning Chinese will help you understand China, its rich culture and fast development. You will also make many friends amongst its hard-working and ingenious people.

Mastery of Chinese will make you proud because you will be able to speak not only the most widely used language—English, but also the language used by the largest population—Chinese.

I am glad to learn that Eton was one of the earliest British schools to open Chinese language course and include it into the A-Level curriculum. I have also learned how this has motivated Eton to organise visits to China. These study tours in China and the Chinese summer school are bound to boost students' interest in learning Chinese.

I hope a Confucius Institute will be opened in your college in the not-too-distant future. This will open up another channel to learn Chinese and understand China.

To help you learn Chinese language and understand China, I have brought you some books and discs on Chinese literature, art and folk customs. Some of them are in English. Some are bilingual. I hope you will find them interesting.

Teachers and Students,

China and Britain are both great countries.

We both made great contribution to human civilisation. In this new era, China and Britain should join hands to promote common development. Through our collaboration we can make even greater contribution to world peace and prosperity.

One famous *Old Etonian* was the Duke of Wellington. I believe I will quote him correctly when he said, "The Battle of Waterloo was won on the playing fields of Eton."

Maybe the future of China-UK relations to a large extent also lies here at Eton.

The pattern of history suggests that you will be the major participants and builders of future China-UK relations.

Today, I hope my speech would inspire you to reach out and work with the young people of China.

Together you can build a bright future of China-UK relations.

That is the path to create a peaceful, sustainable and harmonious world.

Thank you!

Now I would like to take your questions.

道路坚定，前途光明*

尊敬的四十八家集团俱乐部主席佩里先生，

尊敬的高盛集团全球资产管理总裁奥尼尔先生，

女士们、先生们：

很高兴应四十八家集团俱乐部邀请出席英国工商界的报告会。

四十八家集团60年前率先开启西方与新中国的经贸往来。多年来，四十八家集团关注中国发展历程，致力于推动中英各领域合作，是中国人民的老朋友、好朋友。

过去几个月中，英国朋友们问我最多的问题就是中国共产党的十八大的问题。英国媒体也高度关注，有评论说，十八大是2012年全世界召开的最重要的政治会议。我本人有幸列席了这次历史性的会议，愿同大家分享一些与会的感受和认识。我认为，十八大很好地说明和解答了四个问题。

第一个问题：中国共产党建党已有91年，为什么始终充满活力、焕发青春？

中国共产党坚持党内民主，不断探索党内民主的实现形式，激发全党的活力和创造力。一些英国媒体将十八大与美国大选相提并论，认为这是2012年世界上最重要的两次选举，他们也比较关心中国共产党新领导人的选举方式，总感到有一层神秘面纱。其实，十八大选举神圣但不神秘，是严格依

* 在英国工商界宣介党的十八大精神报告会上的主旨演讲。2012年12月12日，伦敦年利达律师事务所。

照党章和有关规定来进行的，制度和程序是规范的、清楚的，充分体现了中国共产党党内民主的推进。比如，党的中央委员会和纪律检查委员会，本届一共是 506 人，他们先后经过民主推荐、组织考察、中央政治局研究提名、十八大代表讨论酝酿、差额选举等方式，才最终产生。新一届的中央政治局和中央政治局常委则由新产生的中央委员会第一次全体会议选举产生。

十八大的报告，也就是中国共产党的政治宣言和行动纲领，其整个起草过程始终充分发扬民主，广泛听取意见，集中党内外各方智慧。从 2012 年初成立十八大文件起草组到大会开幕近一年时间里，中共中央组织了几十家单位就十余项重大问题进行调研，包括听取党外人士意见。报告几上几下，在全党范围内充分讨论。在十八大会议期间，又根据代表意见，对报告做了进一步修改。可以说，十八大报告是充分发扬民主的成果，是党内外集体智慧的结晶。

过去 10 年，中共一直在代表选举、干部选拔、党务公开、党内决策和监督等各方面进行积极探索，党内民主不断走向正规化和规范化。十八大提出实行“党代会代表提案制”，这是中国共产党首次正式做出该项涉及党内民主机制的重要决定。今后党代会代表对党的大政方针等都可以以制度化的方式提出意见、建议。十八大报告还明确提出，要提高工人、农民代表比例，表明来自基层的声音将更多地得到反映。

中国共产党一直强调以党内民主带动人民民主，党内民主的推进可谓“牵一发而动全身”。10 年间，选举民主、协商民主、基层民主在实践中稳步向前，干部选拔任用走向公开透明，人大代表实现城乡同比例选举，听证制度不断推进，政务信息逐步公开。如今，民众可以通过网络、微博行使知情权、参与权和监督权，政府部门也在网上晒账本、晾信息、回应民众关切。这样的进步，事实上每天都在中国发生。

十八大明确，中国未来将继续积极稳妥推进政治体制改革，发展更加广泛、更加充分、更加健全的人民民主。未来，“中国式民主”必定会更好地根植于现实国情和文化土壤。

第二个问题：中国共产党为什么能始终得到人民的拥护和支持?

“全心全意为人民服务”，这是中国共产党的宗旨。“人民性”也是十八大的突出特点。胡锦涛总书记在十八大报告中强调，只有植根人民、造福人民，党才能始终立于不败之地。习近平总书记在新一届政治局常委与媒体见面时的讲话只有短短几分钟，“人民”一词先后出现了19次。他说：“人民对美好生活的向往，就是我们的奋斗目标。”语言质朴平实，但传递出执政党视人民的利益高于一切的执政理念，体现出执政党对自身宗旨和使命的清醒认识。

在中国经济总量已经跃居世界第二的今天，中国共产党不但关注推动经济持续发展，而且更注重发展为了人民、发展依靠人民和发展成果由人民共享。十八大顺应人民群众对美好生活的新要求和新期待，对保障和改善民生方面的问题做出了全面具体的部署，强调要努力办好人民满意的教育，推动实现更高质量的就业，千方百计增加居民收入，统筹推进城乡社会保障体系建设以及努力发展医疗事业，提高人民健康水平。特别值得一提的是，到2020年，不仅中国国内生产总值要实现比2010年翻番，城乡居民人均收入也要翻番，这是党的发展规划中首次对居民收入增长制定明确目标。十八大报告明确提出要建立以权利公平、机会公平、规则公平为主要内容的社会公平保障体系，营造公平的社会环境，保证人民平等参与、平等发展的权利。值得一提的是，十八大报告中提出的发展和改善民生的目标并非理想化的“空中楼阁”，更不是给选民开的“空头支票”，都是切切实实的，都是看得见、够得着的，都是在不远的将来有望实现的。

一个以人为本、执政为民的服务型政党，自然得到人民的信任和支持，人民必然授予它执政权、领导权。

第三个问题：中国共产党为什么能始终紧跟时代？

一个政党，先进不先进，落伍不落伍，关键在指导思想。中国共产党的指导思想始终与时俱进。十八大确立了“科学发展观”的新指导思想。这是中国共产党在过去10年坚持勇于推进实践基础上的理论创新。这一理论成果，是马克思主义同当代中国实际和时代特征相结合的产物，对新形势下中国实现什么样的发展、怎样发展等重大问题做出了新的回答。科学发展观为中国现代化建设作了全面布局，就是经济建设、政治建设、文化建设、社会建设和生态文明建设的“五位一体”，即经济持续发展，人民民主不断扩大，文化软实力显著增强，人民生活水平全面提高，资源节约型、环境友好型社会建设取得重大进展。

“五位一体”中的“生态文明建设”是十八大新加入的内容，说明中国把环境保护、可持续发展放在了更加重要的地位。中国不仅要成为“富强中国”“民主中国”，也要成为“美丽中国”。说起“美丽中国”这个概念，可能与英国还有关系。几年前，BBC（英国广播公司）和中国中央电视台联合摄制了一部纪录片 *Wild China*，中文名字就叫《美丽中国》，拍摄了中国壮美的自然风光及其珍稀动植物。这部片子播出后，反响很大。当然，我们今天建设“美丽中国”，不仅是要保持名山大川的秀美，更重要的是，要让生活空间宜居适度，生态空间山清水秀，给自然留下更多修复空间，给农业留下更多良田，给子孙后代留下天蓝、地绿、水清的美好家园。

一个解放思想、实事求是、与时俱进、求真务实的政党，一个认识上不断创新、理论上不断创新、实践上不断创新的政党，一个把握时代发展要求、顺应人民共同愿望的政党，必定是一个先进的政党、走在时代前列的政党。

第四个问题：中国共产党坚持中国特色社会主义道路的底气和信心何在？

不同国家有不同的历史、文化和国情，不同国家所走的道路都是其人民长期探索的结果，我们应当尊重各个民族的自主选择，尊重差异性带来的丰富性，而不是试图划定标准，追求千篇一律。中国古人说：“橘生淮南则为橘，橘生淮北则为枳。”今天，如果我们机械照搬照抄别国经验，难免也会有这样的“水土不服”。中国作为最大的发展中国家，土地辽阔，人口众多，民族多样，经济底子薄弱，城乡和地区发展不平衡，面对这些具有中国特色的挑战，就必须给出“中国式解决方案”。

中国共产党从成立那天起，就把建立社会主义作为自己的纲领。在改革开放 30 多年的实践中，中国共产党人既不走封闭僵化的老路，也不走改旗易帜的邪路，而是走出了中国特色社会主义道路，就是在中国共产党领导下，立足基本国情，以经济建设为中心，坚持改革开放，贯彻科学发展观，促进人的全面发展，逐步实现全体人民共同富裕，建设富强民主文明和谐的社会主义现代化国家。

十八大明确将坚定不移地坚持中国特色社会主义道路、中国特色社会主义理论体系和中国特色社会主义制度。未来的中国将“咬定青山不放松”，毫不动摇地沿着这条道路走下去。中国的发展方向比以往任何时候都更加明朗，中国的前途也将更加光明，我们有这样的道路自信、理论自信和制度自信。

女士们、先生们，

我想，在座各位关注中国共产党的十八大，不仅是对中国未来发展感兴趣，也特别关心这次会议对于中英关系的影响。我认为，十八大给两国关系带来了新的发展契机。会议传递出了明确的信号，中国将坚持在和平共处五项原则基础上全面发展同各国的友好合作，将改善和发展同发达国家的关系，拓宽合作领域，妥善处理分歧，推动建立长期稳定健康发展的新型大国关系。这当然适用于中英关系。

中国将始终不渝地奉行互利共赢的开放战略，欢迎英国参与中国现代化建设。特别是中国加快转变经济发展方式，实施创新驱动发展战略，推进文化建设、生态文明建设，发展教育、医疗等社会事业，与英国的优势强项多有契合，双方合作蕴藏着巨大的潜力。中国也愿同英国一道担负好大国责任，进一步加强沟通协调，携手应对粮食安全、能源资源安全、网络安全等全球性挑战。当然，根深才能叶茂，源远才能流长，深化合作离不开良好的政治互信，离不开两国人民加深相互理解。我们期待中英双方在相互尊重、平等相待的基础上，“不动摇、不懈怠、不折腾”，携手走入富有成果的下一个十年。

谢谢。

下面我愿回答你们的提问。

A Solid Path, A Bright Future *

Chairman Perry,

Chairman O'Neill,

Ladies and Gentlemen,

It gives me great delight to accept this invitation from the 48 Group Club.

Your members embody a spirit of friendship and business exchange with China that reaches back almost 60 years. You should be proud that your Club is famous amongst Chinese people. It is greatly respected as the oldest foreign business association of any in the world with New China.

Throughout this long relationship, the 48 Group Club has been a close observer of the major milestones of the evolution of the People's Republic of China. So, you, above all, will appreciate the great significance of the recent meeting of the 18th CPC National Congress in Beijing.

In past decades the British media paid very little attention to the National Congress of the Communist Party of China. But for the 18th Congress, the British media have closely followed this meeting. This reflects the growing understanding that China has a crucial role in the future of the whole world. So, it was not surprising that some observers said it was the world's most important political conference this year.

I had the honour of attending this meeting. So, it is my pleasure to share my observations with such distinguished and long-time friends of China.

In my view, the 18th CPC National Congress answered four questions.

---

* Speech at Icebreaker Lecture with the 48 Group Club. Linklaters, London, 12 December 2012.

The first question is how the CPC has maintained its vigor and vitality—even though it is now 91 years old.

The CPC adheres to and has continuously explored ways to practice democracy within the Party in order to bring out the dynamism and creativity of the whole Party. Some British media compared the 18th CPC National Congress to the presidential election in the USA, suggesting these are the two most important elections this year. In their reporting and comment the UK media showed intense curiosity about how the CPC leaders are elected. The reason was that for UK media they believe that the CPC is opaque and mysterious.

In fact, the elections at the 18th CPC National Congress were solemn but not at all mysterious. The election took place in strict accordance with the institution and procedure stipulated in the CPC Constitution and other related rules. The whole process was clear and predictable. It fully reflected the progress of democracy in the CPC.

For example, the new CPC Central Committee and Disciplinary Committee have a total of 506 members. They are elected through a lengthy procedure. This includes:

- democratic selection,
- assessment by organisational department,
- nomination by the political bureau,
- deliberations among delegates to the 18th National Congress,
- and multi-candidate election.

In turn, the new Political Bureau and its Standing Committee were elected at the first plenary session of the new Central Committee.

Another vital aspect of the 18th National Congress is the Report that is delivered by General Secretary Hu Jintao. The Report matters as it is the political manifesto and action guideline of the CPC.

The drafting process to create this Report embraced full democracy. It extensively solicited opinions from various sectors and crystallised the wisdom of people inside and outside the Party.

During the one year from the setting up of the drafting team to the opening of the Congress, the CPC Central Committee tasked dozens of institutions to carry out surveys and research on over ten major subjects. This included listening to the views of non-CPC members.

The draft Report then went through several rounds of thorough discussions in the entire CPC. During the 18th Congress, the draft was further revised upon the suggestions and comments of the delegates.

So, we may well say that the Report is the work of full democracy and the brainchild of both the CPC and non-CPC members.

In the past decade, the CPC has introduced numerous new democratic steps. For example:

- electing delegates,
- selecting party officials,
- increasing transparency in its own administration, decision making and supervision.

These efforts have greatly advanced the democracy within the CPC. The 18th National Congress established a system that gives Party Congress delegates the mandate to make written proposals. This is a significant decision on promoting democracy within the Party. It offers an institutional guarantee for every Party Congress delegate to make comments and proposals on the CPC's policies. The report also stressed the need to raise the ratio of ordinary workers and farmers in the Party Congress delegates. This means voices from grassroots level will be better heard.

The CPC has all along insisted on using its democratic process to catalyse democracy across China. So, the progress of the CPC's democracy will have a rippling effect. In the past 10 years, democracy in election, consultation and at community level has steadily advanced.

Selection of party officials has become more transparent. The ratio of People's Congress deputies to local population in rural areas was increased to the same as in cities. The selection system was further improved. Information disclosure of governments at all levels was gradually advanced. Now the general public may exercise their right to information, participation and supervision through the Internet and "Weibo." Many of you will know this as the Chinese version of "Twitter."

Government agencies also make public their budget and expenditure and respond to public concerns through the Internet. Such progress is increasingly widespread across China.

The 18th CPC National Congress made it clear that China would continue to move forward political reform actively and properly. There is a commitment to broaden and promote people's democracy to its full. In the future Chinese style democracy will better adapt to the realities in China.

The second question is why the CPC has enjoyed the continuous support of the Chinese people.

The motto of the CPC is repeated in many signs and posters across China. This is: *To serve the people heart and soul.*

To serve the people is a prominent feature of the Report delivered at the 18th Congress. General Secretary Hu Jintao stressed in the Report that the CPC can only prosper by staying in close contact with the people and serving the people.

When the members of the new Standing Committee of the Political Bureau met the press, General Secretary Xi Jinping spoke for only a short time. But in his brief talk the word "people" was mentioned 19 times.

He said, "People's aspiration for a beautiful life is the goal of our endeavor."

These were plain words, but they showed that the CPC, as the ruling party, put the people's interests above anything else. They are powerful examples of CPC's clear understanding of its own purpose and mission.

China is now the second largest economy in the world. High on the CPC's agenda is not only continued economic growth, but also achieving a development of the people, for the people and by the people. Going along with the people's expectation for a better life, the Report of the 18th Congress set out comprehensive plans for ensuring and improving people's life.

The targets set in the Report include:

- improve education,
- create good jobs,
- increase people's income,
- improve social security system in both rural and urban areas,
- and improve public health and the medical system.

In particular, the Report set the target of doubling, not only GDP, but also incomes by 2020 on the basis of the 2010 level. This is the first time that the CPC has set a clear target for the growth of people's income.

The Report at the 18th Congress also talked about building China into a fair society, a society guaranteed by fair rights, opportunities and rules. People will have equal rights to participation and development.

It must be noted that the goals of improving people's life set out in the Report are not a mirage, nor simply paying lip-service. All of the goals are tangible and attainable. All of these aims are reachable in the near future.

Naturally, a party that puts people first and is committed to serving the people has won the trust and support of the people. In turn, the people will continue to give it the power to govern and the power to lead.

The third question is why the CPC has been able to keep abreast with the time.

Whether a political party is advanced or backward is determined by its guiding thought.

The CPC's guiding thought has been constantly updated. The recent 18th Congress established the "scientific outlook on development" as its new guiding thought. This is an innovation in theory. It is based on the CPC's many explorations in the past decade. This latest theory is Marxism adapted to Chinese realities and matching overriding global trends. This guiding thought sheds new light on some major questions. Such as what kind of development China wants and how China can achieve such development.

The "scientific outlook on development" is an umbrella term that embraces a summary of China's modernisation. It puts equal emphasis on economic, political, cultural, social and ecological development. To be specific, these are the aims:

- sustained economic growth,
- broadened democracy,
- strengthened cultural public diplomacy,
- higher living standards of the people,
- and great progress in building a resource-conserving and environment-friendly society.

Amongst these five aspects, preserving the environment is newly added at the 18th

Congress. It shows that environmental protection and sustainable development assumes greater prominence in China's development. We not only want a rich, strong and democratic China. We also want a beautiful and environmentally sustainable China.

The concept of "Beautiful China" has strong links with Britain. Several years ago, the BBC and China Central Television jointly made a documentary about China. Its English name is *Wild China*. But its Chinese name is *Mei Li Zhong Guo* which translates as "Beautiful China." This highly popular documentary recorded China's spectacular natural landscapes, animals and exceptional biodiversity in flowering and fruiting plants.

When we say we aim at a "Beautiful China," we want those rivers and mountains to be enjoyed by future generations. Moreover, we want to ensure a balance between a clean and pleasant environment and increasing fertile land for farming. We want future generations to enjoy blue sky, green landscapes and pure water. This is precious legacy which future generations are entitled to.

All in all, the CPC is a party with a free and open mind. It is down to earth. It seeks truth from facts and keeps up with the times. It always looks to something new and is fresh in ideals, in theory and in practice. It always echoes the call of the times and follows the wish of the people. A political party with these qualities must be an advanced party.

The fourth question: where does the CPC's confidence come from in its chosen socialist path with Chinese characteristics?

Different countries have different histories, cultures and national conditions. Each country's development path is the choice of its own people after long explorations.

So, it is essential that we should respect the choice of different nations and respect the richness brought by diversity. The alternative is an unacceptable path that is myopic and seeks to impose fixed criteria and seek uniformity.

There is an ancient Chinese saying that goes:

Oranges grown on the south of River Huai taste sweet, while on the north sour.

It means the same fruit may have completely different tastes in different environments. In today's world, if we copy other countries' model, I am afraid it would be a case of oranges grown on the north of River Huai.

China is the largest developing country. It has a vast area, huge population and multiple ethnic groups. Its economic foundation is weak and its development is unbalanced in rural and urban areas. To address these uniquely Chinese challenges, there must be Chinese solutions.

Since its founding, the CPC has taken the realisation of socialism as its mission. In the more than three decades of reform and opening-up, the CPC has neither been rigid and conservative nor radical and subversive. Instead, it has opened a socialist path with Chinese characteristics.

This path means that going forward China will:

- follow the leadership of the CPC,
- take into full account China's national conditions,
- focus on economic growth,
- continue with reform and opening-up,
- implement the "scientific outlook on development,"
- promote all-round development of its people,
- realise common prosperity of all Chinese,
- and build China into a modern socialist country that is rich, strong, democratic, culturally advanced, and harmonious.

The 18th CPC National Congress reiterated:

- that China would stick to the socialist path with Chinese characteristics,
- also the socialist theory with Chinese characteristics,
- and the socialist system with Chinese characteristics.

In the future, China will firmly follow these three principles. We have confidence in our path, in our theory and in our system.

Ladies and Gentlemen,

I believe you are interested in the 18th Party Congress. This is not only because you are interested in China's future development, but also because you want to know what it means for China-UK relations.

In my view the 18th Party Congress has brought new opportunities for our relations.

This Congress sent out a clear message. These key points are:

- China will develop friendly cooperation with all countries on the basis of the five principles of peaceful coexistence.
- China will improve and further develop relations with developed countries, expand cooperation, manage differences and build a new type of relationship that is long, stable and healthy.

This message of course applies to China-UK relations.

China remains firmly committed to a win-win strategy of opening-up. We welcome Britain to play a part in China's modernisation. Many of China's priorities are the strengths of the UK such as:

- A shift in growth model,
- innovation,
- culture,
- environmental protection,
- education,
- and medical care.

All these strengths hold out great potential for our cooperation.

China and Britain are two of the great leading nations in the world. So, China also stands ready to work with the UK in fulfilling the responsibilities of big leading countries through closer communication and coordination.

We are ready to join efforts with Britain in addressing such challenges as food security, energy security and cyber security.

Of course, deepening cooperation would be impossible without political mutual trust between our two countries. Hand in hand with this is better understanding between our two peoples.

As we have differing cultures and histories, there are bound to be issues that pose challenges from time to time. But if we strive to deepen a genuine and sincere understanding, then this should be the way to achieve true harmony in our relations.

The year 2013 will be a major milestone for China with a new leadership taking up their responsibilities. As these leaders take office, we hope China and the UK will neither waver nor invite troubles. We hope the leaders of China and the UK, and all the people of our two countries, will work together for another fruitful decade based on mutual respect and equality.

Thank you. I will be glad to take your questions.

“中国梦”：国家、民族和人民之梦*

尊敬的英国外交大臣特别顾问豪厄尔勋爵，

尊敬的四十八家集团俱乐部主席佩里先生，

“青年破冰者”组织主席岳琳女士，

青年破冰者们：

首先我要热烈祝贺“青年破冰者”组织成立五周年。这是我连续第四次出席你们的“生日聚会”。

今年适逢四十八家集团成立 60 周年，我也要借此机会表示热烈祝贺。60 年来，四十八家集团及其继任者“四十八家集团俱乐部”秉承“破冰者”精神，坚信“世界上没有打不破的坚冰”，坚信中英之间和平发展、互利共赢是大势所趋，为中英经贸领域的合作、为中英关系的发展做出了突出贡献。

佩里先生希望我今天与大家谈谈“中国梦”，这是一个不仅在中国，也在世界上被热议的话题。

说起“梦”，近百年来，中国人对自己的国家做了不少“梦”，比如梁启超先生在 20 世纪初就曾在《新中国未来记》中写出了他对中国未来的期望：“无端忽作太平梦，放眼昆仑绝顶来。”梁启超先生做的是“太平盛世梦”。孙中山对中国的梦想则体现在其著作《建国方略》中，所以，孙中山先生有一个“现代化梦”。当然，中国人还有“三峡梦”“奥运梦”“世博梦”。这些

* 在英国“青年破冰者”组织成立五周年晚宴上的主旨演讲。2013 年 5 月 2 日，伦敦皇朝饭店。

梦想如今都一一成为现实。

那么最近习近平主席提出的“中国梦”，其含义是什么呢？它就是习主席阐述的——国家富强、民族复兴和人民幸福。“中国梦”是“三位一体”，缺一不可。

“中国梦”是发展目标、前进方向，那么它有没有路线图呢？我认为，中国共产党的十八大就已经为“中国梦”的实现制定了蓝图，这就是到2020年中国国内生产总值和城乡居民人均收入在2010年基础上翻一番，全面建成小康社会，简称“双倍增计划”；到21世纪中叶建成富强民主文明和谐的社会主义现代化国家。上述这两个目标，一个的完成期正好是中国共产党成立百年，另一个的目标期正好是中华人民共和国建国百年，所以又叫“两个一百年”目标。然后，在“两个一百年”目标的基础上，实现中华民族的伟大复兴。这就是实现“中国梦”的“三步走”战略。

说起“中国梦”，大家不免会想起“美国梦”。那么“中国梦”与“美国梦”的区别是什么呢？“美国梦”是1931年美国历史学家亚当斯首先提出来的概念。“美国梦”就是指一个人无论什么背景，只要通过个人奋斗，就能实现自己的梦想。而“中国梦”则是国家的梦、民族的梦和人民的梦，也是每一个中国人的梦，是个人之梦的集合、是共同的梦。正如习主席所说的：“国家好，民族好，大家才会好。”如果说“美国梦”体现了美国文化和美国国民性格的话，那么“中国梦”则充满着中华文明“家国天下”的理性光辉。

如何才能实现“中国梦”？习主席说：“空谈误国，实干兴邦。”中国已经确定在三个方面真抓实干、治国兴邦。

一是抓好经济、政治、文化、社会和生态五个建设。中国将加快转变经济发展方式，调整经济结构；大力发展人民民主，坚持走中国特色政治发展道路；促进文化繁荣发展，大力弘扬中华优秀文化；提高保障和改善民生水平，着力提高人民生活水平；努力建设美丽中国。因此，“中国梦”是民富国强之梦，是政通人和之梦，是山清水秀之梦。

二是深化改革开放。中国过去30多年的发展得益于改革开放，中国未来的发展仍要靠改革开放。“开弓没有回头箭”，改革只有进行时，没有完成时；开放的大门已经打开，就将始终敞开。改革开放将为中国未来发展提供源源不断的动力。可以说，“中国梦”也是改革之梦，开放之梦。

三是坚持走和平发展道路。“中国梦”不是要“独步武林”，独霸天下，而是要实现民族的复兴，承担大国的责任。中国的发展对世界不是威胁，而是机遇。中国将继续是世界和平的倡导者、维护者，是世界经济的增长动力。中国将继续积极参与国际政治、安全和发展事务，为维护世界和平与地区稳定发挥建设性作用，为推动公正合理的国际体系建设和全球治理做出积极努力，为促进各国合作和世界经济增长做出贡献。今后 5 年中国将进口 10 万亿美元左右的商品，中国对外投资将达到 5 000 亿美元，出境游人次可能超过 4 亿，这无疑将有力带动全球经济发展。所以,“中国梦”也是和平之梦、合作之梦、共赢之梦。

我最近访问了英吉利海峡中的根西岛，参观了法国大文豪雨果被流放期间的故居。正是在那里，他创作了传世名作《悲惨世界》。《悲惨世界》中有一句名言：“世上没有什么比梦想更能创造未来；今天看似乌托邦，明天却将是活生生的现实。”

在座的吉姆·奥尼尔先生，可能当年你提出“金砖国家”一词的时候，也不会想到今天“金砖国家”非但成为一个家喻户晓的概念，而且已经成了一个实实在在的合作共同体，成为当今世界的重要一极，重构了世界的版图。

“中国梦”也是这样，它今天是梦想，明天将是现实。

青年破冰者们，

理解“中国梦”，就是理解中国的发展动力和前进方向，就是理解中国的今天与未来。英国思想家培根说，青年擅长创造，擅长行动，擅长革新。所以我期待着你们来创造，来行动，来革新，抓住“中国梦”带来的机遇，筑就我们共同的“中英关系之梦”，为开创中英关系更加美好的明天做出贡献。

谢谢。

下面我愿回答各位的提问。

"Chinese Dream": The Dream of a Country, a Nation and a People*

Lord Howell,

Chairman Stephen Perry,

Chair Lin Yue,

Young Icebreakers,

I warmly congratulate you all on the fifth anniversary of the "Young Icebreakers."

It has been my privilege to attend four of your "birthday parties."

I also want to take this opportunity to congratulate the 48 Group Club.

This year marks your 60th anniversary. Over the six decades, the 48 Group and its successor the 48 Group Club have carried on the spirit of the "Icebreakers."

I admire your conviction that "there is no unbreakable ice in the world."

I applaud your belief in peaceful development and mutual benefit between China and UK.

During the past 60 years you have made outstanding contributions to China-UK economic cooperation and overall bilateral relations.

Chairman Perry has asked me to talk about the "Chinese Dream." I am very glad to respond to his request. This is a topic that is currently generating much interest both in China and around the world.

Dreams about China are not new. Over the past century Chinese people have dreamed a lot of dreams about our country.

---

* Speech at the Dinner Marking the Fifth Anniversary of Young Icebreakers. Royal China Restaurant, London, 2 May 2013.

For example, in the early 20th century the Chinese scholar and reformist Liang Qichao described his "Chinese Dream" in the political novel *The Future of New China*. He wrote with reference to one of the longest mountain ranges in China:

"I dreamed of standing on the summit of the Kunlun Mountains and seeing a peaceful China."

So, Mr. Liang's dream was about peace and prosperity.

For Dr. Sun Yat-sen, "Chinese Dream" was reflected in his work called *the Fundamentals of National Reconstruction*. That book was mostly about modernisation.

In more recent times Chinese people also had other dreams. For example:

- The "Three Gorges Dam Dream."
- The "Olympic Dream."
- And then the "World Expo Dream."

Today all these dreams have come true.

Then what is the meaning of the "Chinese Dream" recently initiated by President Xi Jinping?

As President Xi has explained, it means:

- A prosperous and strong China.
- The revival of the Chinese nation.
- And a contented life for the Chinese people.

These aspects are three-in-one. None of them are dispensable.

The "Chinese Dream" sets the goal and direction. So, is there a roadmap?

The 18th Congress Report of the Communist Party of China has drawn up a very clear roadmap. The Report includes two main goals:

- The first goal is to double both GDP and per capita income by 2020 on the basis of the 2010 level. This means that the building of a "well-off society" will be completed. This goal is simplified as the "Two Doubles."
- The second goal is to turn China into a socialist modernised country. It means

that, by the middle of this century, China will be rich, strong, democratic, culturally advanced and harmonious.

The accomplishment of these two goals will coincide respectively with two centenary celebrations:

- First, the centenary of the Communist Party of China.
- And second the centenary of the People's Republic of China.

So, these aims are also known as the "Two Centenary Goals."

Through building on the two goals, China will advance to achieve the great revitalisation of the Chinese nation. This is the three-step strategy for fulfilling the "Chinese Dream".

Many people will inevitably compare the "Chinese Dream" with the "American Dream."

What is the difference between the two?

The "American Dream" was first advanced in 1931 by American historian James Adams. His description suggests an individual will realise his dream through honest work irrespective of colour or faith.

This definition of the "American Dream" provides a sharp focus on the cultural difference between China and the USA. In China the "Dream" is driven by the communal interest of all the people.

The "Chinese Dream" is the dream of a country, a nation and a people.

The "Chinese Dream" is not just the dream of the government and leaders of China.

The "Chinese Dream" is also very much the heartfelt dream of every Chinese. It is a common dream.

President Xi embraced the spirit of the "Chinese Dream" when he said,

"Only when the country and the nation are better off, can every one of us be better off."

The "American Dream" embodies American culture and national character.

In turn, the "Chinese Dream" is anchored within, and reaches out from Chinese philosophy. That can be defined in this way:

"One nation is one family and each member is responsible for its prosperity."

How will the Chinese people come together to achieve the "Chinese Dream?"

Again, let me quote President Xi to give an answer. He said,

"Empty talk makes a country suffer, while hard work makes a country prosper. "

Building on the words of President Xi, the Chinese government has decided to work hard in three areas.

First, to make advancements in economic, political, cultural, social and ecological fields. To be specific, China will do the following:

- Transform its economic growth model and readjust the economic structure.
- Press ahead with people's democracy and stick to the political system with Chinese characteristics.
- Advance cultural development and take a deeper understanding of China to the world through its long and rich culture.
- Step up efforts to improve people's welfare and raise living standards.
- Strive to build a beautiful China through sustainable development.

From the above you can see that the "Chinese Dream" is about these main elements:

- National and individual prosperity.
- Good governance.
- And a beautiful environment.

The second area of hard work is to deepen reform and opening-up.

China's rapid growth in the past three decades is attributable to reform and opening-up.

China's future development still hinges on reform and opening-up.

Here I draw on an analogy. Once the arrow is released from the bow it can never return.

In the grammar for reform, there is only "continuous tense," no "perfect tense."

In turn, once the door is open, it will always be open.

Reform and opening-up offers an inexhaustible driving force for China's future development.

In this sense the "Chinese Dream" is also the dream of reform and opening-up.

The third area of hard work is to stay on the path of peaceful development.

The "Chinese Dream" is not to seek supremacy. It is to regain the worthy status of China and take on the responsibility of a big country.

China's development means opportunity, not threat to the world.

China will continue to be the champion and guardian of world peace, and the engine of the world economy. China will contribute in the following areas:

- China will continue to play an active part in international political, security and development affairs.
- China will contribute a constructive role in maintaining world peace and regional stability.
- China will promote an equitable and reasonable international order and global governance.
- And China will boost international cooperation and world economic growth.

Looking forward China will continue to be a key driver of the world economy:

- In the coming five years China's imports will amount to 10 trillion US dollars.
- China's overseas investment will reach 500 billion US dollars.
- The number of China's outbound tourists will pass 400 million.

All these factors will undoubtedly stimulate global growth. So, the "Chinese Dream" is also a dream of peace, cooperation and mutual benefit.

I recently have been to Guernsey in the Channel Islands. There I visited the house where the French writer Victor Hugo lived during his exile. It was in that house that he wrote his masterpiece *Les Miserables*. In that book he made a point very relevant to my theme this evening. Victor Hugo wrote:

"There is nothing like dreams to create the future. Utopia today, flesh and blood tomorrow."

I know Mr. Jim O'Neill is with us tonight. He is famous around the world for his concept of the BRIC countries.

When Mr. O'Neill advanced the idea of BRICS, I feel sure he could not have imagined that so soon BRICS would become a household name. I sense he would have been surprised to see the expanded BRICS operating as a group. We saw this very recently in South Africa. The BRICS have become a force for changes big enough to reshape the world landscape.

The same could be true with the "Chinese Dream." Today it is a dream. Tomorrow, it could be reality.

Young Icebreakers,

Through understanding the "Chinese Dream" you will identify China's goal and direction. You will understand China's present and future.

The great British statesman and philosopher Francis Bacon wrote:

"Young men are fit to invent, for execution and for new projects."

Perhaps I can be bold enough to update the spirit of these words and say "Young men and women!"

So, Young men and women "Icebreakers" I give you a challenge:

- I look forward to your creation, action and innovation.
- I expect you to seize the opportunities brought by the "Chinese Dream."
- I encourage you to contribute your part to a brighter future of China-UK relations.
- I urge you to make true our common dream for China-UK relations.

In conclusion I wish you many more successful anniversaries!

Thank you!

Now, I would like to take your questions.

引领中国发展新时代，开启中英合作新征程*

尊敬的英中协会名誉副主席莱特文爵士，

尊敬的各位议员，

女士们、先生们：

很荣幸再次到访英国议会，特别是非常高兴出席英中协会和英国议会跨党派中国小组在这里联合举办的中共十九大精神宣介会。

这几天，我通过撰文、演讲和接受采访等方式，向英国各界人士广泛宣介中国共产党第十九次全国代表大会，目的只有一个，那就是希望大家能更好地了解十九大对中国和世界的影响，更好地了解中国未来发展的新思想、新蓝图和新举措。

作为大会亲历者，我很高兴今天有机会与各位议员分享我的所感、所思和所想。我先做一个开场发言，然后我们进行深入的讨论。莱特文爵士告诉我，议员们对报名参加今天的活动很踊跃，想讨论的问题也很多，希望我多留出提问的时间。我完全同意。一般演讲的“黄金定律”是“七分演讲，三分答问”，今天我们可以“三分演讲，七分答问”。大家可以放开提问，我已留出充分时间，为的是不留下任何未回答的问题。

习近平总书记在十九大报告中做出了“中国特色社会主义进入新时代”的重大判断，那么这个新时代到底意味着什么呢？

第一，新时代意味着新方位。明确方位才能找准方向，把握大势才能赢

* 在英国议会宣介中共十九大精神主旨演讲。2017 年 11 月 21 日，英国议会下院。

得未来。随着近40年的改革开放和快速发展，中国社会的主要矛盾已经转化为人民日益增长的美好生活需要和不平衡不充分的发展之间的矛盾。明确社会主要矛盾的历史性变化，为制定国家大政方针提供了理论依据，标志着中国将在继续推动发展的基础上，着力解决好发展不平衡不充分问题，大力提升发展质量和效益，更好地满足人民在经济、政治、文化、社会、生态等方面的需要，更好地推动人的全面发展、社会全面进步。

第二，新时代产生了新思想。思想是一个政党的灵魂。十九大把习近平新时代中国特色社会主义思想确立为指导思想，深刻回答了新时代怎么坚持和发展中国特色社会主义的根本问题，并对经济、政治、法治、科技、文化、教育、民生、生态、国防、外交、党建等17个方面的工作提出了战略指导和规划，这标志着中国共产党指导思想实现了又一次历史性飞跃。习近平新时代中国特色社会主义思想，是一个系统完整的科学理论体系，是马克思主义与中国实践相结合的最新理论探索和思想创新结晶，将为推进中国特色社会主义事业提供坚强的政治和思想保障。

第三，新时代确立了新目标。目标指向未来，宏图激发信心。十九大提出，从现在到2020年，是全面建成小康社会决胜期；从十九大到二十大，是“两个一百年”奋斗目标的历史交汇期。大会还提出两个“十五年”的战略安排，分两步走实现全面建设社会主义现代化国家的新目标，即从2020年到2035年，基本实现社会主义现代化；从2035年到21世纪中叶，把中国建成富强民主文明和谐美丽的社会主义现代化强国。上述宏伟蓝图确立了中国社会主义现代化新征程的坐标体系，展现了中国人民对国家发展前景的强大信心。

第四，新时代打造了新格局。大格局才能有大作为。十九大按照“五位一体”总体布局，协调推进“四个全面”战略布局，对经济建设、政治建设、文化建设、社会建设、生态文明建设以及党的建设做出新的全面部署。中国将坚定不移推进全面深化改革，不断推进国家治理体系和治理能力现代化；贯彻新发展理念，建设现代化经济体系，坚持经济发展质量第一、效率优先，以供给侧结构性改革为主线，推动经济持续健康发展；实施好乡村振兴、区域协调发展、健康中国等各项发展战略，坚决打好防范化解重大风险、精准脱贫、污染防治等攻坚战。我想强调的是，中国开放的大门不会关闭，只会越开越大，中国将以“一带一路”建设为重点，遵循共商共建共享原则，加强创新能力开放合作，形成陆海内外联动、东西双向互济的开放格局。

第五，新时代迎来了新的中央领导集体。伟大事业离不开坚强的领导核心。十九大选举产生了新一届中央领导集体，一批德才兼备、年富力强的领导干部进入中共中央委员会和新一届中央政治局，再次说明中国共产党具有旺盛生命力和强大凝聚力，充分反映出中国发展事业的蓬勃兴旺。打铁必须自身硬，中国共产党将取得反腐败斗争的压倒性胜利，推动全面从严治党向纵深发展。我相信，在以习近平同志为核心的中共中央新一届领导集体带领下，在13亿多中国人民的努力下，中华民族伟大复兴的“中国梦”必将实现！

女士们、先生们，

我注意到，英国各界高度关注新时代中国外交政策走向，英国媒体做了大量报道，其中既有客观正面的评价，也有一些主观片面的解读。今天，我想着重谈一下这个问题。

十九大报告确定了中国特色大国外交的两大目标，即推动构建新型国际关系，推动构建人类命运共同体。这两个目标分别回答了两个问题，即中国要推动建设一个什么样的世界以及如何建设这个世界。

中国致力于推动建设相互尊重、公平正义、合作共赢的新型国际关系，这三者紧密联系，相辅相成，是一个有机系统的整体。

第一，相互尊重是基础。在当今世界处于大发展、大变革、大调整的背景下，世界各国应顺应时代潮流和大势，尊重彼此自主选择的社会制度和发展道路，尊重彼此核心利益和重大关切，推动不同发展模式取长补短、相互促进、共同发展。

第二，公平正义是准则。中国是讲公平、讲正义、讲法治、讲秩序的国家，一贯认为大小国家一律平等，根据事情本身的是非曲直决定自己的原则立场，主张各方应摒弃冷战思维，树立共同、综合、合作、可持续的新安全观。

第三，合作共赢是目标。各方要扔掉我赢你输、赢者通吃的旧思维，树立做大“蛋糕”、互利合作的新观念。我们要用整体而不是割裂的眼光看待和处理国际关系，倡导各国在维护本国利益的同时增进人类共同利益，实现不同社会制度、不同发展道路、不同文化传统的国家和平共处、和谐共生。

中国致力于构建人类命运共同体，这一理念的核心就是建设持久和平、普遍安全、共同繁荣、开放包容、清洁美丽的世界。政治上，坚持相互尊重、平等协商，走对话而不对抗、结伴而不结盟的国与国交往新路。安全上，坚持以对话解决争端，以协商化解分歧，统筹应对传统和非传统安全威胁。经济上，坚持同舟共济，促进贸易和投资自由化、便利化，推动经济全球化朝着更加开放、包容、普惠、平衡、共赢的方向发展。文化上，尊重世界文明多样性，坚持不同文明文化互学互鉴、取长补短、包容发展。生态上，坚持建设环境友好型社会，各国合作应对气候变化挑战，保护好人类共同的家园。

我相信，随着中国日益走近世界舞台的中央，我们愿意给世界提供更多中国智慧、中国方案和中国经验，给国际社会带来更多正能量，给各国发展带来更多新机遇。

女士们、先生们，

世界在进步，中国在发展。关于如何全面客观地看待新时代中国发展前景，我想给各位议员提三点建议。

一要全面地看，不要局部地看。十九大为中国下一步发展做出的各项战略部署是一个有机整体，习近平新时代中国特色社会主义思想是一个科学完整的理论体系。因此，要联系地而不是孤立地、系统地而不是零散地、全面地而不是局部地看十九大提出的各项新理念和新部署。如果只关注个别事项，就会只见树木、不见森林，就难以看清大局和大势。

二要长远地看，不要短浅地看。当前，中国确实面临着发展不平衡、不充分等挑战，投资环境可能也存在着这样那样的问题。但我认为，中国改革开放近 40 年的经验表明，发展中的问题完全可以在发展中逐步加以解决。

正如在中国传统哲学中，“危”与“机”是可以相互转换的，不仅“危中蕴机”，还可以“化危为机”。如果只关注眼前问题，犹豫不决，瞻前顾后，就难以把握好甚至会错失很多“黄金机遇”。

三要发展地看，不要用旧眼光看。新时代中国特色社会主义建设的一条重要经验，就是立足本国国情，坚持走自己的路。中国特色社会主义建设是一个不断革故鼎新、与时俱进的过程。中国的创新没有穷尽，中国的改革没有止境，中国的发展没有终点。如果仍用冷战时期意识形态之争的旧思维、用“国强必霸”“零和游戏”的旧逻辑看待中国发展和中国道路，必将被滚滚向前的历史车轮抛在后面。

女士们、先生们，

2017 年是中英建立大使级外交关系 45 周年，也是中英关系“黄金时代”深入发展之年。我们对两国关系取得的成绩感到骄傲，更对新时代中英关系的发展前景感到振奋。我认为，中共十九大将为中英关系发展提供三大机遇。

一是中国政策机遇。十九大提出中国将贯彻“新发展理念”，坚定不移地走“创新、协调、绿色、开放、共享”的发展道路，加快建设开放型、创新型国家，全面实行准入前国民待遇加负面清单管理制度，大幅度放宽市场准入，扩大服务业对外开放，保护外商投资合法权益。最近出台的将对外国投资者投资证券等金融领域的比例限制放宽至 51%、三年后不受限制的政策，就得到英国工商界人士的热烈欢迎。未来中国还将出台更多惠民生、促发展的举措，这必将为包括英国在内的各国深化同中国的互利合作开创更多机遇。

二是合作发展机遇。中国是世界第二大经济体，对世界经济增长的贡献率超过 30%。随着中国加快发展和对外开放，中国作为世界经济增长主要引擎的作用将不断提升。富起来的中国为世界和平与发展事业做出了重要贡献，强起来的中国一定会做出更大贡献。预计未来 15 年，中国将进口 24 万亿美元的商品、吸收 2 万亿美元的外来投资，对外投资总额将达到 2 万亿美元；未来 5 年，中国出境旅游将达到 7 亿人次。这些数字本身最有力地说明了中国发展给世界带来的机遇。

三是国际协作机遇。十九大提出中国将秉持共商共建共享的全球治理观，主动参与和推动经济全球化进程，积极参与全球治理体系改革和建设。中英两国作为联合国安理会常任理事国和二十国集团重要成员，在倡导自由贸易、支持经济全球化、完善全球经济治理等方面拥有广泛共识，开展了有效合作。正如梅首相上周在金融城晚宴上演讲时所说，“英中可携手塑造世界格局”。中英两国完全可以加强合作，共同为推动构建新型国际关系和人类命运共同体做出贡献。

女士们、先生们，

正如习近平主席 2015 年对英国进行国事访问在议会演讲时指出的，“议会是各界精英荟萃之地。希望各位议员登高望远，继续做中英关系的积极推动者、中英友好的贡献者、中英合作的支持者，为中英关系更广阔、更光明的未来铺设理解之路、架起合作之桥”。

今天，中国发展进入新时代，中英关系发展迈入“黄金时代”。我们期待与在座的各位议员以及英国各界人士携手努力，并肩前行，推进中英关系“黄金时代”行稳致远，不断打造“黄金成果”，造福两国人民和世界人民。

谢谢。

下面我愿回答各位成员的提问。

New Era for China and New Chapter of China-UK Cooperation*

Sir Oliver Letwin,

Lords and MPs,

Ladies and Gentlemen,

It is a great delight to be back at the House of Commons for this event co-hosted by GBCC and APPCG to talk about the 19th National Congress of the Communist Party of China.

For the past weeks I have been busy sharing information with my British friends about this epoch-making Congress. I published articles on newspapers and delivered a few speeches. And I was on ITV's *Peston on Sunday*. I want to get more people to know why this Congress is significant to both China and the world. I hope to elaborate on China's new thinking, new blueprint and new measures for further development.

I was honoured to have attended the Congress in Beijing in person. And I feel equally honoured to be here today to share my thoughts and observations with the British peers and members of Parliament.

Today, I am going to deliver a speech first, then we get down to further discussion. I completely agree with Sir Oliver's suggestion that I shall leave more time for questions. I know you have come with a lot.

So, despite of the golden rule of 70 percent speech and 30 percent Q&A, today I am going to turn this around by leaving 70 percent of the time to Q&A. Please feel free to

---

* Speech at the British Parliament. House of Commons, 21 November 2017.

raise any questions you may have. I promise I will leave no question unanswered.

Now, let me begin with the core message of the Congress. This is: socialism with Chinese characteristics is entering into a new era.

What does the *new era* mean? I think there are at least five implications.

First, China is at a new historic juncture.

To know where the future lies, you must first know where you are. The 19th Congress sets the direction for China's development in the coming years.

After nearly four decades of reform, opening-up and rapid growth, the principal contradiction facing the Chinese society has evolved. And so has our main task. According to the Congress, China's main task now is to address the imbalances and inadequacies in our development in order to meet the people's ever-growing needs for a better life.

Recognising this change is highly significant. This will determine what policies and overall strategies China will adopt. China continues to push for development. But we will target the imbalances and inadequacies in our development. This means we want higher-quality growth and we want more efficient growth. We want to meet our people's needs for a better life in all respects. This includes economic, political, cultural, social and eco-environmental needs. We want well-rounded development for every individual and social progress in all respects.

Second, in this new era, we have new theories to lead the way.

Theoretical guidance is the soul of a political party.

The new theoretical guidance of our Party is Xi Jinping Thought on Socialism with Chinese Characteristics for a New Era. This was established at the 19th Congress. It answers the fundamental question of how to uphold and develop socialism with Chinese characteristics in the new era. It consists of strategic plans for our work in 17 areas, including the economy, politics, rule of law, science and technology, culture, education, people's welfare, ecology, national defense, diplomacy, party building, etc.

This is a new milestone in the evolution of theoretical thoughts of the Communist Party of China. Xi Jinping Thought is a system of scientific and comprehensive theory. It is the result of adapting Marxism to the Chinese context. It represents our latest efforts in theoretical exploration and creation. It is the political and ideological guarantee for building socialism with Chinese characteristics.

Third, in this new era, we have set new objectives.

These objectives unveil an exciting future and give us great confidence.

The five years between now and the next National Congress are crucial. It is a period in which the time-frames of China's Two Centenary Goals converge.

The first centenary goal is to complete the building of a moderately prosperous society in all respects. This will have been delivered by 2020 before the 100th anniversary of the Communist Party of China.

Then it will be time to move on to the second centenary goal of building a modern socialist country when the People's Republic marks its 100th anniversary.

This will be achieved in two steps from 2020 to 2050, with 15 years for each step, namely:

- realising socialist modernisation by 2035,
- and building China into a great modern socialist country that is prosperous, strong, democratic, culturally advanced, harmonious and beautiful by the middle of this century.

This new blueprint marks out the important signposts for our journey ahead. It demonstrates the Chinese people's strong confidence in their country's future development.

Fourth, in the new era, we have made new action plans.

Big accomplishments always require overall planning. The 19th Congress has made overall plans for China in line with the Five-sphere Integrated Plan and the Four-pronged Comprehensive Strategy. These are new and comprehensive plans. They cover the economic, political, cultural, social, and eco-environmental fields as well as party building.

- China will carry out deeper and more comprehensive reforms to modernise its governance system and capability.
- China will implement the new development concepts and aim at sustainable and healthy growth. This will be achieved by building a modern economy and improving the quality and efficiency of growth.

- China will pursue a rural vitalisation strategy, implement a coordinated regional development strategy and carry out the Healthy China Initiative.
- China will take tough steps to forestall and defuse major risks, carry out targeted poverty alleviation, and prevent and control pollution.

And I want to stress that China will stay open to the world. We will only open wider. Here, the Belt and Road Initiative (BRI) will be a priority. In developing this major Initiative, we will strive for shared growth through discussion and collaboration with partners. And we will open wider to the world in building up our innovation capacity. With these efforts, we hope to break new ground in opening China further through links in all directions, across land and over sea.

Fifth, in the new era, we have a new central leadership.

A great cause calls for strong and firm leadership. The 19th Congress elected a new CPC central leadership. The new Central Committee and Political Bureau are strong and vigorous with political integrity and professional competence. This goes to show the CPC's strong vitality and cohesion. This also goes to show that China's causes are booming.

The CPC will continue to work hard to secure a sweeping victory in the fight against corruption. As the saying goes, it takes a tough blacksmith to make good steel. Strict self-governance will make sure that the Party is tough in dealing with corruption.

Now the 1.3 billion Chinese people are rallying around the new central leadership with General Secretary Xi Jinping at its core. I have every confidence that China is in good hands, and we are well on our way to achieve the "Chinese Dream" of national rejuvenation.

Ladies and Gentlemen,

I noted that many people here in Britain, the media in particular, are following China's foreign policy closely to understand how it will unfold in the new era. Some media reports are fairly objective and positive while others are based on misperceptions. Let me use this opportunity to share my take.

The Congress lays out China's two major diplomatic visions. One is to build a new type of international relations. The other is to build a community with a shared future for mankind. They answer two questions:

- What is China's vision of the world?
- How will China seek to shape the world?

China envisions a new type of international relationship, which has three salient features, namely mutual respect, fairness and justice, and win-win cooperation. These three elements are interconnected and mutually-reinforcing. Together they give us a complete picture of the new type of international relations. Let me go through them one by one.

First, mutual respect. This is the basis for the new type of international relations.

The world today is undergoing major developments, transformation, and adjustment. In this context, all countries should follow the trend of the times, which is peace and development. Therefore, countries must respect each other's independent right to choose their own social system and development path. Countries must respect each other's core interests and major concerns. And countries should try to learn from each other in order to stimulate progress and common development.

Second, fairness and justice. This is the norm of the new type of international relations.

China attaches fundamental importance to fairness, justice, rule of law and order. We believe that all countries are equal regardless of size. We always take position on an issue based on its own merits. We resolutely reject the Cold War mentality and call on all countries to do the same. We stand for a new thinking on common, comprehensive, cooperative and sustainable security.

Third, win-win cooperation. This is the objective of the new type of international relations.

The ideas of zero-sum games or "the winner takes it all" are outdated and should be abandoned. They should be replaced with a new way of thinking, namely making the pie bigger so that everyone gets a larger share. Cooperation should aim at mutual benefits.

Our world is an integrated and interconnected whole. That is the right way to approach state-to-state relations. Countries certainly must uphold their own national interests. But they should not lose sight of the common interests of humanity. After all, despite differences in social system, development path and cultural heritage, we have only one world to share and we should share it in peace and harmony.

Now let me turn to China's other vision, namely building a community with a shared future for mankind. This concept is about building an open, inclusive, clean, and beautiful world that enjoys lasting peace, universal security and common prosperity.

- In the political dimension, the community with a shared future advocate mutual respect and consultation on an equal footing. It calls for a new approach to state-to-state relations based on communication rather than confrontation, partnership rather than alliance.
- In the security dimension, the community with a shared future advocate settling disputes through dialogue, resolving differences through discussion, and joint response to traditional and non-traditional threats.
- In the economic dimension, the community with a shared future advocate trade and investment liberalisation and facilitation, and economic globalisation that is more open, inclusive and balanced and whose benefits are shared by all. In short, we are all in the same boat.
- In the cultural dimension, the community with a shared future advocate respect for cultural diversity, mutual learning and inclusive development.
- In the ecological dimension, the community with a shared future advocate the idea of "a home for all." This calls on countries to build an environment-friendly society and work with each other to tackle climate change.

I believe that as China moves closer to the centre stage, we will be able to share with the world more of China's wisdom, China's solution and China's experience. We will bring more positive energy into the world and we will create new development opportunities for other countries.

Ladies and Gentlemen,

The world is moving on. China is also making progress. When you try to understand China's development prospects in the new era, it is important to take a comprehensive and objective perspective.

Here I have three pieces of advice.

First, it is important to see the complete picture.

The development plans laid out at the 19th Congress formed an integral whole. So is Xi Jinping Thought. It is a system of scientific and comprehensive theory. The new ideas and strategic plans are interconnected rather than isolated. They are part of a systematic structure, not just individual bits and pieces. They should always be seen and understood as part of a complete picture. If one only focuses on the bits and pieces, it is easy to lose sight of the larger picture and the overall trend. As we say in China, "Staring at one tree will make one blind to the whole forest."

My second advice is that it is important to see China in the long run.

China has its share of challenges. There are imbalances and inadequacies in our development. There are also problems of one sort or another with our investment environment. During forty years of reform and opening-up, China encountered and overcame countless difficulties. Our experience speaks loud and clear: When you run into a problem in the process of development, development itself is the solution.

According to the Chinese philosophy, in every crisis there is opportunity if you are ready to see beyond the problems before your eyes. If you cannot, if you hesitate and dare not take action, the many "golden opportunities" will slip away.

My third advice is that it is important to keep our mind open and our thoughts up to date.

There is one most important experience in building socialism with Chinese characteristics for the new era. That is, we have found our own development path, and this path suits us. This is a path of constant reform and innovation. On this path, we must always keep pace with the times. Going forward, China will keep on innovating. China will keep on reforming; China will keep on developing.

When interpreting China's path and China's development, one should abandon the Cold War mentality and do away with the old-fashioned logic of power politics and zero-sum games. Those who cling on to these outdated concepts will end up on the wrong side of history.

Ladies and Gentlemen,

This year marks the 45th anniversary of China-UK ambassadorial diplomatic relations. It is also a year for consolidating the China-UK Golden Era.

We have every reason to be proud of the progress we have made in our bilateral ties, and we have more reason to feel heartened by the prospects of our future relations.

For China-UK ties, I believe the 19th Congress brings at least three major opportunities.

The first opportunity comes from China's development policies.

China will pursue innovative, coordinated, green and open development shared by all. These are what we call new development concepts.

We will stay open. And we will build a country of innovators. To achieve this, we will implement the system of pre-establishment national treatment plus a negative list across the board. This will significantly increase market access, further open up the service sector, and protect the legitimate rights and interests of foreign investors.

An example of this is the recent measure to increase foreign ownership limit in the financial sector to 51%, with the prospect of removing the cap after three years. I believe the British business community will welcome this new move.

Going forward, China will roll out more measures that focus on improving the lives of the people and stimulating growth. These new favourable policies will create more opportunities for closer cooperation between China and the world, Britain included.

Second, there are opportunities in China's booming development.

China is the world's second largest economy. We are on average contributing more than 30% to world growth. As China continues to grow and opens further to the world, its role as an economic powerhouse will be reinforced.

A prosperous China is delivering benefits to world peace and development. A stronger China will certainly make greater contribution.

In the coming fifteen years, China will import 24 trillion US dollars of goods, open up a 2,000-billion-dollar market to foreign investors, and invest about 2,000 billion dollars overseas. In the next five years, Chinese tourists will make more than 700 million overseas visits.

These numbers offer a glimpse of what kind of opportunity China will bring to the world.

Third, there are opportunities for international collaboration.

At the 19th Congress, China highlighted its concepts of global governance. These are extensive consultation, joint contribution and shared benefits.

In line with these concepts, China will work vigorously to advance economic globalisation and play an active part in building and reforming the global governance system.

China and Britain are both permanent members of the UN Security Council and important members of the G20. Our two countries have broad consensus on upholding free trade, supporting economic globalisation and improving global economic governance. And our cooperation in these areas has been effective.

Prime Minister May said this at the Lord Mayor's banquet last week,

"I am committed to maintaining the Golden Era of our relationship with China...whose decisions together with ours will shape the world around us."

I think the Prime Minister's message is loud and clear. I believe China and the UK working together will contribute undoubtedly and enormously to the building of a new type of international relations and a community with a shared future for mankind.

Ladies and Gentlemen,

During his state visit to the UK in 2015, President Xi Jinping delivered a speech here at the Parliament. He said,

"Parliamentarians are the cream of a society. I hope you will, as we Chinese often say, 'scale higher to see further.' I hope that you will continue to promote the UK's relations with China, strengthen our friendship and support our cooperation. And I hope that you will build a bridge of understanding and cooperation so as to help create an even brighter and more promising future of our bilateral ties."

Now, China's development has entered a new era. China-UK relationship is in the Golden Era. We are ready to join hands with each and every one of you present today and with British friends from all sectors to build a lasting China-UK Golden Era that will bear more "golden fruits" and deliver more benefits to the people of our two countries and beyond.

Thank you.

Now, I will be glad to take your questions.

读懂新时代中国，构建人类命运共同体*

尊敬的中宣部副部长、国务院新闻办主任蒋建国先生，

尊敬的中国国家创新与发展战略研究会会长郑必坚先生，

尊敬的西班牙前首相冈萨雷斯先生，

尊敬的意大利前总理蒙蒂先生，

尊敬的芬兰前总理万哈宁先生，

尊敬的贝格鲁恩研究会联合创始人嘉德尔斯先生，

女士们、先生们、朋友们：

大家下午好！

很高兴出席“新时代中国”国际研讨会开幕式。

随着中国进入新时代，今天研讨会的主题可谓恰逢其时，它回答了两个问题：一是为什么要读懂新时代的中国，二是怎样读懂新时代的中国。

关于第一个问题，我有三点建议要与大家分享。

第一，这是抓住“中国机遇”的现实需要。中国是世界第二大经济体，对世界经济增长的贡献率超过30%，已成为世界经济的重要贡献者、世界和平的坚定维护者、全球治理的积极建设者。2017年中共十九大的成功召开，标志着中国特色社会主义进入新时代。新时代中国前进的步伐将更加坚定、更加稳健：2020年全面建成小康社会，2035年基本实现社会主义现代化，到21世纪中叶建成富强民主文明和谐美丽的社会主义现代化强国。新时代

* 在“新时代中国”国际研讨会开幕式上的讲话。2018年4月11日，伦敦克林西亚酒店。

的中国将给各国带来更多新机遇，而只有那些真正了解中国的人，才能抓住“中国机遇”，搭上中国发展快车。

第二，这是构建人类命运共同体的时代呼声。当今世界正处在大发展、大变革、大调整之中。随着经济全球化深入发展，世界已变成地球村，各国成为你中有我、我中有你的命运共同体。新时代中国外交的总目标，就是要推动构建新型国际关系、构建人类命运共同体。这不是一个或几个国家的事情，需要世界各国一道努力，共同参与全球治理，共同分享发展成果，共同推动发展进步。作为世界上最大的发展中国家和全球影响力日益上升的新兴国家，中国更加需要世界，世界也更加需要中国。

第三，这是缩小中西方“认知鸿沟”的必要途径。我从事外交工作 40 多年，对中西方“认知鸿沟”深有感触。40 多年来，我目睹中国走上改革开放的道路，人民生活水平不断改善，国际地位不断提升。但西方对中国的“认知鸿沟”仍然存在。要缩小“认知鸿沟”，需要双方的努力。西方要改变旧思维，摒弃西方中心论，努力从中国历史、文化和传统中寻求今日中国思维、理念和政策的根源，更加全面、客观、深入地了解和理解当代中国。中国则要更加积极主动地向西方民众讲好中国理念、中国观点和中国故事。我想，这正是“新时代中国”国际研讨会的意义所在。

关于如何读懂新时代中国，我也想与大家分享三点建议。

第一，要全面认识中国共产党。要读懂中国，就先要读懂中国共产党。中国共产党不同于西方任何一个政党，是一个拥有近 9 000 万党员、带领近 14 亿中国人民开创美好新时代的政党，是一个具有优良传统、强大生命力、始终全心全意为人民服务的政党，是一个坚持为中国发展谋长远、为中国人民谋幸福、为人类进步事业而奋斗的政党。中国共产党始终把为人类做出新的更大的贡献作为自己的使命。

第二，要深刻研读《习近平谈治国理政》。今天上午我出席了《习近平谈治国理政》第二卷多语种图书首发式。这部著作集中反映了习近平新时代中国特色社会主义思想的发展脉络和主要内容，充分体现了中国共产党为推动构建人类命运共同体、促进人类和平与发展崇高事业贡献的中国智慧和中国方案。这部书是全面了解中国最系统、最权威的著作，是读懂中国的宝典，是解读中国的金钥匙。

第三，要近距离了解中国国情和民情。“百闻不如一见”。我的不少英国朋友对此深有感触，“现场真实版”中国和“西方报道版”中国反差很大。高铁、网购、移动支付、共享单车，这些被称为中国的“新四大发明”，不仅让他们见证了中国在新一轮技术革命中的大发展，更让他们认识到中国是一个发展日新月异、民众活力四射、文化开放包容的国度。

习近平主席指出，“读懂中国是一个双向交流的过程”。历史一再证明，只有与时代同步伐、与世界共命运的人，才能赢得光明的未来。我衷心希望各位专家学者积极投身于“双向交流的过程”，通过各种方式了解和感受中国的新发展、新气象、新宏图，与我们一道讲好中国故事，为促进中国与世界的交流与合作，为构建人类命运共同体，为建设一个更加多彩、光明、美好的世界贡献力量！

最后，我预祝“新时代中国”国际研讨会圆满成功！

谢谢大家！

Understanding China in the New Era is Key to Building a Community with a Shared Future for Mankind*

Minister Jiang Jianguo,

Chairman Zheng Bijian,

Mr. González,

Mr. Monti,

Mr. Vanhanen,

Mr. Gardels,

Ladies and Gentlemen,

Dear Friends,

Good afternoon!

It is a real delight to join you at the opening ceremony of the Seminar on "China in the New Era."

I think this seminar is highly timely as it draws our attention to two very important questions.

- First, why is it important to understand China in the new era?
- Second, what should we do to understand China in the new era?

With regard to the question of why, I have three answers.

---

* Remarks at the Opening Ceremony of the Seminar on "China in the New Era." Corinthia Hotel, London, 11 April 2018.

First, the world needs to understand China in the new era in order to seize the Chinese opportunities.

Today, China is the second largest economy in the world and contributes over 30% to world economic growth. It is an important contributor to world economy, a firm upholder of world peace and an active participant in global governance.

Last year's 19th National Congress of the Communist Party of China ushered in a new era for socialism with Chinese characteristics.

In the new era, China will move forward with firm and steady steps:

- China will complete the building of a moderately prosperous society in all respects by 2020.
- China will realise socialist modernisation by 2035.
- China will strive to become a modern socialist country, namely a prosperous, strong, democratic, culturally advanced, harmonious and beautiful country, by the middle of this century.

In this process, China will create new opportunities for all countries. To be able to seize these opportunities and catch the express train of China's development, one needs to truly understand China in the new era.

Second, the world needs to understand China in the new era in order to appreciate the true meaning of building a community with a shared future for mankind.

The world is undergoing profound changes and transformation. Globalisation has turned the world into a village, namely a community with a shared future.

The overarching goal of China's diplomacy in the new era is to promote the building of a new type of state-to-state relations and a community with a shared future for mankind.

This is not the work for one or a few countries. Everyone must pitch in. We should all take part in the global governance. We should push for common progress. And we could all share the fruits of development.

China is the largest developing country and an emerging economy with growing global influence. China and the world certainly need each other in this great endeavour of building a community with a shared future for mankind.

Third, to understand China in the new era helps bridge the divide in mutual knowledge between China and the West.

In my over 40 years of diplomatic career, I have experienced too much of this divide between China and the West.

China has seen tremendous improvements in the life of its people and a huge increase in its global influence since reform and opening-up policies were introduced 40 years ago. However, there is still a knowledge deficit in the West when it comes to China. Bridging of this divide in mutual knowledge requires the efforts of both sides.

The West needs to change its old mindset and discard Western-centrism. It needs to look for the origin of China's thoughts, principles and policies in its history, its culture and its heritage. This could be the beginning of a comprehensive, objective and deep understanding and appreciation of contemporary China.

China for its part needs to take more initiatives in telling the West about China's thoughts, China's views and China's story. That is why, I think, it is so meaningful and important to have this seminar on China in the new era.

Now, let me turn to the second question, that is, how to understand China in the new era. I want to share with you my three suggestions.

My first suggestion is to fully understand the Communist Party of China.

This is the first step to understanding China.

The Communist Party of China is different from any political party in the West.

This Party has nearly 90 million members and is leading nearly 1.4 billion Chinese people into a beautiful new era.

This Party has fine traditions and strong vitality. It is devoted fully to serving the people.

This is a Party that sets the goal to achieve long-term development for China, to pursue happiness for the Chinese people, and to promote progress of all mankind.

The Communist Party of China takes as its mission to make newer and greater contribution to mankind.

My second suggestion is to read and study the book *Xi Jinping: The Governance of China*.

Earlier this morning I had the honour to attend the launch of the multi-language editions of *Xi Jinping: The Governance of China (Volume II)*.

This book tells the evolvement and reflects the essence of Xi Jinping Thought on Socialism with Chinese Characteristics for a New Era. It embodies the Chinese wisdom and Chinese solution that the Communist Party of China contributes to building a community with a shared future for mankind and promoting world peace and development.

This is the most systematic and authoritative book on China. It offers a golden key to a comprehensive understanding of China.

My third suggestion is to visit China and get to know the country and its people at close range.

Seeing is believing.

Many of my British friends marvel at what they see in China. In their words, the real China is completely different from the Western media version.

They have seen with their own eyes the "four great new inventions" of China, namely high-speed rail, mobile payments, e-commerce and bike-sharing. In these inventions, they have witnessed China's tremendous achievements in the new round of technological revolution. They have also applauded the rapid growth, met the vigorous people and experienced the open and inclusive culture of China.

President Xi said, "Understanding China requires two-way communication."

This is also the requirement of our times and our shared future. As we have learnt from history, only those who follow the trend of the times and care about the destiny of the world will win a bright future.

I sincerely hope that everyone present today will actively engage in this "two-way communication."

I hope you will try to gain a better understanding of China's new development and new plans, and then join us to tell the world about China's story.

With enhanced exchanges and cooperation between China and the world, we could make greater contribution to building a community with a shared future for mankind.

We could make our world a more colorful, more splendid and more beautiful place.

In conclusion, I wish the Seminar on "China in the New Era" a great success!

Thank you!

认识真实的中国，共建友谊的桥梁*

尊敬的哈罗公学校长兰德先生，

尊敬的哈罗公学董事会主席巴廷先生，

老师们、同学们：

大家下午好！

很高兴访问久负盛名、人才辈出的哈罗公学。我出使英国 9 年多来，曾访问过许多知名学府，每次看到这么多青春洋溢、朝气蓬勃的面庞，都感到自己也年轻了许多。

刚才，我参观了贵校旧演讲厅、画廊等标志场所，深切感受到哈罗公学深厚的历史底蕴，领略到这里独具特色的人文环境，也对哈罗公学严谨务实的治学氛围、国际化的办学目标留下了深刻印象。我高兴地得知，近年来哈罗公学不断加大与中国的教育交流合作，取得不少成果。

2015 年，习近平主席对英国国事访问期间，曾谈及不少在中国家喻户晓的历史名人，包括英国首相丘吉尔、著名诗人拜伦等。他们都毕业于哈罗公学，还有深受中英两国青年人喜欢的《神探夏洛克》的主演康伯巴奇，也是哈罗杰出毕业生之一。这充分说明了哈罗的魅力与实力，也从一个侧面反映出中英人文交流的活力与潜力。

作为中国驻英国大使，我的一项重要任务就是推进两国人文交流、讲好中国故事，让更多的英国民众了解中国、支持中英合作。9 年来，我遍访英

---

* 在哈罗公学的演讲。2019 年 9 月 19 日，英国哈罗公学。

国各地，北至最北端的设得兰群岛的耶尔岛，南至英吉利海峡诸岛，远至海外领土。所到之处，我都深刻感受到两国友好日益深入人心，越来越多的英国民众渴望了解中国。那么，中国是一个什么样的国家？如何了解和认识一个真实的中国？我愿从四个方面谈谈中国这个古老又年轻的国家。

第一，中国是一个文明悠久、充满活力的国家。中华民族有着绵延5 000多年、未曾中断的文明史。我曾担任中国驻埃及大使，埃及同样是一个文明古国，有文字记载的历史比中国还要早，但遗憾的是古埃及文明由于外敌的持续入侵而中断了。中国的造纸术、火药、印刷术、指南针、天文历法等文明成果在世界上影响深远。与苏格拉底、柏拉图、亚里士多德等西方哲人大约同一时代的老子、孔子、墨子等中国思想家，曾广泛探讨人与人、人与社会、人与自然关系的真谛，提出了博大精深的思想体系。在哥伦布发现美洲大陆之前数十年，中国明代航海家郑和就率领船队七次远航太平洋和西印度洋，到访30多个国家和地区。

同时，中国也是一个正在发生巨变的年轻国度。2019年是中华人民共和国成立70周年。短短70年间，中国人民用勤劳和智慧取得了举世公认的发展成就，中国从一穷二白成为世界第二大经济体，7亿多贫困人口摆脱贫困。中国现有公共图书馆3 173个，全年出版各类图书95亿册。中国自2013年起成为世界第二大研发经费投入国。中国在载人航天、探月工程、量子科学、深海探测、超级计算、卫星导航等诸多领域均取得重大成果。当然，中国仍是世界上最大的发展中国家，面临的发展不平衡、不充分等挑战依然严峻。虽然GDP总量是英国的6倍，但人均GDP还不到英国的1/4。面对挑战，我们有信心、有能力克服困难，用勤劳的双手苦干加实干，建设好我们的国家，让人民过上更好的生活。

第二，中国是一个饱经苦难、珍爱和平的国家。近代史上，中国人民蒙受外国侵略和内部战乱的苦难。经过前赴后继的抗争，在付出几千万人伤亡的巨大牺牲后，中国人民终于掌握了自己的命运。在第二次世界大战中，中英军民曾并肩作战，抵抗日本法西斯。英国每年8月会举行“战胜日本”纪念日活动，中国则将每年9月3日确定为中国人民抗日战争胜利纪念日，目的就是铭记历史、不忘苦难、珍爱和平。

正是源于对被侵略、被奴役的历史记忆，中国人民格外珍惜今天的和平生活。中国坚定奉行独立自主的和平外交政策，坚定不移走和平发展道路，既通过维护世界和平发展自己，又通过自身发展促进世界和平。中国在国际事务中秉持公平正义，坚持根据事情本身的是非曲直决定自己的立场和政策，绝不把自己的意志强加于人，也绝不允许任何人把他们的意志强加于中国人民。自1990年以来，中国累计派出维和军事人员近4万人次。目前，中国是联合国所有会员国中第二大出资国，也是五个常任理事国中派遣维和人员最多的国家。中国军舰连续10多年在亚丁湾、索马里海域执行护航任务，维护了包括英国商船在内的6 000多艘航船的安全。

第三，中国是一个拥抱世界、勇于担当的国家。近代史上，中国曾因为闭关锁国，落后于时代发展步伐。新中国成立后特别是改革开放以来，我们把对外开放作为基本国策，坚持“引进来”和“走出去”相结合，不断融入经济全球化大潮。2001年加入世贸组织以来，中国忠实、全面地履行自己的义务，已成为120多个国家和地区的最大贸易伙伴。中国还深度参与区域经贸合作，迄今已与25个国家和地区达成了17个自贸协定，有力地促进了贸易投资自由化便利化。中英在基础设施、教育文化、科技创新、金融服务、清洁能源等领域不断深化合作，实现了互利共赢、共同发展。

中国积极融入现行国际体系，参与了当今世界几乎所有重要政府间国际组织，签署了300多项国际公约。我们积极参与应对气候变化、反恐、维护网络安全等领域的国际合作，认真履行国际责任和义务。中国在朝核、伊朗核、阿富汗等国际热点问题上发挥着重要作用，成为维护多边主义、推动国际体系变革的中流砥柱。我们还积极促进南南合作和南北对话，加大对发展中国家的援助力度，通过互利合作带动更多国家共同发展。

第四，中国是一个分享机遇、追求共赢的国家。中国的发展不是自私自利、损人利己、我赢你输的发展，而是始终坚持将维护自身利益和促进人类共同发展相结合，尊重并推动世界文明多样化，践行博施众利、兼济天下的传统理念。中国已连续多年对世界经济增长的贡献率超过30%，成为世界经济增长的主要稳定器和动力源。目前，中国经济正从高速增长向高质量发展转型，中等收入群体已达4亿多人，市场潜力不断释放，投资环境持续优化，中国将给世界带来更多机遇。

当今世界面临很多挑战，应该构建一个什么样的世界是时代之问。中国的答案是——构建人类命运共同体。人类只有一个地球，各国共处一个世界，地球是人类目前唯一的共同家园。我们生活在同一个地球村，越来越成为你中有我、我中有你的命运共同体。中国将与各国一道，努力建设持久和平、普遍安全、共同繁荣、开放包容、清洁美丽的世界。

怎样构建这样的世界？中国的答案之一就是“一带一路”。大家知道，历史上曾有一条古丝绸之路，连接东西方，绵亘万里，延续千年，打开了各国友好交往的窗口，书写了人类交融发展的历史篇章。中国于2013年提出共建“丝绸之路经济带”和“21世纪海上丝绸之路”，也就是“一带一路”倡议。这一倡议就是要赋予古丝绸之路以全新的时代内涵，继承和发扬和平合作、开放包容、互学互鉴、互利共赢的丝路精神，把中国的发展与世界其他国家的发展结合起来，共同促进地区及全球发展振兴。“一带一路”就像一对腾飞的翅膀，引领沿线各国飞向和平、发展、合作、共赢的未来。短短6年来，“一带一路”倡议已成为全球最受欢迎的公共产品和规模最大的合作平台，正迈入高质量发展的新阶段。中国已经同166个国家和国际组织签署了共建“一带一路”合作协议，在沿线国家建设了82个境外经贸合作区，为东道国上缴税收20多亿美元，创造近30万个就业岗位。英国两次参加“一带一路”国际合作高峰论坛，是“一带一路”的天然合作伙伴。英国的经验、设计、创意与中国的智慧、技术、市场完全可以优势互补，形成“1+1＞2”的效果。

老师们、同学们，

2019年是中英建立代办级外交关系65周年。65年来，中英关系历经风雨、砥砺前行。特别是2015年习近平主席的国事访问，开启了中英关系“黄金时代”，两国各领域合作稳步推进。展望未来，中英合作前景广阔。大家都是中英同龄人中的佼佼者，也是两国关系的未来。正如习近平主席所说：“青年是人民友谊的生力军。”我愿就如何建设中英友谊桥梁谈几点希望。

第一，要珍惜韶华，练就过硬的本领。据我了解，哈罗的校训是“虔诚和笃学”，蕴含着勇气、荣誉感、谦虚、归属感等丰富的价值内涵。希望大家秉持校训，努力学习，脚踏实地，求真学问，练真本领，使自己学有所成，成为各行各业的栋梁之材。

第二，要加强沟通，筑牢互信的根基。中英两国社会制度和文化传统不同，在一些问题上存在不同看法很正常，有时还会有误解，关键是要相互尊重、增进了解。希望大家通过互访和交流学习，多了解彼此的历史和现实，加深对自身文明和其他文明的对比认知，努力做促进东西方文明交流互鉴、美美与共的使者。

第三，要勇于开拓，涵养创新的活力。创新是一个国家和民族发展进步的灵魂。人类正经历第四次工业革命，人工智能、大数据、石墨烯技术等将深刻改变人类生活。近年来，中英在教育、科技、文化、创意等领域的合作方兴未艾，为广大青年人才脱颖而出、建功立业提供了广阔舞台。希望大家今天努力学习，将来积极参与中英创新合作，勇当创新创业的弄潮儿。

第四，要放眼全球，培养开放的视野。当今世界正处于百年未有之大变局，人类面临是开放还是封闭、是前进还是倒退的重大抉择。中英都致力于维护多边主义，促进自由贸易和开放合作，实现世界经济强劲、可持续、平衡、包容增长。希望大家把握历史前进的正确方向，为全球合作共赢、共同发展贡献正能量。

最后，我希望大家能多到中国走走看看，更加全面地了解中国、认识中国、喜爱中国，做中英友谊的传承者，用青春和智慧书写人生华章，为两国民心相通添砖加瓦，为中英关系“黄金时代”增光添彩，使我们生活的这个星球变得更加美好！

谢谢！

下面我愿回答同学们的提问。

Know the Real China and Build a Bridge of Friendship*

Headmaster Alastair Land,

Chairman John Batting,

Teachers and Students,

Good afternoon!

It is a real delight to visit Harrow, a prestigious school and home to numerous talents.

In my more than nine years as Chinese Ambassador to the UK, I have visited many well-known schools in this country. Every time I meet students like you with all your youthful vigour, I feel young myself.

Just now I visited Harrow's historical buildings, including the Old Speech Room Gallery. I was deeply impressed with the profound history, unique culture, academic achievements and global presence of Harrow School. I am also pleased to learn about the increasingly close exchanges and cooperation between Harrow and China, and the fruitful results of such endeavour.

Chinese President Xi Jinping paid a state visit to the UK in 2015. During that visit, he mentioned a number of famous names well-known in China. They include Winston Churchill and Lord Byron, both Harrovians. Another outstanding Harrovian, Benedict Cumberbatch, is popular among both Chinese and British young people for his rendition of *Sherlock*.

These famous names show Harrow's charm and strength. Their popularity in China

---

* Speech at Harrow School. Harrow School, 19 September 2019.

reflects the vitality and potential of China-UK cultural and people-to-people exchange.

As Chinese Ambassador to the UK, I regard it as my mission to advance such exchanges and to tell the stories of China. My goal is to help the British people learn more about China and win more support for China-UK cooperation.

Over the past nine years, I visited many places in this country, from Yell of the Shetland Islands in the North to the Channel Islands in the South. I have even been to the British oversea territories far away. Wherever I went, I could feel the deep friendship towards China, and I could see that more and more British people want to learn more about China.

What kind of a country is China? China is an ancient civilisation. Yet it is also a young country. Now I would like to share my views with you about the real China.

First, China is a time-honoured civilisation that is full of vitality.

The Chinese civilisation has more than 5,000 years of uninterrupted history.

I had been Chinese Ambassador to Egypt. Ancient Egypt had a recorded history that dated back to earlier than that of China. But unfortunately, the civilisation of ancient Egypt was interrupted by foreign invasion.

The Chinese civilisation has made contribution to the world with far-reaching impact, including papermaking, gunpowder, printing, compass, astronomical findings and calendar.

China is also known for its ancient philosophers, such as Lao-tse, Confucius and Mo-tse, who lived at roughly the same time as Socrates, Plato and Aristotle. These ancient philosophers had established a profound philosophical system and explored extensively into the relations between individuals, between man and society, and between man and nature.

Decades before Columbus discovered the Americas, Chinese navigator Zheng He had led his fleet on seven voyages down the coast of the Pacific and the Western coast of the Indian Ocean. He reached more than 30 countries and regions.

China is also a young country which is experiencing profound changes.

This year marks the 70th anniversary of the founding of the People's Republic of China. In merely seven decades, the Chinese people, with their wisdom and hard work, have achieved remarkable success.

China has grown from an impoverished country to the second largest economy in the world.

More than 700 million people are lifted out of poverty.

There are 3,173 public libraries in China. 9.5 billion books of various types are published each year.

Since 2013, China has ranked second in the world in terms of R&D spending.

China has also made remarkable achievements in manned space flight, lunar exploration, quantum science, deep-sea exploration, supercomputing and satellite navigation.

That being said, China is still the world's largest developing country. It is faced with daunting challenges due to imbalanced and inadequate development. Although China's total GDP is five times more than that of the UK, in per capita terms, China is less than a quarter of the size of Britain.

Despite of these challenges, China has the confidence and capabilities to overcome all the difficulties, build a better future for our country and create a better life for our people.

Second, China has experienced untold sufferings and cherishes peace.

In modern times, the Chinese people endured foreign invasions and civil wars. Through relentless fights, in which tens of millions of people sacrificed their lives, the Chinese people finally took their destiny in their own hands.

During the Second World War, the military and people of China and the UK fought side by side against the fascists. The UK celebrates "Victory over Japan" Day, or VJ Day, every August, and China celebrates the victory of the war of the Chinese people's resistance against Japanese aggression on September 3rd every year. Our goal is the same, that is, to remember history, keep in mind past sufferings and cherish peace.

It is because of such experience of being invaded and enslaved that the Chinese people especially cherish the peaceful life today; that China resolves to follow an independent foreign policy of peace, and stays committed to the path of peaceful development; that China upholds world peace in order to achieve development, and also promotes world peace through its development.

In international affairs, China upholds fairness and justice. It takes its position and makes policies in accordance with the merits of the issue. The Chinese people never impose their will on others. Nor will they bend to the will of anyone.

Since 1990, China has sent close to 40,000 military personnel on peacekeeping missions of the United Nations. China is now the second largest contributor to the UN regular budget, and the biggest contributor of peacekeeping personnel among the five permanent members of the UN Security Council.

The Chinese Navy has carried out escort missions in the Gulf of Aden and off the coast of Somalia for more than ten consecutive years. They have ensured the safe passage of more than 6,000 ships, including British merchant ships.

Third, China embraces the world and takes up its responsibilities.

After the 18th century, China had lagged behind due to the closed-door policy. Since the founding of New China, especially since the beginning of reform, China has made opening-up its basic national policy. China has welcomed foreign investment and explored the global market. In this process, China has become part of the economic globalisation.

Since acceding to the World Trade Organisation in 2001, China has fulfilled its duty faithfully and fully. It is now the largest trading partner of more than 120 countries and regions.

China also engages deeply in regional trade and economic cooperation. It has signed 17 free trade agreements with 25 countries and regions, which have effectively promoted trade and investment liberalisation and facilitation.

Between China and the UK, we have deepened cooperation on infrastructure, education, culture, science, technology, innovation, financial services and clean energy. This has delivered win-win results and promoted common development.

China actively integrates with the existing international system. It has joined almost all important intergovernmental international organisations and signed more than 300 international conventions.

China shoulders its international responsibilities and performs its duty faithfully by taking an active part in international cooperation on climate change, counter-terrorism and cyber security.

China also plays an important role on international hot-spot issues such as the Korean Peninsula nuclear issue, Iran nuclear programme and Afghanistan issue. It has become a staunch force for upholding multilateralism and promoting reform in the international system.

Moreover, China has vigorously promoted South-South Cooperation and North-South dialogue, increased assistance to fellow developing countries and engaged in mutually-beneficial cooperation for common development.

Fourth, China is ready to share development opportunities with the world and pursue win-win results for all.

China's approach to development is not the selfish, "beggar-thy-neighbour", "I-win-you-lose" way. While we safeguard our own interests, we also believe in the need for common development of all mankind. And we work to promote that. Because the Chinese traditional philosophy values generosity and social responsibility, we respect and encourage diversity of civilisations.

For many years in a row, China has contributed more than 30% of world economic growth. It is now a major stabiliser and powerhouse for world economic growth. As its economy shifts from high-speed growth to high-quality growth, and with a 400 million middle-income population, an expanding market and a friendly environment for investment, China will offer more opportunities to the world.

In face of the numerous challenges in the world, everyone should ask this question: What kind of a world do we want? China's answer is this: We should build a community with a shared future for mankind.

The Earth is our only home. Everyone is a member of our global village, a community where countries are interdependent and share the same future.

China stands ready to work with other countries to build an open, inclusive, clean and beautiful world that enjoys lasting peace, universal security and common prosperity.

If we want to build such a world, what should we do? China gave its answer by proposing the Belt and Road Initiative.

You may have all heard about the ancient Silk Road. It started from China, extended to Europe, connected the East and West, and covered tens of thousands of miles. For thousands of years, it had been a trade route enabling friendly exchanges between China and the countries along the route. It had been a splendid chapter in the annals of the exchanges between civilisations.

In 2013, China proposed to build a new silk road, that is the Silk Road Economic Belt and the 21st Century Maritime Silk Road, which have since been known as the

Belt and Road Initiative, or BRI.

This Initiative enriches and gives a new look to the ancient Silk Road. It carries forward the Silk Road spirit of peace and cooperation, openness and inclusiveness, mutual learning and mutual benefits. It is aimed at achieving common development of China and all other participating countries, and realising regional and global revitalisation. It gives wings to countries along the routes as they strive to achieve economic take-off. It enables them to move ever closer towards a future of peace, development and win-win cooperation.

In merely six years, BRI has become the most popular public goods and the largest cooperation platform in the world. It is stepping onto a new stage of high-quality development.

China has signed agreements on BRI cooperation with 166 countries and international organisations. It has also set up 82 economic and trade cooperation zones in countries along the routes. These zones have paid more than 2 billion dollars in tax to host countries and created close to 300,000 jobs.

The UK government has twice sent a special representative of the Prime Minister to the Belt and Road Forum for International Cooperation. It is a natural partner of China in building BRI. In BRI cooperation, Britain's experience, design expertise and creative ideas, and China's development concept, technology and market make a perfect match. By pooling the strengths of our two countries, we will realise a multiplying effect in our cooperation and contribute our wisdom and strength to BRI.

Teachers and Students,

This year marks the 65th anniversary of China-UK diplomatic relationship at the chargé d'affaires level. In the past 65 years, China-UK relationship has forged ahead despite wind and rain. President Xi Jinping's state visit in 2015 ushered in the China-UK Golden Era. Since then, cooperation between our two countries across the board has been advanced steadily. Looking ahead, China-UK cooperation enjoys a bright future.

You are among the best and brightest. You represent the future of China-UK relationship. President Xi Jinping said, "Young people are the mainstay of friendship between our people." I would like to share my hopes for you to build the bridge of friendship between our two countries.

First, I hope you will cherish the time of youth and strengthen your capability.

The founder of Harrow School established the principles of "Godliness and good learning." They contain the core values of "Courage, Honour, Humility and Fellowship."

I hope you would live up to these principles and values, work hard, take a down-to-earth attitude, learn the knowledge and strengthen your capability, so as to achieve academic success and grow to be the pillars of society in various fields.

Second, I hope you will learn to communicate and cement the foundation of mutual trust.

China and the UK differ in social system and cultural heritage. It is natural that we do not always see eye to eye. Sometimes there might even be misunderstanding. The key is to respect and learn more about each other.

Through mutual visits and exchanges, you will have a deeper understanding of each other's history and current situation, and learn to appreciate the differences between civilisations. I am sure you will grow to be envoys for closer exchanges, mutual learning, and harmonious coexistence between the Eastern and Western civilisations.

Third, I hope you will have the courage to be innovative and explore new frontiers.

Innovation is the spirit behind the progress of a country or nation. As the fourth Industrial Revolution unfolds, new technologies such as artificial intelligence, big data and graphene will bring profound change to our life.

In recent years, China and the UK have engaged in close cooperation on education, science, technology, culture and creative industries. This provides a broad stage for the young people to excel and succeed.

I encourage you to study hard today, engage actively in the future in China-UK cooperation on innovation, and take the lead in the trend of innovation and entrepreneurship.

Fourth, I hope you will adopt a global perspective and have a broad vision.

The world is undergoing profound changes unseen in a century. Mankind is faced with the crucial choice between openness and isolation, between progress and retrogression.

Both China and the UK are committed to upholding multilateralism, promoting free trade and open cooperation, and ensuring the robust, sustainable, balanced and inclusive growth of the world economy.

It is important to keep to the right direction of history. I hope you will make your contribution in the years to come to the win-win cooperation and common development of the world.

In conclusion, I hope you will visit China and see the country with your own eyes. I hope you will have a more comprehensive understanding of China, and I am sure you will fall in love with the country.

I also hope that with your youth and wisdom, you will carry forward the friendship between China and the UK, live your life to the fullest and help build a closer bond between the peoples of our two countries.

I look forward to your contribution to the China-UK Golden Era. I am sure the world can count on your generation to build a better future!

Thank you!

Now I will be happy to take your questions.

把握新机遇，注入新信心，开启新征程*

很高兴再次与中英工商界朋友们在线座谈。今天又是一个特殊的日子，177 年前的今天，上海正式开埠。当时的中国积贫积弱，被西方列强用武力打开了国门。177 年后的今天，世事变迁，沧海桑田，中国实现了从站起来、富起来到强起来的伟大飞跃，正站在新的历史起点上。

2020 年 10 月，中国共产党第十九届中央委员会第五次全体会议在北京召开。这是中国在“两个一百年”历史交汇点上召开的一次具有全局性、历史性意义的重要会议，擘画了中国未来发展蓝图，明确了前进方向和奋斗目标，为今后 5 年乃至更长时期中国经济社会发展提供了行动指南。

会议最重要的成果是审议通过了《中共中央关于制定国民经济和社会发展第十四个五年规划和二〇三五年远景目标的建议》(以下简称《建议》)。我认为,《建议》的重大意义体现为四个“新”。

一是迈入新发展阶段。2020 年是“十三五”收官之年，中国将全面建成小康社会，消除绝对贫困。2021 年中国将进入一个新发展阶段，开启全面建设社会主义现代化国家新征程，这在中国发展进程中具有里程碑意义。《建议》提出了“十四五”时期中国发展的指导方针、主要目标、重点任务、重大举措，展望了 2035 年基本实现社会主义现代化的远景目标，集中回答了在新发展阶段实现什么样的发展、如何实现发展这个重大问题。2020 年，中国国内生产总值将超过 100 万亿元人民币。预计到“十四五”末，中国经济

* 在中英工商界中共十九届五中全会精神在线宣介会上的主旨演讲。2020 年 11 月 17 日。

将达到现行的高收入国家标准，到 2035 年实现经济总量或人均收入翻一番是完全有可能的。

二是贯彻新发展理念。中国社会的主要矛盾已经转化为人民日益增长的美好生活需要和不平衡不充分的发展之间的矛盾，集中体现在发展质量上。“十四五”乃至今后更长时期，中国经济社会发展将以推动高质量发展为主题。我们将更加注重发挥创新、协调、绿色、开放、共享的新发展理念的引领作用，以深化供给侧结构性改革为主线，着力提升发展质量和效益，推动质量变革、效率变革、动力变革，充分激发 14 亿中国人民的活力，使发展成果更好地惠及全体人民。

三是构建新发展格局。当前，世界经济面临严重衰退，经济全球化遭遇逆流，单边主义、保护主义上升，传统的国际循环明显弱化。《建议》提出，中国将加快构建以国内大循环为主体、国内国际双循环相互促进的新发展格局。这一新发展格局强调的是国内国际双循环，不是国内经济的单循环，更不是关起门来搞封闭运行。不管国际风云如何变幻，中国坚持对外开放的基本国策绝不会动摇。我们将深入参与国际循环，使国内循环和国际循环相互促进、相得益彰。

四是明确新发展要求。中国共产党领导中华民族伟大复兴事业，是历史的选择、人民的选择。面对新冠肺炎疫情冲击，中国有力、有序、有效地统筹疫情防控和经济社会发展，率先控制疫情、率先复工复产、率先实现经济正增长，再次彰显了中国共产党的强大领导力。《建议》首次把全体人民共同富裕取得更为明显的实质性进展作为远景目标，充分证明中国共产党坚持以人民为中心的发展思想，发展为了人民、发展依靠人民、发展成果由人民共享，不断满足人民日益增长的美好生活需要，不断增强人民群众的获得感、幸福感、安全感。

当前，世界正经历百年未有之大变局，新冠肺炎疫情正在全球大流行。两者相互交织、相互激荡，给人类带来前所未有的挑战和考验。在这样的时代背景下，今后 5 年乃至更长时期，中国的发展将给世界带来什么影响？我认为，这将增强四方面信心。

一是为世界和平发展注入信心。当今世界不稳定不确定因素增多，有的国家大搞单边主义、保护主义、霸权主义，鼓吹“新冷战”和“脱钩论”，威胁国际社会稳定和安全。《建议》提出，中国将高举和平、发展、合作、共赢旗帜，坚持独立自主的和平外交政策，推进各领域各层级对外交往，推动构建新型国际关系和人类命运共同体。中国坚定不移走和平发展道路，永远不称霸，不扩张，不谋求势力范围，更无意跟任何国家打“冷战”“热战”。中国历来主张中美双方应加强沟通对话，在相互尊重的基础上管控分歧，在互惠互利的基础上拓展合作。我们希望美国新一届政府同中方相向而行，秉持不冲突不对抗、相互尊重、合作共赢原则，推动两国关系沿着正确轨道向前发展。事实已经证明，并将继续证明，中国越发展，就越有利于世界和平与进步力量的发展壮大，就越能为世界和平与稳定注入更多正能量。

二是为世界开放发展注入信心。开放带来进步，封闭必然落后。构建更加开放的国内国际双循环，不仅符合中国自身发展需要，还将更好地造福各国人民。中国有 14 亿人口，中等收入群体超过 4 亿，是全球最具潜力的大市场，未来 10 年累计商品进口额有望超过 22 万亿美元。中国将坚持实施更大范围、更宽领域、更深层次的对外开放，促进国际合作，实现互利共赢，推动贸易和投资自由化、便利化，推动共建“一带一路”高质量发展，为世界经济复苏和发展注入强大动能。

三是为世界创新发展注入信心。创新是引领发展的第一动力。《建议》提出，坚持创新在中国现代化建设全局中的核心地位。中国把科技自立自强作为国家发展的战略支撑，同时与世界各国在科学技术和创新领域加强对话交流合作，分享中国科技成果，贡献更多中国智慧。同时，中国坚持绿水青山就是金山银山的理念，坚持尊重自然、顺应自然、保护自然，构建生态文明体系。不久前，习近平主席宣布，中国将提高国家自主贡献力度，力争 2030 年前二氧化碳排放达到峰值，2060 年前实现碳中和，并将为此制定实施规划。我们将积极参与和引领应对气候变化、保护生物多样性等国际合作，为促进全球绿色发展贡献力量。

四是为世界共治发展注入信心。《建议》提出，积极发展全球伙伴关系，坚持多边主义和共商共建共享原则，积极参与全球治理体系改革和建设。中国将维护以联合国为核心的国际体系和以国际法为基础的国际秩序，维护以世贸组织为核心的多边贸易体制，积极参与重大传染病防控国际合作，推动构建人类卫生健康共同体。中国倡导全球事务由各国商量着一起办，治理体系由大家一起建设，发展成果由各国人民共同分享。中国将始终做世界和平的建设者、全球发展的贡献者、国际秩序的维护者。

展望“十四五”乃至更长时期，中国经济高质量发展将给中英两国工商界带来更多合作机遇。

一是中国庞大的市场机遇。疫情背景下，中国经济率先复苏，是“后疫情时代”世界经济的重要引擎，将给包括英国在内的各国企业带来更多合作机遇和更大发展空间。在上周刚刚结束的第三届中国国际进口博览会期间，英国公司在多个领域签署了总价值超过 4.3 亿英镑的商业订单。中英两国企业界可进一步利用好进博会、服贸会、广交会等平台，扩大双方经贸合作，携手促进两国经济复苏和发展，更好地造福两国人民。

二是合作共赢的开放机遇。中国构建国内国际双循环新发展格局，致力于全面提高对外开放水平，更有效率地实现内外市场联通、要素资源共享。脱欧后的英国致力于打造“全球化英国”，拓展全球合作伙伴，希望英方继续为中国企业在英投资兴业提供开放、公平、公正、非歧视的营商环境。中英应加强政策对接和经验交流，拓展两国及全球贸易投资金融合作，共建“一带一路”高质量发展，推动建设开放型世界经济。

三是优势互补的创新机遇。中国坚持创新驱动发展，加快发展现代产业体系特别是新兴产业。英国是世界创新强国，实施产业发展战略。中英在创新领域优势互补，可以进一步深化科技和产业创新合作，推动疫情催生的新产业、新业态发展，加强地方发展合作，激发源源不断的创新潜能，在世界创新合作大潮中走在前列。

四是“两会”对接的绿色机遇。2021 年中英两国将分别举办《生物多样性公约》第十五次缔约方大会（COP15）和《联合国气候变化框架公约》第二十六次缔约方大会（COP26），双方就两场大会加强对接，实现协同增效。

中国将继续推动绿色低碳发展，促进经济社会发展全面绿色转型。英国在应对气候变化和发展清洁能源、绿色金融等方面具有特色。中英企业应抓住两场大会契机，积极拓展绿色复苏、绿色科技和绿色金融等领域的合作，共同引领全球气候变化治理和绿色发展。

人们常说："信心比黄金更珍贵。"世界正处于动荡变革之中，中国正开启新的历史征程。让我们坚定信心，抓住机遇，共同谱写中英合作共赢的新篇章，共同开创世界和平与发展的新未来！

谢谢。

下面我愿回答大家的提问。

New Opportunities, New Confidence, New Journey*

It is a real delight to join friends from the Chinese and British business communities once again online.

Today is a special day. On this day 177 years ago, China opened the port of Shanghai officially to foreign trade. At that time, China was impoverished and weak. Its door was forced open by Western powers.

Over the past 177 years, profound changes have taken place in the world. In China, there have been great leaps forward, from gaining independence to achieving prosperity and growing strong. The country is now standing at a new historical starting point.

Last month, the Fifth Plenary Session of the 19th CPC Central Committee was held in Beijing. This important conference coincides with a key moment in history where the timeframe of China's Two Centenary Goals converge. Therefore, it bears overall and historic significance. It has outlined the blueprint for China's development in the future, defined the direction and the goals, and set forth a guideline for China's economic and social development in the coming five years and beyond.

Above all, the conference reviewed and approved the CPC Central Committee's Proposals for the Formulation of the 14th Five-Year Plan (2021-2025) for National Economic and Social Development and the Long-Range Objectives Through the Year 2035. This is definitely the most important outcome.

To understand the significance of this document, I have summarised four "NEWs."

---

* Keynote Speech at the Briefing on the Fifth Plenary Session of the 19th CPC Central Committee. 17 November 2020.

First, it unveils a new development stage.

2020 is the last year for the implementation of the 13th Five-Year Plan. This is the year when China will have completed the building of a moderately prosperous society in all aspects and eliminated absolute poverty.

In 2021, China will enter a new development stage and embark on a new journey of building a modern socialist country in all aspects. This will be a milestone in the history of China's development.

The document sets forth the guidelines, main targets, key tasks and major measures for China's development in the 14th Five-Year Plan period. It outlines the long-term vision of basically realising socialist modernisation by 2035. And it answers the important question of what kind of development China is pursuing and how we are going to achieve it.

This year, China's GDP will exceed 100 trillion RMB yuan. By the end of the 14th Five-Year Plan period, China's economy is expected to reach the current level of high-income countries. Hence it is certainly possible that China's GDP or per capita income could double by 2035.

Second, the Proposals embody the new development concept.

Unlike in the past, the principal contradiction in the Chinese society now is the one between unbalanced and inadequate development and people's ever-growing aspiration for a better life. The resolution, of course, lies in high-quality development.

In the 14th Five-Year Plan period and beyond, the theme of China's economic and social development will be none other than high-quality development.

We will let the new development concept lead the way, namely innovative, coordinated, green, open and shared development.

We will focus on deepening supply-side structural reform.

We will promote transformation in quality, efficiency and driving forces so as to achieve higher quality and better efficiency.

We will rely on the creative vigour of 1.4 billion Chinese people.

And we will ensure everyone has a share in the outcomes of development.

Third, the Proposals set up a new growth pattern.

At the moment, the world economy is experiencing grave recession; economic globalisation is encountering headwind; and unilateralism and protectionism are on the rise. All these have resulted in an obvious weakening in the traditional international circulation.

The Proposals suggest that China will accelerate the building of the "dual circulation" growth pattern in which the domestic market will play a leading role, with international and domestic markets reinforcing each other. This new growth pattern is not a closed domestic circulation but an inclusive one that connects domestic and international markets.

The world may have changed, but China will not change its basic national policy of opening-up. We will engage more deeply in the international circulation and enable the domestic and international circulations to complement each other and achieve multiplying effects.

Fourth, the Proposals lay out new requirements for development.

The great rejuvenation of the Chinese nation under the leadership of the Communist Party of China is the choice of history and the choice of the people.

In the face of the outbreak of Covid-19, China has balanced epidemic response and economic and social development in an effective and orderly manner. It is the first country in the world to get the epidemic under control, bring economic activities back on track and achieve positive growth. This bears witness to the strong leadership of the CPC.

In the Proposals, notable and substantial progress in common prosperity is clearly marked as a long-term goal. This is a brand-new definition of China's long-term goal and it goes to show that putting the people at the centre is the development philosophy of the CPC.

The CPC believes that development is for the people and by the people; and development outcomes shall be shared by all. The CPC has spared no effort to meet people's ever-growing needs for a better life and to work for greater benefit, happiness and security for the people.

The profound changes unseen in a century are compounded by the raging pandemic across the world. This is posing unprecedented tests and challenges.

Against this background, how will China's development affect the world in the coming five years and more? I think China's development will strengthen confidence in the following four aspects:

First, it will strengthen confidence in the peaceful development of the world.

The world is now facing increasing instabilities and uncertainties. Some countries are pushing for unilateralism, protectionism and hegemony, and clamouring for a "new Cold War" and "economic decoupling." As a result, the stability and security of the international community has come under threat.

The Proposals emphasise that China will hold high the banner of peace, development and win-win cooperation, adhere to an independent foreign policy of peace, advance external exchanges in all areas and at all levels, and promote the building of a new type of international relations and a community with a shared future for mankind.

China is firmly committed to the path of peaceful development. It never seeks hegemony, expansion or sphere of influence, let alone start a "cold war" or "hot war" with any other country.

On relations with the United States, it is China's consistent position that the two countries should enhance communication and dialogue, manage differences while maintaining mutual respect, and expand cooperation based on mutual benefit. We hope that the next administration of the United States will work with the Chinese side in the same direction, and uphold the principles of non-conflict, non-confrontation, mutual respect and win-win cooperation, so as to move China-US relationship forward on the right track.

Facts have proven and will continue to prove that a more developed China will be a stronger force for world peace and progress, and will inject more positive energy to international peace and stability.

Second, China's development will strengthen confidence in the open development of the world.

Openness brings progress while isolation results in backwardness. Under "dual circulation," China will be more open. This not only meets domestic needs for development but also brings more benefits to the people around the world.

With a population of 1.4 billion, including a middle-income group of over 400 million, China is a huge market with the greatest potential in the world. In the coming ten years, it is expected to import goods worth over 22 trillion US dollars.

Going forward,

China will open up more areas and more sectors at a higher level.

We will advance international cooperation for win-win results.

We will promote trade and investment liberalisation and facilitation.

And we will pursue high-quality development of the Belt and Road Initiative.

All these will provide strong impetus for world economic recovery and growth.

Third, China's development will strengthen confidence in global growth driven by innovation.

Innovation is the primary driving force for development. The Proposals suggest that China will put innovation at the centre of its modernisation drive.

China regards self-reliance in science and technology as a strategic pillar of its national development. At the same time, it stands ready to step up dialogue, exchanges and cooperation with the rest of the world in science, technology and innovation (STI), to share its STI achievements and to contribute its wisdom to the world.

We believe that lucid waters and lush mountains are just as precious as mountains of gold and silver. Based on this belief, China respects, protects and follows the Law of Nature, and strives to protect ecological environment.

Not long ago, President Xi Jinping announced that China will scale up its Intended Nationally Determined Contributions (INDCs). It aims to peak CO_2 emissions by 2030 and to achieve carbon neutrality by 2060. We will make implementation plans for achieving those goals.

China is determined to take an active and leading role in international cooperation on climate change and biodiversity, and make its contribution to global green development.

Fourth, China's development will strengthen confidence in building better global governance.

According to the Proposals, China will actively build partnerships with countries of the world, remain committed to multilateralism and the principles of extensive consultation, joint contribution and shared benefits, and take an active part in the reform and development of the global governance system.

China will uphold the international system with the United Nations at its core, uphold the international order based on international law and uphold the multilateral trade system with the WTO at its centre. China will also take an active part in international cooperation on the prevention and control of major infectious diseases, and advance the building of a global community of health for all.

China advocates a multilateral approach in global affairs:

- Every country has a say in addressing global challenges through consultations.
- Every country has a role in building global governance system.
- And the people of every country have a share in the benefits of development.

China will always be a defender of world peace, a contributor to global development, and an upholder of international order.

During the 14th Five-Year Plan period and beyond, the high-quality growth of China's economy will create more opportunities for cooperation between Chinese and UK businesses.

Opportunity number one: China's huge market.

China is the first country in the world to achieve economic recovery amid the pandemic. It will be a major powerhouse for global growth in the post-pandemic era. It will create enormous cooperation opportunities and development space for businesses of all countries, including the UK.

At the Third China International Import Expo (CIIE) concluded last week, British businesses signed contracts worth more than 430 million pounds in a wide range of areas.

Going forward, Chinese and UK businesses can seize the opportunities of platforms such as CIIE, the China International Fair for Trade in Services and the China Import and Export Fair to expand trade and economic cooperation. Working together, the business communities could contribute to recovery and growth of both our economies and bring more benefits to our peoples.

Opportunity number two: open and win-win cooperation.

In building the "dual circulation" development paradigm, China is committed to opening up at a higher level on all fronts. This will enable better connection and sharing of production factors and resources between the domestic and international markets in a more efficient way.

The UK aims to build a global Britain after Brexit and find more partners for cooperation around the world. We hope that the UK will continue to provide an open, fair, just and non-discriminatory environment for Chinese businesses to invest and operate here in this country.

China and the UK can do more to match our policies, share our experience, expand bilateral and international cooperation in trade, investment and financial services, pursue high-quality cooperation on the Belt and Road Initiative, and contribute to building an open world economy.

Opportunity number three: China-UK complementarity in innovation.

China is pursuing innovation-driven development and speeding up the development of modern industries, especially emerging ones. The UK leads the world in innovation and is implementing a strategy for industrial development.

With complementary strengths in innovation, China and the UK are well positioned to deepen cooperation in science, technology and industrial innovation. Our two countries can work together to boost the development of emerging industries and business models in response to the pandemic, enhance cooperation on development at the local level, and unlock the potential of innovation, so as to always be at the forefront of international cooperation in innovation.

Opportunity number four: green development and synergy between COP15 and COP26.

In 2021, China and the UK will host COP15 and COP26 respectively. Our two sides are enhancing synergy between the two conferences to achieve greater results.

China is pursuing green and low-carbon development, and promoting a full transition to green economic growth and social progress. The UK has unique strengths in climate response, clean energy and green finance.

Businesses from our two countries should seize the opportunities of COP15 and COP26 to expand cooperation in green recovery, green technology and green finance, and take the lead in the global governance on climate change and green development.

As people often say, confidence is more precious than gold.

Today, the world is undergoing dramatic transformations. China is embarking on a new, historical journey.

Let's join hands to seize opportunities with greater confidence. Let's work together to write a new chapter for China-UK win-win cooperation and embrace a brighter future for world peace and development!

Thank you!

Now, I would like to take your questions.

第二章

治国理政

党的十八大以后，外界渴望了解中国新一届领导人，特别是习近平总书记的治国理政理念。历史上，伦敦是孕育思想、启蒙文明、激发思潮的地方。170 年前,《共产党宣言》在这里诞生；150 多年前，马克思在这里完成《资本论》。我在伦敦先后主持《习近平谈治国理政》推介会，参加《习近平谈治国理政》第二卷多语种图书首发式，向英国各界宣介这两部著作。指出它们是认知中国、引领思想的指南，是传承文明、引领时代的宝典，是启迪智慧、引领世界的钥匙，是彰显担当、引领行动的号角。

我还在使馆主持习近平外交思想主题座谈会，向英国政界、理论界、教育界、工商界、舆论界讲解习近平外交思想核心要义，阐述习近平外交思想的世界意义。出席座谈会的英国各界人士纷纷表示，我的讲解使他们对习近平外交思想的深刻内涵和重要意义有了更深入、更全面的了解。他们在发言中畅谈对习近平外交思想的理解和认识，分析中国“天下大同”“和衷共济”等传统哲学思想的现实意义，对习近平主席的“世界情怀”表达钦佩，对“一带一路”倡议和构建人类命运共同体理念表示赞同。

读懂当代中国，领略领袖风范*

尊敬的英国前副首相杰弗里·豪勋爵，

尊敬的英国前副首相约翰·普雷斯科特勋爵，

尊敬的中国外文局陆彩荣副局长，

各位议员，

女士们、先生们、朋友们：

欢迎各位出席中国驻英国大使馆和中国外文局在伦敦国际书展期间联合主办的《习近平谈治国理政》推介会。

伦敦国际书展已有 40 多年的历史，是全球图书业最重要的春季盛会，也是全球出版业最具影响力的交易平台之一。今天，习近平主席治国理政重要思想的著作——《习近平谈治国理政》一书亮相伦敦国际书展，不但为书展增添了一大亮点，而且也是中英关系中的一件大事、好事。

2012 年 11 月中国共产党召开十八大以来，以习近平为总书记的新一届中央领导集体带领中国人民走上了全面建成小康社会、全面深化改革、全面依法治国、全面从严治党的新征程。国际社会日益关注中国的这一伟大“新政”及其对中国乃至世界的影响。《习近平谈治国理政》一书，记录了习近平主席有关治国理政的思考与实践，回应了一个时期以来国际社会对中国的各种看法和疑惑，提供了一个集中感知和认识今日中国的窗口。

通过这个窗口，读者可以了解中国从哪里来，中国向哪里去，中国人民

* 在《习近平谈治国理政》推介会上的讲话。2015 年 4 月 15 日，中国驻英国大使馆。

将走一条什么样的发展道路。习近平主席在书中全面回答了这些问题。他深刻阐释了“中国梦”的本质，那就是国家富强、民族振兴、人民幸福，他向世界表明了中国人民坚定不移走自己道路的自觉和自信，描绘了中华民族走向伟大复兴的美好愿景；他探讨了中国悠久的文化传统、独特的历史命运和复杂的基本国情，指出了我们走适合自己的发展道路的必然性，“穿合脚的鞋”，那就是坚持中国特色社会主义；有关全面深化改革、适应经济新常态、保障和改善民生、建设法治国家、建设文化强国、建设生态文明等方面的思想他在书中也有全面阐释。这些重要论述体现了中国对破解发展难题、实现美好愿景有着系统的战略思考，有着清晰的发展路径，有着全面的工作部署，有着坚强的领导能力。

通过这个窗口，读者可以认识中国的世界观、中国对世界的责任观、“中国梦”与世界梦的交汇融合。书中有 5 个专题 20 篇文章专门谈外交战略和国际关系，集中反映了习近平主席对地区和国际事务的主张和理念，清晰阐释了世界问题的中国观点和中国办法，也表达了中国与国际社会共享机遇、共同发展、共同进步、共同繁荣的美好愿望和心声。两年半来，习近平主席共出访 11 次，到访 31 个国家，在国内外会见外国元首和政府首脑约 300 人次，参加 20 多场重要的多边外交活动，实现对五大洲、不同类型国家高层交往的全覆盖。习近平主席多次强调中国坚定不移走和平发展道路，永远不称霸，永远不搞扩张。从倡导坚持正确义利观到命运共同体理念，从阐述“亲、诚、惠、容”周边外交理念到构建以合作共赢为核心的新型国际关系，从共建“丝绸之路经济带”到建设“21 世纪海上丝绸之路”，一系列充满智慧的新理念、新倡议，宣示了中国走和平发展道路的坚定决心，表达了中国发展将造福世界的真诚意愿，向国际社会展示了中国勇于担当的大国胸怀。习近平主席的外交思想和外交实践集中体现了新时期中国外交鲜明的中国特色、中国风格和中国气派。

通过这个窗口，读者可以领略习近平主席的卓越智慧、个人魅力和领袖风范。中国有句古语：“文如其人。”厚重的文化积淀、丰富的生活阅历、长期的基层和地方工作经验，形成了习近平主席真诚坦率、平实生动的文风。

在这本书收录的演讲、谈话和采访中，习近平主席把深刻的道理阐述得通俗易懂、以小见大、以事明理；他还把中华文化与各国文明融会贯通，既弘扬传统，又兼容并包。研读《习近平谈治国理政》一书，人们可以感受到习近平主席作为一位大国政治家的风范和魅力，认识到他的学贯古今、融通中西，感受到他的平实自然和坦诚谦和。

这些就是《习近平谈治国理政》的真谛所在、意义所在和魅力所在。

女士们、先生们，

习近平主席说，中英都是世界上有影响力的大国，拥有广泛共同利益，肩负着促进世界和平与发展的重要责任。当前，中英关系正处在一个“黄金时期”，尤其是2015年好事不断，喜事连连。从剑桥公爵威廉王子成功访华，到英国宣布加入亚洲基础设施投资银行；从中英经贸合作捷报频传，到中英文化交流年活动蓬勃开展。《习近平谈治国理政》一书亮相伦敦书展，将进一步促进英国公众更好地了解当代中国，认识当代中国，进而深化中英之间的相互理解与信任。

最后，让我们共同期待习近平主席2015年应伊丽莎白女王邀请对英国进行国事访问，共同祝愿访问为中英关系的发展开启新愿景，谱写新篇章。

谢谢！

A Window for Better Understanding of Today's China and its Leader*

Rt Hon Lord Howe,

Rt Hon Lord Prescott,

Vice President of China Foreign Languages Publishing Administration Lu Cairong,

Lords and MPs,

Ladies and Gentlemen,

Friends,

First of all, let me extend my warmest welcome to all of you.

The Chinese Embassy and China Foreign Languages Publishing Administration are delighted to have you with us here for the formal launch of the book *Xi Jinping: The Governance of China* during the London Book Fair.

The forty-year-old London Book Fair is the most important spring gathering of international publishers and one of the most influential global book trading platforms. Today's launch of the book *Xi Jinping: The Governance of China* is both a highlight of this prestigious book fair and a major event in China-UK relations.

This book is a compilation of works of President Xi Jinping. It embodies President Xi's governance philosophy.

Since the 18th National Congress of the Communist Party of China in November 2012, the new central leadership with Xi Jinping as general secretary has led the people of China on a new long march. On this new long march, China will strive:

---

* Speech at the Book Launch of *Xi Jinping: The Governance of China*. Chinese Embassy in London, 15 April 2015.

- to build moderate prosperity in all respects,
- to deepen reforms in an all-round way,
- to advance rule of law in every aspect,
- and to strengthen all-round Party self-conduct.

These new governance measures have drawn increasing international interest in how they will influence China and indeed the world.

Xi Jinping: The Governance of China is a collection of works that record the President's thoughts and practices in governing China. For those who may have various questions and doubts about China, this book offers an authoritative response. For those who would like to learn more and get a better understanding of the country, this book opens a window on today's China.

Through this window, readers will be able to see where China has come, where China is going, and what kind of road the people of China will take in pursuit of development. This book has all the answers to these questions.

In the book, the President expounds on the nature of the "Chinese Dream." It is a dream of prosperity for the country, renewal of the nation and happiness for the people. He shows the world that the people of China have taken a development path of their own choice with determination and confidence. He shares a vision of the great renewal of the Chinese nation.

He explores China's time-honoured cultural tradition, unique historical mission and complex national condition. China will inevitably follow a development path that is suitable to the country, or in the words of the President, "wear the shoes that fit." And what fits China is socialism with Chinese characteristics.

Many other thoughts of President Xi are also found in this book, including:

- comprehensive and deeper reforms,
- adaptation to economic new normal,
- better welfare and better life for the people,
- stronger rule of law,
- cultural advancement,
- and ecological conservation.

His analysis on these important issues reveals China's complete strategic thinking, clear roadmap, coordinated action plan and strong leadership in breaking through development bottlenecks and turning the nation's vision into reality.

Through this window, readers will also be able to see China's view of the world. They will be able to understand China's sense of responsibility as a member of the international community. They will be able to appreciate how the "Chinese Dream" and the world's dream go hand in hand.

Twenty articles in five chapters of the book were devoted to diplomatic strategy and international relations. Here, one can read about President Xi's propositions and philosophy on regional and international affairs. There are clear explanations of China's views and solutions on global issues. There are pledges and aspirations of China to share opportunities with the international community and seek common development, common progress and common prosperity.

Over the past two and a half years, President Xi has taken 11 overseas trips and visited 31 countries. He has met with some 300 foreign heads of state or heads of government either in China or during overseas trips. He has also attended over 20 important events of multilateral diplomacy. These high-level diplomatic activities have taken him to all five continents and different types of countries.

President Xi has stressed on many occasions that China will steadfastly pursue peaceful development:

- China will never seek hegemony.
- China will never follow expansionist policy.
- China will never pursue interests at the expense of justice.

President Xi has clearly outlined what China advocates:

- China advocates the idea of a community with a shared future.
- China advocates the principle of amity, sincerity, mutual benefit and inclusiveness in its relations with neighbours.
- China advocates a new type of international relations built around win-win cooperation.

- China advocates the building of the Silk Road Economic Belt and the 21st Century Maritime Silk Road.

These new ideas and new initiatives reflect centuries-old Chinese wisdom. They are a clear-cut announcement of China's resolve to pursue peaceful development. They are a passionate expression of China's sincerity to share the benefits of its development with the world. They are a courageous demonstration of China's vision and sense of responsibility.

As we can see from President Xi's diplomatic philosophy and practice, they embody a distinct Chinese characteristic, Chinese touch and Chinese style.

Also, through this window, readers will appreciate President Xi's wisdom, charisma and leadership style. As the Chinese idiom goes, a man is what he writes.

President Xi has a literary style that is sincere, candid, unadorned and vivid. This is accredited to the many years he spent living and working at the grass roots level and going back to the roots of the Chinese culture.

In the speeches, talks and interviews in this book, President Xi always takes an easy-to-understand approach to profound concepts. He has a way with big ideas and abstract theories, always able to find small words and vivid examples to get the message across. His deep roots in tradition and genuine appreciation for different cultures can also be felt in the great care he takes to bridge gaps and highlight the linkages between different civilisations. Readers of this book will certainly have an opportunity to appreciate the quality and charisma of a statesman in close range as well as to benefit from his wisdom, his knowledge and his natural, candid and modest style.

These are the essence, the significance and the fascination of reading the book, *Xi Jinping: The Governance of China.*

Ladies and Gentlemen,

As President Xi put it, both China and the United Kingdom are major countries with global influence. Our two countries have extensive common interests and shoulder important responsibilities for world peace and development.

We are now in a golden time for China-UK relationship. There has been one good news after another since the beginning of this year—from the successful royal visit by the Duke of Cambridge to UK's announcement on joining AIIB, from fruitful business cooperation to flourishing events of the China-UK Year of Cultural Exchange.

Now, with the launch of the book *Xi Jinping: The Governance of China* here at the London Book Fair, it is one more good news for people here in Britain who want to learn more about today's China. And this will certainly further strengthen the mutual understanding and trust between China and the UK.

In conclusion, let us look forward to the forthcoming state visit by President Xi Jinping at the invitation of Her Majesty Queen Elizabeth II. Let us wish the visit success in outlining a new vision and writing a new chapter for China-UK relations.

Thank you!

领悟中国智慧，感知世界情怀*

尊敬的英国约克公爵安德鲁王子殿下，

尊敬的中宣部副部长、国务院新闻办公室主任蒋建国先生，

尊敬的中国国家创新与发展战略研究会会长郑必坚先生，

女士们、先生们、朋友们：

大家上午好！

今天是一个非常特殊和重要的日子，《习近平谈治国理政》第二卷多语种图书首发式在这里隆重举行。我谨代表中国驻英国大使馆向出席今天首发式的中外嘉宾致以热烈的欢迎！

习近平主席指出："这是一个需要理论而且一定能够产生理论的时代，这是一个需要思想而且一定能够产生思想的时代。" 2017 年 10 月，中国共产党第十九次全国代表大会成功召开，确立了习近平新时代中国特色社会主义思想，为中国未来发展指明了前进方向，也为世界进步事业提供了中国智慧。《习近平谈治国理政》凝聚了习近平新时代中国特色社会主义思想的精华，无论对中国还是世界，都具有极其重要的意义。

第一，这是认知中国、引领思想的指南。《习近平谈治国理政》第二卷是 2014 年出版的《习近平谈治国理政》的延续，收录了从 2014 年 8 月至中共十九大召开前习近平主席的各类重要文稿 99 篇和图片 29 幅。全书分为 17 个专题，包括阐明大政方针的重要讲话、讲述中国故事的精彩演讲、研究部

---

* 在《习近平谈治国理政》第二卷多语种图书首发式上的讲话。2018 年 4 月 11 日，伦敦乔治大街 1 号。

署工作的谈话要点等篇目，每一个专题都聚焦一个重大理论和现实问题，思想深刻精辟、语言生动鲜活、寓意深长高远。《习近平谈治国理政》第一、二卷共同构成一个全面丰富的思想理论体系，清晰展现了习近平新时代中国特色社会主义思想的发展脉络和精髓要义，为国际社会深入了解新时代中国道路、中国理念、中国方案提供了最权威的读本。

第二，这是传承文明、引领时代的宝典。一个国家选择什么样的发展道路和治理体系，是由这个国家的历史传承、文化传统、经济社会发展水平决定的。《习近平谈治国理政》第二卷引用了诸多中国历代先贤的经邦济世、治国安民的典籍策论、至理名言，传承了五千年中华文明的人文精神和文化基因；这部著作从中国近代 100 多年来革命、建设、改革的奋斗实践中探寻客观规律，准确把脉中国经济发展的新特征、社会主要矛盾的新变化，科学擘画新时代中国发展的宏伟蓝图；这部著作既有深厚的文明底蕴，又富含强烈的时代气息，是中国共产党和中国人民实现中华民族伟大复兴“中国梦”的行动纲领。

第三，这是启迪智慧、引领世界的钥匙。改革开放 40 年来，中国经历了不同寻常的发展历程，经济总量从世界第十跃升为世界第二，7 亿多人摆脱贫困，创造了人类社会发展史上的奇迹。很多人感到好奇：中国成功的秘诀是什么？“中国奇迹”不是天上掉下来的，而是中国共产党带领 13 亿多中国人民艰苦奋斗、不懈努力取得的。《习近平谈治国理政》就是诠释中国奇迹、讲述中国故事、传播中国精神的最佳读本。中国共产党人的治国理政经验，丰富了发展中国家走向现代化的路径乃至全人类的治理思想宝库，为促进人类和平与发展事业贡献了中国智慧和中国方案。

第四，这是彰显担当、引领行动的号角。人民利益至上是贯穿《习近平谈治国理政》这部著作的主线。“始终把人民放在心中最高的位置”“人民对美好生活的向往就是我们的奋斗目标”“民心是最大的政治”等朴素语言，饱含着一个大国领导人亲民、爱民、为民的真情实感，展现了习近平主席对全心全意服务广大民众的执着和担当。更重要的是，习近平主席站在人类前途命运的高度，把中国人民的梦想同世界各国人民的梦想紧密相连，为中国将向何处去、世界将向何处去、我们怎么办等重大课题指明了方向，给出了答案，彰显了一位卓越领导人和政治家的战略眼光、全球视野和世界情怀。

女士们、先生们，

历史上，伦敦是孕育思想、启蒙文明、激发思潮的地方。170 年前，《共产党宣言》在这里诞生；150 多年前，离这里不远的英国博物馆见证了马克思的代表作《资本论》的完成。

今天，我们在伦敦举办《习近平谈治国理政》第二卷多语种图书首发式，对促进东西方思想对话、文化交流、文明互鉴具有重要而深远的意义。

今天的首发式对中英关系也是一件大事。中英关系一直走在中国与西方大国关系前列，两国人文交流为双边关系发展做出了重要贡献。2018 年初，英国首相梅成功访华，两国领导人再次确认打造中英关系“黄金时代”大方向，并就提升两国关系的战略性、务实性、全球性和包容性达成重要共识。我衷心希望，双方能以此次活动为契机，进一步加强人文交流和文明互鉴，努力将两国关系打造成为大国之间相互尊重、平等互信、合作共赢的典范，使“中国梦”与“英国梦”相映生辉、携手同行。

莎士比亚曾说：“书籍是全世界的营养品，生活里没有书籍，就好像没有阳光；智慧里没有书籍，就好像鸟儿没有翅膀。”我相信，面对世界百年未有之大变局，《习近平谈治国理政》将给全世界带来“知识的营养”“时代的阳光”“智慧的翅膀”，既帮助国际社会更加全面深入地了解中国的过去、今天和未来，也必将推动国际社会携手努力，一道为构建人类命运共同体、开创人类社会更加美好的未来做出新贡献！

最后，预祝《习近平谈治国理政》第二卷多语种图书首发式圆满成功！

谢谢！

Chinese Wisdom and Global Vision*

Your Royal Highness,

Minister Jiang Jianguo,

Chairman Zheng Bijian,

Ladies and Gentlemen,

Dear Friends,

Good morning!

It is a real pleasure to join you at this special and important event: the launch of the multi-language editions of *Xi Jinping: The Governance of China (Volume II)*. On behalf of the Chinese Embassy, I would like to extend my warm welcome to everyone present today.

President Xi said: "This is a time that calls for theories and will surely produce theories; this is a time that calls for thoughts and will surely produce thoughts."

In response to the call of the times, last October's 19th National Congress of the Communist Party of China proposed the Xi Jinping Thought on Socialism with Chinese Characteristics for a New Era. It serves as a guide for China's future development and shares the Chinese wisdom with the world.

The book *Xi Jinping: The Governance of China (Volume II)* embodies the essence of Xi Jinping Thought on Socialism with Chinese Characteristics for a New Era. Its publication is of great importance to both China and the world.

First, this book is a guide to understanding China and China's thoughts.

---

* Remarks at the Launch of the Multi-language Editions of *Xi Jinping: The Governance of China (Volume II)*. One Great George Street, London, 11 April 2018.

The first volume of *Xi Jinping: The Governance of China* was published in 2014. The second volume contains 99 articles and 29 photos of President Xi dated from August 2014 to the 19th Party Congress.

The book has 17 sections, each focusing on a major theoretical or practical issue. The articles include remarks outlining major policies, speeches telling China's story and highlights of discussions regarding implementation of policies. All of them reflect the deep thoughts and the vivid language of the author and far-reaching implications of his insights.

These two volumes form a comprehensive system of rich thoughts and theories. They reveal the evolvement and essence of Xi Jinping Thought on Socialism with Chinese Characteristics for a New Era. For those who are hoping to gain a deeper understanding of China's path, ideas and plans in the new era, these books are the most authoritative works to look to.

Second, this book carries the fine traditions of the Chinese civilisation and will guide China's development in the new era.

The development path and governance system of a country is closely related to its historical heritage, cultural traditions and economic and social development level.

The second volume of *Xi Jinping: The Governance of China* carries forward the humane spirit and cultural heritage of 5,000 years of Chinese civilisation. This is particularly reflected in the author's understanding of the ancient Chinese wisdom on the governance of the country and the people.

In this book, President Xi also reflects on China's efforts in the century of revolution, development and reform in modern times.

He captures the new features of China's economic development and the new changes in the principal contradiction facing the Chinese society.

And he designs a grand blueprint for China's development in the new era.

With its root deep in the Chinese civilisation and its insights into the trend of times, this book can well serve as a guide for the Communist Party of China and the Chinese people in the pursuit of the "Chinese Dream" of national rejuvenation.

Third, this book is a key to understanding China's wisdom and sharing it with the world.

After four extraordinary decades of reform and opening-up, China has grown from the tenth to the second largest economy in the world. More than 700 million people have been lifted out of poverty.

Many people call this a miracle and are curious to know China's secret to success.

This miracle did not fall from the sky. It is the result of the relentless efforts of over 1.3 billion Chinese people led by the Communist Party of China.

Xi Jinping: The Governance of China tells the stories of the China miracle, the China success and the China ethos.

The governance experience of the Communist Party of China is the focal point of this book. It enriches the governance thoughts of mankind. It embodies the Chinese wisdom and Chinese solution that are important contribution to world peace and development.

Fourth, this book is a call for action and a demonstration of the sincerity of a responsible leader.

The principle of "put people first" runs through the whole book of *Xi Jinping: The Governance of China*. Here are a few lines from the book I wish to share with you:

"Always place the people above all else in our hearts."

"The people's aspiration for a better life is our goal."

"The biggest political power lies in winning people's hearts."

These plain words reflect a deep love for the people, and a firm determination and strong sense of responsibility to serve the people wholeheartedly.

More importantly, the book reflects the author's global vision in the articles and paragraphs about the future of the entire mankind. He regards the "Chinese Dream" as part of the larger picture of the World Dream. He points to the direction and gives answers to such major questions as where China should be going, where the world should be going, and what needs to be done.

This is the strategic and global vision of an outstanding leader and statesman for his country and for the world.

Ladies and Gentlemen,

Historically, London has provided breeding grounds for thoughts and inspirations for civilisations and ideologies. It was the birth place of *The Communist Manifesto* 170 years ago. Not far from here, the British Museum witnessed the completion of the masterpiece of Karl Marx entitled *Capital, A Critique of Political Economy* over 150 years ago.

Today, London bears witness to the launch of another important work, the second volume of *Xi Jinping: The Governance of China*. This event is of far-reaching significance to the exchanges and mutual learning between thoughts, cultures and civilisations of the East and the West.

It is also a major event in the China-UK relationship. This relationship has been leading the relations between China and other major Western countries, to which cultural and people-to-people exchanges have been an important contributing factor.

At the beginning of this year, Prime Minister May paid a successful visit to China. During the visit, the leaders of our two countries reaffirmed their commitment to the China-UK Golden Era and agreed to build a more strategic, practical, global and inclusive relationship.

I sincerely hope that China and the UK will seize the opportunity of today's event to enhance people-to-people exchanges and promote mutual learning between different civilisations. I hope we will work together to set our relationship as an exemplar of major-country relations that feature mutual respect, equality, mutual trust and win-win cooperation. And I hope we will support each other in realising the "Chinese Dream" and "British Dream" respectively.

William Shakespeare once said:

"Books are the nutrient of the whole world. A life without books is like a life without sunlight; wisdom without books is like a wingless bird."

As we are faced with the greatest global changes in a century, the book *Xi Jinping: The Governance of China* will bring the nutrient of knowledge, the sunlight of the times and the wings of wisdom to the world.

The book will help the international community gain a full and deeper understanding of China's past, present and future.

And it seeks to urge the international community to come together to build a community with a shared future for mankind and create a more beautiful future for human society.

In conclusion, I wish the launch of the multi-language editions of *Xi Jinping: The Governance of China (Volume II)* a great success!

Thank you!

感知东方智慧，读懂中国未来*

尊敬的英国四十八家集团俱乐部主席佩里先生，

尊敬的英国社会学会荣誉副会长马丁·阿尔布劳教授，

尊敬的马丁·雅克博士，

尊敬的英国中国商会会长方文建先生，

尊敬的各位议员，

各位嘉宾，

女士们、先生们：

欢迎大家出席习近平外交思想主题座谈会。

2019 年是我从事外交工作的第 46 个年头，也是我出任中国驻英国大使的第 10 个年头。不少英国朋友问我：出使英国多年，印象最深刻的事情是什么？我的回答是，习近平主席 2015 年对英国的成功国事访问。这是我作为驻外大使第一次接待我国国家元首到访，至今难忘。这次历史性的访问不仅开启了中英关系的“黄金时代”，也为两国关系在 21 世纪第二个十年的发展指明了方向。

习主席在伦敦金融城市长晚宴上发表演讲时指出，“中国人民走的是历史选择的道路、要的是更加美好的生活、想的是和平与发展的世界”，“中国将同各国一道，逢山开路、遇河架桥”，“世界上的路，只有走的人多了，才会越来越宽广”。这些论述高屋建瓴、掷地有声，既蕴含着兼济天下、包容

* 在习近平外交思想主题座谈会上的主旨演讲。2019 年 4 月 9 日，中国驻英国大使馆。

互鉴的东方智慧，也体现了一位大国领导人的远见卓识和责任担当。

作为驻英国大使，我的使命就是增进中英之间的了解、互信与合作，让英国和世界了解一个真正的中国。近年来，英国媒体对华的报道呈指数级增长，每天翻开报纸都有不少关于中国的新闻。但坦率地讲，报道质量良莠不齐，看法观点也是消极多于积极，有人认为中国发展是机遇，有人认为是挑战，还有人认为是威胁。那么一个富起来、强起来的中国究竟将向何处去？将对世界产生什么样的影响？对于这些问题，习近平外交思想给出了最好的答案。因此，要了解今天的中国，要理解今天的中国外交，就要读懂习近平外交思想。今天，我愿通过回答三个问题谈谈我的几点思考和体会。

第一，习近平外交思想的核心要义是什么？

2018 年 6 月，我回北京参加中央外事工作会议，会上确立了习近平外交思想的指导地位，成为新时代中国对外工作的根本遵循和行动指南，是中国外交理论建设的一次创新、一次突破和一次飞跃。我想从三个角度谈谈我对习近平外交思想的理解。

一是对中国文化和外交传统的继承与创新。对和平、和睦、和谐的追求深深植根于中华民族的血脉之中，“以和为贵”“天下太平”的理念世代相传。中国一向信守“计利当计天下利”的共赢准则，倡导“和而不同”“兼收并蓄”“己所不欲，勿施于人”的包容理念，主张“协和万邦，和衷共济，四海一家”的大同思想。中国外交一直秉持并传承着传统哲学中的这些中国智慧。

2019 年是新中国成立 70 周年。70 年来，我们形成了以独立自主、和平发展、合作共赢为鲜明特色的外交传统和中国风范。几十年前，中国在自身经济十分困难的情况下，依然“勒紧裤腰带”帮助发展中国家推进民族独立事业和经济发展。1976 年我常驻赞比亚期间，亲历了坦赞铁路的交接仪式，60 多名中方人员为了这条铁路长眠在非洲的大地上。这条铁路承载的重义轻利、平等相待、合作共赢的精神，一直流淌在新中国外交政策的脉络中。改革开放后，我们做出了和平与发展仍是时代主题的战略判断。党的十八大以来，中国外交既弘扬优良传统，又展现出与时俱进、奋发有为、开拓进取的崭新风貌，根据不断变化的世情、国情，提出了一系列富有中国特色、体现时代精神、引领人类发展进步潮流的新理念、新主张、新倡议。

二是对外交理论和实践的凝练与总结。习近平外交思想以“十个坚持”为总体框架和核心要义，这“十个坚持”并不是凭空想象的，而是对中国几十年外交理论和实践的“浓缩”“萃取”“升华”，形成了中国特色大国外交的理论与实践基础。在“十个坚持”中，我要着重强调三点。坚持以维护世界和平、促进共同发展为宗旨推动构建人类命运共同体，这是新时代中国外交追求的崇高目标，已被写入《中华人民共和国宪法》和《中国共产党章程》，也被写入联合国等重要国际和地区组织的文件。坚持以共商共建共享为原则推动“一带一路”建设，这是中国今后相当长时期对外开放和对外合作的管总规划。“一带一路”倡议提出 6 年多，这不仅是新时代中国扩大开放的重大举措，也是当今世界最受欢迎的公共产品和最大规模的合作平台。坚持以相互尊重、合作共赢为基础走和平发展道路，这是中国外交必须长期坚持的基本原则，为中国和世界开辟出一条共同发展的康庄大道，走出一条国与国交往的新路。

三是对世界发展和中国角色的判断与定位。习近平主席指出，当今世界正处于百年未有之大变局。20 世纪，人类经历了两次世界大战和长达近半个世纪的冷战。进入 21 世纪，世界多极化加速推进，新兴国家群体性崛起，国际格局深刻调整。与此同时，世界经济增长乏力，金融危机阴云不散，单边主义日益抬头，保护主义甚嚣尘上。在这样的形势下，中国如何看待自己和世界？习近平外交思想给出了最好的答案，那就是服务民族复兴、促进人类进步，用正确的历史观、大局观、角色观看中国、看世界。改革开放以来，中国通过自己的努力不仅让 13 亿多人民过上了好日子，而且为维护世界和平与繁荣、促进各国人民共同利益与福祉做出了重要贡献。无论中国发展到什么程度，都始终是世界和平的建设者、全球发展的贡献者、国际秩序的维护者。

第二，习近平外交思想对世界意味着什么？

2018 年是中国改革开放 40 周年。40 年来，中国国内生产总值增长了 33.5 倍，进出口总额增长了 782 倍。改革开放不仅深刻改变了中国的面貌，也使中国与世界的关系发生了历史性变化。正如习近平主席指出的，“世界好，中国才能好；中国好，世界才更好”。在这样的背景下，习近平外交思想赋予了“中国梦”世界意义，体现了融通中外、天下大同的世界情怀。

一是为人类进步描画新愿景。习近平外交思想本着“以天下为己任”的情怀，提出构建人类命运共同体的倡议。面对“建设一个什么样的世界、怎样建设这个世界”的时代之问，国际社会要风雨同舟，不能各自为营；要患难与共，不能以邻为壑；要合作共赢，不能零和博弈。人类命运共同体理念遵循历史大势，着眼人类共同的未来，强调坚持多边主义，倡导国际公平正义，为人类发展进步开辟了一条康庄大道。

二是为国际关系探索新思路。人类历史上发生过 16 次新兴大国崛起，其中 12 个都与守成大国爆发了战争。一些人认为中国也避不开几百年来其他大国兴衰起落的规律。习近平外交思想提出构建新型国际关系，彻底否定了“国强必霸”“修昔底德陷阱”的旧逻辑，走出了与传统大国不同的发展道路。中国从来没有对外扩张的基因，从来不接受弱肉强食、赢者通吃的丛林法则，而是主张建设相互尊重、公平正义、合作共赢的新型国际关系。

三是为全球治理提供新指引。当今世界不稳定、不确定因素增多，人类面临诸多共同挑战。2017 年，习近平主席在达沃斯的演讲唱响了支持全球化和多边主义的最强音，为世界经济把脉开方，为全球治理贡献中国方案，在全球范围内引起了强烈反响。我们认为，各国应求同存异、聚同化异，积极做行动派，不做观望者，要坚持共商共建共享的全球治理观，坚持全球事务由各国人民商量着办，努力把人类前途命运掌握在自己手中。

第三，如何正确看待习近平外交思想？

近些年来，世界特别是西方国家对中国的关注中，存在不少误解甚至误判，对习近平外交思想的一些认识也不够全面、不够准确。那么，我们应该怎样正确看待习近平外交思想？我认为，把握好三点至关重要。

首先是维护和改进国际秩序，而不是“替代”谁的制度。中国是联合国的创始成员国，是战后国际秩序的开创者、受益者和坚定维护者。迄今，我们参与了几乎所有重要政府间国际组织，签署了 300 多项国际公约。尽管现行国际体系并非百分之百完美，但总体上是行之有效的。中国不会“另起炉灶”，而是寻求推动改革和完善之道，使其向更加公正合理的方向发展，适应当前国际形势需要。

其次是谋求共同发展，而不是“干涉”谁的事务。中国坚持“国不以利为利，以义为利也”的大国义利观，始终本着互利共赢原则与其他国家开展务实合作。我们不搞所谓“债务陷阱”，不会通过经济合作介入他国政治事务。本月下旬，中国将举办第二届“一带一路”国际合作高峰论坛，迄今我们已与124个国家和29个国际组织签署了173份“一带一路”合作文件。我们从未“胁迫”任何人与我们合作，各国都是根据自身需要、独立自主地做出战略判断。

最后是承担应有责任，而不是对谁“示强”。新中国成立70年来，中国没有主动挑起过任何一场战争和冲突。我们坚定维护国家主权、安全、发展利益，也积极提供与自身实力相匹配的国际公共产品。中国是联合国维和行动第二大出资国和五常国中派遣维和军事人员最多的国家，参与了当今几乎所有热点问题的解决进程，积极贡献中国智慧、中国方案。中国承担多少国际责任，既取决于国际社会的期待，也与自身实力、发展阶段相匹配。

女士们、先生们，

历史发展、文明繁盛、人类进步，从来离不开思想引领。英国是近代人类文明的思想库，历来主张开放包容、兼收并蓄，不仅是工业革命的摇篮，还培育出莎士比亚、拜伦、雪莱、洛克、罗素、培根等享誉世界的文学家和思想家。各位嘉宾长期关注中国事务、研究涉华问题，都有许多独到的思考。希望我的介绍有助于大家深入理解习近平外交思想。

一花独放不是春，百花齐放春满园。习近平外交思想是中国外交政策的“指南针”，彰显了中国同世界同舟共济、携手并进、共创人类美好未来的真诚意愿，将引领中国与世界的互动沿着正确的历史方向前行。希望各位嘉宾认真研究、正确解读，以促进中英民心相通、文明互鉴，为推动中国、英国及世界共同发展进步贡献智慧，为推动构建人类命运共同体贡献力量！

谢谢大家！

Learn the Oriental Wisdom and Understand the Future of China*

Chairman Stephen Perry,

Prof. Martin Albrow,

Dr. Martin Jacques,

Chairman Fang Wenjian,

Lords,

Distinguished Guests,

Ladies and Gentlemen,

Welcome to the Symposium on Xi Jinping Thought on Diplomacy.

This is the 46th year of my career as a diplomat, and the 10th year as Chinese Ambassador to the UK. Many British friends asked me what has impressed me most during my tour of duty in the UK. My answer is: the successful state visit by President Xi Jinping to the UK in 2015.

That visit was memorable not just because it was the first time for me to receive a head of state from China as Ambassador. More importantly, this historic visit ushered in the China-UK Golden Era. It also charted the course for China-UK relations in the second decade of the 21st century.

At the banquet held by the Lord Mayor of the City of London, President Xi Jinping said:

"The path that the Chinese people follow has been a choice of history. What the

---

* Keynote Speech at the Symposium on Xi Jinping Thought on Diplomacy. Chinese Embassy in the UK, 9 April 2019.

Chinese people want is a better life. What the Chinese people long for is a world of peace and development."

He also said:

"China will stand firm with all other countries to meet whatever challenges that may lie ahead."

"Roads will only become broader when more people travel on them."

These powerful words reflect a strategic thinking. They embody the oriental wisdom that values the common good, inclusiveness and mutual learning. They also demonstrate President Xi Jinping's vision, courage and responsibilities as a leader of a big country.

As the Chinese Ambassador to the UK, I regard it as my mission to enhance mutual understanding, mutual trust and cooperation between China and the UK, and to tell the story of the real China to the people of the UK and beyond.

In recent years, the increase of media reports on China has been exponential. But to be frank, these reports are not all of good quality. There are more negative voices than positive ones. China's development is regarded as an opportunity by some but a challenge or even a threat by some others.

So, where is a richer and stronger China headed? How will it influence the world? To these questions, Xi Jinping Thought on Diplomacy has provided the best answer. To understand today's China and China's diplomacy, one must study and try to understand Xi Jinping Thought on Diplomacy.

Now I would like to share with you my views by answering three questions.

First, what is at the core of Xi Jinping Thought on Diplomacy?

Last June, I attended the Central Conference on Diplomatic Work in Beijing, where Xi Jinping Thought on Diplomacy was established as the guiding thought that provides basic principles and guidelines for China foreign policy. It is an innovation, a breakthrough and a leap forward in the evolution of the thought on China's diplomacy.

Now I would like to share with you my understanding on Xi Jinping Thought on Diplomacy from three perspectives.

First, Xi Jinping Thought on Diplomacy inherits and develops China's cultural and diplomatic tradition.

The pursuit for peace, good neighbourliness and harmony has been running in the blood of the Chinese nation.

For generations,

- We have prized and pursued "peace for all under heaven";
- We have believed in win-win as embedded in the ancient teaching that "the interests to be considered should be the interests of all";
- We have upheld the ideals of harmony and inclusion rooted in the words of ancient philosophers, such as "there should be harmony without uniformity" and "do not do unto others what you would not have them do unto you";
- And because of our belief that "all under heaven belong to one big family," we are convinced that countries should always come to each other's assistance and work towards the same direction.

These are the traditional Chinese wisdoms behind China's diplomacy.

This year marks the 70th anniversary of the founding of the People's Republic of China. In the past 70 years, we have formed the diplomatic tradition with unique Chinese features, namely independence, peaceful development and win-win cooperation.

Several decades ago, when China itself was struggling to make ends meet, we shared what little we had with other developing countries striving for independence and economic growth.

In 1976, I was a young diplomat in Zambia, where I had the honour of attending the handover ceremony of Tazara, a railway linking Tanzania and Zambia. More than 60 Chinese workers sacrificed their lives for building Tazara and were laid to rest on the African continent. Tazara highlights the value of putting righteousness above material gains. It embodies the spirit of equality and win-win cooperation. These ideas have always been deeply embedded in China's foreign policy.

Following the adoption of the policies of reform and opening-up, China came to the strategic conclusion that peace and development were the theme of the times. This fundamental judgment continued to be the bedrock of China's diplomacy up to and after the 18th National Congress of the Communist Party of China.

At the same time, China's diplomacy has also kept abreast with the changing times and made new progress in line with the evolving landscape abroad and reality at home. We have put forward a number of new ideals, proposals and initiatives that are imbued with Chinese characteristics, embody the spirit of our times and provide guidance to the progress of mankind.

Second, Xi Jinping Thought on Diplomacy encapsulates the concepts and practice of China's diplomacy.

At the centre of Xi Jinping Thought on Diplomacy are ten key concepts known as ten persistent efforts. These concepts are the essence of China's diplomacy that are extracted and distilled from China's long-held principles and decades of practice.

Together they constitute the foundation of the idea and practice of major-country diplomacy with Chinese characteristics.

Out of the ten concepts, I would like to stress three.

First, making persistent effort to build a community with a shared future for mankind, with the aim of safeguarding world peace and promoting common development.

This lofty goal of China's diplomacy in the new era has been written into the Constitution of China and the Constitution of the Communist Party of China. It is also endorsed in the documents of important regional and international organisations including the UN.

Second, making persistent effort to advance the Belt and Road Initiative in line with the principle of achieving shared growth through discussion and collaboration.

BRI is the overarching design for China's opening-up and international cooperation and will remain so for a considerable period of time to come. This is an important measure to open up China wider to the world in the new era. More than six years after it was proposed, BRI is becoming the most popular public goods and largest platform for international cooperation.

Third, making persistent effort to follow a path of peaceful development based on mutual respect and win-win cooperation.

This is a basic principle that must be upheld in China's diplomatic initiatives on a long-term basis. Peaceful development is a path to common development. It is leading to a new type of state-to-state relations.

The third perspective of my understanding of Xi Jinping Thought on Diplomacy is that it provides an assessment and definition on the development of the world and the role of China.

President Xi Jinping pointed out that the world is undergoing profound changes unseen in a hundred years:

Last century, mankind experienced two world wars and a Cold War that lasted for nearly half a century.

The 21st century is witnessing accelerated multi-polarisation, the rise of emerging countries and profound adjustments in the international landscape. At the same time, the world economic growth remains sluggish, the financial crisis is taking its toll, and unilateralism and protectionism are on the rise.

Under such circumstances, how does China see itself and the world? Xi Jinping Thought on Diplomacy provides the best answer:

- We should strive for national revitalisation.
- We should promote the progress of mankind.
- We should adopt a historical perspective, see the big picture and play our role.

China's hard work over the past decades has not only brought about a better life for its more than 1.3 billion people. It is also an important contribution to peace and prosperity in the world and the common interests and benefits of people of all countries.

No matter what development stage China reaches, it will continue to be a builder of world peace, a contributor to global development and a defender of international order.

Now we come to the second question: what does Xi Jinping Thought on Diplomacy mean to the world?

The year 2018 marked the 40th anniversary of China's reform and opening-up. In the past 40 years, China's GDP increased by 33.5 times, and its total export and import increased by 782 times. Reform and opening-up have not only transformed China profoundly but also brought about historic changes to the relations between China and the world. As President Xi Jinping pointed out, "China will do well only when the world does well, and vice versa."

Born against this backdrop, Xi Jinping Thought on Diplomacy gives a global significance to the "Chinese Dream." It emphasises ever close ties between China and the world. It advocates the ideal of "one world, one family."

First, it draws a new blueprint for human progress.

Xi Jinping Thought on Diplomacy is based upon the belief that "it is our duty to work for the common good of all people in the world." That is the rational behind the concept of building a community with a shared future for mankind.

- What kind of a world do we desire?
- What should we do to build a world that we want?

To these important questions of our times, Xi Jinping Thought on Diplomacy gives the following answer:

- Instead of minding one's own business and rocking the boat, the international community should come to each other's aid and row together.
- Instead of taking a "beggar-thy-neighbour" approach, we should stand side by side in time of hardship.
- Instead of playing a zero-sum game, we should engage in win-win cooperation.

Building a community with a shared future for mankind answers the call of the times, focuses on the shared future, upholds multilateralism and advocates international fairness and justice. This is a road to human progress.

Second, Xi Jinping Thought on Diplomacy explores a new thinking on international relations.

In the past 500 years, there were 16 cases in which a rising power confronted the established power. 12 cases ended with war. This has led some people to think that China would not be an exception.

But China strives to avoid the beaten track and blaze a new trail. In history, China never sought expansion. Today, China does not accept the law of the jungle, namely the weak falls prey to the strong and the winner takes it all.

In order to bring to an end the old logic that "a strong country is bound to seek hegemony" and "an emerging power and an established power are bound to fall into the Thucydides's Trap," Xi Jinping Thought on Diplomacy proposes to build a new type of international relations.

This is the new trail. This new type of international relations features mutual respect, fairness, justice and win-win cooperation.

Third, Xi Jinping Thought on Diplomacy provides a new guideline for global governance.

With rising instabilities and uncertainties in the world, mankind is faced with increasing and common challenges, and in need of a joint response. This is exactly why President Xi Jinping's speech at Davos back in the 2017 received enthusiastic response from all over the world.

In that speech, President Xi analysed the problems in the world economy, endorsed globalisation and multilateralism, and contributed China's solution on global governance.

China believes that in global governance:

- countries in the world should seek common ground while narrowing differences;
- take actions rather than just standing by,
- and uphold the principle of shared growth through discussion and collaboration.

Only in this way will mankind take the future in their own hands.

Now let's come to the third question: how to obtain an accurate and comprehensive understanding of Xi Jinping Thought on Diplomacy?

In recent years, there have been misunderstandings, even misjudgment, about China in some countries, especially Western countries. Some of the interpretations of Xi Jinping Thought on Diplomacy are not comprehensive and lack accuracy.

In understanding Xi Jinping Thought on Diplomacy comprehensively, I believe the following three points are crucial.

First, Xi Jinping Thought on Diplomacy is aimed at safeguarding and improving the international order rather than replacing the existing system.

China is one of the founding members of the United Nations. It is a creator, beneficiary and firm defender of the international order established after the Second World War. As of today, China has taken part in almost all the major intergovernmental international organisations and signed more than 300 international conventions.

The current international system may not be perfect, but on the whole it is effective. China stands for reform and improvement, not "reinventing the wheel." We would like to see a more equitable and reasonable international system that meets the needs of the current international situation.

Second, Xi Jinping Thought on Diplomacy is aimed at common development, rather than interfering in the affairs of other countries.

China believes that a country should never sacrifice the greater good for material interests. In our business cooperation with other countries, we follow the principle of win-win results. We do not interfere in other countries' political affairs through economic cooperation or by creating the so-called "debt trap."

Later this month, China will host the second Belt and Road Forum for International Cooperation. As of today, China has signed 173 documents on BRI cooperation with 124 countries and 29 international organisations. We have never forced any country to cooperate with China. These countries and organisations signed those documents based on their independent strategic judgments and in line with their own needs.

Last but not least, Xi Jinping Thought on Diplomacy is aimed at shouldering responsibility rather than flexing muscles.

In the past 70 years since the founding of the People's Republic of China, China has never launched a single war or conflict.

We have been firm in safeguarding our national sovereignty, security and development interests. At the same time, we have provided public goods to the international community to the best of our capabilities.

China is the second largest contributor to the UN peacekeeping budget, and the largest contributor of peacekeepers among the five permanent members.

China has also taken part in the settlement of almost all the hot-spot issues in the world, and has actively contributed China's wisdom and solutions.

As for what international responsibilities that China should shoulder, it depends on both the expectation of the international community and the capability and development stage of China.

Ladies and Gentlemen,

Thoughts have always played a crucial part in leading the development of history, in making the achievements of civilisations and in promoting the progress of mankind.

In modern times, the UK is known for being a treasure house of thoughts. Its open and inclusive spirit has not only nurtured the Industrial Revolution but also fostered great writers and thinkers such as Shakespeare, Byron, Shelley, Locke, Russell and Bacon.

You have all been following and studying China and China-related issues for a long time. I am sure you have your own understanding on Xi Jinping Thought on Diplomacy. I hope you will find my introduction helpful in facilitating a deeper understanding on this topic.

Just as a single flower does not make a spring, the progress of mankind depends on the efforts of all countries.

Xi Jinping Thought on Diplomacy is the “compass” for China’s foreign policy. It demonstrates China’s sincerity to join hands with other countries to create a better future for mankind. It will ensure that China takes the right side of history and its interactions with the world head in the right direction.

I hope that your earnest study and accurate interpretation of Xi Jinping Thought on China’s Diplomacy will help strengthen the bond between the people of our two countries, and enhance mutual learning between our two civilisations. I look forward to your wisdom on how to seek common progress for China, for the UK and for the world, and I count on your contribution to the building of a community with a shared future for mankind!

Thank you!

中国为什么选择马克思主义*

女士们、先生们，

朋友们：

欢迎大家出席中国驻英使馆举办的“马克思主义在中国”座谈会。很高兴见到这么多英国从事研究马克思主义的专家与学者。今天活动的举行，我认为是：天时、地利、人和。

一是天时。2011 年是中国共产党成立 90 周年，不久前中国隆重举行了庆祝纪念活动。中国共产党作为一个马克思主义理论孕育催生、历经各种血与火考验的政党，其 90 年波澜壮阔的历史，可以说就是一部马克思主义真理在中国的发展史、实践史。

二是地利。英国是马克思和恩格斯的“第二故乡”，马克思主义在这里成型、成熟，从这里传向世界、播至东方。我记得，到任英国不到半个月，我就曾同使馆青年一道拜谒了坐落于海格特公墓的马克思墓；我也参观过伦敦市中心索霍区的马克思故居、英国博物馆内著名的“马克思的脚印”，踏寻伟人的历史足迹。

三是人和。大家或是长期从事马克思主义的研究，或是长期探索实践马克思主义，或是参与马克思主义政党的领导和组织工作，正是马克思主义使我们大家坐到一起，共同讨论。

关于“马克思主义在中国”这个主题，我想谈三点。

---

* 在“马克思主义在中国”座谈会上的主旨发言。2011 年 7 月 20 日，中国驻英国大使馆。

第一，中国为什么选择马克思主义？

中国选择马克思主义，是在近代以来中国社会发展进步的壮阔进程中，在经历艰苦顽强的上下求索后，人民和历史做出的抉择。20世纪初的中国内忧外患，但无论是旧式的农民革命，还是资产阶级改良，抑或资产阶级革命，都没有也无法改变中国的命运。直到俄国十月革命爆发，马克思主义这一系统的、科学的世界观和方法论传入中国，人们才看到了漫漫黑夜中的明灯，迎来了中国共产党成立这一开天辟地的大事变。

从此，中国共产党以马克思主义为基本理论指导，团结带领人民在中国这块古老沧桑、饱经磨难的土地上，完成和推进了三件大事。一是完成了新民主主义革命，实现了民族独立、人民解放。二是完成了社会主义革命，确立了社会主义基本制度。三是进行了改革开放新的伟大革命，开创、坚持、发展了中国特色社会主义，推动现代化建设取得了举世瞩目的伟大成就。中国从90年前的一盘散沙、四分五裂、封闭愚昧、温饱不足，经历了最广泛、最深刻的社会变革，变成了今天的团结和谐、统一强大、自信开放和总体小康。

第二，马克思主义怎样在中国发展？

马克思主义不是僵硬刻板的教条和一成不变的公式。马克思和恩格斯在1872年《共产党宣言》德文版序言中指出，由于时代的变迁和实践的发展，宣言中“这些基本原理的实际运用，正如《共产党宣言》中所说的，随时随地都要以当时的历史条件为转移”，一些论述“有的地方已经过时了”，“在今天看来是不完全的”。恩格斯1895年在致威纳尔·桑巴特的信中亦指出：“马克思的整个世界观不是教义，而是方法。它提供的不是现成的教条，而是进一步研究的出发点和供这种研究使用的方法。”

马克思主义自来到中国的那一天起，就开始了与中国实际和时代特征有机结合的进程，就在不断进行“马克思主义中国化”，并实现了两次历史性飞跃。第一次历史性飞跃，主要解决了在半殖民地半封建的中国进行什么样的革命、怎样进行革命这一根本问题，成功开辟了中国新民主主义革命道路，并初步探索了社会主义建设道路，形成了毛泽东思想这一伟大理论成果。第二次历史性飞跃，主要解决了在社会主义初级阶段的中国，什么是社会主义、怎样建设社会主义，建设什么样的党、怎样建设党，实现什么样的发展、怎样发展等重大理论和实际问题，成功开辟了中国特色社会主义道路，形成了包括邓小平理论、“三个代表”重要思想以及科学发展观等重大战略思想在内的中国特色社会主义理论体系，这也是马克思主义中国化的最新理论成果。

中国共产党坚持运用马克思主义的立场、观点和方法，来观察、分析和解决中国的问题，同时创造性地运用马克思主义，推动马克思主义中国化，为马克思主义注入了强大生机和活力，使马克思主义的真理力量和巨大威力得到了充分发挥和体现。

第三，中国共产党人在推进马克思主义中国化、发展马克思主义的不懈探索中，获取了哪些宝贵基本经验?

我认为，主要有三条。一是解放思想。马克思在《黑格尔法哲学批判导言》中指出：“理论在一个国家实现的程度，总是决定于理论满足于这个国家的需要的程度。”如何在一个落后的东方大国进行无产阶级革命、建设社会主义、实现国家现代化，马克思著作里没有现成答案，人类发展史上也没有现成经验。中国共产党人将马克思主义的基本规律运用于实践，超越“本本”，摆脱教条，无畏探索，大胆创新，开创了中国特色社会主义道路，形成了中国特色社会主义理论体系，确立了中国特色社会主义制度。

二是实事求是。中国共产党人运用马克思主义创造了光辉成就，但前进的道路并非总是一帆风顺。中国共产党也曾经历挫折、出现失误、付出代价，但我们总是能直面错误、承担责任、拨乱反正。有学者指出，中国共产党似乎有一种“内在抗体”，总是能够战胜各种“致命病毒”，我认为，这种“内在抗体”就是实事求是的政治勇气。中国共产党在90年历程中，就是用实事求是这把钥匙，不断自我总结、反思和革新，打开了中国历史发展的一个又一个关键锁扣，开启了马克思主义中国化的一个又一个全新境界。

三是与时俱进。马克思主义中国化，同时也是马克思主义时代化的过程。不同时代、不同历史阶段的世情、国情和党情，都给中国共产党人提出了新课题和新挑战。中国共产党在90年历程中能够始终挺立在时代潮头、引领中国进步，关键在于始终坚持与时俱进，正确判断时代特征，准确把握发展趋势，科学制定目标任务，始终保持一个马克思主义政党的先进性。我们清醒地认识到："一个政党的先进性不是一蹴而就的，也不是一成不变的，过去先进不等于现在先进，现在先进不等于永远先进。"我们一直告诫自己，一个只会躺在功劳簿上的政党是没有前途的政党，我们必须"勇于变革、勇于创新，永不僵化、永不停滞"。

正因为中国共产党人坚持解放思想、实事求是、与时俱进，推动马克思主义中国化和时代化，在实践中丰富和发展马克思主义，中国共产党才会从成立之初50多人的小党发展成拥有8 000多万党员的世界第一大执政党，中国才会从积贫积弱的落后国家发展成为世界第二大经济体，中华民族才能从处于危亡局面走向伟大复兴之路。

历史之河不会停滞，理论之树永葆常青。展望未来，中国将继续坚持马克思主义的基本原理，坚持中国特色社会主义理论体系，坚持适合中国国情的发展道路，在建设社会主义的进程中不断发展马克思主义。

这意味着中国将继续坚持生产力是人类社会发展的根本动力，坚持发展是硬道理，坚持以经济建设为中心，以科学发展为主题，加快转变经济发展方式，加快经济结构战略性调整，加快科技进步与创新，促进经济长期平稳较快发展，为社会发展奠定坚实的物质基础。

这意味着中国将继续发展社会主义民主政治，把中国共产党的领导、人民当家作主和依法治国三者有机统一起来，积极稳妥地推进政治体制改革，健全民主制度、丰富民主形式、拓宽民主渠道，保证人民依法实行民主选举、民主决策、民主管理和民主监督。

这意味着中国将继续大力保障和改善民生，着力解决好人民最关心、最直接、最现实的利益问题，坚持发展为了人民、发展依靠人民、发展成果由人民共享，永葆马克思主义政党的政治本色。

这意味着中国将继续坚持独立自主的和平外交政策，始终不渝地走和平发展道路，奉行互利共赢的开放战略，在和平共处五项原则基础上同所有国家友好合作，维护世界和平，促进共同发展，推动建设和谐世界。

这意味着中国共产党将在独立自主、完全平等、相互尊重、互不干涉内部事务原则的基础上，同各国各地区政党和政治组织发展交流合作，相互学习借鉴治国理政经验，促进国家关系发展。

最后，我想说，认识马克思主义在中国的发展对中英关系具有特殊意义。因为只有从深层次认识了马克思主义中国化问题，才能正确认识中国共产党在中国的作用，客观、全面看待当代中国的发展，从而增进彼此的理解和尊重，减少偏见和误解，为中英合作增添动力和润滑剂，推动中英关系不断向前发展。

谢谢！

Why Did China Choose Marxism*

Ladies and Gentlemen,

Dear Friends,

First of all, a very warm welcome to all of you to the Chinese Embassy. It's a great pleasure to meet so many British scholars of Marxism and share thoughts with you on Marxism in China.

It strikes me that the timing, venue and participants of our event are well-chosen, relevant and impressive. Let me explain why.

First, we meet at the right time. This year marks the 90th anniversary of the Communist Party of China, or the CPC. High-profile celebrations have been underway across China. The CPC was born out of Marxism and has stood the tests of time and adversity. The extraordinary 90 years since its founding have been a history of development and practice of Marxism in China.

Second, we have chosen the right place. Britain is the second home of Karl Marx and Friederich Engels. This is the land where Marxism took shape and matured. It was from Britain that Marxist theory spread worldwide.

Within two weeks of my arrival in London as Ambassador, I visited the Highgate Cemetery. I went with my young colleagues in the Embassy to pay tribute to Marx.

I went further to retrace the steps of this great thinker and mentor. I visited his central London home in Soho and toured the British Museum to see where Karl Marx did his research.

---

* Keynote Speech at the Marxism in China Seminar. Chinese Embassy in the UK, 20 July 2011.

Third, we bring together the right people. Many of you are scholars of Marxism, long time campaigners for Marxism or leaders and participants in Marxist parties. It's Marxism that gives us this opportunity to exchange ideas together.

Regarding the theme of our discussion today, Marxism in China, I would like to make three points.

First, why has China chosen Marxism?

Marxism became the choice of the Chinese people following a painstaking journey of exploration and perseverance since the second half of the 19th century.

The early 20th century saw China and its people in deep crisis, both internal and external.

Neither old-style peasant revolts or bourgeois reform or revolution could make any difference to China's plight and destiny.

The October Revolution in Russia made a profound impression on many Chinese people. It pointed to a solution to free the Chinese people from their terrible predicament. That solution was the theory of Marxism as a systematic, scientific outlook of the world and methodology that could be spread to China.

Four years later, in 1921, the Communist Party of China was founded in Shanghai. It was to become a party that has profoundly changed the history and the destiny of China.

Since then, using Marxist theory as its guide, the party has evolved through tremendous challenges.

The Party has led China and her people through three great revolutions, one after another, amid many trials and tribulations.

First, the new democratic revolution achieved national independence and people's liberation.

Second, the socialist revolution established socialism as the basic political system.

Third, the new, great revolution of reform and opening-up put China on a path of socialism with Chinese characteristics. The third revolution has been fundamental to the great success of the drive to modernise China.

These three revolutions witnessed China's rebirth through 90 years of social transformation. No country in history of the world has ever experienced such widespread and profound change in such a short period of time.

When the CPC was founded in 1921, China was a land divided, isolated and impoverished. China has now emerged as a united, harmonious, confident and prosperous country open to the entire world.

My second question for you today is this: how did Marxism match with the reality of China?

As you will know Marxism is by no means a set of rigid dogmas. You can read this in the preface to 1872 German Edition of *The Communist Manifesto*. Here Marx and Engels made this very important observation that relates to changes of time and development of practice.

Marx and Engels wrote: "The practical application of the principles will depend, as the Manifesto itself states, everywhere and at all times, on the historical conditions for the time being existing."

They continued with: "This programme has in some details been antiquated and some literature is deficient in relation to the present time."

In his letter to Werner Sombart in 1895, Engels wrote: "The entire conception of Marx is not a doctrine but a method. It does not offer made dogmas, only starting points for subsequent investigation and the method for such investigation."

In China, the steps taken to tailor Marxism to Chinese national and historical circumstances started from very early in the history of the CPC. You can trace back these adjustments to when Marxism first arrived in China. Such efforts to adjust Marxism for China's needs have never ceased.

In this process, two historic breakthroughs were made. The first breakthrough answered the fundamental question China was pondering in the early 20th century:

What kind of revolution did a semi-colonial, semi-feudal China need and how to get there?

The breakthrough led to the blazing of the trail for the new democratic revolution and the building of socialism. In turn this contributed to the formation of an important theory—Mao Zedong Thought.

The second breakthrough addressed a whole range of major theoretical and practical puzzles in the primary stage of socialism. Examples of these are:

- What is socialism and how to build it?

- What kind of Party should be built?
- How to build the Party?
- What kind of development should be achieved?
- And how to achieve that development?

The revolution charted a clear path for socialism with Chinese characteristics:

- It built up an entire theoretical system including the Deng Xiaoping Theory.
- It added the important thought of Three Represents and the Scientific Thinking on Development.
- All these are the latest outcomes in adapting Marxism to China's realities.

Since its founding, the Communist Party of China has developed a proud tradition. It makes analysis and seeks to solve China's problems with Marxist positions, views and methodologies.

More important, the Party applies Marxism creatively and in light of China's realities.

As a result, Marxism is much more vibrant today and its capacity to foster positive change is there for all to see.

My third question about Marxism in China today is this: What have the Chinese Communists learnt as they practice and develop Marxism in China?

I believe that there are three essential conclusions.

First, free the mind.

I draw your attention to the introduction by Marx in the Contribution to the Critique of Hegel's *Philosophy of Law*. Here Marx pointed out: "Theory can be realised in a people only insofar as it is the realisation of the needs of that people."

So, using that thought as a guide, how were the Chinese people to follow the theories of Marx? How was China to start a proletarian revolution, build socialism and modernise a poor, large Oriental country?

There is no ready answer in Marx's writings.

Nor can any precedent be found in human history.

In their application of the laws of Marxism, the Chinese communists ditched dogmas and made courageous exploration and innovation.

The CPC found the path toward Chinese-style socialism, developed a whole set of theories, and built the socialist system with Chinese features.

My second conclusion about evolving Marxism in China today is this: take a realistic approach.

Yes, the Party has had enormous success. But the road to that success was full of severe challenges. The Party had setbacks, made mistakes and paid the price.

However, the CPC and the Chinese people have always been able to face mistakes head on, assume their responsibilities and find a new way forward.

Some scholars point out that the CPC seems to have some sort of "antibody" to combat all sorts of viruses. In other words, the Party has an in-built resistance to threats to its continuity. I believe the so-called "antibody," if any, must come from the political courage of seeking truth from facts.

In its 90 years of history, the Party kept on taking stock of and reflecting on its experience, and had been brave enough to reform and renew.

With the key of seeking truth from facts, the Party opened one critical lock after another in the Chinese history. In this process Marxist theory was elevated to a new height again and again.

My third conclusion about adapting Marxism to China today is this: keep up with the changes of time.

To apply Marxism in Chinese context is to fit it into the circumstances of the time.

Different historical stages and conditions left quite different marks on the CPC, China and the world.

Confronted with new challenges and situations, the Party was always able to ride the tide of history and lead China toward progress. This was possible because as time changed, the party could always change with it.

The Party set out scientific goals and tasks and remained an advanced Marxist party. We are soberly aware that:

- A party is not to become advanced overnight.
- And its advanced nature must not be taken for granted.
- An advanced party today may not be advanced tomorrow.

Therefore, what we keep telling ourselves is this:

- A party that rests on its laurels has no future.
- We must be ready to change and bold enough to break new ground.
- And we must not stand still.

The party's commitment to free the mind, its realistic approach and refusal to stand still are the three key points to understand Marxism in China today.

Those three points explain the CPC's success in applying Marxism in China under different historical circumstances.

In the process Marxism itself got enriched and improved.

In 1921 the CPC started with 50 members. Today, 90 years after its birth the CPC has become the world's largest ruling party with over 80 million members.

Over the same period, China has been utterly transformed. In 1921 China was a poor, weak and underdeveloped country. Today, 90 years on, China is the second largest global economy. The Chinese people, once on the verge of crisis, are well on the path toward a great rejuvenation.

As time marches forward theory must never lose touch with reality.

Looking forward, China will stick to the basic principles of Marxism and the theoretical framework of socialism with Chinese features.

China will continue to follow the path tailored to our realities. China will further refine Marxism to build a socialist future.

So, what does this all add up to in this analysis of China and Marxism?

It means the Chinese people will follow these principles:

- Productivity is regarded as the driver of social development.
- China believes in the overriding importance of development.
- The economic agenda is a prime focus.
- There will be a pursuit of scientific development.
- The growth model of China will be reorientated.
- Restructuring of the economy will be done in a strategic manner.
- We will push for technological progress and innovation.

- China will sustain steady, fast economic growth and lay a solid economic foundation for social development.

It means China will further strengthen its socialist democracy, defined by the Party's leadership, people's ownership of China's development and rule of law.

As the political reform moves steadily forward, we will improve democracy, enrich its format and widen the channels for public participation.

The lawful rights of the people in democratic election, democratic decision making, democratic management and democratic supervision will be further strengthened.

It means China will further improve her people's livelihood, address the major concerns in their day-to-day life and protect their interests.

Under the Party's leadership, China's development is for the people, by the people, and all the benefits of development are shared among the people. This is what a Marxist ruling party is all about.

It means China will continue to pursue an independent, peaceful foreign policy and a win-win opening-up strategy. The Chinese people will continue to go down the path of peaceful development.

We seek friendship and cooperation with all countries based on the Five Principles of Peaceful Coexistence. China is committed to joining hands with the international community in contributing to world peace, common development and world harmony.

It also means the Party will develop exchanges and cooperation with all other political parties and organisations worldwide. Such exchanges will follow the principles of independence, equality, mutual respect and non-interference in internal affairs.

The Chinese people recognise all nations can learn from each others' experience and cultures. China believes there is much to gain through study of different governance philosophies. These studies offer considerable potential to explore how to move state-to-state relations forward.

Last but not least, I'm convinced that understanding Marxism in China plays an important role in China-UK relations.

A grasp of Marxism in China today is the only path to a clear understanding of the Chinese nation today. I believe it is essential to realise what the CPC means to China.

That is the way to truly see China as it is.

Exchanges strengthen understanding and respect.

Dialogue reduces bias and misunderstanding.

A comprehensive and objective understanding of today's China provides a driving force to the further growth of our bilateral relations.

Thank you!

2010年5月26日

在白金汉宫向英国女王伊丽莎白二世递交国书。女王生前曾接受12位中国大使递交国书，我是最后一位当面向她递交国书的中国大使。

2011 年 7 月 20 日

在“马克思主义在中国”座谈会上作主旨发言：《中国为什么选择马克思主义》。

2012 年 1 月 18 日

在英国帝国理工学院发表主旨演讲：《创新是中国发展的关键》。

2012年2月9日

在英国国防大学联合指挥与参谋学院发表主旨演讲：《〈孙子兵法〉与中国的外交国防政策》。

2012年12月12日

在英国工商界宣介党的十八大精神报告会上发表主旨演讲：《道路坚定，前途光明》。

2013 年 4 月 17 日

在伦敦国际战略问题研究所发表主旨演讲：《新时期的中国外交》。

2013 年 11 月 20 日

在英国改革俱乐部发表主旨演讲：《全面深化改革是中国发展的强大动力》。

2014年1月25日

在英国剑桥大学发表主旨演讲:《中国发展前景光明》。

2014年5月20日

在英国国防大学联合指挥与参谋学院发表主旨演讲：《“中国梦”引领中国安全观与国防建设》。

2014年6月26日

在英国苏格兰国家博物馆“明朝：黄金帝国”展开幕式上发表讲话：《观察中英文化交流的窗口》。

2014年9月5日

在美国塔夫茨大学弗莱彻法律与外交学院授奖仪式暨开学典礼上发表主旨演讲：《使命与梦想》。

2015 年 4 月 15 日

在《习近平谈治国理政》推介会上发表讲话：《读懂当代中国，领略领袖风范》。

2016 年 1 月 25 日

在英国四十八家集团俱乐部春节晚宴上发表主旨演讲：《充满期待的2016》。

法治照耀中国*

尊敬的年利达律师事务所全球事务负责人戴仕文先生，

各位英国企业界、金融界、法律界的朋友，

女士们、先生们：

首先感谢年利达律师事务所邀请我参观在英国图书馆举办的英国《大宪章》展览并出席今天的晚宴。这是我第二次近距离接触《大宪章》。2014 年夏天，我访问了英格兰南部的索尔兹伯里大教堂，那里长眠着英国前首相希思先生，同时存放着《大宪章》的一份手抄副本。今天，在世界历史上产生过深远影响的《大宪章》两份存世副本和美国《独立宣言》《权利法案》原件同时展出，非常难得。

800 年前的《大宪章》在英国历史上具有崇高的政治、法律地位，据说对美国的《独立宣言》和《权利法案》也有较大的影响。就法律层面来说，《大宪章》影响最为深远的是它明确了非经依法审判，不能剥夺他人的自由和财产。这体现了英国早期的法治思想。

法治思想并非英国或西方独有。中国法治理念源远流长，早在两千年前就有了自成体系的成文法典。中国古人认为“法者，治之端也”，主张“一断于法”，不分贵贱尊卑。不过，在中国数千年历史上，人治多于法治，法治往往受到这样或那样的束缚或干扰。这就表明为什么 2014 年年底召开的

---

* 在英国年利达律师事务所晚宴上的主旨演讲。2015 年 5 月 13 日，伦敦圣潘克拉斯万丽酒店。

中国共产党十八届四中全会如此重要，因为会议就全面推进依法治国做出了一系列重大决定，这是中国法治建设的里程碑。

《大宪章》的另一个重要历史意义是，它最早对君权做出了限制，对此后数百年英国政治体制演变产生了深刻影响，成为今天英国君主立宪制的基石。英国的政治演变史是英国历史的主要看点，英国的这条渐进式改革道路，世界上没有任何国家能够照搬模仿。

中国近现代史上的发展道路也是独特的。中国近代以来，许多仁人志士曾苦苦寻找适合中国国情的政治体制。中国试图实行君主立宪制、议会制、多党制和总统制，甚至还复辟帝制，但都行不通。最后中国人民选择了中国共产党，建立了新中国。

65年来，在中国共产党领导下，中国从积贫积弱的半殖民地半封建社会发展成为繁荣昌盛的发展中大国。中国不仅成为世界第二大经济体，还成为世界第一大贸易体、世界第三大对外直接投资国。世界上还没有哪个国家工业化的速度和规模能够与中国媲美。中国的发展不但使中国人民受益，而且给世界带来机遇。这说明，一个国家走什么样的发展道路，实行什么样的社会政治制度，是要靠自己探索走出来的。

历史发展到今天，中国共产党将如何推进依法治国？一些西方人看中国时，总是有意无意地将中国共产党领导与依法治国对立。我认为，如果不抱偏见，这个问题不难回答，也不难理解。我们先看西方，比如在英国，执政党组成的政府在议会提出法案，法案在议会通过成为法律后，无论是执政党还是政府都必须遵守。中国也是一样，中国要厉行法治，需要一个总揽全局、协调各方的领导核心，而这一重大历史使命只有中国共产党及其领导的政府才能担当，才能胜任。同时，中国共产党必须在宪法和法律范围内活动，党的政策、党的任何组织和个人都不能凌驾于法律之上。中国共产党的成员触犯法律，不论其职务和地位有多高，都必须受到法律惩处。过去两年来，一大批“老虎”与“苍蝇”被打，这既是反腐匡纪，剜除党内毒瘤，也体现了中国共产党对法律的尊崇与恪守。

中国将如何在中国共产党的领导下推进依法治国，十八届四中全会都做出了明确的规划，包括要完善以宪法为核心的中国特色社会主义法律体系，加强宪法实施；深入推进依法行政，加快建设法治政府；保证公正司法，提高司法公信力；增强全民法治观念，推进法治社会建设。中国将适应对外开放不断深化，完善涉外法律法规体系，促进构建开放型经济新体制。中国也将借鉴不同国家包括英国法治的有益经验，服务于自身法治建设。十八届四中全会召开半年多以来，中国法治建设和改革加速推进，已经取得了明显进展，比如最高法院设立巡回法庭，建立跨行政区划法院，设立知识产权法院，建立以审判为中心的诉讼制度，实行办案质量终身负责制和错案责任倒查问责制。这些司法改革措施以提高司法公信力为根本尺度，既符合国情又遵循司法规律。

70 多年前，一本令世人瞩目的书最先在英国出版，这就是美国记者埃德加·斯诺所著的《红星照耀中国》。他在访问中国西北地区后，写下了这部报告文学，对中国共产党和中国革命作了真实介绍，一问世便轰动世界。当时舆论普遍认为这是一部杰作，标志着西方对中国的了解进入一个新时代。

今天，中国共产党励精图治，为实现“中国梦”的目标，正在全面建成小康社会，全面深化改革，全面推进依法治国，全面从严治党。应该说，今天依然是“红星照耀中国”，同时中国共产党正在续写一部全新的篇章——法治照耀中国。

谢谢。

现在我愿回答大家的提问。

Rule of Law —"Shining Over China" *

Mr. Simon Davies,

Business and Financial Leaders,

Ladies and Gentlemen,

This is a special evening. I was fascinated to see the largest exhibition ever staged about the world-famous Magna Carta. I wish to congratulate Linklaters for sponsoring this inspiring exhibition at the British Library.

I am most grateful to Linklaters for the invitation to view the exhibition and then inviting me to join you for dinner.

This was my second time to view Magna Carta close up. Last summer, I visited Salisbury Cathedral. I was there to pay tribute to the late Prime Minister Sir Edward Heath who had a home close by. Afterwards I viewed one of the original Magna Carta kept in the Cathedral.

Today on display at the British Library are two of the four original 1215 Magna Carta and the original copies of the American Declaration of Independence and The Bill of Rights. Seeing these side by side is indeed very special as these documents have had a profound impact in shaping the world history.

This 800-year-old Magna Carta is highly significant in British history, both politically and legally. Many believe Magna Carta to have had a big impact on the American Declaration of Independence.

In terms of legal significance, Magna Carta's most far-reaching impact is the

---

* Speech at the Dinner Hosted by Linklaters. St. Pancras Renaissance Hotel, London, 13 May 2015.

establishment of the principle that no one shall be deprived of life, liberty or property without due process of law. Magna Carta marked the earliest practice of rule of law in Britain.

Rule of law is not an exclusively British or western idea. China is known for having a long history of legal practice and principles.

2,000 years ago, China had its own complete system of written code of law. The Chinese have always believed in these principles:

- Good governance begins with enforcing the law.
- And all are judged by law, not by wealth or status.

However, in thousands of years of Chinese history, rule of man often prevailed while rule of law was subject to restrictions or disruptions of various sorts.

Today, the Communist Party of China, or the CPC, takes rule of law as a paramount principle of importance. That is exactly why the Fourth Plenary Session of the 18th CPC Central Committee, convened at the end of last year, was especially important. That meeting came to a series of major decisions on comprehensive advancement of rule of law in China. That meeting was nothing short of a milestone in the history of establishing rule of law in China.

This evening our thoughts are very much focused on Magna Carta. Another historical significance of Magna Carta is that it was the first to provide for restrictions on the power of monarchs. That had a profound impact on the evolution of the British political system over hundreds of years. The pattern of influence of Magna Carta is perhaps the most fascinating part of the evolution of British history.

Today, Magna Carta remains the cornerstone of the British constitutional monarchy. It is also fascinating to observe how the unique experience of Britain following incremental reform has not been replicated elsewhere in the world.

Likewise, China's path in modern times has also been unique. During the past century, numerous Chinese pioneers have made painstaking efforts in search of a political system suited to the Chinese people. China experimented with a number of solutions—from constitutional monarchy to parliamentary, multi-party and presidential systems. At one time, autocratic rule was restored. When it became clear that none of these worked, the people of China chose the Communist Party and founded a new China.

After sixty-five years, under the leadership of the CPC, the once weak, poor, semi-feudal and semi-colonial country has been transformed. No country in history has industrialised on such a scale and at such a speed. The outcome is a China that is now a major and prosperous developing country. It is not only the world's second biggest economy but also the largest trading nation and third largest investor in FDI. China's development has not only benefited the Chinese people but also brought many opportunities to the world.

With evolution of rule of law, the British and Chinese experience proves these principles:

- A country always relies on its own trial and error as it explores a path of development.
- Each nation shapes a social system that suits its reality.

After sixty-five years, how will the CPC promote rule of law today?

Some people in the West, intentionally or unintentionally, always see the leadership of the CPC in opposition to good governance with rule of law.

For those who approach China with an open and fair mind, they can observe interesting parallels between the Western countries and China.

Let us first take a look at how political parties work in the West. In the UK, for example, the government formed by the ruling party is empowered to make proposals on legislation. When a bill passes the Parliament and becomes law, it will be binding for the ruling party and the government.

It is the same in China. To enforce rule of law in China, a strong leadership is needed—a leadership that has the overall picture in mind and is capable of rallying various groups. This historic mission is now on the shoulders of the CPC and the government under its leadership.

The CPC will lead, and it must lead within the framework of the Constitution and laws. Neither the Party's policy nor any party organisation or individual is above the law. Party members, rank and file, are subject to the same scrutiny and punishment in case of offences.

Over the past year, a large number of "tigers" as well as "flies," metaphors for corrupt officials, have been dealt with according to Party discipline and brought to justice according to law. This is a clear demonstration that the CPC respects and abides by the law.

The Fourth Plenary Session of the 18th CPC Central Committee has made clear-cut plans for advancing rule of law in China. These measures include:

- To improve a socialist system of laws with Chinese characteristics centred around the Constitution, and to strengthen the implementation of the Constitution.
- To ensure law-based administration and to put government under rule of law.
- To safeguard judicial justice and to strengthen judicial credibility.
- And to promote the public awareness of rule of law and to enhance the building of a law-based society.

China will also improve laws and regulations with regard to foreign businesses in order to facilitate further opening-up. This will also advance and build a new system of an open economy.

Those who study the history of China will know that it has a consistent pattern of absorbing ideas from outside its borders. So, it should not surprise that China will learn from countries, like Britain, to improve its rule of law.

It is just a little over half a year since the important meeting of the Fourth Plenary Session of the 18th CPC Central Committee. Yet China has accelerated the advancement of rule of law and reform. There has been tangible progress:

- The Supreme Court has created the first Circuit Courts, the first IPR courts, and courts with trans-regional jurisdiction.
- The People's Courts have adopted a case-filing registration system.
- The litigation process now focuses on courtroom hearings.
- A lifelong accountability system to guarantee prudent handling of cases and a system to retrospectively hold judges accountable for erroneous rulings have been adopted.

These judicial reform measures are aimed at strengthening judicial credibility. They suit China's national condition and are in line with general judicial practice.

Seventy years ago, a book published in Britain became a global sensation. This was Edgar Snow's *Red Star over China*—an account of his visit to the revolutionary base in China. Its investigative reporting about the CPC and China's revolution attracted world attention. The book was regarded as an influential masterpiece and a milestone marking the beginning of a new era of Western understanding of China.

Many extraordinary events have unfolded in China since *Red Star over China* was published seventy years ago.

Today, the CPC is leading the country in a grand project called the "Chinese Dream." To accomplish this project, China will strive to advance rule of law and enforce stricter Party discipline. At the same time China will build moderate prosperity and deepen reforms.

So, the "red star" is still shining over China!

And in this new chapter of Chinese Dream, rule of law will "shine over China."

Thank you!

Now, I would like to take your questions.

第三章

和平发展

西方社会对中国的崛起存在许多误解、疑虑，甚至恐慌。由于少数反华势力恶意炒作“中国威胁论”和一些媒体歪曲报道，多数西方民众不了解中国的实情，很容易被误导。针对这种情况，我利用各种机会讲中国和平发展的故事。首先讲文化。中华传统文化崇尚“和为贵”，中国人民爱好和平、珍惜和平。和平已融入中华民族的血脉中，刻进中华文化的基因里。其次讲历史。近现代以来，中国饱受欺压和侵略，深知战争的伤痛与和平的可贵。新中国成立以来，中国从未主动挑起一场战争，从未侵占别国一寸土地。再次讲现实。中国的发展需要一个和平的国际环境，中国的和平发展也促进了世界和平与稳定，给世界经济带来了增长动力和发展机遇。最后讲未来。中国将来无论发展到什么程度，都无意取代谁，都永远不扩张、永远不称霸。

和平、发展、合作——中国外交的主题*

女士们、先生们：

很高兴有机会来到牛津大学这座英语世界中最古老的高等学府演讲。

牛津大学有着800多年历史，产生过26位英国首相和47位诺贝尔奖获得者。伦敦《旗帜晚报》的一位专栏作家曾发现一个有趣的规律，每个在牛津上过学的人都会在与他人交谈开始后的11分钟内提及这一事实。这可能有所夸张，但也从一个侧面说明牛津大学是每个从这里走出去的学子一生的骄傲。

牛津大学与中国的渊源是在1687年，当时一个叫沈福宗的中国人来到牛津，他用拉丁语告诉人们应该用怎样的顺序去阅读博德利图书馆中的中文书籍，并且为图书馆制作了中文书籍目录。在他离开200多年以后，陆续有中国人到这里求学任教，包括陈寅恪、钱钟书、吕叔湘、许地山和杨宪益等著名学者。如今，牛津大学已经有超过2 000名中国毕业生，正在就读的有732名，是第二大海外留学生群体。我也高兴地得知，牛津大学与北京大学建立了多年的校际合作关系，双方保持密切的学术交流，联合培养高层次人才。

今天，我演讲的主题是中国的外交。主题是贵校提出的，我明白为什么大家会对这个题目感兴趣，因为目前大家对中国外交有各种看法、有不少争论。

---

* 在牛津大学的演讲。2010年6月10日，牛津大学。

当前中国的外交政策是什么？我认为就是坚持走和平发展道路，奉行互利共赢的开放战略，在和平共处五项原则基础上同所有国家发展友好关系，参加应对全球性问题的国际合作，努力推动建设持久和平、共同繁荣的和谐世界。简而言之，中国外交主张和平、发展和合作。

中国的外交政策基于中国的现实国情，扎根于中国的历史文化，反映中国与世界的紧密关系，是时代的要求和必然选择。

第一，中国的发展中国家属性要求外交为发展服务。

国际上一些媒体、学界和政界人士对中国的国家属性有疑问，认为中国经济、科技、军事及文化软实力发展迅速，特别是 GDP 总量坐三望二，已经跨入发达国家门槛，是“世界强国”之一。

的确，从历史纵向来看，中国改革开放 32 年来的变化是惊人的，成就是骄人的，但如果与世界横向相比，我们的差距又是显然的。我不妨举一些数据。

从人均 GDP 看，根据国际货币基金组织的数据，2009 年中国仅有 3 678 美元，排名居世界第 100 位，在阿尔巴尼亚之后，属于中等收入区间的偏低水平。

从人口结构看，中国 13 亿多人口中，农村人口 7 亿多，比重为 58%，远远高于发达国家水平；按照联合国每人每天 1 美元的贫困线标准，中国仍有 1.5 亿贫困人口。

从发展水平看，中国城乡、地区发展很不平衡，东部和西部的人均 GDP 差距在 3 倍以上。我曾在位于中国西部的甘肃省担任省长助理，那里文化底蕴深厚、人民勤劳朴实，但受自然条件等限制，至今人均 GDP 只有 1 280 美元。

从社会发展成熟度看，中国的教育、医疗和社会保障体系尚待完善和发展。消费结构中食品仍是主要部分，2008 年恩格尔系数为 33.1%。

从科技创新能力看，2008 年中国研发投入仅占 GDP 的 1.45%，尚未跨过标志国家进入技术创新阶段的 2% 的门槛。

所以，综合上述各项指标，中国仍然是名副其实的发展中国家，发展是第一要务。中国外交在维护国家的主权和安全利益的同时，必须将创造长期和平稳定的国际环境、平等互利的合作环境作为一项中心任务。

第二，中国的历史文化奠定了中国外交的和平性和平等性。

中华民族是热爱和平的民族。在五千年传统文化中，“和为贵”“和而不同”“以和邦国”“亲仁善邻”等思想深入中华民族的内心世界，形成中华民族热爱和平、崇尚和谐的民族性格、价值观念和心理情感。6个世纪前，郑和率领当时世界上最强大的舰队7次远航，最远到达了非洲东海岸，带去了贸易和文化，但没有侵占别国的一寸土地，更没有在海外派驻一兵一卒。

中国的历史遭遇使我们深知和平的宝贵、平等的价值。中国近现代屡遭蹂躏，饱受屈辱，1949年新中国成立前的一百多年里，中国遭受大规模的侵略战争就有6次之多，被迫对外签订了大大小小343个不平等条约。孔子说：“己所不欲，勿施于人。”这句话既是中国人崇尚的做人准则，也是中国外交实践中的重要理念。

第三，中国与世界的利益依存更加紧密，你中有我，我中有你。

人类进入21世纪，经济全球化深入发展，科技革命加速推进，全球和区域合作方兴未艾。中国的发展离不开世界，世界的繁荣稳定也离不开中国。中国关起门来搞建设的日子早已一去不复返，世界经济的发展也不能缺少中国的强劲增长。比如，中国房地产市场的冷热，可能会影响世界铁矿石市场的走势，同时欧洲不少国家实行紧缩政策、削减财政赤字，可能会直接影响中国的出口制造业订单。这种“利益共生”格局正在逐步形成。

第四，中国与世界面临的共同挑战增加，一荣俱荣，一损俱损。

借用狄更斯所写的，“它是最美好的时代，它是最糟糕的时代”，人类在不断取得进步，也总是遇到新的烦恼。恐怖主义、金融安全、水资源、粮食、能源、环境、网络等非传统安全问题近年来凸显，带来日益复杂的全球性挑战。任何国家不可能单独解决这些问题，任何国家也不可能置身事外，需要各国同舟共济，合作应对。

女士们、先生们，

丘吉尔有一句名言：“伟大、高尚的代价是责任。”中国积极承担与自己国际地位和国家实力相匹配的责任，努力维护世界和平，促进共同发展。

中国致力于和平解决国际争端和热点问题，推动国际和地区安全合作。中国是联合国安理会常任理事国中派出维和人员最多的国家，累计向 24 项联合国维和行动派出上万人次，现正在执行维和任务的有 2 100 多人。就在 2010 年 1 月，8 名中国维和警察在海地地震中献出了生命。

中国以实际行动推动国际防扩散进程。中国参加了防扩散领域的所有国际条约和相关国际组织，并与其他国家和有关多国就出口控制机制积极开展交流与合作。中国大力倡导朝核问题六方会谈，努力推动实现半岛无核化。中国积极参与伊朗核问题六国磋商，坚持“双轨”战略，支持外交努力。

中国对世界经济增长的贡献率位居第一，世界银行预测，2010 年这一比率可能高达 30%。中国大力倡导国际社会携手应对国际金融危机，共克时艰，加强与主要经济体宏观经济政策的协调，积极参与二十国集团峰会进程，承诺购买 500 亿美元的国际货币基金组织债券。

中国积极支持国际减贫事业，推动实现千年发展目标。中国向包括非洲国家在内的广大发展中国家提供了超过 2 000 亿元人民币的援助，免除了 49 个重债穷国和最不发达国家的债务。我与非洲有很深的感情，作为外交官首次常驻的国家就是赞比亚，目睹了中国援建的坦赞铁路，这条被非洲人民称为“自由之路”的铁路建设完成后，当地人民欢庆通车的激动场面至今令我记忆犹新、难以忘怀。

中国高度重视气候变化问题。中国在《联合国气候变化框架公约》对发展中国家没有任何强制和约束性要求的情况下，承诺到 2020 年使单位 GDP 二氧化碳排放量比 2005 年降低 40%~45%。这一承诺不附加任何条件，不与任何国家的减排目标挂钩。

女士们、先生们，

英国是政治、经济、文化上有重要影响的世界大国，中国始终将英国视为和平发展进程中的重要合作伙伴。两国都具有悠久的历史和丰富的文化，双方经济互补性强，经贸、金融、教育、科技和低碳等各领域合作潜力大。两国关系的全球性和战略性日益突出，双方在预防和制止地区冲突、推动世界经济增长、支持自由贸易体系、促进多边主义、改革国际经济金融体系、维护核不扩散体系等领域具有相似或共同语言。进一步发展中英关系，不仅符合两国的利益，也有利于世界的和平、稳定和繁荣。

我作为中国新任驻英大使，抵英3个多月，很多人都问我，我的使命和目标是什么。

我告诉他们，我的使命就是实现“IDEA”。

“I”代表利益（Interests），即要扩大中英的共同利益，将中英在双边和多边合作中的蛋糕越做越大。

“D”代表对话（Dialogue），即要促进中英间各层次、各领域的对话与交流，特别是充分发挥两国高层互访、中英经济财金对话和战略对话等重要机制的牵头作用。

“E”代表探索（Exploration），即要不断探索合作新领域，创造合作新亮点，特别是努力寻求中英间突破性的经贸大项目，推动开展前沿的低碳和绿色技术合作。

“A”代表互谅（Accommodation），即要增进彼此理解，尊重对方关切。中英不可能在所有问题上看法一致，但双方应在相互尊重的基础上，倾听对方观点，了解对方关注，增强换位思考，合理照顾彼此利益。

我高兴地看到，英国新政府成立后，中英关系开局良好。卡梅伦首相就职次日即与温家宝总理通电话，黑格外交大臣也与杨洁篪外长通了电话，奥斯本财政大臣上周还访问了中国并与王岐山副总理会晤，双方一致表示将进一步拓展和提升中英关系。

我也高兴地看到，上海世博会已成为中英展现各自现代形象、增进两国人民了解、促进经贸、科技和文化合作的平台。目前，英国馆——“蒲公英”的观众每天超过5.3万人，网站点击量超过8 000万次，相关经贸推介活动已吸引了来自中国的25个投资项目。

多年来，牛津大学凭借其深厚的学术基础和前瞻的学术思维，在中国研究方面居英国和欧洲前列。我也高兴地得知牛津大学前年成立了“中国中心”，整合研究资源，加大研究投入。我衷心地希望牛津大学今后继续发挥对华研究的领头羊作用，创造更加丰富和更高价值的学术成果，增进英国、欧洲及世界对中国的了解，促进中英和中欧关系的发展。

女士们、先生们，

我相信，只要我们满怀希望，共同努力，中英关系的未来一定更加美好，世界的未来一定更加和谐。

谢谢。

下面我愿回答大家的提问。

Peace, Development and Cooperation: Themes of China's Foreign Policy*

Ladies and Gentlemen,

I am very pleased to speak at your prestigious university.

Oxford is not only the oldest institution of higher learning in the English-speaking world, but has produced in its 800 years, 26 British prime ministers and 47 Nobel laureates.

According to an interesting discovery made by a columnist with Evening Standard, Oxford graduates will mention something about their Oxford roots within 11 minutes of starting a conversation. That may be a slight exaggeration; yet having studied at Oxford must be a source of life-long pride to you all.

China's association with Oxford dates back to 1687, when a Chinese scholar Shen Fuzong came to Oxford. He assisted in cataloguing the Chinese books in the Bodleian Library. More than 200 years later, quite a few Chinese scholars have come to study or teach here in Oxford. Chen Yinque, Qian Zhongshu, and Lv Shuxiang, along with many others, were among the well-respected in China.

Today, over 2,000 Chinese have graduated from Oxford, and 732 are studying here as we speak, making China the second largest source of overseas students for Oxford. The diversity of the student population here is truly impressive. We feel very much at home here in Oxford.

In addition, I was delighted to hear that Oxford has developed a successful partnership with Peking University and I do hope that such mutually beneficial

* Speech at the University of Oxford. University of Oxford, 10 June 2010.

educational and academic links between Oxford and the Chinese universities will continue to flourish.

Over the years, Oxford has also been a leading institution in the UK and Europe for China studies. With your China Centre set up in 2008, I sincerely hope that Oxford will stay at the forefront in helping the UK, Europe and the rest of the world to know and understand more about China.

Today, I am asked to talk about China's foreign policy. As there has been a great deal of interest, discussion and even debate about China's foreign policy in recent months.

How do I characterise China's foreign policy? My analysis is that China's foreign policy is all about pursuing the path of peaceful development, through an open-minded global approach based on mutual benefit, and by actively participating in the addressing global issues, to build a harmonious world of lasting peace and common prosperity.

What do we mean by a harmonious world? It is not a world free of problems or conflicts, nor a world of uniformity, but rather a world of peaceful coexistence of countries that cooperate in solving problems despite their diversity. In short, the themes of China's foreign policy boil down to Peace, Development and Cooperation.

Firstly, China's foreign policy in the context of its developing country status aims first and foremost at promoting the country's development.

Some in the world are not sure about China being a developing country, pointing to the increasing strengths of its economy, science and technology, along with defense and soft power. So, with its GDP now ranking 3rd with the potential of rising to the 2nd, they tend to describe China as a global power.

While this is flattering, and China has gone through a huge transformation in the past 30 years, China is still lagging behind in many areas. Let me give you some examples:

- According to the IMF, China's per capita GDP was $3,678 in 2009, ranking behind Albania at the 100th in the world.
- Out of a population of 1.3 billion, 700 million or over half of the population live in rural areas, which is much higher than in developed countries; 150 million people still living on less than a dollar a day, the poverty line set by the UN.
- Serious disparities also exist between rural and urban areas as well as between

regions in China. In per capita, the GDP of eastern China is at least 3 times higher than that of western China. As I used to be an assistant Governor of Gansu, a western province, I know the per capita GDP there was merely $1,280.

- Education, medical care, and social security systems remain underdeveloped, and food takes up the lion's share in household spending, with Engel's coefficient at 33.1%.
- With R&D input accounting for only 1.45% of the total GDP in 2008, we are lower than the 2% threshold expected for countries with a reasonable innovative capacity.

This is why development is the primary objective for China, and its foreign policy is largely aimed at fostering a peaceful, stable and cooperative external environment which will support its internal development efforts.

Secondly, peace and harmony lie at the centre of China's foreign policy.

Throughout its 5,000-year-old culture, China has always treasured peace and benevolence. There are many teachings that reflect this, such as "peace comes first," "run the country with harmony" and "treat thy neighbour with kindness." Six centuries ago, Admiral Zheng He led the world's strongest fleet on 7 expeditions into the western seas as far as the horn of Africa. He brought with him goods for trade and culture, but never took an inch of foreign land.

China went through a lot in the 100 years before the founding of the People's Republic of China in 1949. With 6 major wars of foreign aggression and 343 unequal treaties being imposed on China, the experience has taught us to value peace and equality even more. As Confucius told us, "Don't do to others what you don't want others to do to you." This is a moral principle for every Chinese in his daily life, and is an important principle in China's foreign policy.

Thirdly, China's foreign policy is very much influenced by its close interdependence with the rest of the world.

In the age of globalisation, China's development would not have been possible without the world and the world would not be as prosperous and stable without China. Closing its doors has long been a thing of the past. China's strong growth has become indispensable to the global economy. For instance, fluctuations in the Chinese real estate market could impact the worldwide price of iron ore; or the economic belt tightening in European countries could reduce orders for Chinese manufactured products.

As Charles Dickens once wrote, "It was the best of times. It was the worst of times."

Our world has made unparalleled progress in standards of living and in science and technology, yet it is also plagued by new scourges, such as terrorism, financial instability and environmental challenges, to mention just a few. These challenges by their very nature defy single country solutions. Cooperation has become an imperative for us all.

Ladies and Gentlemen,

Winston Churchill once said, "The price of greatness is responsibility." As I will illustrate, China is actively fulfilling its responsibilities consistent with its strength and capacity, to uphold world peace and promote common development.

- China is committed to peaceful and cooperative solutions to conflicts and hotspot issues, and is the largest contributor of peacekeepers amongst the P5 nations at the UN Security Council, with 10,000 peacekeepers sent to 24 UN missions so far. As we speak, 2,100 peacekeeping positions are manned by Chinese personnel. Unfortunately, as we know even peacekeeping has its danger: eight Chinese peacekeepers lost their lives in the Haiti earthquake last January.
- China is also committed to non-proliferation, and has acceded to all international treaties on non-proliferation and is a member of many relevant international organisations. It has cooperated with other countries in multilateral export control regimes, and is a strong advocate for the Six-Party Talks on the denuclearisation of the Korean Peninsula. As an active player in the P5+1 talks on the Iranian nuclear issue, China supports the dual-track approach and diplomatic efforts.
- China is now the biggest contributor to world economic growth. According to the World Bank, 30% of global growth this year may come from China and China has worked hard to promote coordinated actions by major economies against the global financial crisis and pledged to buy up to $50 billion in IMF bonds.
- China is also actively supporting international efforts to alleviate poverty and achieve the UN's Millennium Development Goals, by providing other developing countries, including many in Africa, with 20 billion pounds in assistance and

cancellation of debts by 49 heavily indebted poor countries (HIPCs) and least developed countries (LDCs). I have a close personal bond to Africa, because my first posting as a young diplomat was Zambia. And I still remember vividly the enthusiastic celebrations of the local people when the Tanzania-Zambia railway became operational.

- China is serious about addressing climate change. Although developing countries are not subject to mandatory targets under the United Nations Framework Convention on Climate Change (UNFCCC), China has pledged to reduce its carbon intensity by 40%~45% compared to its 2005 level by 2020. This is a pledge that is not predicated on the efforts of other countries.

Ladies and Gentlemen,

China sees the UK as an important partner in its process of peaceful development. The two countries enjoy strong economic ties and there is still a huge potential for cooperation in trade and investment, education, science and technology, as well as in low-carbon projects. Our relationship is increasingly becoming global and strategic in nature, as our two countries advocate multilateralism and have overlapping positions and interests in major global issues. We both work hard to boost world economic growth and reform of the international economic and financial systems. We both support free trade and the nuclear non-proliferation regime. Further development of our relationship is in the interest of our two countries, but it also serves peace, stability and prosperity of the world.

Since I arrived in the UK as the new Chinese Ambassador a little over 3 months ago, I have been asked frequently about my mission and priorities. Well, I can sum these up in one word: IDEA. With the:

"I" standing for interests. We need to expand our common interests and make the areas of our cooperation larger both bilaterally and multilaterally.

"D" for dialogue. We need to step up dialogue at all levels, especially through high-level visits, and by using mechanisms such as the Economic and Financial Dialogue and the Strategic Dialogue.

"E" for exploration. We need to explore new areas of cooperation, not least by identifying new projects in cutting-edge areas such as low-carbon and green technology.

"A" for accommodation. We need to enhance mutual understanding and respect each other's concerns and culture. China and the UK do not see eye to eye on everything, but it is important for us to listen to and respect each other, to ensure we appreciate and accommodate the other's concerns.

I am heartened by the good start on our relations with the new British government. Prime Minister David Cameron talked on the telephone with Premier Wen Jiabao as soon as he took office; Foreign Secretary William Hague has had two telephone conversations with our Foreign Minister Yang Jiechi and Chancellor George Osborne has met with Vice Premier Wang Qishan just last week in Beijing. Both sides have expressed a commitment to further expanding and upgrading our relations.

The ongoing World Expo in Shanghai has also offered both countries an opportunity to showcase their skills and imagination, as well as increasing understanding between our two peoples by facilitating business, technological and cultural cooperation. The UK national pavilion, which has been nicknamed "dandelion" by Chinese Internet users, is receiving 53 thousand visitors a day and more than 80 million website hits. The business events built around the Expo have already led to Chinese investment in 25 British projects.

Ladies and Gentlemen,

It has been a real pleasure talking to you, future leaders of the next generation. China-UK relations lie in your hands. I do hope you will visit China, work and trade with China.

I am confident that by working together, we will build a better relationship between our two countries and a more harmonious world for all.

Thank you.

Now I would like to take questions from the audience.

从全面、纵深的角度认识和平发展的中国*

尊敬的博斯沃思院长，

各位校友：

很高兴出席弗莱彻学院第八届伦敦专题研讨会，这使我有机会与一些老朋友重逢，同时又结识一些新校友。感谢博斯沃思院长的盛情邀请。

28 年前，在中国改革开放和中美建交之初，我作为最早的几批中国留学生中的一员，来到了美丽的弗莱彻学院，在这座全美历史最悠久的外交学与国际关系研究生院，度过了自己青年时期的一段美好时光，学习了一些外交知识特别是国际关系理论，至今感到受益匪浅。

毕业后，我曾先后在四大洲任职，虽然外交工作繁忙，但我始终未中断对国际关系的理论学习和思考，并努力在外交实践中不断探索新的理论和理念。

近一个时期以来，我一直在思考中国与世界的关系问题。改革开放 30 多年来，中国与世界的关系可以说已经发生了历史性的变化。以我个人的一些亲身经历和直接感受来说，1982 年我在弗莱彻留学时，中美刚刚建立了外交关系，当美国人听说我来自中国后，第一个问题就是“哪一个中国”（Which China）；20 世纪 80 年代末至 90 年代初，我首次到美国常驻，适逢东欧剧变、苏联解体，西方热议的是中国什么时候步苏联的后尘；又过了 10

---

* 在美国塔夫茨大学弗莱彻法律与外交学院第八届伦敦专题研讨会上的演讲。2010 年 12 月 4 日，伦敦希腊中心。

年，21世纪初，我出任中国驻埃及大使，在金字塔下，导游或商贩首先问我是不是日本人，再问是不是韩国人，最后才想到问是不是中国人。今天，如果有人再问"你来自哪个中国"，人们一定会认为他来自外星；西方现在热议的已不是所谓中国的崩溃，而是中国的崛起；中国年出境旅游者数量超过5 000万，世界各地早已对中国游客的到来习以为常，当地的商贩已学会用中文讨价还价。

然而，如何认识和把握今天中国与世界的关系，我感到目前西方国际关系主流理论难以充分解释，理论与现实之间存在着严重的脱节和滞后问题。

我在弗莱彻学习时，肯尼斯·沃尔兹创立的结构现实主义刚刚兴起，如今这一新现实主义学派成为美国国际关系研究的一大主流，深刻影响着美国的外交政策制定。从结构现实主义来看，国际政治系统处于无政府状态，国家的功能基本相似，即国家必须依靠自身力量捍卫本国的生存和安全，并最大限度地追求国家利益。国家间能力的分配决定国际政治结构。一个国家的崛起必然打破天平的平衡，引起别国的恐惧，从而激发别国增强自身实力或与他国结盟，以恢复均衡局面。按照这样的历史循环理论，中国的崛起对国际体系来说，就自动构成了一种威胁，尤其是安全威胁。

不仅是结构现实主义理论，即使是根据后起的国际关系另一大主流学派——新自由主义，有人也得出结论，或是经济市场化的中国必然完全照搬西方的政治模式，最终被西方"同化"，或是中国的身份受意识形态的影响，难以融入西方主导的国际社会。

当上述现有国际关系两大主流理论遇到中国，其分析看法不是感到悲观，就是感到失望，这与上述两大理论的先天性缺陷密不可分。比如，结构现实主义完全无视国家的个性和内部特征，新自由主义的利益倾向性十分明显。更何况两者都产生于20世纪70年代至80年代，没有脱离冷战的时代背景。在今天多极化、全球化的时代，老观念碰到了新现象，恐怕就难免会陷入一些旧的思维定式。

歌德曾说："理论是灰色的，但生命之树常青。"世界上的事物，总是在不断地发展变化，理论总是需要适应实际不断更新发展。国际关系理论同样必须与时俱进，一成不变的国际关系学说不是张冠李戴，就是此路不通。

当观察分析今天的中国，研究思考中国的发展给国际关系带来的变化影响时，我认为必须把握以下三个特点。

第一，中国的发展是一种和平状态的发展。保罗·肯尼迪在其《大国的兴衰》中总结了人类近500年来的大国发展史，尽管该书的要义是经济基础决定国家的盛衰，但也不无例外地表明了大国的崛起从历史上看总是伴随着掠夺、冲突和战争。13亿多人口的大国，对外不搞军事扩张，不抢占一寸别人的土地，不从别国掠夺资源，而是依靠改革开放，依靠政治社会的稳定，依靠人民的勤劳，依靠自由开放的全球贸易，逐渐实现民族复兴和成为世界强国，这种崛起方式从历史上看前所未有，但中国的确已经走出了这样一条和平发展的全新之路。

无先例可循，不等于不会产生先例。横向地看，欧盟从20世纪50年代的“煤钢联营”，到此后的“欧共体”，及至今天发展成为有27个成员国的“欧洲联盟”，成为世界政治中具有重要影响的一“极”，其诞生和一体化进程始终是在和平条件下实现的，同时也促进了欧洲60多年的和平。历史上何曾有这样的先例?

中国的和平发展，体现在中国外交政策的各个方面：我们奉行独立自主的和平外交政策，在和平共处五项原则的基础上同世界各国发展友好合作关系。我们倡导互信、互利、平等、协作的新安全观，既维护本国的安全，又尊重别国安全关切，促进人类共同安全。我们奉行防御性的国防政策，军费开支占国内生产总值的比重不足1.5%，不到世界平均水平的一半。中国是联合国安理会常任理事国中派出维和人员最多的国家，累计参与24项联合国维和行动，派出上万名维和人员。中国向索马里海域派出护航舰队，与多国舰队一道打击海盗，维护国际水域的安全。中国大力倡导朝核问题的六方会谈，努力维护半岛和地区的和平稳定，我在担任中国驻朝鲜大使3年半的时间里对此深有体会。中国积极参与伊朗核问题的六国磋商，致力于维护核不扩散体制以及中东、海湾地区的稳定。中国还积极与世界各国共同应对气候变化、能源资源安全等全球性问题。

中国的和平发展是对国际关系理论的一大突破和一大贡献。人类社会总是在这样的“破”与“立”中前行。

第二，中国的和平发展基于中国的“世界观”。国际关系理论发源于西方，根植于西方的价值观、历史文化和对世界的看法。用西方的国际关系理论解释中国的发展，难免会水土不服，似是而非。

中国的“世界观”简单来说，就是我们认为当今世界处在大变革和大调整之中，和平与发展是时代的主题。影响中国“世界观”的要素主要是中国的传统文化、自身近现代历史和对时代潮流的判断。从传统文化来说，中国人提倡“己所不欲，勿施于人”，追求“和为贵”，“讲信修睦、亲仁善邻”。与西方崇尚个人英雄主义不同，中国人的立身美德是谦逊，主张依靠集体而生存和发展。从近现代历史看，中国饱受欺压和侵略，深知战争的伤痛与和平的可贵。邓小平说，“中国永远不称霸”。这既是中国人的心声，也是历史的经验。从时代潮流看，我们认为求和平、谋发展、促合作已经成为不可阻挡的趋势，国与国的相互依存更加紧密，中国的发展离不开世界，世界的繁荣稳定也离不开中国。

和平发展理念是建立在中国的“世界观”基础上，因而不是空洞的理论，更不是“烟幕弹”，而是中国的国家信念和战略目标。

第三，中国积极促进国际体系良性发展。中国与国际体系的关系是外界比较关注的问题，也是中国在认真思考和着力解决的问题。以 2001 年中国加入世界贸易组织为标志，中国全面进入国际体系，迄今为止共参加了 130 多个政府间国际组织，缔结了 300 多项多边条约。因而，今天中西方已经较为一致的观点是：中国正在融入国际体系，中国不是国际体系的破坏者。现在的问题是：中国融入国际体系后该发挥什么样的作用？

西方提出了“中国责任论”，要求中国与西方一道维护现有国际体系。对中国来说，并不是这么简单，这里存在一个自我定位和身份认同的问题，也就是哲学中所说的“我是谁”。中国成了世界第二大经济体，但中国还是发展中国家这一点并未改变。中国的人均 GDP 只有 3 700 美元左右，只有世界平均水平的 1/3 多一点，排在世界百位之后。中国也向来认为，所有国家不分大小、强弱和贫富，都是国际体系的平等成员，各方利益都应当得到合理的尊重和维护。

因此，中国致力于在国际体系中发挥负责任和沟通协调的作用，成为国际体系的参与者、建设者和贡献者。我们在与西方发达国家广泛开展合作的同时，继续加强与发展中国家的传统友谊，帮助其开发和减贫。国际金融危机后，中国向国际货币基金组织增资 500 亿美元，明确要求将资金优先用于最不发达国家。我们支持、倡导并践行多边主义，建设性地参与国际体系变革进程，就国际规则的制定与修改提出合理的政策主张，主张增加发展中国家在国际体系中的代表性和发言权，推动国际关系民主化，促进国际体系更加有效地解决各种问题和挑战。

目前气候变化坎昆会议正在举行，各方都很关注。在气候变化问题上，中国的立场和行动无可指摘，努力和成绩有目共睹。我们坚定维护“共同但有区别的责任”原则，同时根据自己的国情采取自主减排行动，承诺到 2020 年单位国内生产总值二氧化碳排放比 2005 年下降 40%~45%。目前，中国水电装机容量、风电的新增容量、核电在建规模、太阳能热水器集热面积均居世界第一。中国既呼吁发达国家向发展中国家切实履行资金承诺，提供 300 亿美元快速启动资金，也明确表示绝不同其他发展中国家争一分钱，而且一如既往地在中非合作及中国与周边国家双边框架内向欠发达国家提供应对气候变化的物质和能力支持。

中国在国际体系中发挥积极作用，促进国际体系的良性发展，这既是对自己负责，也是对世界负责。

从事中国的外交事业，在这个时代，是一件幸事，也是一件乐事。中国的发展给了中国外交官广阔的舞台，更重要的是，我们在突破历史和创造历史。

从实践中促进世界的和平、稳定与繁荣，从实践中丰富国际关系理论，推进国际体系的积极发展，这应当是每位弗莱彻学子的目标和骄傲。因为弗莱彻的办学宗旨就是“为有志于维护一个复杂、富有挑战和日益全球性的社会之稳定与繁荣的学生们提供广泛而专业的国际关系教育”。

我也衷心地希望各位弗莱彻校友从全面和纵深的角度多认识和了解发展中的中国，让我们在各自的领域里共同促进中欧关系、中美关系及整个东西方关系的发展。

谢谢。

下面我愿回答大家的提问。

Understanding China's Pursuit of Peace and Development from a Comprehensive and in-depth Perspective*

Dean Stephen Bosworth,

My fellow Fletcher alumni,

It is a great honour for me to address the 8th Annual London Symposium of the Fletcher School. It is a real pleasure to catch up with old friends and get to know new ones. I wish to thank Dean Bosworth for his kind invitation.

28 years ago, I came to the beautiful campus of the Fletcher School as one of the early groups of Chinese students there. That was not long after China started the reform and opening-up and established diplomatic relations with the United States. I still recall fondly the time I spent as a young student in Fletcher. I learnt a great deal about diplomacy, especially theory of international relations, from which I have benefited even to this day.

After Fletcher, I started a busy diplomatic career, which took me to the postings in four continents. All this time I continued to learn and think about IR theories and tried to come up with my own ideas as my diplomatic experience grew.

These days I have been studying China's relationship with the world. This relationship has gone through tremendous changes in the past three decades.

Back in 1982 when I studied at Fletcher, it was only three years after China and the

* Speech at the 8th Annual London Symposium of the Fletcher School of Law and Diplomacy. The Hellenic Centre, London, 4 December 2010.

US established diplomatic ties. When I told people I came from China, the question was always: "Which China?"

Seven years later, I went to Washington DC for my first diplomatic posting in the US at a time of East European upheavals and Soviet disintegration. The hotly discussed question in Western capitals was: "When will China follow suit?"

Another ten years later, I was appointed Chinese Ambassador to Egypt. When I visited the Pyramids and other tourist attractions, local vendors always asked,

"Are you from Japan?" "No."

"Are you from Korea?" "No."

They finally asked "Are you from China?"

Today, if someone asks me which China I am from, he must be from another planet.

The hot topic in the world today is more about the rise of China than its fall. Furthermore, with over 50 million Chinese travelling overseas each year, many local vendors can bargain in Chinese for a good profit.

Nonetheless, my feeling is that when it comes to China's relationship with the world, there seems to be a gap in mainstream IR theories in the West, as it is quite hard to explain the nature of this relationship today according to existing theories.

When I was studying in Fletcher, Kenneth Waltz had just advocated the theory of structural realism. This became a leading neo-realist theory, playing a big part in shaping US foreign policy. According to structural realism, the international politics is in perpetual anarchy and individual states are all driven by a desire to ensure their survival and security and maximise their national interests. The distribution of power among states is the determining factor in international politics. The rise of one state will inevitably tip the balance, and lead other states to strengthen themselves or seek alliances with others to restore the balance of power. If this theory is valid, China's rise will automatically pose a security threat to the international system.

Apart from structural realism, neo-liberalism, another major school of IR studies, also leads some to conclude that the embrace of the market economy in China will either result in a westernised China, or a China that is permanently detached from the western-dominated international system due to ideological constraints.

If one judges the relationship between China and the world on the basis of these two major IR theories, one would either feel pessimistic or disappointed. This, I believe, is largely the result of the inherent flaws of these two theories. For example, structural realism ignores the internal features of individual states, while neo-liberalism is biased towards Western interests. Moreover, both theories emerged in the 1970s and 1980s, when the world was still in the Cold War. Now we live in an era of multi-polarity and globalisation. These old ideas are no longer sufficient to explain new realities. We really need to think out of the box.

Goethe said, "All theory is grey, but the golden tree of actual life springs ever green." Theories should be adapted to a constantly changing world. Otherwise, they will lead to the wrong conclusion or create confusion.

For those who observe today's China and analyse the impact of China's development on international relations, the following three aspects merit special consideration.

First, China's development is peaceful.

According to Paul Kennedy in the *Rise and Fall of the Great Powers*, the rise of dominant powers for the past 500 years has, with no exception, come hand in hand with plunder, conflict and war. China, a country with 1.3 billion people, has never pursued military expansion, or snatched any territory or resource from other countries. Instead, we tried to achieve national rejuvenation and play our role on the world stage through reform and opening-up in the context of political and social stability, through the hard work of the Chinese people, and through free and open trade. This may have never happened before, but it does not make it less true: China has blazed a new path of development that is peaceful.

Take the European Union for example. It started in the 1950s as the Coal and Steel Community and later as the European Community. Now it has 27 states as its members. The EU, an important pole in international politics, was born and integrated into the international system under totally peaceful conditions. It contributed to over six decades of peace in Europe. There is no historical precedence for this great endeavour.

China's peaceful development can be seen in every aspect of its foreign policy. We pursue an independent foreign policy of peace and develop friendly and cooperative relations with all countries on the basis of the Five Principles of Peaceful Co-existence. We believe that security should be based on mutual trust, mutual benefit, equality and coordination. While safeguarding our own security, we respect the security concerns of others and endeavour to promote common security. We follow a national defense policy solely for the purpose of self-defense. China's military expenditure accounts for less than 1.5% of GDP, not even half of the world average.

China is the largest contributor of peacekeepers among the five permanent members of the UN Security Council. It has sent over 10,000 peacekeepers to 24 UN missions. It has dispatched escort fleets to the waters off the coast of Somalia to work with other naval fleets to combat piracy and safeguard international waters. China has played a major role in the Six-Party Talks on the Korean nuclear issue, working tirelessly for peace and stability on the Peninsula and in the region. As Chinese Ambassador to the DPRK for over three and half years, I know perfectly well China's efforts in this regard.

China has also taken an active part in the P5+1 consultations on the Iranian nuclear issue. We stay committed to the integrity of the nuclear non-proliferation regime and stability in the Middle East and the Gulf region. China has also engaged with other countries to jointly tackle climate change, energy and resource security and other global issues.

China's peaceful development can serve to further refresh and enrich IR theories. Such refreshing and enriching of theory and practice is necessary for us to keep abreast with new times.

Second, China's peaceful development is based on China's world view.

IR theories have their roots in Western values, histories, cultures and world views. That is why attempts to frame China's development in Western IR theories often end up in mismatches and confusion.

China believes that our world is in the process of major change and transformation. Peace and development are the defining features of our times. The main factors shaping China's world view include its traditional culture, modern history and perception of the trend of the times. Traditionally, the Chinese people believe that peace is precious and that "you do not do to others what you would not want others to do to you." And we believe in good faith and good neighbourliness. Unlike the individualism valued by Western societies, the Chinese take modesty as a virtue and stand for collective survival and prosperity. Having suffered from foreign invasion in its modern history, China understands the misery of war and the value of peace.

Mr. Deng Xiaoping once said, China will never seek hegemony. This statement is not only what the Chinese people think, but is also supported by what happened in the past. We believe that the pursuit of peace, development and cooperation has become an irresistible trend of the times. As countries in the world get increasingly interconnected, it is impossible for China to develop in isolation from the world, and the world's prosperity and stability also requires the contribution from China.

Peaceful development is no empty talk or smoke screen of China. It is a national belief and strategic objective anchored on China's view of the world.

Third, China is an active contributor to the international system.

Many people are interested in China's relations with the world. In fact, this is also an issue on our mind. China became a full participant in the international system with its entry into the WTO in 2001. So far China has joined over 130 intergovernmental organisations and acceded to more than 300 multilateral treaties. The West now largely recognises that China has become part of the international system, contributing to it rather than undermining it. The only question is: what role should China play in the world?

Many in the West believe that China has the responsibility to join the West in upholding the existing international system. For China, defining its responsibilities in the international system is not as easy as it appears. This is closely related to China's understanding of itself and its identity. To borrow a philosophical term, it is a question of understanding "Who am I?" Although China is the second largest economy in the world, it is still a developing country. Its per capita GDP was about 3,700 US dollars in 2009, less than 1/3 of the world average and behind 100 countries in the world. China always believes that countries, big or small, strong or weak, rich or poor, are equal members of the international community. Their interests should be duly respected and protected.

Therefore, China endeavours to play a responsible and coordinating role in the international system, not only participating in but also contributing to the international system. While engaging in extensive cooperation with Western countries, we continue to strengthen traditional friendship with other developing countries and help them develop themselves and reduce poverty. In the wake of the international financial crisis, China contributed 50 billion US dollars to the IMF. We have asked to give priority to the least developed countries in the use of these funds. As a supporter and advocate for multilateralism, we played a constructive part in the reform of the international system. We stand for increased representation of developing countries and greater democracy in international relations. In this way the international system will be better able to address problems and challenges.

The UN Climate Change Conference in Cancun is watched closely by people around the world. China's actions and contribution to addressing climate change are now widely acknowledged. We firmly uphold the principle of "common but differentiated responsibilities." We have taken voluntary emission control actions in line with our national conditions and pledged to reduce CO_2 emission per unit of GDP by 40%~45% in 2020 against the 2005 level. China now ranks the first in the world in terms of installed hydropower capacity, newly added wind power capacity, nuclear power capacity under construction, and the use of solar panels. We call on developed countries to honour their commitment to provide fast-start climate funds worth 30 billion US dollars to developing countries. At the same time, we have made clear that we will never compete for these financial resources with other developing countries. We will only continue to provide material support and capacity building for less developed countries in addressing climate change, within the framework of China-Africa cooperation and through bilateral channels.

China is committed to playing a positive role in the international system and contributing to its sound development. We owe it not only to ourselves but also to the world.

I feel I'm very fortunate to be a Chinese diplomat at this important time. China's development has provided a platform for Chinese diplomats to use their talents, and more importantly, to participate in the shaping and making of history.

I believe all Fletcher students should embrace the ambition of promoting world peace, stability and prosperity, enriching the theories of international relations, and contributing to the development of international system. This is exactly the aim of the Fletcher School, which is "to offer a broad professional education in international relations to students committed to maintaining the stability and prosperity of a complex, challenging, and increasingly global society."

I sincerely hope my fellow Fletcher alumni will look at China's development from a comprehensive perspective and have a better understanding of today's China. It is also my hope that no matter where we are and what we do, we as Fletcher alumni will work together to promote China-Europe relations, China-US relations, and China's relations with the rest of the world.

Thank you.

Now, I would like to take your questions.

从“十二五”规划看中国的科学发展与和平发展*

尊敬的尼布利特所长，

女士们、先生们：

今天能在英国皇家国际事务研究所这个具有近百年历史、全球知名的国际关系研究机构演讲，我深感荣幸。我对皇研所是未谋其面，先闻其名。20多年前我在美国工作时，经常参加一些学术活动，研讨中不时提到的一个专有名词是“皇研所规则”（Chatham House Rule），从中我得知了隔着大西洋的皇研所。来英国后，通过与尼布利特所长等皇研所专家的交流，我对贵所独立思考、深入分析的传统也有了更多了解。

今天我演讲的主题是“未来中国的发展”。刚刚结束的中国全国人大审议通过了“十二五”规划，这是中国未来5年的发展蓝图。因此，我认为，讲中国未来的发展，最好就是解读一下“十二五”规划，从中管窥中国的发展思路和方向。

我认为，“十二五”规划释放的发展思路主要就是两点，一是科学发展，二是和平发展。

关于科学发展，可能一些西方人都不是太理解“科学”这个词，我想再用四个关键词来解释一下，这就是：平衡、包容、全面和绿色。

说“平衡”，就是说中国经济发展方式要转型，经济结构要调整。当前中国经济发展速度和经济规模均位居世界前列，但中国目前“低价工业化”

---

* 在英国皇家国际事务研究所的演讲。2011年3月17日，英国皇家国际事务研究所。

发展模式正受到严峻挑战，“大而不强、快而不优”的发展现状亟须改变。“十二五”规划中将未来5年中国经济增速目标定为7%，这相比改革开放30年来中国平均年增长10%明显放缓，也略低于上一个五年规划时确定的7.5%的目标。这一“量”的减慢将为“质”的提升留出空间，我们就可以抓住时机促进经济发展方式实现四个重大转变。一是从依赖投资和出口拉动的增长方式向消费、投资、出口相协调转变。二是从凭借廉价劳动力优势向创新驱动、内生增长方式转变。三是从传统产业为主向发展战略性新兴产业和现代服务业，形成多元支撑的方式转变。四是从“透支”资源和环境的粗放增长方式向低碳、绿色的发展方式转变。

说“包容”，就是要让每一个中国人生活得更加幸福、更有尊严，使发展成果惠及全体人民。当前，中国国民收入分配中存在居民收入和劳动报酬占GDP比重过低、基尼指数偏高等问题，同时公共服务水平尚未适应经济发展的步伐。如何迈过所谓的“中等收入陷阱”?“十二五”规划明确提出，我们将大力发展社会事业，保障和改善民生。一是要促进民富，让老百姓“钱袋子”尽快鼓起来，力争用三到五年的时间把城乡居民收入占GDP的比重提高10个百分点。二是加强社会建设，提高公共服务能力。政府要知民情，解民忧，化民怨，暖民心。三是提高社会保障水平，让老百姓安居乐业。未来5年，中国将重点在农村社会保险体系、城镇职工和居民社会保险制度以及最低生活保障制度这三个方面迈出更大步伐，从而更好地实现“学有所教、劳有所得、病有所医、老有所养和住有所居”这一目标。

说“全面”，是指经济、社会、政治、文化建设要齐头并进，缺一不可。“十二五”规划明确提出中国将以更大的决心和勇气全面推进经济、政治、文化、社会等各方面改革创新，提高改革决策的科学性，增强改革措施的协调性，从根本上破除体制机制障碍，最大限度地解放和发展生产力，促进社会公平正义。西方一些人总认为，中国只发展经济，不重视社会建设；只搞经济改革，不进行政治改革。这是对中国全面改革和全面发展的一种误解。中国改革开放30多年来，政治体制改革一直随经济体制改革推进、深化。我们的人民代表大会制度、中国共产党领导的多党合作和政治协商制度，在中国政治生活中的地位越来越高，作用越来越大。我们的民主法制建设不断加强，几千年形成的人治社会正在向法治社会转变。我们的党内民主越来越生动，引进竞争上岗机制，实行任前公示，扩大基层党组织直选和中央、地方党委的差额选举比例。我们的基层民主越来越活跃，在中国农村，村主任现在都是由村民直选，村务都要向村民公开。“十二五”规划重申了中国将积极稳妥推进政治体制改革，扩大社会主义民主，完善社会主义法制，使上层建筑更加适应经济基础发展变化，为科学发展提供有力保障。我们将不断加强政府自身改革建设，牢记政府的一切权力都是人民赋予的，必须对人民负责，为人民谋利益，接受人民监督。我们将最广泛地动员和组织人民依法管理国家和社会事务，管理经济和文化事业。我们将坚持依法治国基本方略，加强维护群众利益的法规建设，推进依法行政。中国政治体制改革的步伐从来没有停滞，今后也不会停滞。

说“绿色”，就是要考虑生态成本，重视生态效益。“十二五”规划提出，未来5年中国将加快建设资源节约型、环境友好型社会，大力发展循环经济，加大环境保护力度，积极应对全球气候变化，增强可持续发展能力，切实遵守为应对气候变化问题而向国际社会做出的庄严承诺。具体目标是非化石能源占一次能源的消费比重提高到11.4%，单位国内生产总值能耗和二氧化碳排放分别降低16%和17%，主要污染物排放总量减少8%~10%，森林蓄积量增加6亿立方米，森林覆盖率达到21%以上。我经常提醒英国企业家们，过去，中国先看投资项目能否产生经济效益，现在首先要看是否符合环保要求。对外来投资，中国现在再也不是来者不拒，而是严格限制高污染、高能耗和资源型项目，鼓励外资投向符合发展潮流的高端制造业、高新技术产业、现代服务业、新能源和节能环保产业。

“十二五”规划释放的第二大信息就是：和平发展。中国将继续奉行独立自主的和平外交政策，坚持走和平发展道路，坚持互利共赢的开放战略，同世界各国一道推动建设持久和平、共同繁荣的和谐世界。

认识中国的“和平发展”，我认为主要应把握三点。

第一，“和平发展”是“科学发展”的必然要求。当今的时代是全球化的时代，中国与世界的关系日益紧密，中国的前途命运日益同世界的前途命运紧密联系在一起。中国要实现科学发展，必须有一个和平的国际环境，必须加强同世界各国的合作。我们睦邻友好，与周边国家加强务实合作；与发达国家增强互信，深化合作；与广大发展中国家巩固传统友谊，扩大互利合作。我们将以自己的科学发展促进地区和世界的共同发展，以自己的和平发展促进地区稳定和世界和平。

第二，和平发展的基本要义是开放、合作和互利共赢。

中国的和平发展是开放的发展。关起门来搞建设的时代已经一去不复返。中国需要对外开放，世界也需要一个开放的中国。“十二五”规划强调中国必须实行更加积极主动的开放战略，拓展新的开放领域和空间，积极参与全球经济治理和区域合作，不断提高对外开放水平。

中国的和平发展是合作的发展。中国是国际大家庭的一员，只有风雨同舟、利益共享、责任共担，才是最符合自己和别国利益的。我们主张对外要友好，不要敌视；要合作，不要对抗；要互相信任，不要相互猜疑；要平等相待，不要强加于人。

中国的发展是互利共赢的发展。中国坚持自身利益与世界利益的一致性，在自身发展的同时，努力与世界各国实现共同发展，决不做损人利己、自私自利的事。我们知道，要想自己发展，必须让别人发展；要想自己安全，必须让别人安全；要想自己活得好，必须让人家也活得好。

第三，中国和平发展，对世界是好事，是机遇。中国越发展，对世界的贡献也就越大。

一是中国发展本身就是人类进步事业的重要组成部分。中国实行改革开放 30 多年，3 亿多人摆脱贫困，用占世界 7% 的耕地解决了世界 1/5 人口的吃饭问题，经济总量跃升至世界第二，政治社会保持稳定。根据路透社与伊普索斯最近联合进行的一项民调，中国 78% 的民众对未来充满信心。世界上 1/5 的人口安居乐业，本身就是对世界和平的重要贡献。

二是中国的和平发展给世界带来了增长动力和发展机遇。中国是世界第一大出口国，也是世界第一制造业大国。中国制造和出口的物美价廉的商品使世界各国消费者受益。中国同时还是世界第二大进口国，去年进口总额近1.4万亿美元，增长38.7%。中国进口的增加有力地拉动了其他国家的出口，促进了其经济增长。2010年欧盟对华出口增加31.9%，英国增长42%。随着中国大力促进内需和扩大消费，中国有望成为世界最大的消费市场，进口必然还会增加。

在过去10年里，中国吸收了7 000多亿美元的外资，各国企业在参与中国建设的同时，也获得了丰厚的回报。2010年，中国对外直接投资接近600亿美元，在发展中国家中居第一位。中国对外投资和中国企业积极“走出去”，有力促进了所在国经济增长、就业增加和社会事业发展。2009年，中国企业的海外分支向所在国纳税总额达到109亿美元，雇佣所在国员工43.8万人。2000年以来中国企业在非洲建设了6万公里道路和7 000万平方米房屋。据《金融时报》的研究，中国在过去两年里向其他发展中国家至少发放了1 100亿美元贷款，作用超过了世界银行。

在1997年亚洲发生金融危机时，中国发挥了中流砥柱的作用。在此次国际金融危机中，中国实行大规模刺激政策，保持经济较快增长，为世界经济提供了强劲增长动力。2009年中国对世界经济增长的贡献率高达50%，2010年亦达到20%。在欧洲爆发债务危机后，中国也坚定支持欧元区和IMF联手救援机制，不但不抛售欧元资产，而且“雪中送炭”，主动向欧洲国家伸出援助之手，帮助欧洲克服困难、实现复苏。

三是中国和平发展有力地促进了世界和平与稳定。中国奉行独立自主的和平外交政策，庄严地向世界承诺永远不称霸，永远不搞扩张；主张不干涉别国内部事务和谈判解决国际争端；倡导互信、互利、平等、协作的新安全观。中国积极参与国际维和行动，是联合国安理会常任理事国中派出维和人员最多的国家，累计参与24项联合国维和行动，派出上万名维和人员；中国向索马里海域派出护航舰队，与多国舰队一道打击海盗，维护国际水域的安全；中国大力倡导朝核问题六方会谈，推动伊朗核问题的谈判和对话，努力维护地区的和平与稳定。中国积极参加二十国集团峰会等多边机制建设，推动世界经济治理机制改革不断深化。中国与国际社会一道努力应对气候变化、能源和资源、粮食安全、恐怖主义等全球性挑战。最近，中国尽管自身也遭受了地震灾害，但我们仍然派出救援队奔赴新西兰、日本抗震救灾，并提供现汇和物资援助。无论从中国的外交思想，还是外交行动来看，中国都是世界和平的维护者、稳定的促进者。

展望今后5年，中国将统筹好科学发展与和平发展的同向、互动关系，真正做到内外兼顾、均衡和谐，使我们的发展道路走得越来越宽广、越来越平坦。

女士们、先生们，

中国的发展和复兴，这是人类历史近几百年来的新现象；中国所走的道路，也是前人从未走过的道路。中国古人说："不闻不若闻之，闻之不若见之，见之不若知之，知之不若行之；学至于行之而止矣。"我发现这段话有一个非常简洁和传神的英文译文："I hear，I forget. I see，I remember. I do，I understand."我衷心希望，各位有识之士能站在时代潮流的前沿，打破思维定式，开创全新视角，理解中国的发展道路，抓住中国发展带来的机遇，深化与中国在各领域的合作，与我们一道携手共建一个更加和平、更加繁荣、更加和谐、更加美好的世界。

谢谢。

现在我愿回答大家的提问。

The 12th Five-Year Plan: China's Scientific and Peaceful Development*

Dr Robin Niblett,

Ladies and Gentlemen,

It is my great honour to address at Chatham House, an institute with a world reputation and a long history. I first heard about Chatham House more than 20 years ago when I was working in the United States. Chatham House Rules was often applied in the academic events I attended. Thanks to Dr Niblett and his colleagues, I have learned much more about Chatham House and its proud tradition of independent thinking and profound scholarship since I came to the UK.

My topic today is China's future development. To understand the thinking and the direction of China's development for the next 5 years, we need to take a closer look at the 12th Five-Year Plan that was adopted at the recent annual parliamentary session in China.

As far as I can see, the 12th Five-Year Plan boils down to two key terms—scientific development and peaceful development.

Some people in the West may be curious about the term "scientific development." I think it can be explained in four words: "balanced, inclusive, comprehensive and green development."

Balanced means China must upgrade its growth model and economic structure. Being the second largest economy, China may lead the world in growth rate and economic size, yet its low-cost industrialisation model is exhausting its potential. So,

* Speech at the Royal Institute of International Affairs. Chatham House, 17 March 2011.

China must go beyond size and speed to achieve strength and quality. This is why the economy is set to grow by 7% annually in the next 5 years, which is a marked slowdown from the double-digit growth over the past 3 decades, and lower than the 7.5% target for the previous Five-Year Plan period. This slower quantitative growth will make more room for higher qualitative growth and create conditions for 4 major transitions:

- a move from reliance on investment and export to balanced growth driven by consumption, investment and export;
- a shift from low labour cost to home-grown innovation;
- a change from traditional industries to emerging strategic industries and modern services;
- and an evolution from energy and resources consuming development to low-carbon and green growth.

By inclusive, we mean we want to deliver a happier and more dignified life for every Chinese and make sure that we all share in the benefits of our development. The ratio of earnings to GDP in China remains low, and the Gini Coefficient is high. The quality of public services is far from matching the pace of economic growth. To overcome the "middle income trap," the 12th Five-Year Plan rightly gives priority to strengthening social programmes and improving people's living standards. To this end, we need to put more money in people's pockets and raise the ratio of income to GDP by 10 percent over the next 3 to 5 years, and provide better public services. The government must listen to the people, understand their hopes and worries and try its best to help them. Major steps will be taken in the next 5 years to strengthen the social safety net for farmers, urban workers and residents, and put in place a mechanism that ensures the minimum living allowance. In this way, we will make steady progress towards providing all our citizens with a good education, a decent income, quality health care, an old age pension and suitable housing.

By comprehensive, we want to ensure progress on every front, be it economic or social, political or cultural. The 12th Five-Year Plan calls for bolder steps in reform and innovation across all of these areas. This will help improve coordination and decision-making, break institutional barriers to productivity and promote social justice. Some people in the West believe that China only focuses on economic growth and ignores social progress, and that it only carries out economic reform, not political reform. This is a misunderstanding. Over the past 30 years, political reform has come with economic changes every step of the way. We have seen the growing role of the National People's Congress and multi-party cooperation and political consultation under the leadership of the Communist Party. Democratic decision making and the legal system have been strengthened, with the millennium-old pattern of rule by man giving way to rule of law. Democracy within the party is also developing rapidly. Competitive promotion with public consultation is becoming the norm. Direct election at village level was expanded and multi-candidate elections for offices at both central and local levels have been expanded. The 12th Five-Year Plan reaffirms that China will move ahead with political reform, and improve socialist democracy and rule of law. We will increase government accountability, subject officials to scrutiny by the general public and build a government of the people, by the people and for the people. The people's participation in state as well as economic and cultural affairs is also being encouraged and protected. We will stay committed to rule of law. China's political reform has never stopped and will not stop in the future.

By green, we are stressing the need to reduce environmental costs of development. The 12th Five-Year Plan calls for building a resource-efficient and environment-friendly society, that is to say, we need to better protect the environment and address the issues around climate change. This has resulted in specific targets, which include:

- Raising the share of non-fossil fuels in primary energy consumption to 11.4%.
- Reducing energy and carbon dioxide intensities by 16% and 17% respectively.
- Cutting the discharge of main pollutants by 8%~10%.
- Increasing forest stock by 600 million cubic metres and forest coverage to 21%.

I often remind business leaders in this country who are interested in doing business in China that in the past, foreign-invested projects were evaluated on the basis of their economic returns. Now it is environmental impact, as China no longer welcomes polluting, energy-and-resources-consuming businesses. Instead, it encourages foreign investors to channel their capital into high-end manufacturing, high-tech industries, modern services, new energy and environment-friendly projects.

The 12th Five-Year Plan also sends another message—peaceful development. China remains committed to an independent and peaceful foreign policy. It believes in win-win opening-up and hopes to work with countries to build a harmonious world of lasting peace and common prosperity.

To understand China's peaceful development, we need to be aware of three key points:

First, peaceful development is a natural extension of our scientific development. We live in a globalised world and in an era of increasing independence among countries. China's future has never been so closely linked to that of the rest of the world. China's scientific development calls for international cooperation and a peaceful environment. China has worked hard to deepen its friendship and cooperation with its neighbours, with developed countries and other developing countries. China will, through its scientific and peaceful development, contribute ever more to peace and development of the region and the world.

Second, China's peaceful development is open, cooperative and win-win to others.

China's development is an open development, as development behind a closed door has long been a thing of the past. China needs to open up and the world needs an open China. This is recognised in the 12th Five-Year Plan, as it emphasises the need to open more industries up to the world and to be an active player in global economic governance and regional cooperation.

China's development is a cooperative development. Being a member of the international community, China understands too well that the interests of all countries can be best served when countries stand together through thick and thin and when they share both interests and burdens. China advocates amity not animosity; cooperation not confrontation; mutual trust not suspicion; and treating each other as equals not imposing on others.

China's development is a win-win development, as it encourages a synergy between its own interests and the interests of others, and seeks mutual development. It will never follow a "beggar-thy-neighbour" approach. It understands that China can develop and enjoy security and prosperity only when other countries enjoy the same.

Third, China's peaceful development is a blessing and opportunity to the world. The more developed China becomes, the greater its contribution to the world will be.

China's development is an important part of human progress. Since reform and opening-up was initiated more than 30 years ago, 300 million people have been lifted out of poverty. China has managed to feed one fifth of the world's population with only 7% of the world's arable land. It is now the second largest economy, and enjoys political and social stability. A recent Reuters/Ipsos Poll showed that 78% of the Chinese people surveyed are confident about their future. With one fifth of the world's population enjoying a peaceful and prosperous life, China has made a big contribution to world peace and prosperity.

China's peaceful development is an engine and opportunity for world economic growth. As the world's largest exporter and manufacturer, China produces affordable and quality goods to the benefit of consumers across the world. At the same time, China is the world's No.2 importer, having imported nearly 1.4 trillion US dollars' worth of goods last year, an increase of 38.7%. These imports have boosted economic growth in its trade partners. Last year EU's export to China increased by 31.9%, and the figure for the UK was as high as 42%. As China continues to stimulate demand and consumption at home, it is well on the way to becoming the world's largest consumer market.

China has attracted over 700 billion US dollars of foreign investment over the past decade. This has enabled foreign businesses to be an important part of China's development and to share in the growing boom of the Chinese market. Last year, China invested nearly 60 billion US dollars overseas, ranking first amongst developing countries. China's economic growth has encouraged Chinese businesses to go-global and contributed to economic and social progress and job creation across the world. In 2009, overseas branches and subsidiaries of Chinese companies paid a total of 10.9 billion US dollars in local taxes and hired a local work force of 438 thousand people. Over the past decade, Chinese businesses have helped to build 60 thousand kilometres of road and 70 million square metres of housing across Africa. Research by the *Financial Times* shows that in the past two years, China has given record loans of 110 billion US dollars to other developing countries, higher than the World Bank.

China played a pivotal role during the Asian financial crisis in 1997. As the financial crisis of 2008 hit developed countries, China provided a strong boost to the global economy by adopting a huge economic stimulus package and maintaining rapid growth. It contributed 50% to global growth in 2009 and 20% in 2010. It stood firmly by Europe during the European debt crisis last year. Instead of selling Euro assets, it offered a helping hand to its European partners and supported their efforts to recover from the crisis.

China's peaceful development has proved to be a strong force for world peace and stability. China has solemnly pledged to the world that hegemony or expansion is not an option for China. China stands for non-interference in others' internal affairs and negotiated solutions to international disputes. China believes that security should be based on mutual trust, mutual benefit, equality and coordination. China is the largest contributor of peacekeepers among the five permanent members of the UN Security Council. We have sent 10,000 peacekeepers to 24 UN missions and escort ships to the waters off the Somali coast to work with the navies of other countries to combat piracy and improve safety in international waters. China has actively worked to facilitate the Six-Party Talks and negotiations over the Iranian nuclear issue to uphold peace and stability in the region. China has played an active part in the G20 summits and other multilateral institutions, and helped strengthen the reform of global economic governance. It is working with the international community to find a more effective way to meet global challenges such as climate change, energy, resources and food security and terrorism. Recently, despite its own losses and sufferings in earthquakes, China has sent rescue teams to New Zealand and Japan, as well as offering them assistance in cash and in kind. China is in every way an upholder of peace and a facilitator of stability.

Looking into the future, China's task in the next 5 years is to ensure that scientific and peaceful development is both achievable and mutually reinforcing. There is every reason to be confident that China's road ahead will be broader and even more promising.

Ladies and Gentlemen,

China's development and rejuvenation has been new to the world, and there has been no historical parallel to the road China has travelled.

So, how should people see China's development? Let me quote an ancient Chinese saying, "To hear about something is better than not hear about it, to see it is better than hear about it, to know it still better than see it, yet to fulfil it through action is the ultimate form of knowledge."

Interestingly this saying happens to have a very close English equivalent, "I hear and I forget, I see and I remember, I do and I understand."

I do hope that people will reject stereotyped thinking, try to hear, to see and to understand China with an open mind, and seize opportunities presented by China's development. I am confident that by sharing opportunities and working together, we will make our world a better place of peace, prosperity and harmony.

Thank you.

Now I would like to take your questions.

中国让世界更安全*

尊敬的亚当·李主席，

尊敬的尼古拉斯·贝尔先生，

女士们、先生们：

最近，我与“查塔姆”（Chatham）很有缘分，因为就在上周四，我在“查塔姆宫”（Chatham House，英国皇家国际事务研究所别称）发表了一个演讲，今天很高兴又来到具有101年历史的查塔姆俱乐部（Chatham Dining Club）。

我在皇研所讲的题目是《从“十二五”规划看中国的科学发展与和平发展》。据我所知，贵俱乐部最早是由一批军队将领创立的，目的是研讨国际关系和世界安全。尽管100多年过去了，俱乐部不断扩大，会员已从军人发展到政界、学界和舆论界，但这一传统一直延续至今。所以，今天我想谈谈中国的发展对全球安全到底有何影响。

当前，外界特别是西方对中国总是有担心，既有经济上的担心，也有安全上的担心，担心中国发展的不确定性，担心中国成为威胁。我上周在皇研所回答提问时，就有人提出了这一问题，问中国如何消除这种担心。我当时就回答说，这种担心没有必要，中国的发展不会威胁到任何人。相反，中国的发展对各国是机遇，中国的发展有利于世界的和平与繁荣。而我作为中国大使，就是要努力使外界消除这种莫名的担心，让越来越多的人了解到中国的发展对世界具有积极意义。

---

* 在英国查塔姆俱乐部的演讲。2011年3月24日，伦敦卡利多尼亚会所。

这里，我想讲个中国古代故事。古时候杞国有个人担心天会塌，自己无处存身，便食不下咽，寝不安席。有朋友就去开导他，说天不过是积聚的气体罢了，填满了四处，天怎么会塌下来呢？你有什么可担心呢？经过一番开导，那个杞国人才放下心来，恢复了正常生活。这个故事后来浓缩成一个成语“杞人忧天”。其含义恰恰就是我最近常引用的富兰克林·罗斯福的一句话：“我们唯一恐惧的就是恐惧本身。”

我认为，一个发展、进步、繁荣、富强的中国，只会使世界更加安全。

第一，中国是世界和平与稳定的利益攸关者。中国要实现不断发展，必须要有一个和平的国际环境。在全球化时代，中国与世界的利益关系日益紧密。中国现在是世界第一大出口国和第二大进口国，外贸依存度超过60%。截至2009年年底的统计数字显示，中国投资者在境外设立了1.3万家企业，遍布170多个国家和地区。中国的原油、铁矿砂等能源和资源的对外依存度超过50%。中国能否持续发展，越来越取决于地区是否稳定、世界是否太平。

第二，中国是和平外交政策的积极倡导者。孔子说：“己所不欲，勿施于人。”中国近代饱受欺凌和战火涂炭，因此深知战争的残酷和和平的宝贵。中国最早提出了“和平共处五项原则”，并切实遵守《联合国宪章》；中国主张不干涉别国内部事务及和平谈判解决国际争端；中国庄严地向世界承诺永远不称霸，永远不搞扩张；中国是世界核武器国家中唯一承诺不首先使用核武器、不向无核国家使用核武器的国家；中国倡导“互信、互利、平等、协作”的新安全观。

第三，中国是防御性国防政策的坚定奉行者。中国有限的军事力量完全是为了维护国家独立、主权和领土完整，不会对任何国家构成威胁。中国在军事战略上坚持防御、自卫和后发制人的原则。最近媒体十分关注中国军费问题。这个问题，我想特别说明一下。

一是目前中国军费水平在世界各国中处于较低水平。根据伦敦国际战略研究所（IISS）最新发布的《全球军力报告》，中国2010年军费占同年GDP的1.3%，不仅远远低于美国（4.7%）、英国（2.5%）、俄罗斯（2.8%）等传统军事强国，也低于印度（2.5%）、巴西（1.7%）这样的新兴大国。即使中国 2011 年的国防预算增加 12.7%，也只占到 GDP 的 1.4%。如果从人均军费看，中国则更低。美国是中国的 38 倍，英国是 20 倍。

二是增加的费用中很大一部分用于提高军人的生活水平。受国际金融危机影响，中国近年通货膨胀有所上升，同时，中国正大力促进民生，提高民众收入水平，2010 年中国农民的平均收入增长 10.9%。军人职责神圣，有其独特的一面，但同时军人也是普通人。用我们中国人的话来讲，他们是“上有老、下有小”，是要承担家庭责任的人。因此，我们适当改善军人的生活条件，理所当然。关于这一点，在座的不少有军旅生涯的查塔姆俱乐部会员，一定会更容易理解。

第四，中国是国际安全的重要贡献者。中国是联合国安理会常任理事国中派出维和官兵最多的国家，累计参与 24 项联合国维和行动，派出上万名维和人员。在刚果（金），在苏丹，在利比里亚，在黎巴嫩，在海地，到处都可见到中国维和军警的身影。就在 2010 年海地地震中，中国牺牲了 8 名维和警察。目前，中国仍有 10 支维和分队 1 546 人部署在 4 个联合国任务区。

中国大力倡导朝核问题六方会谈，努力维护半岛和地区的和平稳定。2010 年，“天安号”事件后，半岛局势一触即发，中国加大斡旋力度，防止了局势紧张升级。

在南海问题上，我们主张通过谈判和平解决争议，在争议解决之前，可以“搁置争议，共同开发”。正是由于中国的努力，南海作为世界较繁忙的国际海运航道之一，其航行自由安全从未因争端受到影响。

在亚丁湾，中国海军持续参与索马里海域护航行动，至 2010 年年底，已为包括英国在内的 50 多个国家的 3 000 多艘船舶护航。

总之，无论是从中国的发展需要，还是从中国的外交思想和国防战略，或者从中国的外交行动来看，中国都是世界和平与安全的倡导者、维护者和促进者。

最后，我愿用中国改革开放和现代化建设的总设计师邓小平先生的话来结束今天的演讲。他说：“中国现在是维护世界和平和稳定的力量，不是破坏力量。中国发展得越强大，世界和平就越靠得住。”

谢谢。

现在我愿回答大家的提问。

China Makes the World a Safer Place*

Mr. Adam Lee,

Mr. Nicholas Bell,

Ladies and Gentlemen,

It is a privilege for me to be a guest of this distinguished Chatham Dining Club.

It has been a Chatham week for me.

I spoke at Chatham House just last Thursday, and now here I am at the 101-year-old Chatham Dining Club.

Last week, I spoke at Chatham House about the 12th Five-Year Plan—China's Scientific and Peaceful Development. I understand that Chatham Dining Club was founded by a group of army officers to discuss matters outside the military world. Now the membership is much wider, but this interest in world affairs has persisted to this day. So today I will talk about what China's development means to global security.

The outside world, especially the West, appears to be concerned about China's development both in the economy and in the security fields. Last week at Chatham House I was asked these questions:

Should the world fear the rise of China?

How can China assure the world that its rise is peaceful?

My response was this: China's development presents opportunities for peace and prosperity, not threats.

I will develop my theme for you this evening. I will start with an ancient Chinese story.

---

* Speech at the Chatham Dining Club. Caledonian Club, 24 March 2011.

Long, long ago in China in the State of Qi, there was a man who was worried that the sky would fall down on him. He was so concerned that he couldn't eat or sleep. A friend of his told him the sky was just a cluster of clouds. It was everywhere and how could it ever fall down? This finally put an end to his anxiety. This is the origin of the Chinese proverb "Qi Ren You Tian," and exactly what Franklin Roosevelt meant when he said "the only thing we have to fear is fear itself."

I truly believe that a more developed, forward-looking and prosperous China will make the world a safer place.

First, China is a stakeholder in world peace and stability.

Over the past 30 years a peaceful international environment has enabled China to reform, open up and develop. In an age of globalisation, China's interests are increasingly linked to those of the world. As the world's number one exporter and number two importer, 60% of the economic growth of China has been driven by trade. By the end of 2009, Chinese investors had set up thirteen thousand businesses in more than 170 countries and regions. In addition, more than half of the crude oil and iron ore consumed in China was imported. China has a growing stake in regional stability and world peace if it is to sustain its development.

My second major point is that China is an active advocate of a peaceful foreign policy.

Confucius said, "Do not do to others what you do not want others to do to you." China went through foreign aggression and humiliation in its modern history during the past two hundred years. As a result, the Chinese people know as well as any nation the cruelty of wars and the value of peace. China was the first to propose the Five Principles of Peaceful Coexistence that arose out of dialogue between China and India in 1954. China always abides by the UN Charter. China stands for non-interference in others' internal affairs and peaceful settlements to international disputes. China solemnly proclaimed to the world that neither hegemony nor expansion is an option for China. China was the only nuclear-weapon state to commit itself to no first use of nuclear weapons and no use of such weapons against non-nuclear-weapon states. China believes that security should be based on mutual trust, mutual benefit, equality and coordination.

The third point I want to share with you is about defense.

China is a staunch practitioner of a defensive national policy. China has no offensive defense strategies. China has limited military capabilities which do not pose a threat to others. The Chinese military capabilities are solely for safeguarding independence, sovereignty and territorial integrity. China follows the principles of self-defense and a reactive approach in its military strategies. Let me say a few words about China's military spending, which has attracted some interest lately.

First and foremost, China's military spending is kept at a low level in comparison with other countries. The IISS compiles the international military report. The latest Military Balance 2011 shows that China's military expenditure in 2010 only accounted for 1.3% of its GDP. This is much lower than 4.7% in the US; 2.5% in the UK; or 2.8% in Russia. China's military expenditure was even lower than emerging countries such as India and Brazil, whose military spending took up 2.5% and 1.7% of their respective GDPs. Even if we take into account the 12.7% growth in military budget this year, the figure is only 1.4%. Calculated in per capita terms, the US military spending is 38 times that of China and the UK 20 times. Apart from this international comparison, a fairly large portion of the increased military budget will be used to improve our servicemen's lives. One reason for this is to take account of rising inflation since the financial crisis.

At the same time, China is working hard to improve people's livelihood and increase their income. Last year the farmers' income increased by 10.9%. We don't see why we should not improve our servicemen's life. They deserve a pay raise for their service to the country, not to say many of them have to take care of their children and aging parents. For those of you who have a military career, this might be easier to understand.

My fourth point for you to consider this evening is that China is an important contributor to international security.

China is the largest contributor of peacekeepers among the five permanent members of the UN Security Council. It has sent 10,000 peacekeepers to 24 UN missions. You will find Chinese peacekeeping officers in Congo, Sudan, Liberia, Lebanon or Haiti. Last year eight Chinese peacekeepers laid down their lives in the Haiti earthquake. As we speak 1,546 people are working on ten peacekeeping contingents in four regions.

As I said earlier China is committed to a peaceful development. As a result, China advocates the Six-Party Talks as a channel for upholding peace and stability in the Korean Peninsula and Northeast Asia as a whole. Chinese mediation efforts after the

Cheonan incident helped ease tension in the region. China stands for a peaceful South China Sea and negotiated solution to disputes. Pending a final solution, we can put aside differences and go for common development. Thanks to China's efforts, freedom and safety of navigation in the South China Sea have never been affected. This is of global importance as this is one of the busiest shipping lanes in the world. In the Gulf of Aden, Chinese naval ships have been part of the escort missions in the waters off the Somali coast. By the end of last year, our naval ships had escorted over 3,000 vessels from more than 50 countries, including Britain.

To put it simply, China is a positive force for world peace and security in every aspect.

I will conclude by quoting Mr. Deng Xiaoping, the chief architect of China's reform, opening-up and modernisation: "China seeks to preserve world peace and stability, not to destroy them. The stronger China grows, the better the chances are for preserving world peace."

Thank you.

Now, I would like to take your questions.

中国是亚洲的和平稳定力量*

尊敬的尼布利特所长，

女士们、先生们：

很高兴应尼布利特所长邀请再次来到皇家国际事务研究所。今年是“一战”爆发100周年，而皇研所的成立与“一战”有着密不可分的关系。正是在讨论“一战”后国际秩序安排的巴黎和会上，出于防止战争的目的，英美代表团决定成立国际问题研究机构，皇研所由此应运而生，并发展成为世界国际问题研究领域较著名、较有影响力的智库之一。在纪念“一战”爆发百年之际，我们在皇研所讨论亚洲的稳定与发展具有特殊的历史意义。

有人说，21世纪是亚洲世纪，正如19世纪是欧洲世纪，20世纪是美国世纪。无论这个观点是否正确，可以肯定的是，亚洲正日益成为国际社会关注的焦点之一。围绕亚洲，目前讨论最多的有三个问题。

第一个问题：当前的亚洲是不是“一战”前的欧洲？

近来，政界和学术界对“一战”历史的总结和反思不断增多。有人将“一战”前的欧洲和现在的亚洲进行对比，认为当前亚洲国家在历史、领土、领海、军事等各领域矛盾呈多发、群发和上升状态，亚洲有可能像“一战”前的欧洲国家那样最终滑向冲突和战争。最近，日本首相安倍甚至把当前的中日关系类比为“一战”前的英德关系。我认为，如果说学术界的人士执上述看法可能是由于过于片面，以偏概全，“只见树木，不见森林”；那么政治

* 在英国皇家国际事务研究所的演讲。2014年2月5日，英国皇家国际事务研究所。

领导人执这种观点，则不能不让人怀疑其真正的动机。

当前，亚洲形势总体稳定，和平、发展、合作仍是亚洲国家的主流。我想用三个以“S”开头的英文单词来描述当前的亚洲。

一是“稳”（stable），这指的是亚洲的总体形势。求和平、谋稳定、促发展，通过友好协商妥善处理分歧是亚洲国家的广泛共识，特别是大国关系良性发展是地区局势稳定的“压舱石”。中俄全面战略协作伙伴关系深入发展。中美共同致力于构建不冲突、不对抗、相互尊重、合作共赢的新型大国关系。中国和东盟各领域的务实合作不断迈上新台阶。

二是“亮”（shining），这指的是亚洲的经济形势。当前，全球经济金融形势仍不容乐观，但亚洲对拉动世界经济恢复和发展的作用日益明显，成为难得的亮点。亚洲新兴经济体继续保持较快增长，是当今世界最具活力和潜力的地区，前景看好。国际货币基金组织统计，亚洲新兴经济体 2013 年增长 6.3%，是 2013 年世界平均增速的两倍多。亚太地区的商品产量、贸易额、外汇储备、吸引的外国直接投资，均占世界的一半或一半以上。

三是“实”（solid），这指的是亚洲的区域合作。亚洲区域合作基础扎实，内容不断充实，层次持续提高，活动越来越频繁和制度化，展现了巨大生机和良好前景，并将在整体上提升亚洲的发展速度和质量。亚洲不仅是世界上自贸合作最活跃的地区，近年来在区域经济一体化体系建设、互联互通、安全等领域的合作也日益完善。

与此同时，亚洲也面临一些安全挑战，既有“二战”残余、冷战积怨、海上“暗礁”等历史遗留的安全矛盾，更有自然灾害、跨国犯罪、网络安全、能源和粮食安全等日益突出的非传统安全挑战。需要特别指出的是，一个时期以来，以安倍为代表的日本领导人企图为侵略历史翻案，挑战世界反法西斯战争胜利成果和以《联合国宪章》为基础的战后国际秩序，导致日本与邻国关系紧张，成为亚洲最大的不稳定因素。

总的来看，和平与发展是当今时代的主题，这一主题在亚洲表现得尤其明显。亚洲国家在政治、经济、人文、安全等领域的合作正处于历史上最好的时期，且合作水平仍不断提升。个别国家企图破坏亚洲稳定大局的言行受到亚洲国家和国际社会的一致谴责和反对，其企图是不会得逞的。因此，今天的亚洲与“一战”前欧洲的那种恶性、无序竞争在本质上是完全不同的。

第二个问题：新形势下，中国的亚洲和周边政策有何变化?

周边是中国安身立命之所、发展繁荣之基。中国历来重视与邻国的友好关系，始终把周边外交摆在中国外交的优先位置。中国越发展，就越体会到和平稳定的周边环境之可贵。2013 年 10 月，中国召开了新中国历史上首次周边外交工作座谈会，确立了今后 5 至 10 年中国周边外交的战略目标、基本方针和总体布局，强调要坚持与邻为善、以邻为伴，坚持睦邻、安邻、富邻，并创新提出要在与周边国家各领域合作中突出体现亲、诚、惠、容的理念，为中国周边外交开辟了更加广阔的前景。

中国新一届政府上任以来，中国周边外交开创出新局面，同周边国家关系进入深化睦邻友好、全面拓展合作的新阶段。新形势下，中国周边外交将秉持“四个坚持”。

一是坚持睦邻友好，提升政治互信，为亚洲国家世代友好承担应尽之责。“远水难救近火，远亲不如近邻”。中国与周边国家地缘相近，人缘相亲，长期守望相助，肝胆相照，睦邻友好、互利合作是周边国家对华关系的主流。习近平主席、李克强总理就任后首访、首站都选择了周边国家。过去 1 年，中国同周边 21 个国家开展国家元首和政府首脑级别交往，基本实现了高层交往全覆盖。

中国将多做得人心、暖人心的事，像“走亲戚”一样加强与周边国家高层和各领域交往，不断增强亲和力、感召力、影响力，争取更多朋友和伙伴。中国绝不做损人利己、以邻为壑的事情。

二是坚持合作共赢，强化利益纽带，为亚洲繁荣发展注入强劲动力。英语有句谚语：“一燕不成夏。”中文同样有一句：“一花独放不是春，百花齐放春满园。”中国与亚洲国家经贸联系非常紧密，已成为许多国家最大贸易伙伴、最大出口市场和重要投资来源地，对亚洲经济增长的贡献率已经超过 50%。同时，中国周边充满生机活力，有明显的发展优势和潜力。中国提出建设丝绸之路经济带、21 世纪海上丝绸之路、设立亚洲基础设施投资银行、打造中国–东盟自贸区升级版、建设孟中印缅经济走廊、中巴经济走廊等一系列重大合作倡议，向周边国家展示了施惠的诚意，在周边国家产生热烈反响。

中方将坚持正确义利观，在深化与周边国家务实合作的同时，欢迎其分享中国发展所带来的机遇和红利，中国也将向其提供更多力所能及的帮助，既使中国从周边国家共同发展中获得裨益和助力，也使中国发展更多地惠及周边国家，把双方利益融合提升到更高水平，不断做大利益蛋糕，打造命运共同体，实现共同发展。2014 年中国将主办亚太经合组织领导人非正式会议及相关活动，我们将以此为契机，勾画亚太长远发展愿景。

三是坚持和平稳定，深化安全合作，为亚洲热点、难点问题的妥善解决贡献智慧与力量。“铁肩担道义，妙手著文章”。中国大力倡导开放包容、求同存异的地区精神，推动 10+1、10+3、东亚峰会、东盟地区论坛、上海合作组织等各种区域合作机制相互促进，为维护地区和平、促进地区发展做出了重要贡献。中国在朝核问题、阿富汗问题上做出了积极努力。2014 年我们将办好阿富汗问题伊斯坦布尔进程第四次外长会，努力推动阿政治和解与经济重建。

中国坚持互信、互利、平等、协作的新安全观，将通过今年在华主办的亚信峰会，深化与周边国家的安全合作。作为安理会常任理事国，中方愿继续发挥建设性作用，发出中国声音，提出中国方案，贡献中国智慧，为维护地区和平与安全做出新的努力。

四是坚持人文交流，搭建友谊桥梁，为亚洲不同文明间的对话树立光荣典范。“国之交在于民相亲，民相亲在于心相通”。亚洲人民创造了丰富多彩、享誉世界的辉煌文明，各种文明在相互影响中融合演进，和谐共处。中国将加强公共外交、民间外交和人文交流，促进青年、智库、议会、非政府组织和社会团体的友好交流，广交朋友，广结善缘，增进民间了解和友谊，取长补短，包容互鉴，亲上加亲，谱写人文交流新篇章，把“中国梦”同周边各国人民过上美好生活的愿望、同地区发展前景对接起来，让命运共同体意识在周边国家落地生根，结出硕果。

第三个问题：如何维护亚洲的和平与稳定？

亚洲越来越成为世界上各种力量的利益汇合点，对全球形势发展具有举足轻重的影响。亚洲稳，则世界稳。亚洲强，则世界强。我认为，维护亚洲的持久和平与稳定，既需要中国的努力，也需要地区国家和域外大国相向而行。

一是树立以史为鉴、面向未来的历史观。丘吉尔曾经说过，“不从历史中吸取教训的人注定重蹈覆辙”。我们应从维护人类和平事业的角度，充分肯定亚洲各国人民对世界反法西斯战争所做出的巨大贡献，进一步认识和平发展对于日本以及亚洲所具有的重要意义。日本军国主义对外侵略和殖民统治历史必须引以为鉴，日本法西斯战争给包括中国在内的受害国人民带来的深重灾难必须牢记。日本须真正拿出诚意，承认历史错误，改弦易辙，以实际行动取信中、韩等亚洲邻国。只有真正做到正视历史、以史为鉴，日本同亚洲邻国的关系才有未来，日本才能让亚洲人民放心。希望有关国家也本着对历史负责的态度，汲取“二战”前对德国实行绥靖政策的教训，不要两面下注，对日本军国主义倾向持姑息纵容态度，否则亚洲恐将难有宁日。国际社会应当保持高度警惕，坚决反对和谴责任何企图否定世界反法西斯战争胜利成果、挑战战后国际秩序的言行，共同捍卫《联合国宪章》的宗旨和原则。只有这样，亚洲的稳定才能维护，世界的和平才有保障。

二是树立休戚与共、互利共赢的合作观。亚洲国家相互联系、相互依存不断加深，政治、经济等领域合作潜力无限，深化互利合作是亚洲国家共同发展的正确选择。亚洲各国应树立命运共同体意识，以各国人民的长远和根本利益为出发点，创新合作模式，丰富合作内涵，不断扩大共同利益汇合点，以合作促发展，以合作增互信，不断提升亚洲合作水平。

同时，地区国家应通过谈判以和平的方式妥善解决有关分歧，探索解决领海、领土争议从零和博弈向互利共赢转变的有效途径。近年来，一些地区国家单方面挑起岛屿争端，并蓄意炒作“中国威胁论”，加紧扩充军备，加大制造地区紧张，与亚洲求和平、谋合作、促发展的大潮背道而驰。各种外部势力出于多重目的“拉偏架”，推波助澜，加剧局势恶化。中国不会放弃正当权益，不会牺牲国家核心利益。同时，中国立足于对话大门始终敞开。

中国在和平解决争议的问题上展现出真诚意愿，已同文莱、越南就推进共同开发与海上合作达成一致，同东盟启动“南海行为准则”磋商进程。希望有关国家摒弃零和思维，与我们相向而行，共同维护亚洲安全稳定大局。

三是树立互利互信、平等协作的安全观。亚洲是亚洲人的亚洲，也是世界的亚洲。太平洋足够宽广，亚洲也足够大。维护亚洲的和平稳定，不仅需要地区国家齐心协力，也需要美、欧等域外力量以积极的姿态在地区事务中发挥建设性作用。亚洲国家对此应敞开胸怀欢迎，同时，域外国家也应尊重亚洲的多样性特点和已经形成的合作传统。

当前亚洲安全稳定面临新的挑战，热点问题此起彼伏，传统安全和非传统安全威胁都有新的表现。没有安全稳定，发展就无从谈起。域内外国家须摒弃冷战思维，增强战略互信，倡导综合安全、共同安全、合作安全的理念，在尊重和照顾对方核心利益与关切基础上开展合作，使亚洲成为共谋发展的大舞台，而不是相互排斥、相互角力的竞技场，更不能为一己之私拉帮结伙，把亚洲搞乱。

女士们、先生们，

中国的发展离不开亚洲，亚洲的发展也需要中国。中国坚持走和平发展道路，坚持全面深化改革、扩大开放，这不仅为中国自身发展注入强大动力，也将为亚洲的稳定与繁荣带来新的重要机遇。中国强则亚洲强，一个更加精彩的中国一定也会让亚洲更加精彩。中国作为亚洲大家庭的一员，愿与各国一道，为创建一个和平、发展、合作、共赢的新亚洲而共同做出努力。

谢谢！

下面我愿回答大家的提问。

China is a Force for Peace and Stability in Asia*

Dr. Robin Niblett,

Ladies and Gentlemen,

It is a real pleasure for me to return to the Chatham House on a special occasion.

This year marks the centenary of the First World War. As you will know the founding of Chatham House was largely attributable to that war. Then as now many people were searching for a rationale to prevent such wars.

In 1919 British and American delegates attended the Paris Peace Conference where the post-war international order would be discussed. These representatives conceived the idea of an Anglo-American institute of foreign affairs to study international problems with a view to preventing future wars.

That institute, better known as Chatham House, is now among the world's most prestigious and influential international affairs think-tanks.

This history means we are gathered in a most fitting place to discuss Asian stability and development. It means we can draw on the very foundations of Chatham House for wisdom and insights.

Some people say the 21st century is the Asian century, as the 19th was the European century and the 20th was the American century.

Perhaps it is too early to tell if the 21st is the Asian century. But one thing is for sure. Asia is increasingly becoming one of the centres of international attention. In

* Speech at Chatham House. Chatham House, 5 February 2014.

turn, there are three questions frequently asked about Asia.

First, is today's Asia like Europe on the eve of World War I?

As the centenary of World War I approaches, both political and academic circles are reflecting on that past.

Some have compared today's Asia to pre-World War I Europe. Many of these analysts argue that Asia is facing rising conflicts. These are compared to relations between nations in Europe a hundred years ago.

In recent years there have been escalating tensions among Asian nations. These issues concern history, military issues as well as land and sea boundaries. So, the analysts reason that it is very likely that Asia will end up in conflict and war just as Europe did in the late 19th century.

Japanese Prime Minister Shinzo Abe himself drew an analogy between current China-Japan relations to Anglo-German relations before World War I.

However, if scholars believe this view, I would say they are not seeing the wood for the trees. If a political leader supports such argument then one must be suspicious of his real motive, because the facts simply do not support the views of Mr. Abe.

Then what are the facts about Asia? The basic fact is Asia enjoys a generally stable situation today. Peace, development and cooperation are still the prevailing trend. I will use three words beginning with "S" to present you an analysis of Asia.

The first word is *Stable*.

There is a broad consensus amongst Asian countries to pursue stability. This is delivered by policies that seek peace, development and properly handling differences through friendly consultation. In particular, sound relations between large countries are the ballast of regional stability. Here are some examples:

- The China-Russia strategic partnership of cooperation is deepening.
- China and the US are committed to building a new power relationship featuring non-conflict, non-confrontation, mutual respect and win-win cooperation.
- Practical cooperation between China and ASEAN countries has scaled new heights.

The second word is *Shining*.

In the global economic and financial landscape, Asia has been outshining the other regions.

The role of Asia in powering world economic recovery and growth has become an accepted trend. This has come from emerging economies in Asia maintaining fast growth. This makes Asia the world's most dynamic and most promising region for sustained economic growth. The IMF figures show that in 2013 Asian emerging economies grew by 6.3%, more than two times of the average world economic growth. The volumes of trade, foreign exchange and inbound FDI of Asia-Pacific all made up half, or more than half, of the world's total.

The third word is *Solid*.

Regional cooperation within Asia enjoys a solid foundation. The content of such cooperation has been enriched. The quality has been raised. The cooperation has become regular and institutionalised. Thriving regional cooperation and exciting prospects will boost the growth rate and quality of Asian advance. One driver is trade agreement. Here, Asia leads the world in free trade arrangements. In addition, Asia has made great advances in regional economic integration, transport connectivity and security cooperation.

At the same time Asia also has some security challenges to tackle. These challenges have various causes. Some are legacies left over from World War II and the Cold War. Some arise from historical issues. Other challenges take the form of unconventional security challenges. Examples are natural disaster, transnational crime, cyber security, energy security and food security.

It is worth a special mention that some Japanese political leaders, especially Mr. Abe, have taken blatant steps to deny Japan's aggressive past. The evidence is denial of outcomes of the anti-fascist war. Also, challenges to the post-World War II international order based on the UN Charter. These actions have caused tensions between Japan and its neighbours. The result threatens to become the biggest destabilizing factor in Asia.

However, on balance, peace and development remain the theme of the times. Political, economic, cultural and security cooperation among Asian countries has never been closer and more effective. Such cooperation is still growing.

Certain country's attempt to derail Asian stability has been condemned by Asian countries and the entire international community. Such attempts are doomed to failure.

For these reasons, today's Asian situation is starkly different from the rivalry between nations in Europe before World War I.

Let me now turn to the second question frequently asked about Asia today. That is, what are the changes in China's Asia and neighbourhood foreign policy under the new circumstances?

Asia is China's neighbourhood. It is critical to China's development and prosperity. China is deeply committed to friendly relations with its neighbouring countries. China's foreign policy places top priority on the neighbouring countries.

The more developed China becomes, the better China appreciates the value of a peaceful and stable neighbourhood.

Last October, China held a conference on neighbourhood foreign policy. This was the first of its kind since the founding of the People's Republic. This conference set out the strategic goals, basic guidelines and overall planning for China's neighbourhood policy in the coming 5 to 10 years. The main principles are as follows:

- Build good neighbourly relationships and partnerships with neighbouring countries.
- Develop an amicable, peaceful and prosperous neighbourhood.
- And stress affinity, sincerity, mutual benefit and inclusiveness.

These principles have opened a broader prospect for China's neighbourhood diplomacy.

Since the new Chinese leadership took office, China's neighbourhood diplomacy has made fresh progress. Our friendship and cooperation with neighbouring countries has deepened. We will continue to make efforts in the following four areas:

First, continue to build good-neighbourly relations and enhance political mutual trust with neighbouring countries.

China will fulfill its responsibility in cementing lasting friendship among Asian countries. As a Chinese saying goes:

"Water afar will not put out a fire at hand. A distant relative is not as helpful as a close neighbour."

China and its neighbours enjoy geographic proximity and close people-to-people exchanges. We have supported each other in times of need and shared weal and woe.

Good-neighbourly friendship and win-win cooperation is the hallmark of Asian countries' relations with China. After taking office, both President Xi Jinping and Premier Li Keqiang chose neighbouring countries for their first overseas trips. In the past year, China exchanged visits with 21 neighbouring countries at head-of-state and head-of-government level. This shows high level exchanges between China and its neighbours have reached out to almost all its neighbouring countries.

Going forward, China will do more to build friendship and trust with its neighbours. We will have regular exchange of visits. We will win more friends and partners with our own sincerity, integrity and impact. China will never harm its neighbours to serve its own interests.

Second, continue with win-win cooperation and lend a strong impetus to Asian prosperity. As you say in English:

"One swallow does not make a summer."

In China we have a similar saying:

"One flower does not make a spring. One hundred flowers in blossom together show the full glory of spring."

China attaches great importance to strengthening economic links with other Asian countries. China has become the largest trading partner, the biggest export market and an important investor for many Asian countries. China contributes more than 50% to Asian economic growth.

Meanwhile, China's neighbourhood has clear advantages and great potential for growth. China has proposed a series of cooperation initiatives to boost development of the entire neighbourhood. These include:

- A Silk Road economic zone.
- A Silk Road using sea routes.
- An Asian Infrastructure Investment Bank.
- Upgrading the China-ASEAN Free Trade Area.
- A Bangladesh-China-India-Myanmar economic corridor.
- And a China-Pakistan economic corridor.

These initiatives fully demonstrate China's sincerity to create mutual benefit for all neighbouring countries. These initiatives have been warmly welcomed by our neighbouring countries.

China will stick to the principle of righteousness and carry forward its tradition of sharing. We will share opportunities and benefits with our neighbouring countries through deepening practical cooperation. China will provide more support to its neighbours. China's interests and those of its neighbours will be more closely interwoven. The aim is to achieve common development and prosperity of China and its neighbouring countries.

This year, China will host the APEC Economic Leaders' Meeting and related activities. We will take this opportunity to outline the vision for Asia Pacific long-term development.

Third, continue to safeguard peace and stability.

We will deepen security cooperation with our neighbouring countries and contribute to solving hotspot issues in Asia. China will take up its responsibilities in maintaining regional peace. We have been an advocate of openness and inclusiveness. We insist on the principle of seeking common ground while shelving differences. We have made tremendous efforts to advance regional cooperation arrangements like ASEAN+1, ASEAN+3, East Asian Summit and Shanghai Cooperation Organisation. These mechanisms have enhanced each other and are pivotal to maintaining regional peace and promoting regional development.

China has taken an active part in defusing the Korean Peninsula nuclear issue and Afghanistan issue. This year, China will host the 4th Foreign Ministers, Meeting of the Istanbul Process on Afghanistan. We will work to make this meeting successful and productive. The aim is to facilitate political reconciliation and economic reconstruction in Afghanistan.

China is a champion of the new security concept that underlines mutual trust, mutual benefit, equality and cooperation. China will host the Summit of the Conference on Interaction and Confidence Building Measures in Asia this year. We will take this opportunity to deepen security cooperation with neighbouring countries.

Turning to the role of China within the United Nations. China is a permanent member of the UN Security Council. China will continue to play a constructive role.

We will project China's voice, put forward China's proposals, contribute China's thinking and make new efforts to safeguard regional peace and security.

Fourth, continue to build bridges of friendship by increasing people-to-people and cultural exchanges.

We will endeavor to create a model of cross-cultural dialogue in Asia. Friendship between peoples is the foundation of relations between countries. In turn, friendship between peoples hinges on mutual understanding. People of Asia have profound and proud civilisations. Over centuries, these different civilisations have enhanced each other and coexisted harmoniously in Asia.

China will make greater efforts in public diplomacy, non-governmental diplomacy and people-to-people exchanges. We will encourage more exchanges between youth, think-tanks, parliaments, NGOs and social organisations among Asian countries. The aim is to make more friends, sow the seeds of kindness, and build a family-like neighbourhood. We will align the "Chinese Dream" with the people's aspiration for a better life in neighbouring countries and with the prospects of regional development. We want our neighbours to better appreciate that the interests of us all are closely interwoven and all countries in the region are highly interdependent.

I have now reached the third question that is frequently asked about Asia: How to maintain the peace and stability of Asia?

Asia is now the meeting place of interests of all kinds of stakeholders from across the world. Asia now holds sway in the evolution of global advance.

A stable Asia means a peaceful world. A strong Asia means a prosperous world. In my observation, lasting peace and stability of Asia requires China's efforts. At the same time, it is essential that other countries in the region and powers outside the region work together towards the same goal.

First, we should take inspiration from a famous Chinese saying: "One must use history as a mirror."

In this way we can learn from the past and so travel forward with more clarity and certainty.

Winston Churchill said,

"Those who failed to learn from history are doomed to repeat it."

The world needs to fully recognise Asian peoples' tremendous contribution to the victory of the World War II against fascism. We should view sacrifice and sufferings by Asian people in the context of maintaining peace for all mankind. We should fully appreciate the importance of peaceful development to Japan and to Asia.

The lessons of Japan's history of militarist aggression and colonial rule must be learned. The tribulations of Chinese people, and the people of other countries, caused by Japanese fascism must not be forgotten:

- Japan should show its sincerity.
- Japan must willingly admit its past mistakes caused by its militarism.
- And Japan has to earn the trust of China, Korea and other Asian neighbours with credible actions.

Only when the lessons of history are truly learnt can Japan's relations with its Asian neighbours have a future and Asian people feel reassured.

We hope that relevant countries will shoulder their responsibilities and learn the lesson of appeasement on the eve of World War II.

We also hope that other countries will not attempt to have a foot in both camps and connive at Japan's rising militarism. Otherwise, these risks will take Asia once again on a road into war and conflict.

This means that the international community should stay on high alert about the developments in Japan:

- The international community must resolutely oppose and condemn any words or actions that negate the outcomes of the global war against fascism.
- The international community must challenge any moves to change the post World War II international order.
- And the international community should work together to uphold the principles and purposes of the UN Charter.

Only these principles can maintain stability of Asia and guarantee world peace.

Let me now give you the second reason why regions and powers outside Asia should work together towards the same goal. All should fully recognise that our interests are intertwined and win-win cooperation will make us all winners.

Asian countries are becoming increasingly interdependent. Our political and economic cooperation has great potential. Deepening mutually beneficial cooperation is the right choice for all Asian countries to achieve common development. We should bear in mind the fundamental and long-term interests of Asian countries. We should promote development through cooperation, enhance mutual trust through exchanges and raise the level of Asian collaboration.

At the same time, countries in the region should properly handle differences through peaceful negotiation. We should explore ways to turn disputes on land and sea territories from zero-sum games to win-win situation.

In recent years, certain countries in the region have made unilateral provocations on disputed islands and hyped up a so-called "China threat." They have built up their military and so created regional tension. What they have done runs counter to the overriding trend of peace, cooperation and development in Asia.

For various purposes, some forces outside Asia have taken partial positions. This has aggravated a complicated situation and escalated tensions.

My message today is clear. China will not give up its lawful rights and interests, nor compromise its core national interests.

Meanwhile, China keeps the door to dialogue open. China has demonstrated sincerity of its commitment to peaceful solution of disputes. For example, we have reached agreement with Brunei and Vietnam on joint development and maritime cooperation. We have launched a negotiation process with ASEAN on COC. China hopes that the related countries will discard the zero-sum game mentality, work with us towards the same goal. This goal is to maintain peace and stability of Asia.

Now, I would like to turn to the third reason why regions and powers outside Asia should work together towards the same goal.

We should uphold the new security concept featuring mutual trust, equality and cooperation.

Asia belongs to Asian people. Asia also belongs to the world. The Pacific is vast. Asia is spacious. Asia's peace and stability call for concerted efforts from countries in the region. It also requires outsides forces like the USA and Europe to play a positive and constructive role in Asian regional affairs. Asian countries should welcome this.

At the same time, outside countries should also respect Asia's diversity and its long-standing traditions of cooperation.

At present, Asia's security faces new challenges. Hotspot issues flare up one after another. Security challenges have taken on both traditional and non-conventional manifestations.

Without security or stability, there is no development to speak of. Countries inside and outside the region need to reject the Cold War mentality and strengthen strategic mutual trust. They also need to advocate the concept of comprehensive security, common security as well as cooperative security.

Countries should actively engage in cooperation while respecting and accommodating each other's core interests and main concerns. We should make Asia a big stage rather than a boxing ring. Still less should we favor the selected ones or gang up to serve selfish interests at the cost of Asia's stability.

Ladies and Gentlemen,

China's development cannot be achieved without the rest of Asia.

Asia's development also needs China.

China is committed to the path of peaceful development. It is also committed to comprehensively deepening reform and opening-up. This will not only advance China's development but also create new and important opportunities for Asian stability and prosperity.

A strong China will bring a strong Asia. A more successful China will make Asia more successful.

China is a member of the big Asian family. We stand ready to work with our neighbours to achieve a new Asia of peace, development, cooperation and win-win results.

Thank you!

Now, I will open the floor for questions.

和平发展与共享共赢*

尊敬的英国联合部队司令巴伦斯上将，

尊敬的英国皇家国防研究院院长汤姆·菲利普斯爵士，

各位将军，

女士们、先生们：

很高兴来到英国皇家国防研究院。这是我第三次到英国军事院校演讲，前两次都是在国防大学联合指挥与参谋学院，我讲的分别是中国的国防政策和安全观，听众都是青年校级军官。这次是英军最高研究学府，听众都是英军高级将领和政府高级官员。菲利普斯院长希望我能谈一谈中国对当今世界重大战略性问题的看法。显然，你们是想了解“中国观点”和听到“中国声音”。今天，我也很愿意就中国对一些战略性问题的看法与各位进行交流。

既然是讲战略性问题，首先我就想谈一下当前国际格局和体系的演变问题。关于这个问题，学术界或媒体有很多不同表述，如“东升西降”、多极化、国际关系民主化等，究其本质是相同的，就是以金砖国家为代表的新兴经济体和发展中国家在国际体系中的地位上升和作用增强，世界进入了冷战结束以来最广范围和最大限度的一次“再平衡”。同时随着全球化和信息化的深入发展，人类社会越来越成为你中有我、我中有你的命运共同体，任何国家或国家集团都再也无法单独主宰世界事务，国际力量对比出现“均衡化”趋势。

---

* 在英国皇家国防研究院的演讲。2014 年 11 月 12 日，英国皇家国防研究院。

我们认为，这种再平衡和均衡化将使国际体系更加公平、公正，符合国际社会大多数成员的利益。面对国际形势的这种深刻变化，中国主张“三个共享”。

一是各国和各国人民应该共同享受人类尊严。要坚持国家不分大小、强弱、贫富，一律平等，尊重各国人民自主选择发展道路的权利，反对干涉别国内政，维护国际公平正义。

二是各国和各国人民应该共同享受发展成果。每个国家在谋求自身发展的同时，也要积极促进其他各国共同发展，实现互利共赢。那种以邻为壑、转嫁危机、损人利己的做法既不道德，也难以持久。

三是各国和各国人民应该共享安全保障。面对错综复杂的国际安全威胁，单打独斗不行，迷信武力更不行，合作安全、集体安全、共同安全才是解决问题的正确选择。

当然，有些人担心新旧格局的转换会带来“新兴大国”与“守成大国”之间的战争和冲突，人类再次掉入“修昔底德陷阱”。必须指出的是，21 世纪不同于以往，世界已成为一个相互依存的“地球村”。在这个“地球村”里，新老大国之间的关系不是一个“零和游戏”，不是简单的你升我降，你得利我受损，而是需要共同做大蛋糕，共同分享发展成果。为此，中国提出愿与世界主要力量构建不冲突不对抗、相互尊重、合作共赢的新型大国关系。这不仅符合各方利益，符合国际社会期待，也是大国为维护世界和平、促进世界发展和避免人类重蹈覆辙的应尽责任和担当。

女士们、先生们，

战略性问题并不总是表现为体系或格局问题，也经常表现为一些具体问题，这些具体问题往往牵一发而动全身。比如，当前世界上就有四个突出具体问题，分别是乌克兰、恐怖主义、埃博拉疫情和网络安全。尽管它们似乎是具体的、局部的，但又是重大的，需要采取全球性、战略性措施来应对解决，我把它们称为战略性热点问题。中国对这些问题的态度非常鲜明，也积极、建设性地参与应对，体现了我前面讲到的“三个共享”。

关于乌克兰问题，显然这不是单纯的乌克兰内政问题，背后有大国因素，关系到欧洲的地缘政治版图，人们仿佛从这里又看到了“冷战”的影子。中国在乌克兰问题上没有私利。从危机爆发以来，中方始终坚持客观均衡立场，坚持不干涉别国内政、尊重各国主权和领土完整的国际关系基本准则。我们始终认为，要从根本上解决乌克兰危机，需要兼顾历史和现实，兼顾有关各方关切，特别是俄罗斯同乌克兰的传统历史联系。中国愿意看到一个各民族和谐相处，与周边国家和平共处的乌克兰，这也是乌克兰实现国家长治久安的根本之计。

关于恐怖主义，我们认为，恐怖主义是人类的公敌，中方反对一切形式的恐怖主义。恐怖主义的滋生与扩大同发展落后息息相关，要治标更要治本。在反恐问题上应该加强不同文明间的对话，采取政治、经济、外交、安全等手段综合治理，尤其是消除贫困、改善民生和促进发展，从根本上铲除恐怖主义滋生的土壤，防止“越反越恐”。中方将坚决打击国内暴力恐怖活动，并愿与各国加强国际反恐交流与合作，推动国际反恐合作不断取得新进展。我们反对一些国家在反恐问题上采取双重标准。我们主张在国际反恐斗争中切实尊重《联合国宪章》宗旨、原则和国际关系基本准则，尊重有关国家的主权、独立和领土完整。

关于埃博拉疫情问题，埃博拉疫情在西非持续肆虐蔓延，成为现代社会“最严重的公共卫生安全危机”，不仅威胁着疫区国家人民的生命和健康安全，且已威胁到国际和平与稳定。中国政府和人民感同身受，率先行动，紧急驰援，与国际社会共同帮助非洲国家抗击疫情蔓延。2014 年 3 月埃博拉疫情发生后，中方第一时间就提供了疫区国家最急需的现汇和物资援助，并根据疫情发展和有关国家的愿望不断调整和追加援助清单，至今已提供 4 轮援助，共计 1.25 亿美元。中国提供的援助不仅有防疫物资、现汇、粮食等实物和现金援助，还派出专家和医护人员，在塞拉利昂援建移动实验室和留观中心，在利比里亚援建治疗中心。除了疫区三国，中国还向科特迪瓦等疫区周边 10 个国家及时提供防疫物资援助，同时也向联合国、世卫组织和非盟等国际和地区组织提供资金和政治支持，为遏制疫情扩散做出了积极贡献。中方也着眼长远，第四轮援助方案已开始着眼于“后埃博拉时期”，努力帮助疫区和非洲国家加强公共卫生安全体系和能力建设。可以说，在抗击埃博拉疫情上，中国真正做到了与非洲国家患难与共、风雨同舟，充分体现了中国负责任大国的作用。

关于网络安全问题，这不是一个存在于虚拟世界的问题，而是对人类构成了现实威胁。最近，英国政府通信总部负责人汉尼根（Robert Hannigan）在《金融时报》撰文指出，社交媒体已成为恐怖极端组织煽动暴力思想的阵地、策划恐怖袭击的手段、招募恐怖分子的平台。下个月，英国政府将在伦敦召开“打击网上儿童色情国际峰会”。这说明，网络安全问题，不仅仅是网络本身这一技术性安全，更重要的是网络传播内容的安全。“东伊运”等东突恐怖组织就通过互联网传授、煽动恐怖暴力行为。互联网中还充斥着色情内容，给青少年、儿童健康成长带来威胁，网络贩毒、贩枪也屡见不鲜。维护网络安全已经成为一个世界性和综合性问题。需要指出，一些西方媒体肆意编织网络安全领域的“中国威胁论”，在拿不出任何真凭实据的情况下宣称中国政府组织大规模窃取外国机密，或是将中国依法管理互联网的行为说成中国限制互联网自由等。这些说法与事实严重不符。中国是网络安全的坚定维护者，中国政府和军队及其相关部门从不从事或参与通过网络窃取商业秘密的活动。中国不久前召开的十八届四中全会提出全面推进依法治国，其中就要求加强互联网领域立法，完善网络信息服务、网络安全保护、网络社会管理等方面的法律法规，依法规范网络行为。

中国主张国际社会加强合作，共同构建和平、安全、开放、合作的网络空间，为此应当在联合国框架内制定相关国际规则，建设多边、民主、透明的国际互联网治理体系。要实现这一目标，必须处理好四对关系：既互联互通又尊重主权；既加快发展又确保安全；既享有自由又遵守秩序；既自主自立又开放合作。只有这样，互联网才能给人类带来福祉，而不是成为相互攻击的利器、犯罪的温床，更不应成为传播和实施恐怖主义活动的工具。

女士们、先生们，

了解中国的外交主张很重要，理解中国的行动同样重要。中国的外交行动是建立在中国的发展理念基础上的。

中国作为一个发展中国家，发展经济、改善民生始终是我们的第一要务。要加快发展，就需要有一个和平稳定的国际环境，需要我们坚持并践行和平发展理念，让其他国家切实认识到我们的发展是和平友好、互利共赢的。总结过去几十年的成功实践，中国走和平发展道路有以下几个特点。

第一，中国不搞穷兵黩武，不建势力范围。中国在国际事务中的做法充分体现了中国“不称霸”的决心。除了参与联合国维和行动外，中国在国外未驻一兵一卒，未建任何军事基地，并且始终坚持不结盟、不对抗、不称霸、不搞扩张、不使用武力或以武力相威胁，从未寻求建立势力范围。中国通过友好协商与14个邻国中的12个彻底解决了陆地边界问题，倡导通过当事方直接对话谈判和平解决领土主权和海洋权益争端，主张在争端解决前“搁置争议、共同开发”。中国提出共同、综合、合作、可持续的亚洲安全观，在弘扬亚洲人民智慧和能力的同时，也欢迎各方为亚洲安全和合作发挥积极和建设性作用。中国从来没有，今后也不会主张亚洲版的“门罗主义”。

第二，中国坚持与国际社会共赢发展。中国是经济全球化的受益者之一，同时，中国也通过自己的发展反哺世界经济。2008年国际金融危机以来，中国两次向国际货币基金组织注资，金额达到930亿美元，支持欧元区国家应对危机的努力。根据国际货币基金组织的研究，中国对世界经济增长的贡献率目前已达到30%。中国加大海外投资，成为世界最大的5个资本输出国之一，对相关国家和地区的经济复苏、就业增加、民生改善发挥了积极促进作用。我们倡议建立丝绸之路经济带和21世纪海上丝绸之路，用“一带一路”把东边的亚太经济圈与西边的欧洲经济圈连接起来，通过互利共赢的合作使沿线国家从中国的发展中受益。为此，我们倡导成立了亚洲基础设施投资银行，宣布出资400亿美元设立丝路基金，目的就是要利用中国的资金实力直接支持“一带一路”建设。就在昨天，中国作为东道主举办了亚太经合组织第二十二次领导人非正式会议，积极致力于推动区域经济一体化，促进成员国经济创新发展、改革与增长，大力支持亚太基础设施与互联互通建设，为共同建设互信、包容、合作、共赢的亚太伙伴关系和打造开放型亚太经济格局做出了重大贡献。

第三，中国积极承担与自身能力相适应的国际责任。中国自 1990 年开始参与联合国维和行动，是派遣维和人员最多的联合国安理会常任理事国。中国在伊拉克、乌克兰、叙利亚、伊朗核、朝核、南北苏丹等热点问题上发挥了建设性作用。上月底，中国主持召开了阿富汗问题伊斯坦布尔进程第四次外长会，表明中国与地区国家和国际社会一道，坚定支持阿政治和解、和平重建。在气候变化问题上，中国将减排视作自身可持续发展的内在要求和负责任大国应尽的国际义务，在发展中国家中最早制定实施应对气候变化的国家方案，设立了 2020 年碳排放强度比 2005 年下降 40%~45% 的目标，并积极致力于推进节能减排、低碳发展和生态建设。

第四，中国坚定维护自身主权、安全与发展利益。中国的发展不以牺牲别国利益为代价，不做损人利己、唯我独尊的事情。同时，中国绝不会放弃自己的正当权益，不会拿自己的核心利益做交易。也就是说，我们不惹事、不生事，但也不怕事。一段时间以来，中国针对东海、南海争端采取一系列维权行动，这些争端没有一次是中国主动挑起的，相反中国一贯主张通过和平谈判解决争端。但面对个别国家的不断挑衅，中国岂能对自己的利益受损坐视不管？在座大多数都是军人，其中的道理不言自明。这说明，中国坚定走和平发展道路，其他国家也应当走和平发展道路，只有各国都走和平发展道路，世界才能共同发展，国与国才能和平相处。

综上所述，在当今世界，中国不是国际体系的无关者、搅局者或破坏者，中国不再是一头沉睡的狮子，也不是一头闯进瓷器店的大象，更不是伺机要寻仇报复的“卧虎藏龙”。中国是国际体系的参与者、建设者和维护者，是伸张正义的“功夫熊猫”，是“和平的、可爱的和文明的狮子”。世界对中国的发展不必担心，更不必恐慌。

女士们、先生们，

外交官和军人，虽是两种不同的职业，但从古至今，两者关系密切。过去，人们常说，战场上得不到的东西，谈判桌上也很难得到；今天，听到的更多的说法是，谈判桌上得不到的东西，战场上也很难得到。前一种说法，强调的是军事实力，可能军人更爱听；后一种说法则强调国际争端需要外交解决、和平解决，更反映了时代的进步。

我认为，外交官和军人，尽管一文一武，但都是责任重大、使命光荣的职业，都肩负着捍卫国家主权与安全、维护地区与世界和平的重任。我衷心希望当今世界的大多数问题都能通过政治家、外交官和军人们的不懈努力，以和平方式加以解决。为此，中国愿发挥中国影响和中国作用，与国际社会共同努力，使我们的世界更加稳定、更加和平、更加繁荣、更加美好！

谢谢。

下面我愿回答各位将军的提问。

Peaceful Development and Shared Win-Win*

General Barrons,

Sir Tom Phillips,

Generals,

Ladies and Gentlemen,

It is a real pleasure for me to visit the Royal College of Defense Studies.

This is the third time I have spoken in a British military institution. Previously, I spoke at the Joint Services Command and Staff College of the UK Defense Academy. There I have twice reflected about China's national defense policy and China's security outlook. The audiences were mainly young field officers.

Today I am in the UK's most prestigious institution of military studies. This time Sir Tom has asked me to talk about China's views on the current major strategic issues of the world. The choice of the theme reflects the high status of the audience who are mostly British senior military commanders and government officials as well as your interest in hearing the voice of China.

So, I am very glad to have this opportunity to share with you China's strategic thinking and actions.

Since I have been asked to talk about strategic issues, I want to start with the changing world situation and evolving international system.

Global think-tanks and the media have many theories on this subject, for example, the rise of the East and the decline of the West, the multi-polarisation and

---

* Speech at the Royal College of Defense Studies. Royal College of Defense Studies, 12 November 2014.

democratisation of international relations, and so on.

All of these refer to one fact: the ascent of the emerging economies represented by the BRICS countries, as well as developing countries.

The world is going through a rebalancing of a magnitude never seen since the upheavals after the Cold War.

Meanwhile, globalisation is hurtling forward driven by the immense forces of the digital and knowledge economic revolution. The result is that the world has increasingly become a community where:

- All countries are extremely interdependent.
- National interests are interwoven.
- No single country or grouping can dominate world affairs alone.
- And the international balance of power is moving towards equilibrium.

In China we believe this rebalancing will make the international system fairer and more equitable. It serves the interests of most members of the international community. In response to such profound changes, China proposes three "shares."

First, all countries and peoples should share respect. The meaning of "share" in this context is this:

- All countries, big or small, strong or weak, rich or poor, are equal.
- People should have the right to independently choose their own development path.
- And all nations should oppose interference in internal affairs of other countries and uphold international justice.

The second "share" is about joint development:

- All countries and peoples should share development fruits.
- While seeking its own development, each country should also work to promote development of others for mutual benefit.
- And the "beggar-thy-neighbour" approach, and any attempt to divert crisis to

others, is neither moral nor workable.

The third "share" is about joint security:

- All countries and peoples should have a shared security guarantee.
- In the face of varied and complex international security challenges, going it alone does not work.
- A show of force is no solution.
- Cooperative security, collective security and common security are the right choice.

Of course, some people worry that the shifting of gravity in the world will lead to war and conflict between established powers and emerging powers. Mankind will therefore once again fall into the "Thucydides's Trap."

However, for these observers it must be pointed out that the world in the 21st century is very different from the ancient world.

The world has become a "global village" of interdependence:

- In this "village," the relationships between established powers and emerging powers are no longer a zero-sum game.
- It is not the rise of some and the fall of others.
- It is not the gain of some at the cost of others.
- Instead, we should work together to make the pie larger and share the benefits of development.

To this end, China has proposed a new model of major power relations. It features these principles:

- No conflict.
- No confrontation.
- Mutual respect.
- Cooperation.

- And shared benefit.

This new model of power relations serves the interests of all parties and meets the expectations of the international community. It reflects a strong sense of responsibility of great powers. The rationale is that it helps to preserve world peace, promote growth and prevent humanity from repeating past mistakes.

Ladies and Gentlemen,

Strategic issues not only show in the evolving international system, but also in specific issues. Specific as they are, they have much wider ramifications. For example, the world now faces four pressing issues:

- Ukraine.
- The Islamic State.
- Ebola.
- And cyber security.

All these issues seem specific and local. Yet much is at stake in each of them. I call them the specific issues of strategic significance:

- It takes global and strategic measures in response.
- China's position on these issues is clear-cut.
- China has taken part in addressing each of them actively and constructively.
- And what China has done directly delivers actions following the principles of the three "shares" I talked about earlier.

On the Ukrainian issue, it is not purely domestic politics of Ukraine. Some powers are at play behind the scenes.

What is happening in Ukraine will have implications on Europe's geopolitical landscape. It even reminds people of the Cold War. China has no selfish interests on the Ukrainian issue. Since the outbreak of the crisis, China has adopted an objective and balanced position, and called for observing the norms of international relations. These are non-interference in Ukraine's internal affairs and respect for sovereignty and territorial integrity of Ukraine.

China always believes that both history and reality need to be taken into account when seeking a radical solution to the Ukrainian crisis. Concerns of all related parties should be accommodated, especially the traditional and historical links between Russia and Ukraine. China wants to see a Ukraine where all ethnic groups live in harmony, a Ukraine at peace with its neighbours. This is also the fundamental solution for Ukraine's long-term stability and prosperity.

Turning to the matter of the Islamic State. The advent of such a terrorist organisation as the Islamic State of Iraq and Levant shows that terrorism has risen to a new level.

Across the world, extreme terrorism keeps spreading. The form of terrorist activities continues to evolve and rise in the level of horror. This means that counter-terrorism is no longer an emergency response, but a long-term task.

Terrorism is a scourge for all mankind. China opposes terrorism in all its manifestations. China maintains that poverty and backwardness are catalysts for terrorism. The response must be to tackle both the symptoms and the root cause:

- That requires an increase in dialogue between different civilisations.
- There needs to be a holistic approach through political, economic, diplomatic and security means.
- Coordinated international action is needed especially to eradicate poverty, improve people's life, promote development and remove the breeding ground of terrorism.
- And "the more we fight, the worse terrorism becomes" is the last thing we want.

China has and will continue to resolutely crack down on violent terrorist activities at home.

Across the world China also stands ready to strengthen counter-terror exchanges and cooperation with other countries. China will proactively work for new progress in international cooperation against terrorism.

China opposes any countries adopting double standards on the fight against terror. We believe that in fighting against terrorism we should respect the principles and purposes of the UN Charter, follow the norms governing international relations, respect sovereignty, independence and territorial integrity of related countries.

On the Ebola virus disease, it is rampaging through West Africa and has become the worst ever public health crisis in modern society. Ebola does not only endanger the life and health of people in affected countries, but also menaces international peace and stability.

The Chinese government and people are deeply sympathetic and were quick to act. Together with the rest of the international community, China has assisted African countries in stemming the epidemic. Since the onset of the epidemic last March, China has provided assistance in cash and in kind. These resources were so badly needed by the stricken countries and at the earliest possible time.

Moreover, China has adjusted and increased aid based on the changing epidemic situation and the request of the related countries. So far China has provided four rounds of aid totaling 125 million US dollars. China's aid includes:

- Epidemic control and prevention materials, cash and food.
- China also sent experts and medical staff and set up a mobile lab and emergency observation wards in Sierra Leone.
- China has also funded a treatment centre in Liberia.

Apart from the three stricken countries, China also provided material assistance for epidemic prevention in Cote d'Ivoire and the other nine neighbouring countries.

Meanwhile, China provided funding and political support to international and regional organisations, such as the United Nations, World Health Organisation and African Union.

China's efforts have made a positive contribution to curbing the epidemic. As these efforts go on, China is already looking beyond. Our Fourth Aid Plan focuses on the post-Ebola period and aims to help stricken areas and African countries strengthen public health systems and capacity building.

On the Ebola crisis, it is fair to say that China has truly shared sympathy with African countries. And China has played the role expected of a responsible power.

Turning to cyber security, this is not a problem existing only in the virtual world. It poses a real threat to all mankind.

Recently, the GCHQ Chief, Robert Hannigan, published an article in the *Financial Times*. In the article, he pointed out these harsh facts:

- For terrorist organisations social media has become a battleground to spread violence.
- Social media provides the means to plot terrorist attacks.
- And social media creates a platform to recruit new terrorist members.

Next month, the British government will host the International Online Child Sexual Exploitation Summit.

This initiative shows that cyber security is not only about technology, but more importantly about the content. The Internet has been contaminated by porn and other content harmful to children and young people.

The evidence reveals that the East Turkistan Islamic Movement and other terrorist organisations used the Internet to incite and spread violence and terrorism. Then there is the evil that comes from on-line trafficking of drugs and guns which has become very common.

This all adds up to the fact that ensuring cyber security has become a global and comprehensive challenge.

However, some Western media has promoted the "China threat theory" on cyber security. Without being able to produce any evidence, these journalists claim that the Chinese government has organised large scale theft of foreign secrets. In addition, they label China's lawful management of the Internet as restricting web freedom. These claims could not be farther from the truth.

The facts are that the Chinese government and military authorities never engage in or take part in theft of commercial secrets through the Internet. The recent Fourth Plenary Session of the 18th CPC Central Committee stressed rule of law. This included:

- Strengthening Internet legislation.
- Updating laws and regulations on Internet information service.
- Reinforcing Internet safety guarantees.
- And social management of Internet.

China calls for building a peaceful, safe, open and collaborative cyber space through closer international cooperation. To achieve this goal, there is a need to make international rules within the framework of United Nations, build a multilateral, democratic and transparent international Internet governance regime.

To reach this target all nations must properly handle the following relationships:

- Facilitate on-line communication while respecting sovereignty.
- Speed up development while ensuring security.
- Enjoy freedom while maintaining order.
- And promote open cooperation while ensuring independence.

Only by doing so, can we make sure Internet is a blessing for mankind, not a bane, nor a vehicle to circulate and execute terrorism.

Ladies and Gentlemen,

China is a developing country. Our primary task is to grow the economy and deliver a better life for our people. To achieve faster growth, China needs these factors:

- A peaceful and stable international environment.
- China needs to follow the policy of peaceful development.
- And China needs to assure other countries that China's development is peaceful, friendly and mutually beneficial.

Taking stock of the success of China in the past decades, China's path of peaceful development has the following characteristics.

First, China never goes for militarism nor spheres of influence:

- China's conduct of international affairs fully demonstrates China's firm position of never seeking hegemony.
- China has not sent abroad a single soldier except on UN peacekeeping missions, nor built any military base on foreign soil.
- China has observed the principles of non-alliance, non-hegemony, non-expansion and no use or threat of use of force.

- China never seeks to establish spheres of influence.
- Through friendly consultations, China has resolved boundary issues with 12 of its 14 neighbours.
- China advocates peaceful resolution of disputes on territorial sovereignty and maritime rights and interests through direct dialogue and negotiations between the parties.
- China calls for shelving differences and joint development pending a solution.
- China has initiated a collective, comprehensive, cooperative and sustainable Asian security concept.
- And, while drawing on the wisdom of Asian people, China also welcomes all parties to play a positive and constructive part in Asian security and cooperation.
- China has no interest in an Asian version of Monroe Doctrine. Never did, never will.

The second characteristic is that China shares development benefits with the rest of the international community:

- China is one of the beneficiaries of economic globalisation. In turn, China has contributed to the world economy with its own growth.
- Since the 2008 international financial crisis, China has contributed to the IMF a total sum of 93 billion US dollars.
- China has supported the Eurozone countries' efforts to tackle the financial crisis.
- According to the IMF, 30% of world economic growth now comes from China.
- China has increased investments overseas and become one of the world's top five capital sources.
- And, as a result, Chinese investment promotes local economic recovery, jobs and welfare.
- We initiated the Silk Road Economic Belt and 21st Century Maritime Silk Road to integrate Asia-Pacific and European economies.
- These two initiatives are designed to promote economic growth of countries along the route through mutually beneficial cooperation.
- To ensure financial support for these two initiatives, we set up Asian Infrastructure Investment Bank and contributed 40 billion US dollars to the Silk

Road Fund.

- Just yesterday, China hosted the 22nd APEC Economic Leaders' Meeting. The meeting was committed to advancing regional economic integration, promoting innovative development, reform and growth in member economies, and strengthening infrastructure and connectivity in the Asia-Pacific region.
- The 22nd APEC Economic Leaders' Meeting made a huge contribution to an Asia-Pacific Partnership featuring mutual trust, inclusiveness, cooperation and mutual benefit. It also increased the openness of Asia-Pacific economy.

The third characteristic is that China has fulfilled international responsibilities commensurate with its own capacity:

- China has been taking part in UN peacekeeping missions since 1990.
- China is the largest contributor of peacekeeping personnel among the five permanent members of the UN Security Council.
- China has played a constructive role on hot spot issues such as Iraq, Ukraine, Syria, Sudan and Iranian and Korean Peninsula nuclear issues.

Late last month, China hosted the Fourth Foreign ministers, Meeting of the Istanbul Process on the Afghan issue. This shows China will continue to work with regional countries and the international community to firmly support the political reconciliation and peaceful reconstruction in Afghanistan.

On climate change, China sees emission reduction as a must for China's own sustainable development. This action is domestically driven but also matches our international obligations as a responsible big country.

Among developing countries, China is the first to formulate and implement a national plan on tackling climate change:

- China has set the goal of reducing carbon intensity by 40% to 45% on the basis of 2005 level by 2020.
- China is committed to energy conservation, emission reduction, low carbon growth and ecological preservation.

Turning to the fourth characteristic of Chinese peaceful development:

- China is resolute in safeguarding its own sovereignty, security and development interests.
- China does not achieve development at the expense of the interest of others.
- At the same time, China will never give up its legitimate rights and interests.
- China will not trade its core interests.
- China will never provoke conflicts with other countries.
- And yet, China is not afraid of them either.

In recent years China has taken a series of steps to safeguard its rights in East China Sea and South China Sea:

- None of the disputes was started by China.
- On the contrary, China always calls for resolving disputes through peaceful negotiation.
- But in the face of the repeated provocations by some countries, there is no way that China will not react.

Most of you gathered here are in military uniform. So, as part of the UK defense capability, I am sure you will understand the actions of China to defend its core interests. Also, this shows that while China is firmly committed to peaceful development, other countries should also aim for comparable objectives.

Only when all countries are committed to peaceful development can the world achieve common development and so enable all countries to live together in peace.

In a nutshell, in the international system:

- China is neither an onlooker nor a trouble-maker, nor a spoiler.
- China is no longer a "sleeping lion," nor an "elephant in a china shop," nor a "crouching tiger" or a "hidden dragon" that seeks revenge.
- China is a participant, a builder and maintainer of the international system.
- China can be compared to the Kongfu Panda that upholds justice.

- China can be likened to a peaceful, lovable and amicable lion.

In summary, the world has no need to worry about China's development. And there is no need for panic or knee-jerk reaction to the rise of China.

Ladies and Gentlemen,

Diplomats and soldiers are different professions. Yet they have been closely linked since ancient times. People used to say:

"What cannot be achieved on the battleground is hardly achievable at the negotiation table."

Nowadays, people more often say:

"What cannot be achieved at the negotiation table is hardly achievable on the battleground."

The first saying stresses the importance of military might. It might please you more. But the latter one stresses the need for diplomatic and peaceful solution. I suggest that reflects the progress of the times we are living in.

In my opinion, diplomats and soldiers both have great responsibilities to fulfill. We both have glorious missions to accomplish. And we are all duty-bound to safeguard national sovereignty and security, maintain regional and world peace.

It is my very hope that the most problems of the world will be solved peacefully by relentless efforts of politicians, diplomats and military men.

To achieve this goal:

- China will exercise its influence.
- Play its role.
- Work with the international community.

Together, we can make our world a better place.

Together, we can build a world that is more stable, more peaceful and more prosperous!

Thank you!

Now, I will be glad to take your questions.

中国将坚定不移走和平发展道路*

尊敬的英联邦秘书长斯科特兰女男爵，

尊敬的巴基斯坦前总理阿齐兹先生，

尊敬的澳大利亚前外长唐纳先生，

尊敬的各位使节，

女士们、先生们：

很高兴出席2018年英联邦外交官年度培训会。

斯科特兰秘书长告诉我，今天在座的不少是刚刚履新的英联邦国家使节和外交官。在此，我谨对各位同事表示热烈欢迎。英国文学巨匠塞缪尔·约翰逊曾说："如果你厌倦了伦敦，你就厌倦了生活。"我在伦敦8年多的工作和生活充分证明了这一点。我祝愿大家在伦敦工作顺利、生活愉快、诸事顺遂。

当前，我们生活在一个快速变化的时代。国际格局深刻演变，和平与发展仍是时代的主题，但逆全球化趋势愈演愈烈，保护主义、单边主义、民粹主义甚嚣尘上。人类社会正站在历史的十字路口，是开放还是封闭？是前进还是后退？是坚持多边主义还是搞单边主义？是坚持合作共赢还是搞"零和游戏"？

这些问题，不仅考验世界各国领导人的胸襟、格局和气魄，也考验我们每位外交官的眼界、胆识和智慧。作为这个变化时代的外交官，我们面临前所未有的挑战，也面临前所未有的机遇。关键在于如何认清世界大势、把握

---

* 在2018年英联邦外交官年度培训会上的主旨演讲。2018年9月19日，英联邦秘书处。

历史潮流，抓住机遇、化解挑战。我认为，这是每一位外交官的职责。

美国前国务卿基辛格曾说，当今国际体系正在经历四百年来未有之大变局，中国是国际新秩序的最大变量。也有人说，中国的崛起是21世纪最伟大的奇迹。面对中国的崛起，有人认为是机遇，有人认为是挑战，甚至有人认为是威胁。那么，中国的发展对世界到底意味着什么？对于这个问题，中共十九大报告给出明确的回答，即中国坚持和平发展道路，推动构建新型国际关系、构建人类命运共同体；中国共产党始终把为人类做出新的更大的贡献作为自己的使命。这就意味着，中国的发展将使世界更加和平、更加美好。今天，我愿从五个方面阐释中国发展对世界的意义。

第一，中国始终坚持以“自身发展”促进和平。和平是人类的永恒追求。走和平发展道路，是对几千年来中华民族热爱和平传统的继承和发扬。在五千多年历史长河中，中华文明始终崇尚和平、和睦、和谐，这种追求已经深深植入中华民族的血脉之中。中国历史上曾经长期是世界上较强大的国家之一，但没有留下殖民和侵略他国的记录。中国人民近代曾历经苦难，因而更加珍惜今天和平安定的生活，求和平、促稳定、谋发展是人民的最大心愿。

走和平发展道路也是中国自身发展的内在需求。没有和平，发展就无从谈起；没有发展，和平就无法持久。尽管经济总量上升到世界第二位，但中国是世界上最大发展中国家的定位没有变。目前，中国人均国内生产总值仅排在世界第71位，还有3 000万贫困人口、8 000多万残疾人，每年需要解决1 500万人的就业。作为一个拥有13亿多人口的大国，我们对前进道路上的挑战和困难有清醒认识。我曾在中国较贫穷省份之一甘肃省担任省长助理，深刻体会到中国发展任务之艰巨、挑战之巨大。中国要聚精会神搞建设，既需要一个和谐稳定的国内环境，也需要一个和平安宁的国际环境。

中国不会走国强必霸的老路，而是坚持走一条对话而不对抗、结伴而不结盟的国与国交往新路。无论中国发展到什么程度，中国都永不称霸、永不扩张、永不谋求势力范围。走和平发展道路，是中国根据时代发展潮流和本国根本利益做出的战略抉择，是中国向世界做出的庄严承诺。中国将始终是世界和平的建设者，既通过维护世界和平发展自己，又通过自身发展促进世界和平。

第二，中国始终坚持以“开放合作”引领和平。2018年是中国改革开放40周年。40年的成功经验证明，只有改革开放，才能发展中国；只有开放合作，才能互利共赢，世界各国才能共享发展红利，共享持久和平。40年来，中国积极发展全球伙伴关系，扩大同世界各国的利益交汇点，不搞霸王条款，不图占别人便宜。我们不认同你输我赢、赢者通吃的旧逻辑，在自身富起来、强起来的同时，希望世界各国搭乘中国发展便车、分享中国发展红利。

2013年9月，习近平主席提出的“一带一路”倡议，是中国扩大对外开放与合作的重要举措，也是中国为国际社会提供的重大公共产品。5年来，“一带一路”建设已从理念转化为行动，从愿景转变为现实，从“大写意”走向“工笔画”。“一带一路”正推动中国开放空间从沿海、沿江向内陆、沿边延伸，形成陆海内外联动、东西双向互济的开放新格局。目前，已有103个国家和国际组织同中国签署了118份“一带一路”方面的合作协议，其中就包括不少英联邦国家。5年来，中国与“一带一路”相关国家货物贸易额累计超过5万亿美元，对沿线国家的直接投资超过600亿美元，建立了82个境外经贸合作区，上缴东道国税费22亿美元，为当地创造20多万个就业岗位。

上周，我出席了英国议会跨党派“一带一路”和中巴经济走廊小组成立仪式，着重介绍了中巴经济走廊项目。目前，走廊22个合作项目中有9个已完工，13个正在建设，每年可带动巴基斯坦经济增长1~2个百分点。

中国与斯里兰卡合作建设运营的汉班托塔港仅2018年上半年就完成散货吞吐7.66万吨，未来有望成为印度洋的重要世界级大港；科伦坡国际集装箱码头全部完成“油改电”，二氧化碳排放减少95%，成为南亚地区规模最大的“绿色码头”。

中国公司承建的尼日利亚阿卡铁路（阿布贾至卡杜纳）通车运营两年来，已累计运送旅客近100万人次，还在沿线建设了一批学校、道路、医疗设施等。中国公司在坦桑尼亚投建的国家光纤骨干传输网覆盖全国21个行政区，联通坦桑尼亚周边6国。中国在卢旺达首都基加利市投建的市政道路扩建工程将于明年竣工，建成后将有效缓解城市交通压力。

当然，与任何新生事物一样，人们认识“一带一路”有一个过程，难免会出现这样或那样的误解甚至疑虑。我想强调的是，“一带一路”倡议虽源于中国，但机遇和成果属于世界。中国不打地缘政治的小算盘，不搞封闭排他的小圈子，不做凌驾于人的强买强卖。“一带一路”坚持共商共建共享，绝不是什么“债务陷阱”、资源掠夺，而是与世界各国共谋发展、共迎挑战、共享繁荣的合作平台。

未来，中国改革的步伐会越走越实，开放的大门会越开越大。中国将于 2018 年 11 月在上海举办首届国际进口博览会，这是世界上首个专门以进口为主题的博览会，充分展现了中国进一步扩大开放的决心。我们欢迎包括英联邦国家在内的各国企业积极参展，把优质产品和服务带给中国 13 亿人口的大市场。

第三，中国始终坚持以“国际规则”支撑和平。在国与国交往中，存在差异和出现分歧在所难免，关键在于在相互尊重的基础上，按照公认的国际规则，以务实和建设性方式管控和化解分歧。中国始终做国际秩序的维护者，坚持多边主义，维护以联合国为核心的多边体制权威性和有效性，反对任何一方按照自己的意愿随意取舍或选择规则。

2018 年以来，有的国家执意奉行“本国优先”政策，大搞单边主义、保护主义，四处挥舞“关税大棒”，挑起“贸易战”，给世界经济秩序和多边贸易体系带来严峻挑战。昨天，美国政府不顾国际国内绝大多数意见反对，宣布自 9 月 24 日起对 2 000 亿美元中国输美产品加征 10% 的关税，进而还要采取其他关税升级措施。中方将不得不进行反制，坚决捍卫自身正当合法权益，维护全球自由贸易秩序。

我要强调的是，中国改革开放以来取得的一切发展成就，都是中国人民用勤劳的双手干出来的，归根结底是因为中国走在了正确的发展道路上。中国的奇迹是中国人民创造出来的，不是靠“偷窃”谁的财富、“盗取”谁的技术，更不是被吓出来的。中国人民不信邪也不怕邪，不惹事也不怕事。所谓“极限施压”根本吓不倒中国人民。

美国秉持的是“零和博弈”“以邻为壑”的旧思维，反映出来的世界观、合作观、发展观、输赢观都与中国截然不同。2018年以来，我就中美贸易争端在英国主流媒体发表了6篇文章，强调维护以联合国为核心的国际体系和以国际法为基础的国际秩序，指出合作是唯一正确的选择，共赢才能通向更好的未来。

中国秉持共商共建共享的全球治理观，积极参与全球治理体系改革和建设，努力为改革和完善全球治理贡献中国智慧和力量。我们将推动构建新型国际关系，推动构建人类命运共同体，与各国共同建设持久和平、普遍安全、共同繁荣、开放包容、清洁美丽的世界。无论国际风云如何变化，中国始终是全球化和自由贸易的坚定捍卫者，主张开放、融通、互利、共赢的合作理念，维护世界贸易组织规则，支持多边贸易体制，推动国际治理体系朝着更加公正合理的方向发展，为构建开放型世界经济做出积极贡献。

第四，中国始终坚持以“义利兼顾”维护和平。“国不以利为利，以义为利也”。中国古人的义利观讲究“义中之利，君子所贵也”。在国际合作中，只有义利兼顾才能义利兼得，只有义利平衡才能义利共赢。当代中国外交政策充分吸收传统文化精髓。作为联合国安理会常任理事国和最大发展中国家，中国始终牢记自身特殊责任和重要使命，坚持在国际舞台上为发展中国家主持公道；在联合国、二十国集团等场合同发展中国家加强战略合作，密切协调配合，共同探索和拓展发展中国家走向现代化的有效途径，推动全球治理体系朝着更加公正、合理和平衡的方向发展和完善，旗帜鲜明地维护发展中国家的共同利益和集体诉求。

以非洲国家为例，在座的英联邦国家使节有不少来自非洲。中非是互帮互助的好伙伴，双方友好源远流长，特别是在争取民族独立解放、实现发展振兴的道路上，始终患难与共、相互支持，结下了深厚的兄弟情谊。我曾两度在非洲常驻，对非洲有深厚的感情。20世纪70年代，我在赞比亚工作期间曾有幸参加坦赞铁路的交接仪式，见证了这座象征着中非友谊的历史丰碑。21世纪初，我出使埃及，见证了中埃关系在新世纪的蓬勃发展。

40多年过去了，世界形势风云变幻，但中非友好情谊不但没有变，而且历久弥坚，更加牢不可破。2018年9月3日至4日，中非合作论坛北京峰会成功召开，达成一系列重要成果。中非双方一致同意构建更加紧密的命运共同体。双方见证签署的各类合作协议近150份，特别是28个国家和非盟委员会同中方签署共建“一带一路”的合作文件。非方高度赞赏中方为下阶段中非务实合作提出的“八大行动”。作为中非“十大合作计划”的升级版，“八大行动”规划了中非共同发展的具体路径，强调中方将致力于加强中非在产业产能、基础设施、贸易等领域的合作，同时拓展双方在绿色发展、能力建设、健康卫生、人文交流、和平安全等领域的合作潜能，特别是推动“一带一路”建设与非盟《2063年议程》、联合国2030年可持续发展议程和非洲各国发展战略深入对接，将极大地促进中非合作更好更快发展，更多惠及非洲人民。

这次峰会进一步凝聚了中非合作论坛框架下55方、26亿人民团结合作的意愿和共识，是中非友好大家庭的一次历史性聚会，也是中非促进共同发展的一座新的历史丰碑。习近平主席在峰会讲话中强调，中国在对非合作中坚持做到“五不”，即不干预非洲国家探索符合国情的发展道路，不干涉非洲内政，不把自己的意志强加于人，不在对非援助中附加任何政治条件，不在对非投资融资中谋取政治私利。这是中非关系不惧风雨、历久弥坚的根本原因，也是中非合作欣欣向荣、长盛不衰的“独家秘籍”。任何人都无法阻挡中非合作和非洲发展的大势。

第五，中国始终坚持以“严守底线”捍卫和平。中国坚持走和平发展道路，其他国家也要走和平发展道路，这样世界和平才有保障。中国决不会以牺牲别国利益为代价来发展自己，同时也决不会允许别国损害中国的核心利益，决不会放弃自己的正当权益。我们将坚持以国家核心利益为底线维护国家主权、安全和发展利益，坚定捍卫国家领土主权，维护国家统一，这本身也是维护和平、捍卫和平之举。

近来，南海问题被炒得沸沸扬扬。实际情况怎样呢？事实胜于雄辩。在中国和东盟各国共同努力下，南海形势持续向好，各当事国重回谈判磋商解决有关争议的正轨，中国同有关国家之间的关系健康稳定发展。中国与东盟各国正在全面有效落实《南海各方行为宣言》，积极推进“南海行为准则”磋商。最近，中国与东盟各国已就“南海行为准则”单一磋商文本草案达成一致。这充分说明，地区国家有信心、有能力、有智慧妥善处理好南海问题，实现本地区长久稳定、发展与繁荣。

令人不解的是，一些域外大国似乎并不想看到南海风平浪静，他们派军舰和飞机不远万里来南海制造事端，放着广阔宽敞的南海正常航道不走，偏要打着“航行自由”旗号非法进入中国岛礁邻近海域“耍枪弄棒”，侵犯中国主权，威胁中国安全，破坏地区和平稳定。事实上，南海航行自由从来不存在任何问题。南海每年十几万艘商船安全顺利通行，从没有哪艘遇到过所谓航行自由问题。中国对外贸易和能源运输 70% 以上通过南海，没有任何国家比中国更关心南海航行和飞越自由。中方一贯尊重和维护各国依据包括《联合国海洋法公约》在内的国际法，在南海享有航行和飞越自由，但前提是要尊重沿岸国的主权和安全。航行自由绝不是“横行自由”，绝不是乱闯别国领海、侵犯别国主权的自由。这样的“自由”必须制止，否则南海将无宁日。任何人都不要低估中国维护国家主权、安全和发展利益的意志，任何人都不要低估中国维护南海和平稳定的决心。

女士们、先生们，

英联邦有 53 个国家，绝大多数成员国都与中国建立了外交关系。我们愿在“一个中国”原则基础上与所有国家发展互利合作关系，不断增进互信、深化友谊、扩大合作，特别是在减贫、卫生、气候变化、可持续发展以及全球治理等领域深化务实合作，成为携手同行、合作共赢的好朋友、好伙伴。

习近平主席指出，“世界繁荣稳定是中国的机遇，中国发展也是世界的机遇。和平发展道路能不能走得通，很大程度上要看我们能不能把世界的机遇转变为中国的机遇，把中国的机遇转变为世界的机遇”。让我们共同努力，变世界机遇为中国机遇，变中国机遇为世界机遇，共享机遇、共促和平、共谋发展，为构建新型国际关系，为构建人类命运共同体做出贡献！

谢谢！

现在，我愿回答大家的提问。

China Stays Committed to Peaceful Development*

Baroness Scotland,

Mr. Shaukat Aziz,

Mr. Alexander Downer,

Your Excellencies,

Diplomatic Colleagues,

Ladies and Gentlemen,

It is a real delight to join you at the annual Commonwealth Diplomats Induction Programme.

Baroness Scotland told me that many of you present today have just arrived in London. I would like to extend my warmest welcome to you. Samuel Johnson said, "When a man is tired of London, he is tired of life." Having spent more than eight years in London, I know Johnson was right. I wish you a fantastic tour in London.

We are living in a time of rapid changes. Amid evolving international landscape, peace and development remain the theme of our times. At the same time, anti-globalisation is rising, and protectionism, unilateralism and populism are surging. The international community is standing at a historical crossroads. Should we stay open and move forward, or shut ourselves in and turn back? Should we uphold multilateralism and win-win cooperation, or choose unilateralism and zero-sum games?

These questions are not reserved for the leaders of our countries only. They are

---

* Keynote Speech at the Annual Commonwealth Diplomats Induction Programme. Commonwealth Secretariat, 19 September 2018.

also tests for us, the diplomats. They test our vision, courage and wisdom. The fast-changing time brings unprecedented challenges as well as opportunities. As diplomats, it is our duty to follow the overarching trend of the times, seize the opportunities and address the challenges.

Henry Kissinger once said, the current international system is experiencing "the biggest change in 400 years," and China is the largest variable in the new international order. Others have referred to the rise of China as the greatest miracle in the 21st century. So, what would you say? Is the rise of China an opportunity, a challenge, or a threat? What does China's development mean to the world?

The 19th Congress of the Communist Party of China gave a clear answer to this question:

- China will stay committed to peaceful development. It will work with other countries to build a new type of international relations, and a community with a shared future for mankind.
- The Communist Party of China regards as its mission to make new and greater contribution to mankind.

This means that China's development will make the world a more peaceful and better place. Let me elaborate on this from the following five aspects.

First, China has promoted peace through its own development.

Peace is the ever-lasting pursuit of mankind. By keeping to the path of peaceful development, we have carried on the peace-loving tradition of the Chinese nation.

In its more than 5,000 years of history, China has always valued peace, good-neighbourliness and harmony. This pursuit of peace runs deep in the genes of the Chinese nation. Historically, China had been one of the most powerful nations in the world for a long time, but it had never colonised or invaded other countries.

The Chinese people experienced intense sufferings in modern times, and therefore value deeply the peace and tranquility we now enjoy. Peace, stability and development are the biggest aspirations of the Chinese people.

Peaceful development meets the inherent need of China in the pursuit of its own growth. Without peace, there could be no development, and without development, peace could not last.

Despite being the second largest economy, China is still the world's largest developing country.

- Our per capita GDP ranks only the 71st in the world.
- There are still 30 million people living in poverty and more than 80 million who are disabled.
- And every year, 15 million people need to find a job.

As a big country with a population of over 1.3 billion, China has a clear idea of the kind of challenges and difficulties awaiting it down the road.

I had been Assistant Governor of Gansu Province, one of the poorest provinces in China. I know from personal experience how arduous the task is and how severe the challenges are for China to achieve development. To concentrate on development at home, China needs a harmonious and stable domestic environment, and China also needs a peaceful and tranquil international environment.

In its relations with other countries, China seeks dialogue and partnership rather than confrontation and alliance. China will never seek hegemony, expansion or sphere of influence even when it grows strong.

Staying committed to peaceful development is a strategic choice of China that is in accordance with the trend of the times and serves China's fundamental interests. It is China's solemn commitment to the world. China will always be a contributor to world peace. We maintain world peace in order to achieve development. We also promote world peace through our development.

Second, China has upheld peace through inclusive cooperation.

This year marks the 40th anniversary of China's reform and opening-up. Forty years of success taught us that reform and opening-up are the only way to development. It also taught us that inclusive and win-win cooperation is the only way for countries of the world to share the benefits of development and enjoy lasting peace.

In the past 40 years, China has worked vigorously to build partnership around the globe.

- We have expanded common interests with other countries.
- We have never imposed unfair deals on others or taken advantage of others.
- We do not agree with the old logic of "you lose, I win" or "the winner takes it all."
- While we want China to become richer and stronger, we are also ready to help other countries board our fast train of development and benefit from China's growth.

In September 2013, President Xi Jinping proposed the Belt and Road Initiative. This is an important measure of China to open up its market further and engage in broader external cooperation. It is also the important public goods that China contributes to the international community.

In the past five years, the BRI has been translated from a concept into actions, from aspirations into reality. To borrow the terms of traditional Chinese painting, we have completed the sketch of the BRI with "freehand brushwork." It is now time to attend to the details with "fine brushwork."

The BRI will enable China to expand the scope of its opening-up from regions along the coast and rivers to the hinterland and border areas. Through the BRI, China will open up on all fronts through links running eastward and westward, across land and over sea.

As of today, 103 countries and international organisations have signed 118 cooperation agreements with China on the BRI, including many Commonwealth countries.

In the past five years,

- China's trade in goods with countries along the routes has exceeded $5 trillion.
- China has invested over $60 billion in these countries.
- China has also built 82 economic and trade cooperation zones along the routes. These zones have contributed $2.2 billion in tax and fees to the host countries, and created over 200,000 jobs locally.

Last week, I attended the launch of the All Party Parliamentary Group for the Belt and Road Initiative and China-Pakistan Economic Corridor (CPEC). Out of 22 CPEC projects, 9 have been completed and 13 are under construction. These projects will boost Pakistan's growth by 1 to 2 percentage points.

BRI projects in other countries have also delivered tangible benefits. Here are some examples:

- The Hambantota Port jointly built and operated by China and Sri Lanka handled 76,600 tons of freight in the first half of this year alone. It is expected to become an important world-class port in the Indian Ocean.
- The Colombo International Container Terminal has completely converted from diesel to electricity, cutting CO_2 emissions by 95%. It has become the largest Green Port in South Asia.
- The Abuja-Kaduna railway in Nigeria has provided services to nearly one million passengers since its launch two years ago. China also helped build many schools, roads and health care facilities along the railway.
- The National ICT Fiber Backbone network in Tanzania covers 21 administrative regions in the country and connects six neighbouring countries.
- The road expansion project in Kigali, the capital of Rwanda, will be completed next year. This project will effectively alleviate the traffic congestion in the city.

Like all things new, BRI has met with its share of misunderstandings and even doubts. It takes some time for people to fully appreciate this Initiative.

Here I want to stress that although the BRI was proposed by China, it creates opportunities and produces outcomes for the world. In this Initiative, China has no geopolitical calculations. China is not building an exclusive bloc. China is not strong-arming anybody to do deals on our terms. Instead, the principles of BRI cooperation are extensive consultation, joint contribution and shared benefits. This means that contrary to allegations of "debt trap" or "plundering resources," the BRI is a platform for countries to achieve common development, address challenges together and share in prosperity.

Going forward, China will take solid steps to deepen reform at home and open its door wider to the world. To show its determination, China will host the first-ever International Import Expo in Shanghai this coming November. This will be the world's first-ever import fair. Companies of all countries, including the Commonwealth countries, are welcome at the Import Expo to introduce their products and services to

China's 1.3 billion-strong market.

Third, China has supported peace through adhering to international rules.

In international relations, it is natural that countries may disagree with each other. What's important is to manage and bridge disagreements in a practical and constructive manner according to universally-accepted international rules and on the basis of mutual respect.

China has always upheld the international order and the authority and effectiveness of the multilateral system with the UN as its core. China opposes the practice of cherry-picking international rules to suit one's own selfish interests.

Some country, however, is bent on "putting itself first," advocating unilateralism and protectionism, wielding the "tariffs baton" and threatening other countries with "trade war." This has posed severe challenges to the world economic order and the multilateral trade regime.

Yesterday, despite the opposition at home and abroad, the US government announced that it would impose 10% of additional tariffs on $200 billion worth of imported Chinese goods starting from 24 September, and that it was preparing for further tariff escalations. China is now forced to take counter-measures in order to safeguard its lawful rights and interests and uphold free trade in the world.

I want to reiterate this: What China has achieved since the introduction of reform and opening-up policies are attributable to the hard work of the Chinese people. The fundamental reason for China's success is that we have found the right path for development. The China miracle is created by the Chinese people. It is not a result of stealing others' wealth or technology. We would not have come so far had we feared threats. We do not create trouble, but we are not afraid of it. The so-called "maximum pressure" will never intimidate the Chinese people into submission.

The US actions are deeply rooted in the belief of zero-sum games and "beggar-thy-neighbour" which are completely out of dated. They are a far cry from China's world view, how China sees international cooperation and development, and how China defines winning and losing.

Earlier this year, I published six articles in British media on the trade disputes between China and the US. In these articles, I stressed the importance of upholding the international system with the United Nation at its core and the international order based on international law; I illustrated why win-win cooperation is the only right path toward a better future.

China believes that in the global governance, all countries should follow the principles of extensive consultation, joint contribution and shared benefits. China has taken an active part in the reform and development of the global governance system. China works to contribute its wisdom and efforts to the improvement of this system.

China is ready to work with other countries:

- to build a new type of international relations;
- to build a community with a shared future for mankind;
- and to build an open, inclusive, clean and beautiful world that enjoys lasting peace, universal security and common prosperity.

Regardless of the changing international landscape, China will:

- remain a firm defender of globalisation and free trade;
- advocate open, interconnected and mutually-beneficial cooperation;
- uphold WTO rules;
- support the multilateral trade regime;
- endorse a fair and reasonable international governance system;
- and contribute to building an open world economy.

Fourth, China has maintained peace through pursuing the greater good and shared interests.

In Chinese culture we believe that a gentleman should value the greater good and that a country should never sacrifice the greater good for material interests. In the international cooperation, pursuing the greater good and shared interests will lead to win-win results.

China's foreign policies fully reflect this spirit. As a permanent member of the UN Security Council and the largest developing country, China always keeps in mind its unique responsibilities and important mission.

China has spoken for developing countries on the international stage and has engaged in strategic cooperation and close coordination with them in the UN and the

G20. China is ready to work with partners of the developing world:

- to explore more effective ways to modernisation;
- to improve the global governance system and make it fair, reasonable and balanced;
- and to safeguard the common interests and aspirations of developing countries.

I know many of you are from Africa, so let me take China's relations with African countries as an example. China and Africa are close partners. Our friendship and brotherhood were forged and deepened in our common pursuit for national independence, development and revitalisation. We supported and helped each other, and shared weal and woe.

I have been posted to Africa twice, and so I have deep emotional bonds with this continent. While working in Zambia in the 1970s, I had the honour to attend the handover ceremony of Tazara, a railway linking Tanzania and Zambia that was built by China. I witnessed the dedication of this historic monument of China-Africa friendship. While working in Egypt at the beginning of the new millennium, I saw with my own eyes a thriving China-Egypt relationship in the new century.

Over the past 40 years, despite changing international landscape, China-Africa friendship has remained stronger than ever.

On 3 to 4 September this year, the Beijing Summit of the Forum on China-Africa Cooperation was held. It was a great success. China and Africa agreed to build a closer community with a shared future. A number of important outcomes were reached.

- Nearly 150 cooperation agreements were signed.
- In particular, 28 countries and the African Union Commission signed cooperation documents with China on jointly building the BRI.

The African side highly appreciated the "eight major initiatives" China proposed for China-Africa cooperation in the next stage. It is an upgraded version of the existing ten cooperation plans. It draws a detailed roadmap for China and Africa to achieve common development.

According to the "eight major initiatives":

- China and Africa will enhance cooperation on industrial capacity, infrastructure development and trade.
- The two sides will tap cooperation potential in areas such as green development, capacity building, health care, cultural and people-to-people exchange, peace and security.
- The two sides will also match the BRI with Agenda 2063 of the African Union, the 2030 Agenda for Sustainable Development and national development strategies of African countries.

These initiatives will facilitate fast-growing and better cooperation between China and Africa and deliver more benefits to the African people.

The big family of China and Africa includes 55 parties and 2.6 billion people. The historic gathering in Beijing of this big family strengthened our consensus on further cooperation. It was a new historic monument to the common development of China and Africa.

In his speech at the Summit, President Xi Jinping said that China will take a "five-no" approach in its relations with Africa, namely:

- No interference in African countries' pursuit of development paths that fit their national conditions.
- No interference in African countries' internal affairs.
- No imposition of our will on African countries.
- No political strings attached to assistance to Africa.
- And no selfish political interests in investment and financing cooperation in Africa.

This "five-no" approach is the fundamental reason why China-Africa relations have been able to withstand the test of time and hardship. It is the secret to the thriving China-Africa cooperation. No one could reverse the trend of China-Africa cooperation and Africa's development.

Fifth, China has safeguarded peace through holding the bottom line.

China will stay committed to peaceful development. Other countries should do the same. World peace could be ensured only if everyone adheres to peaceful development. China will never seek development at the expense of others. At the same time, China will never allow its core interests be undermined, or give up its legitimate rights and interests.

Our bottom line is the core interests of our country. We will stay firm in safeguarding our national sovereignty, unity, security and development interests. This in itself maintains and safeguards peace.

Take the South China Sea as an example. Despite all the recent hyping-up, the facts speak for themselves: thanks to the concerted efforts of China and ASEAN countries, the situation in the South China Sea is improving; relevant parties have returned to the right track of addressing disputes through negotiation and consultation; the relations between China and relevant countries have been sound and stable.

China and ASEAN countries are working on the full and effective implementation of the Declaration on the Conduct of Parties in the South China Sea. We are actively advancing the consultation on the Code of Conduct in the South China Sea (COC). Agreement was reached between China and ASEAN countries recently on a single draft negotiating text of the COC. This has fully demonstrated that countries in the region have the confidence, capability and wisdom to deal with the South China Sea issue properly and achieve enduring stability, development and prosperity.

Yet to everyone's confusion, some big countries outside the region did not seem to appreciate the peace and tranquility in the South China Sea. They sent warships and aircraft all the way to the South China Sea to create trouble. Under the excuse of so-called "freedom of navigation," they ignored the vast sea lane and chose to sail into the adjacent waters of China's islands and reefs to show off their military might. This was a serious infringement upon China's sovereignty. It threatened China's security and put regional peace and stability in jeopardy.

The truth is that the freedom of navigation in the South China Sea has never been a problem. Every year, hundreds of thousands of merchant vessels pass through the South China Sea safely and unimpeded. Never has there been a single case of navigation freedom being affected. With over 70% of its foreign trade and transport of energy passing through the South China Sea, China, more than any other countries, cherishes the freedom of navigation and over flight in the South China Sea.

China has all along respected and upheld the freedom of navigation and over-flight in the South China Sea in accordance with international law, including the United Nations Convention on the Law of the Sea. But the precondition for such freedom is respect for the sovereignty and security of the littoral states. Freedom of navigation is not a license to do whatever one wishes. Freedom of navigation is not freedom to invade in other country's territorial waters and infringe upon other country's sovereignty. Such "freedom" must be stopped. Otherwise, the South China Sea will never be tranquil.

No one should underestimate China's will to safeguard its national sovereignty, security and development interests. No one should underestimate China's determination to uphold peace and stability in the South China Sea.

Ladies and Gentlemen,

The majority of the 53 Commonwealth countries have diplomatic relationship with China. China stands ready to develop mutually-beneficial cooperation with all the countries on the basis of the one-China principle. We want stronger mutual trust. We want deeper friendship. We want broader cooperation, particularly on poverty alleviation, health care, climate change, sustainable development and global governance. I am sure that by working together and pursuing win-win results, we will become good friends and good partners.

As President Xi Jinping said,

"A prosperous and stable world provides China with opportunities, and China's development also offers an opportunity for the world as a whole. Whether we will succeed in our pursuit of peaceful development, to a large extent, hinges on whether we can turn opportunities in the rest of the world into China's opportunities and China's opportunities into those for the rest of the world."

Let us join hands to share opportunities with each other and turn opportunities into success. Let us join hands to promote peace and achieve development. Together we will contribute to the building of a new type of international relations and a community with a shared future for mankind!

Thank you!

Now I am ready to take your questions.

坚持和平发展，推进合作共赢*

尊敬的布莱克维主席，

女士们、先生们：

大家晚上好！

很高兴到访牛津剑桥俱乐部。我出任中国驻英大使以来，牛津和剑桥是我访问次数最多的两个大学，但做客牛剑俱乐部还是第一次。俱乐部的会员告诉我，我是第一位到此演讲的中国大使。因此，今天的访问很有意义。正因为如此，我把 2019 年的第一场演讲选在你们的俱乐部——这个牛津剑桥两大名校精英荟萃的地方。

对中国而言，2019 年是一个大年，我们将迎来新中国成立 70 周年。70 年来，中国发生了翻天覆地的变化，从一个积贫积弱的“东亚病夫”发展成为世界第二大经济体，堪称人类发展史上的奇迹。

对英国民众而言，中国从“远在天边”变得“近在眼前”，英国媒体每天都有关于中国的报道，中国的发展与英国越来越息息相关。那么，中国的发展对英国到底意味着什么？是机遇、挑战还是威胁？要回答这个问题，就要认识中国是个什么样的国家，搞清楚中国从何处来，又向何处去。

回顾 70 年来的发展历程，中国的成功之处就是找到了一条适合本国国情的道路，即中国特色社会主义道路。这是认识中国的关键。这条中国特色社会主义道路有四个鲜明特点，可以用四个“P”来概括。

---

* 在英国牛津剑桥俱乐部的主旨演讲。2019 年 1 月 8 日，牛津剑桥俱乐部。

第一个是“PARTY”，即中国共产党是中国的“主心骨”。对于中国这样一个近14亿人口的大国来说，发展道路没有先例可循，也没有金科玉律的教科书，只能在实践中不断探索。中国近代曾历经深重苦难，人民流离失所，国家山河破碎。不少志士仁人发起一系列救亡图存的斗争，各种努力都尝试过，无论是太平天国、义和团，还是洋务运动、戊戌变法、辛亥革命，最终都失败了。只有在中国共产党领导下，中国才实现从站起来、富起来到强起来的伟大飞跃。可以说，中国共产党是历史的选择、人民的选择。20世纪90年代初苏联解体时，西方一些人认为“中国共产党挺不了多久”，提出“历史的终结”，这些看法最终被证明都是错误的，根本原因在于他们对中国共产党缺乏正确认识。中国共产党虽然也曾走过一些弯路，但勇于坚持真理、直面问题、修正错误，不断开拓创新、与时俱进，始终保持与人民的血肉联系，带领人民克服一个又一个困难，不断从胜利走向胜利。

第二个是“PROGRESS”，即把经济建设作为中心。在70年的探索过程中，中国不断认识并发展社会主义。1978年，中国认真总结国内外改革发展经验，“以经济建设为中心”取代“以阶级斗争为纲”，开启了中国改革开放的伟大进程。通过40多年改革开放，中国不断解放和发展社会生产力，国内生产总值年均增长约9.5%，总量达12万亿美元，远高于同期世界经济2.9%的年均增速；占世界经济的比重从40年前的2%，增至今天的15.2%。中国已成为世界第二大经济体、制造业第一大国、货物贸易第一大国、商品消费第二大国、外资流入第二大国，外汇储备连续多年位居世界第一。

第三个是“PEOPLE”，即把让人民过上“好日子”作为奋斗目标。习近平主席指出：“人民对美好生活的向往就是我们的奋斗目标。”中国始终坚持以人民为中心的发展思想，在发展中保障和改善民生。这不仅是我们一切工作的出发点和落脚点，也是中国发展的根本目的。70年来，中国从一个难以解决温饱问题的低收入国家跃升为一个生活宽裕的中等收入国家，7.4亿人摆脱贫困，3亿多人进入中等收入群体；建成了包括养老、医疗、低保、住房在内的世界最大的社会保障体系；居民预期寿命由1981年的67.8岁提高到2017年的76.7岁。

第四个是“PEACE”，即把和平发展作为基本国策。中国始终坚持独立自主的和平外交政策，始终不渝走和平发展道路。中国的发展需要一个和平安宁的国际环境，同时中国又以自身发展促进世界和平。近年来，中国参与了当今几乎所有国际和地区热点问题的解决进程，为世界和平与发展不断贡献中国智慧，提出中国方案。新年伊始，中国已超过日本成为联合国常规预算第二大出资国，贡献份额从 7.9% 上升至 12%。中国还是联合国维和行动第二大出资国和安理会五常国中派遣维和军事人员最多的国家，累计派出 3.7 万人次军警官兵参与维和行动。中国军舰连续 10 年在亚丁湾、索马里海域执行护航，先后保护了 6 000 多艘船舶安全，其中也包括英国商船。

女士们、先生们，

尽管中国发展取得了不少成就，但我们清醒地知道，中国还是一个发展中国家，是世界上最大的发展中国家，发展依然任重道远。

首先，发展不充分，人均水平低。中国人均国内生产总值排在世界第 60 多位，只有美国的 1/7，不到英国的 1/4，人类发展指数位列全球第 90 多位。中国还有 3 000 多万贫困人口、8 000 多万残疾人，需要照顾的老年人口超过 2 亿，每年需要解决的就业人口就达 1 500 万。

其次，发展不平衡，地区差距大。以东西部差距为例，东部沿海地区广东省 GDP 相当于世界排名第 14 的西班牙，而西部地区国土面积占全国 72%，人口占 27%，经济总量仅占 20%，对外贸易和投资只占 7%。我曾在中国西部省份甘肃省担任省长助理，80 多个县我跑过 60 多个，目睹了甘肃省脱贫任务之艰巨。甘肃省扶贫目标仍是保证人民“一日有三餐，四季有衣穿”。

此外，发展仍面临不可持续的问题。中国社会生产力总体水平仍不高，生产力结构还不够合理，高投入、高消耗的增长方式尚未得到根本改变，科技创新能力仍显不足。中国制造业、贸易规模很大，但经济仍“大而不强”。在国际贸易中，中国出口的是廉价“体力劳动”，进口的是高昂“脑力劳动”，服务贸易仍存在巨额逆差。中国的文化建设、国防实力、科学技术、社会治理现代化水平都有待进一步提升。

我们对前进道路上的困难和挑战有清醒的认识，正如习近平主席指出的，中国发展到了“愈进愈难、愈进愈险而又不进则退、非进不可的时候”。在中国共产党领导下，我们有信心、有能力攻坚克难，开创更加美好的未来。展望未来，中国将在世界舞台上扮演什么角色呢？概括起来就是四个“B”。

第一个是“BOOSTER”，中国要做全球经济增长的“推进器”。中国在发展中遇到的问题都是“成长中的烦恼”，只有通过进一步发展来解决。中共十九大为中国未来发展确定了“三个目标”，即到2020年全面建成小康社会，到2035年基本实现社会主义现代化，到21世纪中叶建成富强民主文明和谐美丽的社会主义现代化强国。要实现这些目标，中国将进一步深化改革，扩大开放。正如习近平主席在新年贺词中所说：“中国改革的脚步不会停滞，开放的大门只会越开越大。”中国的发展将继续为世界经济增长提供充足动力。近年来，中国对世界经济增长的贡献率超过30%。越来越多的中国人走出国门，从事商贸、投资、求学、旅游等活动。2017年中国在境外设立企业超过3万家，在海外的劳务人员约100万，留学生约137万。2018年11月，我们成功举办首届中国国际进口博览会，这是迄今世界上第一个以进口为主题的国家级展会。未来15年，也就是中国基本实现社会主义现代化的15年，中国将进口24万亿美元商品，吸收2万亿美元境外直接投资。中国现在是120多个国家和地区的最大贸易伙伴。我想未来15年，这个数字还要进一步扩大。

第二个是“BUILDER”，中国要做人类命运共同体的“构建者”。中国的成功发展得益于和平的国际环境，中国的未来发展仍需要稳定的外部环境。当前，世界正面临百年未有之大变局，单边主义、保护主义肆虐，不稳定性、不确定因素增多，地区热点问题此起彼伏，恐怖主义、网络安全、重大传染性疾病、气候变化等非传统安全威胁持续蔓延，人类社会面临许多共同挑战。没有哪个国家能够独自应对这些挑战，也没有哪个国家能够退回自我封闭的孤岛。因此，中国呼吁各国携手行动，维护世界和平、促进共同发展，推动建设相互尊重、公平正义、合作共赢的新型国际关系，构建人类命运共同体。

第三个是“BACKER”，中国要做现行国际秩序的“支持者”。中国与世界的关系已发生了历史性变化，中国积极融入现行国际体系，参与了当今世界几乎所有重要政府间国际组织，签署了300多项国际公约，在全球治理体系中发挥着越来越重要的作用。当前，世界正处于重要十字路口，现行国际秩序面临重大挑战。在此形势下，中国没有迷惘，也没有退缩，而是站在历史发展进步的一边，更加坚定地倡导自由贸易，更加明确地反对保护主义，坚决维护以联合国为核心的多边体制，坚决维护以世贸组织为基础的多边贸易体系。当然，中国亦深知现行国际秩序并不完美，支持对相关国际机构、多边组织进行改革，但不赞同有的国家按照自己意愿对国际规则随意取舍。

第四个是“BRI”，中国要将“一带一路”打造为各国合作共赢的重要平台。中国提出“一带一路”倡议，从根本上是为了解决发展不平衡、不可持续的问题，这是中国经济发展到新阶段的必然选择，也是推进新一轮对外开放的重要抓手。“一带一路”坚持共商共建共享原则，这既符合中国和平发展、合作共赢的外交政策，也是推动构建人类命运共同体的重要尝试。该倡议提出5年来，得到世界各国普遍欢迎，已经成为当今世界最受欢迎的公共产品和最大规模的合作平台。目前已有150多个国家和国际组织与中国签署“一带一路”合作文件。2019年，中国对“一带一路”提出新的更高要求，将全力办好第二届“一带一路”国际合作高峰论坛，集中推进一批重大项目，推动“一带一路”建设向着更高质量、更高标准、更高水平发展。

女士们、先生们，

从我前面所讲的四个“P”和“B”，大家可以看到，中国人民是爱好和平的人民，中国是致力于和平发展的国家。中国正以满腔热忱拥抱世界，热情友好地和所有国家交朋友。我们也希望世界以同样的姿态回应中国。我高兴地看到，英国各界普遍认为中国发展对英国是机遇，英国民众对中国的好感度在西方大国中位居前列。但世界上还有国家将中国的发展视为威胁，甚至提出与中国进行“新冷战”，这种想法与世界大势背道而驰。正如一句西方谚语所说，“如果你手里拿着的是锤子，那你眼里看到的也只能是钉子”。

“天下大势，浩浩荡荡，顺之者昌，逆之者亡。”在世界大变局中，只有保持开放包容，坚持合作共赢，才能把握历史发展大势，抓住历史变革机遇，共同推动人类社会发展进步。牛津和剑桥两大名校桃李满天下，声誉遍全球。我衷心希望牛津剑桥俱乐部能发挥积极作用，增进世界对中国的了解，推动中英两国人民抓住历史机遇，携手书写中英关系“黄金时代”新篇章，共同为构建人类命运共同体做出贡献。

谢谢！

现在我愿回答大家的提问。

China is Firmly Committed to Peaceful Development and Win-Win Cooperation*

Chairman Joanna Tudor-Blakeway,

Ladies and Gentlemen,

Good evening!

It is a real delight to join you at the Oxford and Cambridge Club.

Oxford and Cambridge are the two universities that I have visited most frequently since becoming the Chinese Ambassador to the UK. But this is my first visit to the Oxford and Cambridge Club. I was told that I am the first Chinese Ambassador to speak at the Club. So, today's event is very special and significant. Therefore, I have decided to make my very first speech of 2019 at your club, the home of outstanding alumni from both these two world-renowned universities.

2019 is an important year for China. It marks the 70th anniversary of the founding of the People's Republic of China. The past 70 years have seen China going through profound changes and growing from "the Sick Man of East Asia" ridden with poverty and weakness to the second largest economy in the world. This has been a miracle in the history of human development.

For people here in Britain, China is no longer a far away land. China is right here before your eyes. It is in your newspapers every day. And more and more people feel closely connected with what is going on in China.

So, what does China's development mean to the UK? Is it an opportunity, a

* Keynote Speech at the Oxford and Cambridge Club. Oxford and Cambridge Club, 8 January 2019.

challenge or a threat? To answer this question, one must first try to understand China—to know where it has come from and where it is going in the future.

The key to understanding China is to understand that China's success of the past 70 years is attributed to its development path that suits China's national conditions. This path is known as socialism with Chinese characteristics. It has four salient features, which can be summarised as four P's.

The first P stands for "PARTY." The Communist Party of China is the backbone of the nation.

For a big country with nearly 1.4 billion people on its way to development, there is no precedence or text book to follow. The only way forward is through trial and error.

Since modern times, China has gone through numerous trials and errors. From the peasant uprisings known as the Taiping Rebellion and Boxer Rebellion to the Westernisation Movement, from the Hundred Day's Reform to the Revolution of 1911, generations of Chinese sought unsuccessfully to free the country from devastation and dismemberment, and to save the people from destitution and displacement.

It is under the leadership of the Communist Party of China that the nations have achieved independence and grown prosperous and strong. The Communist Party of China is the choice of history and the choice of the Chinese people.

When the Soviet Union disintegrated in early 1990s, some people in the West reckoned, "the days for the Communist Party of China are numbered," and forecast the "end of history." Their predictions have been proven wrong and the reason lies in their lack of understanding about the Communist Party of China.

Indeed, the Party had stumbles, falls and even wrong turns along the way, but it has the courage to admit its mistakes, make corrections and continue to seek truth. It has kept renewing itself in order to stay abreast with the times. And it has maintained close links with the Chinese people. These qualities have enabled the Communist Party of China to lead the Chinese people in overcoming the difficulties and achieving one success after another.

The second P stands for "PROGRESS." Economic progress is the central task.

For China, the past 70 years have been an ongoing exploration of and experiment with socialism, in which we have sought ever deeper understanding of it and added new dimensions to it.

In 1978, China embarked on the great journey of reform and opening-up after a thorough review of both domestic experience and overseas practice in reform and development. The focus of the nation was shifted from class struggle to economic development.

In the past 40 years, China has kept emancipating and developing the productive forces, and achieved tremendous progress:

- China's GDP has reached 12 trillion US dollars.
- It has been growing at an average annual rate of 9.5%, which is much higher than the 2.9% concurrent rate of the world economy.
- Its share in the global GDP has increased from 2% forty years ago to 15.2% today.

China is now the world's second largest economy, largest manufacturer, biggest trader in goods, second biggest consumer of goods, No. 2 destination for foreign investment, and No. 1 in foreign exchange reserve for many years in a row.

Now let me come to the third P, which stands for "PEOPLE."

President Xi Jinping has given the best explanation of this point. He said, "The aspirations of the people to live a better life must always be the focus of our efforts." The people and their wellbeing have always been the ultimate goal of all our efforts to achieve development.

In the past 70 years, China had grown from a low-income country that could barely provide food and clothing to its people to a middle-income country enjoying moderate prosperity.

- 740 million people are lifted out of poverty.
- The middle-income population totaled more than 300 million.
- The world's largest social security system is established, covering old-age pension, health care, basic allowances and welfare housing.
- And the average life expectancy had gone up from 67.8 in 1981 to 76.7 in 2017.

The fourth P stands for "PEACE." Peaceful development is China's basic national policy.

China is committed to an independent foreign policy of peace and stays on the path of peaceful development. China needs a peaceful and tranquil international environment for its development, and its development in turn helps maintain world peace.

In recent years, China has been a partner in the international response to almost all regional and international hotspot issues. China has contributed its wisdom and proposed its solutions.

At the beginning of 2019, China overtook Japan to become the second largest contributor to the United Nations regular budget, increasing its contribution from 7.9% to 12%.

China is the second largest contributor to the UN peacekeeping budget and the largest contributor of peacekeeping personnel among the P5. A total of 37,000 Chinese military and police troops have served or are still serving in various UN missions.

In the Gulf of Aden and off the coast of Somalia, the Chinese Navy has carried out escort missions for ten consecutive years, ensuring the safe passage of more than 6,000 ships, including British merchant ships.

Ladies and Gentlemen,

Despite our enormous achievements, we are clearly aware that China is still a developing country, and the largest one in the world. We still face daunting tasks in our development.

First, China's development is inadequate and at a low level in per capita terms.

China's per capita GDP is only one seventh of that of the United States and one fourth of the UK, and ranks behind more than 60 other countries in the world. In human development index, China is just about managing to join the club of top 100.

At home, there are still 30 million Chinese living in poverty, more than 80 million people with disabilities, over 200 million pensioners in need of care, and about 15 million new workforces in need of a job every year.

Second, China's development is imbalanced, with huge disparities between different regions.

Let me give you a comparison between the eastern and western regions of China: the GDP of Guangdong Province in the eastern coastal region is the same as the GDP of Spain, the 14th largest economy in the world; but the western region, which covers 72% of China's land area and is home to 27% of China's population, only contributes 20% of the national economy and accounts for 7% of the country's foreign trade and investment.

I once served as Assistant Governor of Gansu, one of the poor provinces in China's western region. I have been to more than 60 of the over 80 counties in that Province, and I know from personal experience the daunting task of poverty alleviation that people in Gansu face. As we speak, Gansu is still working hard to ensure adequate food and clothing for its people.

Third, sustainability remains a tough issue in China's development.

- China's overall productivity remains low.
- The structure of productive forces needs rational adjustment.
- The shift away from capital-driven and resource-intensive growth model is yet to be completed.
- The capacity for scientific and technological innovation falls short.
- As a result, China's manufacturing and trade are large but not strong.
- Exports are more labour-intensive while imports are more value-added, and service trade is in huge deficit.
- In other areas, such as culture, defense, science, technology and modern social governance, upgrading is badly needed.

These are some of the difficulties and challenges we face.

As President Xi Jinping pointed out, going forward, the difficulties and risks facing China's development will become more and more severe, but without progress we will fall behind, so we must press on. Under the leadership of the Communist Party of China, we have the confidence and capability to overcome the difficulties and create a brighter future.

As China is going forward, what role is China going to play in the world? I would like to use four B's to answer this question.

First, China will be a "BOOSTER" for world economic growth.

The problems in China's development are growing pains, which will be addressed as China continues to develop.

One year ago, at the 19th National Congress of the Communist Party of China, three goals were set for China's development in the years to come, namely:

- Complete the building of a moderately prosperous society by 2020.
- Realise socialist modernisation by 2035.
- And build China into a great modern socialist country that is prosperous, strong, democratic, culturally advanced, harmonious and beautiful by the middle of this century.

To achieve these goals, China will continue to deepen reform and open up wider to the world. President Xi said in his New Year message, "China's reforms will never stop, and its doors will only open even wider." This means that China's development will continue to provide strong impetus for world economic growth.

In recent years, China has been contributing more than 30% to world economic growth. More and more Chinese are trading, investing, studying or holidaying abroad. As of 2017, there were more than 30,000 Chinese companies, about one million Chinese contract workers and 1.37 million Chinese students all over the world.

A recent demonstration of China's resolve to share its development benefits with the world is the first China International Import Expo held last November. This was the first-ever national-level Expo dedicated solely to import.

In the coming 15 years, China will strive to realise socialist modernisation. And in this process, China plans to import 24 trillion dollars of goods and open up a 2-trillion-dollar market for foreign direct investment. China is already the largest trading partner of more than 120 countries and regions. I believe that this figure will become bigger in the next 15 years.

Second, China will be a "BUILDER" of a community with a shared future for mankind.

China's success is attributable to a peaceful international environment. Going forward, China will still need a stable international environment to achieve greater success.

The world is undergoing profound changes unseen in a century:

- Unilateralism and protectionism are raging.
- Instabilities and uncertainties are rising.
- Regional hotspot issues keep cropping up.
- Non-traditional security threats such as terrorism, cyber risks, pandemics and

climate change continue to spread.

These are the common challenges to human society. No country could address these challenges alone. Nor could anyone hide behind closed doors or retreat into isolation.

Therefore, China calls on all countries in the world to join hands. Together, we can:

- Safeguard world peace and promote common development.
- Shape a new type of international relations featuring mutual respect, fairness, justice and win-win cooperation.
- And build a community with a shared future for mankind.

Third, China will be a "BACKER" of the existing international order.

The relationship between China and the world has seen historic changes as a result of China's vigorous integration with the existing international system. China has joined almost all the important intergovernmental organisations in the world and has signed more than 300 international conventions. It is playing an increasingly important role in the global governance system.

The world has come to an important crossroads. The existing international order is facing severe challenges. China has not lost its way. China will not falter. China is looking forward, not backward, by firmly advocating free trade and opposing protectionism. China is upholding the multilateral regime with the UN at its core. China is safeguarding the multilateral trade system based on the WTO.

Of course, the existing international order is not perfect. We know that all too well, and that's why we support reforms in the relevant international institutions and multilateral organisations. But we cannot agree with certain countries' cherry-picking international rules at will.

Fourth, China will promote "BRI" as an important platform for win-win cooperation between all countries.

BRI stands for the Belt and Road Initiative. For China, proposing BRI is a natural step as its economy enters a new stage. It helps address China's own problems of imbalanced and unsustainable development. It is also an important measure in China's new round of opening-up.

BRI follows the principles of extensive consultation, joint contribution and shared benefits. These principles are in line with China's foreign policy which advocates peaceful development and win-win cooperation. BRI is an important effort in building a community with a shared future for mankind.

In the past five years since it was proposed, BRI has been warmly received around the world. It is now the world's most popular public goods and largest platform for cooperation. More than 150 countries and international organisations have signed agreements with China on BRI cooperation.

In 2019, China will aim for higher goals in building BRI. We will do our best to make the second Belt and Road Forum for International Cooperation a success. We will also push for progress in a number of key projects. These will ensure higher quality and higher standards at a higher level in BRI development.

Ladies and Gentlemen,

I hope from the above four P's and four B's, you will see that the Chinese people are peace-loving people. China is a country that is committed to peaceful development. China wants to embrace the world and wishes to make friends with all countries. We hope that the world will respond in the same spirit.

I am pleased to see that there is a broad consensus in Britain that China's development is an opportunity for the UK. I am also pleased that here in Britain, China enjoys a higher favourability rating than in most other major Western countries.

To those who insist on calling China's development a threat, and even clamouring for a "new Cold War," I would say that they are going against the trend of the times. For such a mindset, there could be no better description than this western saying, which goes, "If all you have is a hammer, everything looks like a nail."

This reminds me of a famous saying by Dr. Sun Yat-sen, which goes, "The trend of the times moves on like a mighty river. It is our choice to go along and prosper, or go against it and perish." Now we are in the 21st century, faced with the profound changes in the world. Countries must go along with the historic trend by remaining open and inclusive, and engaging in win-win cooperation, seize the historic opportunities for reform, and achieve progress for all mankind.

Oxford and Cambridge, as world-renowned, prestigious institutions, have outstanding alumni all over the world. I sincerely hope that the Oxford and Cambridge

Club will play a positive role in helping the world understand China. I also hope that you will bring the people of our two countries along to seize the historic opportunities, work together to write a new chapter of the China-UK Golden Era and contribute to building a community with a shared future for mankind.

Thank you!

Now, I will open the floor for questions.

第四章

中国外交

随着中国日益走近世界舞台中央，各国更加关注中国的外交。有善意的，有恶意的，有敌意的。有的认为中国外交“更加咄咄逼人”，有的给中国外交贴上各种标签：“战狼外交”“胁迫外交”“霸凌外交”，不一而足。针对不实之词，我利用各种讲坛阐述中国的外交政策。在西方著名智库伦敦国际战略问题研究所，我从中国外交的目标、任务和行动，阐述中国致力于建立的“三个世界”，一是和平发展的世界，二是开放合作的世界，三是多彩和谐的世界。

在美国名校塔夫茨大学弗莱彻法律与外交学院，我讲述“中国梦”是和平与发展之梦、合作与共赢之梦。指出“中国梦”与“美国梦”不仅并不冲突，而且能够交相辉映。习近平主席提出中美发展以“不冲突、不对抗、相互尊重、合作共赢”为特征的“新型大国关系”，不仅为中美关系发展指明了方向，也是中国外交的一大创举。

新时期的中国外交*

尊敬的奇普曼所长，

女士们、先生们：

很高兴应奇普曼博士邀请来到伦敦国际战略问题研究所（IISS）。国际战略问题研究所是世界政治和安全领域知名研究机构。你们出版的《军事力量对比》和《战略研究》是许多国际问题学者的必读刊物。记得我在以前的演讲中就曾引用2011年《军事力量对比》中关于中国军费开支的相关内容，那份年度报告清楚地表明中国的军费在世界各国中处于较低水平，2010年仅占GDP的1.3%，不仅远低于美国、英国、俄罗斯等传统军事强国，也低于印度、巴西等新兴国家。如果从人均军费角度看，中国则更低，仅有美国的1/38，英国的1/20。由于这些内容非常具有说服力，所以我一直记忆犹新。

我今天演讲的主题是“新时期的中国外交”。为什么说是“新时期”，我想主要有三个因素。

第一，众所周知，从2012年底到2013年初，中国刚刚进行了党和国家领导人的换届。随着中国新一代领导人的执政，中国外交在继承和延续的基础上，必然会创新和发展。

第二，今天的中国与五年前、十年前都不可同日而语。中国现在已是世界第二大经济体，中国的对外贸易量基本与美国持平，中国具有世界上最多的外汇储备。我最近看到的一个消息是，2012年中国超过美国成为世界第一

* 在伦敦国际战略问题研究所的主旨演讲。2013年4月17日，伦敦国际战略问题研究所。

大国际旅游消费国，中国海外旅游的游客人数达到了 8 300 万，境外消费达 1 020 亿美元。

第三，今天的世界格局正经历前所未有的变化。全球几十亿人口和大批发展中国家正加速迈向现代化；新兴市场国家和低收入国家第一次占全球 GDP 权重的一半以上；全球增长重心发生转移，发展中国家对全球经济增长的贡献率已超过 50%。同时，各国相互联系、依存程度空前加深，人类越来越成为命运共同体。

新时期的中国外交是什么？回答这个问题，我认为要把握两条主线：一是中国外交的目标；二是中国外交的行动。

中国外交追求的目标，也就是说中国希望建立一个什么样的世界，什么样的世界最符合中国的利益、有利于中国的发展，我的回答是："三个世界"。

第一是和平发展的世界。过去 30 多年是中国发展最快的时期，这得益于中国自身的改革开放，也得益于世界总体保持了和平稳定。但是今天的世界并不安宁，各种全球性威胁和挑战层出不穷，局部动荡和热点问题复杂难解。国际恐怖势力、民族分裂势力、宗教极端势力在一些地区仍很猖獗。前天在美国波士顿发生的爆炸事件再次证明了这一点。没有天下太平，中国和世界都不可能顺利发展。中国古语说："覆巢之下，岂有完卵。"中国要实现国家富强、民族复兴、人民幸福的"中国梦"，就必须致力于营造一个持久和平稳定的外部环境，就必须努力推动和平与发展始终成为世界的主题，就必须促进世界各国与中国一起走和平发展的道路。

第二是开放合作的世界。过去几十年，中国积极参与全球化进程并从中受益。全球化的特点就是开放与合作，中国紧跟这一时代潮流，将自己的命运和世界的命运紧密结合在一起，实现了开放的发展、合作的发展。今天的中国是世界数十个主要贸易国家的第一大贸易伙伴。当前，国际金融危机影响深远，世界经济增长不稳定、不确定因素增多，保护主义有所抬头，在这样的情况下，中国更加主张和支持一个开放、自由、便利的多边贸易体系，一个前进而不是倒退的全球化进程。就在两天前，中国与冰岛签署了自由贸易协定，这是中国与欧洲国家完成的首个双边自贸协定，是中国倡导中欧互利合作及贸易投资自由化的具体落实，对促进世界自由贸易的发展也具有积极意义。

第三是多彩和谐的世界。今天的世界，既有南与北，也有东与西。不少人曾引用英国诗人吉卜林的《东西方民谣》中的第一句话“东是东，西是西，两者永不相期”，来强调东西方之间的对立与隔阂。殊不知，吉卜林所指的隔阂仅仅是地理意义上的，而这首诗的下面几句才是作者的本意：“但当两位巨人相对而立，无所谓东也无所谓西，也别在意那种族与血裔，尽管他们来自世界的两极。”中国主张世界文明应保持多样性，只有保留各国各民族的特色，世界才是丰富多彩的。中国也认为天下没有放之四海皆准的模式，各国应当选择适合自己国情的发展道路。正如习近平主席指出的，“鞋子合不合脚，自己穿了才知道”。

这“三个世界”也可以说就是中国的“世界梦”。中国如何去实现这个“世界梦”？也就是中国外交将做什么？我认为主要是三个方面。

第一个方面是贯彻互利共赢精神，全面发展与世界各国的友好合作关系。

布热津斯基写过一本书《大棋局》，将欧亚大陆视作美国外交的地缘战略大棋盘。中国外交的这盘棋则超出了欧亚大陆，要宽广得多。

我们将改善和发展同发达国家之间的关系，拓宽合作领域，妥善处理分歧，不走大国争霸、对抗的历史老路，而是建立开放、包容、互信的“新型大国关系”。最近习近平主席和奥巴马总统通话，两国领导人就中美构建新型大国关系达成重要共识。中欧建有全面战略伙伴关系，双方互为最大贸易伙伴。中国一贯坚定地支持欧洲应对债务危机的努力，也正在与欧方商谈中欧中长期合作的机制建设，双方在城镇化、新能源、科技创新和绿色发展等领域的合作正在积极推进。

中国将坚持与邻为善、以邻为伴的周边政策，巩固睦邻友好，深化互利合作，努力使自身发展更好地惠及周边国家。现在，中国同周边国家的贸易额达 1.3 万亿美元，超过中欧、中美贸易之和。中国将积极参与亚洲区域合作进程，坚定支持亚洲地区对其他地区的开放合作，欢迎域外国家为本地区稳定和发展发挥建设性作用。不可否认，当前中国与一些邻国存在领土争议，在这个问题上，中国不会放弃自身的正当权益，不会牺牲国家核心利益，但中国始终致力于和平协商谈判，妥善处理和解决争议，努力维护地区和平与稳定。中国也高度关注近来出现的周边不稳定因素，中国不会允许任何人在中国家门口生事，也不能允许任何国家把亚洲搞乱。

中国将加强同广大发展中国家的团结合作，永远做发展中国家的可靠朋友和真诚伙伴。习近平主席最近访问非洲时，表示中国将加大与非洲国家发展“真、实、亲、诚”的关系，深化中非友谊与合作。为此，未来 3 年内，中国将向非洲提供 200 亿美元贷款，为非洲国家培训 3 万名各类人才，提供 1.8 万个奖学金留学生名额。

中国将加强与金砖国家等新兴经济体的携手合作、共同发展，使金砖国家经济增长更加强劲，合作架构更加完善，合作成果更加丰富。中国将积极推进金砖国家新开发银行、外汇储备库等项目，加快各领域务实合作，把政治共识转化为具体行动。

第二个方面是积极参与多边事务，努力为新时期国际体系建设和全球治理做出贡献。中国认为面对国际形势深刻变化和世界各国同舟共济的客观要求，21 世纪的国际多边体系应与时俱进，朝着公正合理的方向有序发展，应当扩大代表性，提升公正性，增强实效性。

中国作为国际体系的参与者、建设者、贡献者，将坚持把中国人民利益同各国人民共同利益结合起来，以更加积极的姿态参与国际政治、安全和发展事务，发挥负责任大国作用，同各国一道共同应对全球性挑战。

中国将继续支持联合国、二十国集团、上海合作组织、金砖国家机制等发挥积极作用，将继续主张完善国际货币体系、加强各国宏观经济政策协调、强化国际金融监管、增加发展中国家在国际金融机构中的发言权和代表性。中国将在国际和地区热点问题上继续发挥建设性作用，推动问题的解决。

中国将努力维护朝鲜半岛和平稳定，促进通过对话谈判解决伊朗核问题，推动叙利亚问题政治解决进程。中国将继续积极参与国际裁军与军控、核不扩散、反恐、打击海盗等领域的国际安全对话与合作。

第三个方面是大力开展公共外交和人文交流，促进中国与世界的相互了解。今天，在不少西方国家，对中国的负面消息传播得多，正面信息报道得少。这其中很大一个原因是西方传媒的报道倾向，其认为媒体就是要专报坏消息。这使我想起英语有句谚语：“好消息不出门，坏消息到处传。”也许西方媒体认为坏消息更能吸引读者，更有利于报纸的销量，但结果是西方读者看不到一个全面的中国，西方民众了解不到一个真正的中国。

今天，中国外交的一项重要任务就是要让世界听到中国的声音，听到中国的好消息，就是要向世界各国的民众全面、客观地介绍中国，大力推进中国与世界各国的人文交流，使各国民众了解中国的历史变革、文化传统和制度特色；了解中国发展全貌、进步轨迹和前进方向；了解中国的经济、政治、社会和外交政策；了解中国的民情、民意和民生。只有这样，世界才会少一些对中国的误解，多一些对中国的理解；少一些“中国威胁论”的论调，多一些“中国机遇论”的声音。

我今天与大家交流，也可以说是一次公共外交和人文交流，让大家更加深入地了解中国外交。

今天上午，我作为中国政府代表出席了英国前首相撒切尔夫人的葬礼。关于撒切尔夫人的评价很多，英国公众和媒体看法也不尽一致。我们充分肯定她为中英关系的发展，特别是为香港地区问题的解决所做的历史性贡献。我读到《金融时报》的一篇文章，称撒切尔夫人的重要外交遗产就是坚定的原则和信念及必要的灵活性。这是不是对撒切尔夫人外交的准确评价人们还可以讨论，但我认为外交的确要兼顾原则性与灵活性。纵观 60 多年新中国的外交，一大特点就是坚持原则，秉承理念，同时强调原则性与灵活性的结合。在新的时期，中国外交有目标、有行动，我们既要保持连续性，又要不断创新。我相信，中国外交将更有作为。

谢谢。

下面我愿回答大家的提问。

China's Diplomacy in the New Era*

Director General Dr. John Chipman,

Ladies and Gentlemen,

It is a real pleasure and privilege for me to speak at the International Institute for Strategic Studies (IISS). I want to thank Dr. Chipman for his kind invitation.

Being a world-leading institute in strategic studies, IISS's research and analysis on global security, world politics and military conflict is held in high regard worldwide. The publications *The Military Balance and Strategic Review* are on the must-read list of many scholars in international affairs.

Take *Military Balance 2011* for example, which I quoted many times in my speeches.

Military Balance 2011 showed clearly China's defense spending was low compared with other major countries.

In 2010 Chinese defense spending made up only 1.3% of China's GDP. This figure was much less than that of traditional military powers like the US, UK and Russia. In addition, the data showed that Chinese defense spending was comparatively lower than emerging economies like India and Brazil.

Military Balance 2011 also revealed that on per capita terms China's military spending was even lower. It accounted for merely one thirty eighth of the US and one twentieth of Britain. I am deeply impressed by *Military Balance 2011* as these figures are so striking and convincing.

Now back to the theme of my speech today. That is "China's Diplomacy in the New

* Speech at the International Institute for Strategic Studies. IISS, 17 April 2013.

Era."

There are three reasons why I stress the "new era."

First, there has been a major leadership change in China in recent months.

As these new leaders take office we can expect them to maintain overall consistency with China's foreign policies. However, inevitably there will be some new features in China's diplomacy.

Second, today's China is very different from the China of ten years ago, or even five years ago.

China is now the second largest economy of the world. China's foreign trade volume is basically on a par with the United States. China has the world's largest foreign exchange reserve. Last year China had overtaken the United States and became the largest international tourism consumer. The number of outbound Chinese tourists reached 83 million. They spent 102 billion US dollars.

Third, the world today is undergoing unprecedented changes.

Billions of people and a large number of developing countries are marching towards modernisation. For the first time emerging market economies and low income countries make up over half of global GDP.

These trends show global growth gravity is shifting.

Developing countries contribute more than 50% to global economic growth. At the same time interdependence among countries are deepened as never before. Interests of all peoples are increasingly intertwined.

So, what do all these global changes mean for Chinese diplomacy? To understand China's diplomacy in the new era, I believe we need to grasp the goals and actions of China's diplomacy.

The goals of China's diplomacy explain what kind of world China wants to build. This raises the question of what kind of world best serves the interests and development of China. My answer is China needs three kinds of world.

First, it should be a world of peace and development.

The past three decades saw the unprecedented growth of China. This directly evolved from China's reform and opening-up policies.

It is also well worth stressing that this growth of China is equally attributable to the overall peace and stability in the world.

However, today's world is far from being tranquil:

- Global threats and challenges of various kinds crop up one after another.
- Local turbulence and hotspot issues remain intractable.
- International terrorists, ethnic separatists and religious extremists are still rampant in some regions. The Boston bombings two days ago are just a case in point.

Without peace, neither China nor the world can achieve its development goals.

As an ancient Chinese saying goes:

"When a bird's nest is overturned, no egg can survive."

China wants to realise its dream of economic growth, national revival and the contented life for its people.

However, to realise this dream China has to do the following:

- China must strive to create an external environment of lasting peace and stability.
- China must work hard to make sure that peace and development will prevail in the world.
- China must also work to get other countries on board for a path of peaceful development.

The second kind of the world China needs is a world of openness and cooperation.

In the past decades, China has taken an active part in globalisation and benefited a great deal from it.

A striking feature of globalisation is openness and cooperation.

China has followed this trend and fully integrated itself into the world. The result is that China has achieved development through openness and cooperation. Today's China is the largest trading partner of dozens of major trading countries.

If we take a look at the world economic landscape, we will see that the international financial crisis has wreaked great damage.

Uncertainties and destabilising factors in global economic growth are on the rise.

It is, and should be, of very deep concern that the spectre of protectionism is looming.

In such circumstances China even more strongly advocates and supports a multilateral trading regime. There is compelling evidence of the mutual global benefits of a trading system that is open, free and facilitating. It is critical that globalisation advances and does not retreat.

Two days ago China and Iceland signed a free trade agreement. This is the first bilateral free trade agreement China has concluded with a European country. It is one of the concrete actions that China has taken to promote China-Europe win-win cooperation. The aim is to advance trade and investment liberalisation. I believe it will play a positive role in promoting free trade in the world.

The third kind of the world we need is a world of diversity and harmony.

Today's world is moving towards multi-polarity. This means we feel the presence of not only the East and the West, but also the South and the North.

Many have quoted from *The Ballad of East and West* by British poet Rudyard Kipling to accentuate the estrangement and confrontation between the East and the West.

This is the most famous line from the poem:

"East is East, and West is West, and never the twain shall meet."

But, this is only the first stanza of the poem.

The division it talks about is limited to geography. Many have failed to get the real import of this poem expressed in the lines that follow:

"But there is neither East nor West, Border, nor Breed, nor Birth, When two strong men stand face to face, though they come from the ends of the earth!"

China believes that there should be diversity in world civilisation.

The world is rich and diverse only when nations and peoples maintain their distinct characteristics.

Along this line of thinking China also believes that there is not a one-size-fits-all model.

Countries should be allowed to choose their development paths based on their own national conditions. As Chinese President Xi Jinping has recently pointed out:

"Only the wearer knows whether the shoes fit."

What I have described above is China's dream about the world.

Then how will China make this dream come true? That leads to the question what China's diplomacy will do. I believe China's diplomatic actions will concentrate on three areas.

First, we will carry out the spirit of mutual benefit and pursue friendship and cooperation with all other countries in the world.

In his book *The Grand Chessboard*, Zbigniew Brzezinski describes the Eurasia continent as the geopolitical chessboard or focal point for American diplomacy.

China thinks much more broadly. The Chinese diplomatic chessboard reaches far beyond the Eurasia continent.

China will improve and develop relations with developed countries. We will broaden cooperation areas and properly manage differences.

More importantly, China will not repeat the history of the current established powers that confronted each other and fought for ascendancy.

Rather China will build a new type of relations between big countries that feature openness, inclusiveness and mutual trust. In their recent telephone conversation, President Xi Jinping and President Obama have reached important agreement on this new type of relations between China and the United States.

China and the EU have established a comprehensive strategic relationship. This is very significant as we are each other's largest trading partner.

China firmly supports the EU efforts to tackle debt crisis. We are now discussing with the EU about institutional building for China-EU mid- and long-term cooperation. At the same time, we will redouble efforts to advance cooperation in urbanisation, new energy, scientific innovation and green development.

China will stick to the policy of developing friendly and good-neighbourly relations with its surrounding countries.

Following this policy, China will strengthen friendship with its neighbours. Also, China will deepen mutually beneficial cooperation so that China's development will bring greater benefits to countries in our neighbourhood.

China's trade with its neighbours now stands at 1.3 trillion US dollars. This is more than the combined volume of China-EU and China-US trade.

China will take an active part in Asian regional cooperation. We also firmly support an open Asia that cooperates with other regions.

We welcome countries out of the region to play a constructive role in Asian stability and development.

Of course, there is no denying that China has territorial disputes with some neighbouring countries. On these territorial disputes there are clear principles:

- China will not compromise its legitimate rights and interests.
- Nor will China sacrifice its core national interests.
- But China is always committed to handling and resolving disputes through peaceful consultation and negotiation.
- China will always be a force for regional peace and stability.
- We are keeping a close eye on the recent destabilising factors in our neighbouring area.
- China will not allow anyone to make trouble on its doorstep.
- Nor will we allow any country to disturb Asia.

Turning to relations with other developing countries.

China will consolidate its solidarity with developing countries. We will always be a reliable friend and sincere partner of developing countries.

President Xi Jinping recently visited Africa. There he stated that in deepening friendship and cooperation with Africa, China would stress "sincerity, real results, affinity and good faith."

In this spirit, in the coming three years China will provide Africa with strong support. This includes:

- Provide 20 billion US dollars of loans.
- Train 30 thousand personnel of various specialties for African countries.
- And offer 18 thousand scholarships for African students.

China will step up cooperation with emerging economies like the BRICS countries to achieve common development.

Our objective is to boost economic growth of BRICS countries, improve the cooperation mechanism and make our collaboration more fruitful.

China will push forward the initiatives of the New Development Bank and Contingent Reserve Arrangement. China will work to speed up practical cooperation in a wide range of areas so that political consensus can be translated into actions.

The second area of China's diplomatic action is in multilateral diplomacy.

- China will actively participate in multilateral affairs.
- China will contribute to the building of international system and global governance in the new era.

Profound changes have taken place in the international situation. The result is that all countries need to work together as passengers in the same boat.

China believes that the multilateral system in the 21st century should keep pace with the times and be more just and reasonable. To this end, it needs to be more representative, fairer and more effective.

China is a player, builder and contributor of the international system. We will always bear in mind the interests of both the Chinese people and peoples around the world.

To be specific:

- China will take a more active part in international political, security and development affairs.
- China will play the role of a responsible big country.
- China will join hands with other countries to address global challenges.
- China will continue to support the United Nations, G20, Shanghai Cooperation Organisation and BRICS. It will encourage each to play their positive role.
- We believe that efforts should be made to improve the international monetary system. That means to strengthen coordination on macro economic policies; toughen international financial regulation; and increase developing countries' representation and say in international financial institutions.
- China will continue to play a constructive role on international and regional hotspot issues.
- China will help to resolve the issues or ease the tension.
- China will work to maintain peace and stability on the Korean Peninsula.
- China will promote the settlement of the Iranian nuclear issue through dialogue and negotiation.

- China will help move forward the political process of resolving the Syrian issue.
- China will continue to actively participate in international security dialogue. That means cooperation in disarmament and arms control; nuclear non-proliferation; counter terrorism and combating maritime piracy.

Turning to the third area of China's diplomatic action.

China will redouble its efforts in public diplomacy and people-to-people exchanges.

This will increase mutual understanding between China and the rest of the world.

It must be pointed out that in many Western countries the public are exposed to much more bad news about China than good news. One of the reasons is that Western media tend to be negative. This reminds me of an English saying: "Good news never goes beyond the gate, while bad news spread far and wide."

Maybe it is because Western media believe that bad news is more eye-catching and increases readership. But the result is the public in Western countries has denied a full and true picture of China.

Therefore an important task of China's diplomacy is to make China's voice heard and let the world know good news about China.

This means China must be much more effective in telling the real story about China.

This means that China must energetically promote people-to-people exchanges between China and the rest of the world. Through such efforts:

- People in other countries would know about China's history, culture, tradition and its current unique system.
- They would appreciate the long journey China has traveled, how it has traveled and where it is headed in the future.
- They would understand China's economic, political, social and foreign policies.
- They would get an idea of Chinese people's feelings, thoughts and daily lives.

If we can do this, there will be more understanding, less miscomprehension about China. There will be more people seeing China as an opportunity rather than a threat.

My speech today can be regarded as a part of these efforts. I do hope it will help you with a better understanding of China's diplomacy.

This morning I attended Baroness Thatcher's funeral as representative of the Chinese government. I know there are diverse opinions about her in British public and media.

However, we in China fully acknowledge her historic contribution to the development of China-UK relations, in particular the resolution of the Hong Kong issue.

I read an article in *Financial Times* suggesting that a major diplomatic legacy of Baroness Thatcher was "firm principle, faith and necessary flexibility."

People may debate whether this is an accurate summary of Thatcherite diplomacy. But I do feel that diplomacy needs to allow both principle and flexibility.

A review of China's diplomacy since the founding of the People's Republic shows some striking features. This is that Chinese diplomacy is upholding principles and pursuing ideals.

At the same time we stress combination of principle and flexibility.

In this new era, China's diplomacy has identified its goals and set out its actions.

We will maintain consistency and make innovations.

For these reasons, I am convinced that China's diplomacy will achieve, advance and continue to contribute.

In this way China will help make the world a better place for us all to live in.

Thank you.

Now, I would like to take your questions.

使命与梦想*

尊敬的斯塔夫里迪斯院长，

弗莱彻学院的师生们，

女士们、先生们：

能够回到阔别30多年的美国母校——弗莱彻法律与外交学院，是人生一大乐事。

能够学以致用，一生从事自己热爱的外交事业，更是人生一大幸事。

从我1974年加入中国外交队伍到今天已经整整40年。这40年里，我曾在非洲、美洲、亚洲、欧洲四大洲六次常驻；这40年里，我一半多时间曾从事促进中美关系的工作。

当我收到斯塔夫里迪斯院长的来信，得知学院决定授予我母校最高荣誉——“弗莱彻1947届纪念奖”并请我在开学典礼上发表主旨演讲时，我既感到非常荣幸，同时也在思考应该如何总结这40年来的外交经历，把自己的感悟更好地讲述给母校师生。

盘点下来，我这40年来一直在奋斗的，同时也是众多中国外交官共同辛勤耕耘的，就是谋和平、促发展、推合作、求共赢，这是中国外交一以贯之的追求，也是实现“中国梦”的必然要求。而这些与弗莱彻学院“培养致力于维护国际社会稳定与繁荣的学生”的理念，以及“弗莱彻1947届纪念

---

* 在美国塔夫茨大学弗莱彻法律与外交学院授奖仪式暨2014学年开学典礼上的主旨演讲。2014年9月5日，美国马萨诸塞州梅德福市。

奖”的宗旨存在相当程度的契合。

我在弗莱彻学习虽然只有一年，但所学所获受益良多。当年我的老师中，亨里克森教授和福尔茨格拉夫教授目前仍然在校执教，用他们的学识培养一批又一批年轻外交官，我谨在此向他们致以由衷的敬意。

在我的外交生涯中，我曾许多次与弗莱彻校友有交集。我们或是谈判桌上的对手，或是外交使团中的朋友。共同的经历既使我们彼此容易沟通，但有时也不得不较量争锋。

1995 年，我作为中国外交部北美大洋洲司副司长，陪同中国副外长李肇星在纽约与美国副国务卿塔尔诺夫举行中美副外长级磋商，讨论的主题是关于中国国家主席江泽民对美国进行国事访问。

当时，中美关系刚刚经历曲折逐步恢复，中国国家主席已有 10 年未对美国进行过国事访问，但是美方认为国事访问“时机不成熟”，只同意安排正式工作访问。

双方各持已见，争执不下。这时美方代表团二号人物，助理国务卿洛德要求发言。他是弗莱彻 1960 届校友，也是“弗莱彻 1947 届纪念奖”得主，还担任过驻华大使。洛德列举了五条理由，说明为什么正式工作访问是“最佳选择”。

李副外长随即给我写了一张纸条，说“你的老校友发言了，你是否也说几句？”我接受了这个挑战，列了七条理由，说明为什么国事访问是“唯一选项”。

洛德还要发言，但被塔尔诺夫副国务卿叫停。他对李副外长说：“我们的副手都毕业于弗莱彻学院，弗莱彻以培养辩论家著称，如果让他们你来我往下去，不知什么时候才是个头？”

这场弗莱彻人对阵弗莱彻人、1960 届对阵 1983 届的辩论虽然未能促成中美副外长磋商达成协议，但对双方增进对彼此立场的了解是有益的。两年后，江泽民主席对美国进行了成功的国事访问，我也有幸参加了代表团。

当然，我与弗莱彻校友的交往不总是那么激烈。

2001 年 9 月，我在埃及向穆巴拉克总统递交国书。同我一道递交国书的就有美国驻埃及大使、弗莱彻1977届校友戴维·威尔士。在共同出使埃及的岁月里，我们经常就各种议题交换意见。

2006年我出使朝鲜，原以为这次与弗莱彻越走越远，没想到却越走越近。首先来了一位弗莱彻1971届校友、新墨西哥州州长比尔·理查德森。他当时率领美国民主、共和两党代表团访朝，一到朝鲜就提出要见我。理查德森先生在欢迎他的招待会上致辞的第一句便是："刘大使和我毕业于同一个学校——弗莱彻法律与外交学院。"

接下来便是我们的老院长博斯沃斯被奥巴马总统任命为美国朝鲜问题特别代表。我们多次就朝鲜问题深入交谈，共同努力推动朝核问题六方会谈进程。

我举这些例子不是想说明弗莱彻的经历教会了我辩论，增加了人脉；而是想说明在弗莱彻学到的东西使我获益匪浅，受用至今；也想说明弗莱彻的毕业生虽然来自不同的国家，"各为其主"，但都在为实现弗莱彻的理念和人类的理想而共同努力。

最近，有人问我40年的外交经历中体会最深的是什么。我说："外交不是个人行为，而是国家行为；外交的成功、外交官的成功，离不开祖国的繁荣与强大。"我作为现任中国驻英国大使，对此感受更加深刻。

中国驻英国使馆的前身是清朝驻英国公使馆，建于1877年，是中国第一个驻外机构，但其创建的历史并不十分光彩。1875年，一支英国远征队从缅甸进入中国云南，随团的翻译马嘉里在和当地居民的冲突中丧生。英国随后强加给清政府不平等的《烟台条约》，除了赔款、增开通商口岸之外，还要求清政府派钦差大臣向维多利亚女王当面道歉。于是我的第一位前任郭嵩焘1877年作为使臣赴英道歉，为冲淡他专程道歉的色彩，清廷决定郭嵩焘道歉后留英作为常驻使节。结果，中国第一位驻外使节的使命是道歉；中国首任常驻外交使节向外国元首递交的第一封信函不是国书，而是道歉信。

2014年是"一战"爆发百年，这使我想起我的另一位前任——中国近代史上杰出的外交家顾维钧，他也曾任民国政府驻英公使和大使，并作为中国代表出席巴黎和会。中国是"一战"的战胜国之一，但中国的主权和利益却在会上被列强私相授受。尽管顾维钧据理力争，无奈国力不济，他能做的仅仅是拒绝在《巴黎和约》上签字，而改变不了丧权辱国的事实。

这些历史让中国人深刻认识到了“弱国无外交”。在中国近代史上相当长的时间里，这对中国人、对中国外交官来说都是撕心裂肺的伤痛。因此，中国把国家主权和领土完整看得比什么都重要，中国对外关系始终将相互尊重国家主权和领土完整视为外交的根本原则和信条。

今天，中国人民站起来了，我们正在朝着实现国家富强、民族振兴、人民幸福，实现中华民族伟大复兴这一“中国梦”而迈进。

我们为实现“中国梦”提出了“两个一百年”的目标，到中国共产党建党100年时建成惠及十几亿人口的更高水平的小康社会，到中华人民共和国成立100年时建成富强民主文明和谐的社会主义现代化国家。习近平主席提出，要让“生活在我们伟大祖国和伟大时代的中国人民，共同享有人生出彩的机会，共同享有梦想成真的机会，共同享有同祖国和时代一起成长与进步的机会”。

有人担心“中国梦”所指向的“中华民族伟大复兴”是中国要复仇雪耻，谋求地区甚至全球霸权地位，这完全是一种旧思维，根本不了解中国。“中国梦”的天生属性是和平发展、合作共赢。

“中国梦”是和平与发展之梦。这是基于中国自身历史国情和对当今时代主题判断做出的战略选择。

从文化基因上看，中华民族是爱好和平的民族，是联合国安理会五常国中唯一没有对外殖民历史，唯一没有海外军事基地和驻军，唯一承诺不首先使用核武器和不对无核武器国家和无核武器地区使用核武器的国家。

从现实条件上看，在中国这样一个人口占世界1/5的大国搞建设，进而实现中华民族伟大复兴，让人民过上美好富足的生活，扩张和侵略的道路注定难以长久。我们只能靠和平条件下聚精会神搞建设，一心一意谋发展。

从历史经验上看，中华文明从亘古走来，“其兴也勃焉，其亡也忽焉”的轮回，使我们深知霸道不是王道，霸者注定衰落。作为殖民侵略和战争的受害者，我们深谙“己所不欲，勿施于人”的古训。过去30多年中国的发展成就，更让中国人对通过和平发展实现国家富强、民族复兴树立了信心。

“中国梦”是合作与共赢之梦。孔子2 500年前提出的“己欲立而立人，己欲达而达人”的理念已经融进我们的民族血脉，也是我们实现“中国梦”的处世之道。“中国梦”不是为了战胜谁、超越谁或取代谁，而是为了造福中国人民，推动世界共同发展。

因此，中国始终注重以合作促发展，以合作化争端，不断寻找合作机会，不断扩大合作领域，不断拓展共同利益。中国人民在实现自身梦想的进程中，与世界的合作之路会越走越宽，在实现自身发展的同时，也为世界和平与发展事业做出重要贡献。

国际货币基金组织数据显示，国际金融危机爆发以来，中国贡献了近1/4的全球经济增长量。今后5年，中国进口商品将达到10万亿美元，对外投资规模将超过5 000亿美元，这将为世界其他国家带来重大发展机遇。

中国对世界的贡献不仅体现在经济数字上，还反映在人们普遍关注的环保等领域。中国是世界最大的清洁能源投资者。中国的太阳能产量已达世界第一，中国出口的太阳能产品已占世界贸易额50%以上。

英国首相卡梅伦曾说，中国的崛起是我们这个时代最具决定性意义的事件之一，中国的发展对英国和世界都是难得的机遇。

我们也深知通往光明未来的旅程从来都不是一帆风顺的，注定会充满各种艰险和挑战。比如，今天不少人都在谈论新兴大国与守成大国之间的“修昔底德陷阱”。

但在我们回顾100年前爆发的第一次世界大战和近70年前结束的第二次世界大战的浩劫之际，在我们忆及“弗莱彻1947届纪念奖”的创立者们珍视和平的初衷之际，我们应当坚信和平与发展是时代潮流，人类具有避免重蹈历史覆辙的能力，外交努力能使各国找到相处之道；我们应当相信，“中国梦”与“美国梦”不仅并不冲突，而且能够交相辉映。

为此，习近平主席提出中美发展以“不冲突、不对抗、相互尊重、合作共赢”为特征的“新型大国关系”。这作为外交上的一大创新，需要中美双方共同相向而行，体现智慧、勇气、信心和艺术，让广阔的太平洋成为中美的纽带，成为真正的“太平之洋”。

在我结束演讲之前，我愿引用我们学校所在的这个州的杰出人物之一——肯尼迪总统的一段话："和平不存在于条款之中，而是在人们心中。与其把希望全部寄托在羊皮和纸面上，不如行动起来建设和平，让对和平的渴望和期待深入所有人的心中。我相信我们可以做到，我相信人类完全可以掌控自己的命运。"

我希望在座的未来外交官们有勇气拒绝任何历史的宿命论，有智慧掌握和塑造人类的命运，努力在各自岗位上构建和平、推动发展、拓展合作、成就共赢，将弗莱彻的精神发扬光大，共同谱写我们共同命运的美好篇章，让我们的世界更加美好安宁。当我们的后人在回顾21世纪的历史时，我希望他们能够这样评价你们："你们为我们树立了楷模！"

对于外交官来说，这或许是最崇高的使命与梦想。

谢谢。

The Noble Mission and Dreams*

Dean Stavridis,

Faculty and Students of Fletcher,

Ladies and Gentlemen,

It's a great pleasure to come back to Fletcher, my Alma Mater in the States after over 30 years.

Better still, it has been a great blessing to apply what I learnt here at Fletcher to my life's work in diplomacy.

A full 40 years have passed since I joined the Chinese foreign service in 1974. I have since served overseas six times on four continents, in Africa, North America, Asia and Europe. More than half of those years have been dedicated to China-US relations.

So, I had two things in mind when I heard from Dean Stavridis, about the decision to accord to me the most prestigious honour of the Fletcher Class of 1947 Memorial Award and the invitation to deliver the keynote address at this Convocation.

The first was of course immense appreciation for the great honour.

The second was a theme for this address. With all these years behind me, how to best present my take on diplomacy to such an informed audience at this Convocation today?

After some thought it became clear to me that a mere account of "been there, done that" would not do the job.

Instead, I have decided to focus on my four missions as a career diplomat, namely:

---

* Convocation Address at the Fletcher School of Law and Diplomacy. Medford, Massachusetts, 5 September 2014.

peace, development, cooperation, and win-win.

These are my lifetime pursuit and the pursuit of my fellow Chinese diplomats. These are also consistent commitments of China's foreign policy. In addition, they are the inherent elements of the "Chinese Dream" which I will come to later.

Moreover, I believe, those four missions match the founding purposes of the Memorial Award, and are in line with the Fletcher commitment, that is,

"To offer a broad professional education in international relations to students committed to maintaining the stability and prosperity of a complex, challenging and increasingly global society."

I studied only one year at Fletcher, but that was such a rewarding experience. I was fortunate to have such inspiring teachers as Professor Alan K. Henrikson and Professor Robert L. Pfaltzgraff Jr. I owe them a deep debt of gratitude. I am delighted they continue to guide and influence new generations of diplomats.

Over the decades, I have crossed paths with Fletcher alumni on many occasions, either across the negotiation table or side by side in the diplomatic corps.

I have found that our shared Fletcher heritage makes it easier to communicate most of the times! There are occasions when it gets intense.

In 1995 I was the Deputy Director General for North American and Oceanian Affairs in the Chinese Foreign Ministry. In that role I travelled to New York with Vice Foreign Minister Li Zhaoxing for political consultations with US Under Secretary of State Peter Tarnoff. The topic of the day was a proposed state visit to the US by Chinese President Jiang Zemin.

China-US relations at the time were just recovering from a rough patch. Also, it had been 10 years since the previous state visit by a Chinese President to the US. But, at the meeting, our American colleagues were of the opinion that "it was not time yet" for a state visit. Instead, they suggested an official working visit.

The discussion was going nowhere. Then the number two in the American delegation volunteered to speak. This was Assistant Secretary Winston Lord. As you may know he is a F60 and a Fletcher class of 1947 Memorial Award recipient. Also, he once served as the American Ambassador in Beijing.

Winston Lord began to speak and offered five reasons why an official working visit served both sides best.

Vice Minister Li passed me a slip, on which he wrote:

"Your fellow alumnus has spoken. What say you?"

I took up the challenge and listed seven reasons why a state visit was the only viable option.

Just as Winston Lord was about to dive into his rebuttal, he was stopped by Peter Tarnoff, who turned to Vice Minister Li and said,

"Our number twos are both graduates of Fletcher and Fletcher is good at producing debaters. If we let Fletcher guys have their ways, we will never see the end of it!"

That debate of Fletcher vs. Fletcher, F60 versus F83 did not bring the two sides to a consensus. But it did help both sides understand each other better. Two years later President Jiang Zemin paid a successful state visit to the States, and I had the honour to be in his entourage.

My engagements with Fletcher alumni were not always so competitive.

In September 2001, I presented my credentials to President Mubarak of Egypt on the same occasion as Ambassador David Welsh, F77. During our days in Egypt, we compared notes quite often on issues of mutual interest.

In 2006 I was appointed the Chinese Ambassador to the DPRK. It was one of the last places where I would expect interactions with Fletcher community. But I was wrong.

First, I had a F71 guest, Governor Bill Richardson of New Mexico. He led a bi-partisan delegation to the DPRK and asked to see me first when he arrived. At the reception in his honour Governor Richardson opened his remarks by saying:

"Ambassador Liu and I went to the same school, that is, the Fletcher School of Law and Diplomacy."

Then in 2009, our Dean Emeritus, Ambassador Stephen W. Bosworth, was appointed the US Special Representative for North Korean Policy by President Obama. We had in-depth discussions on the DPRK on a number of occasions and made joint efforts to advance the Six-Party talks on the Korean Nuclear Issue.

I recall these events not to show that Fletcher taught me debating or broadened my connections, but to emphasise the importance of my year at Fletcher that has contributed to my career to this very day.

Although Fletcher alumni come from and represent many different countries, I find a common bond between us all, which is the core value embodied in Fletcher that ultimately we are all working for the greater good for all humanity.

Recently, I was asked about what strikes me most in my 40 years of diplomatic service. My answer is that diplomacy is never an individual performance, but is much better compared to a national orchestra.

Success in diplomacy, or in a diplomatic career, cannot be separated from the prosperity and strength of the country you represent.

I feel all the more strongly about this as I reflect on my years as Chinese Ambassador to the UK.

The embassy started as the legation of the Qing Dynasty in London in 1877. It was China's first resident mission overseas in the modern sense, but the story of this origin is hardly something to be proud of.

In 1875, a British expedition crossed into China's Yunnan Province from Myanmar. A certain Augustus Raymond Margary, the interpreter dispatched by the British legation in China, was killed in clashes with local people.

The British government reacted by forcing upon the Qing government the Chefoo Convention, which extorted a hefty indemnity and forced open more trading ports. But worst of all an apology was demanded from the Chinese Emperor via his special envoy to Queen Victoria in person.

So, there went my first predecessor Guo Songtao to the UK in 1877. To make his mandate look less apologetic, the Qing government decided to make him stay as the Chinese Minister in London after his apology mission was accomplished.

The rest is the humiliating history. The first resident envoy China sent to a foreign country had a mandate of apology. The first letter he presented to his hosting Head of State was not one of credentials but one of apology.

This year is the centenary of the outbreak of the First World War. That reminds me of another predecessor in London V. K. Wellington Koo, Minister and later Ambassador to the United Kingdom. He was a member of the Chinese delegation to the Paris Peace Conference in 1919. But to his disappointment, though a victor, China's sovereignty and legitimate interests were left at the mercy of Western powers at the Conference. Mr. Koo protested but was ignored. He refused to sign the Treaty of Versailles at the end of the day, but that gesture could not alter a bitter result.

Those episodes of history taught us Chinese a lesson in the hard way, that is, a weak nation does not have diplomacy. For too long a time in modern Chinese history this created deep hurting wounds for the Chinese people, especially Chinese diplomats. That is why sovereignty and territorial integrity are always at the heart of China's foreign policy.

Now China is rising in the world. The Chinese people are standing tall and making efforts towards the "Chinese Dream," the Dream that features national and individual prosperity and the great rejuvenation of the Chinese nation.

We have put forward Two Centenary Goals for the "Chinese Dream":

- By the end of this decade, which marks the centenary of the Communist Party of China, China will build a moderately prosperous country.
- And by mid-century when we celebrate the centenary of the People's Republic, China will become a developed nation.

According to President Xi Jinping, the Chinese people will enjoy:

- The opportunity to a prosperous life.
- The realisation of their ambitions and dreams.

There are some observers who have expressed worries about the "Chinese Dream." Some suggest it means China will seek to avenge past wrongs. Others proclaim that China will eventually seek regional and even global hegemony. Such opinions are an anachronism and a complete misreading of China.

The "Chinese Dream" has peaceful development and win-win cooperation at its very core.

The commitment to peace and development is a strategic choice based on our own past and present, and our judgment on the call of the times.

Loving peace is built into our culture. China is the only permanent member of the UN Security Council:

- That has no history of colonisation.

- That has no overseas military bases or troops stationed abroad.
- China alone is committed to no use of nuclear weapons first and no use of them against non-nuclear weapon countries and regions.

Peaceful development is anchored in sound logic. In a country of China's size, national rejuvenation and individual prosperity for 1/5 of humanity cannot be built on expansion and exploitation. It calls for undivided attention to development which is only viable in peaceful times.

Peaceful development is our conclusion from lessons learned from history. China has seen too many powers coming and going, rising and falling, each as swift as the other. We know domination is not the way, and hegemony does fall.

China has far too much experience of being on the receiving end of colonialism and invasions. China understands, and all too clearly, the ancient teaching of:

"Do not do to others what you don't want others to do to you."

What China has accomplished in the last three decades and more makes us all the more confident about achieving national prosperity through peaceful development.

To make our dream come true, we opt for win-win cooperation.

As early as 2,500 years ago, Confucius espoused the idea of:

"Helping others in order to help oneself."

This philosophy is in our DNA and is our desired pathway to the "Chinese Dream." China will never aim to dominate others but will seek to build a better future for others and ourselves.

To that end, China values cooperation in promoting development, solving disputes and expanding opportunities and common interests. We have reason to believe that our own development and the prosperity of the world are mutually beneficial.

According to the IMF, China accounts for a quarter of world economic growth since the outbreak of the international financial crisis. It is projected that in the coming five years, China will procure up to 10 trillion dollars' worth of goods and will invest over 500 billion dollars overseas. This means enormous opportunities for other countries in the world.

China's contribution to the world is not limited to economics. It has made huge contributions to international efforts in tackling environmental challenges. China is the world's largest investor in clean energy. It also leads all other countries in the development of solar energy. China's exports of solar products account for over half of the world's total.

British Prime Minister David Cameron once commented:

"China's transformation is one of the defining facts of our lifetime."

He went on to say:

"I see China's rise as an opportunity, not just for the people of this country but for Britain and the world."

We in China know too well that the voyage to that bright future is never going to be easy sailing. Hardships and challenges are guaranteed.

A most discussed issue is the so-called "Thucydides's Trap," which suggests that emerging powers and established powers are doomed to clash.

In this context, there is much reflection about the First World War that broke out 100 years ago. Then there is the enduring task of dealing with the legacy of the Second World War that ended almost 70 years ago. Both these wars had immense influence on the founding purposes of the Fletcher Class of 1947 Memorial Award. With this hindsight we should all the more renew our faith in peace and cooperation as the call of the times.

The spirit of Fletcher should be a constant guide about the wisdom of mankind, and skills of diplomats in particular, to find a way around the follies of the past. We have reason to believe that the "Chinese Dream" and the "American Dream" are not destined to collide, but are fully capable of interacting and working to each other's enhancement.

To this end, President Xi Jinping advocates the development of a new type of relationship between major powers that features:

- no conflict,
- no confrontation,
- mutual respect,
- and win-win cooperation.

For this diplomatic innovation to work, we need China and the United States to work together. This will take optimal wisdom, courage, confidence and a pinch of diplomatic art.

Together, we can make the vast Pacific Ocean the joiner of our two great nations, so that it truly lives up to its name.

Before I wrap up, I wish to quote President John F. Kennedy, one of Massachusetts' favourite sons:

"But peace does not rest in the charters and covenants alone. It lies in the hearts and minds of all people. So let us not rest all our hopes on parchment and on paper, let us strive to build peace, a desire for peace, a willingness to work for peace in the hearts and minds of all of our people. I believe that we can. I believe the problems of human destiny are not beyond the reach of human beings."

With these words of Kennedy in mind, I hope our future diplomats here have the courage to reject any fallacy that we are doomed to repeat the past, and have the wisdom to command and shape the destinies of our nations.

Whatever you do and wherever you go, I urge you to strive for peace, to work for development, to build cooperation and to achieve win-win.

Through your life you will do humanity a great service if you live up to the ideal of Fletcher at its best.

Together we can make our world a better and safer place.

Fletcher encourages us to aim high.

So let us aspire to create a record of success in history. When future generations talk about your time, they will see examples to follow, not follies to avoid.

To a career diplomat, there is perhaps no mission more noble and no dream more desirable.

Thank you.

共答“时代之问”，同创美好未来[*]

尊敬的“亚洲之家”主席格林勋爵，

尊敬的各位使节，

各位“亚洲之家”会员，

各位来宾，

女士们、先生们：

大家上午好！

感谢格林勋爵的热情介绍。我曾多次做客“亚洲之家”，与大家探讨共同关心的重大问题，每次都有新启发、新收获。

当今世界正处于百年未有之大变局，变局与乱局相互交织，全球化与反全球化相互激荡，单边主义与多边主义相互碰撞，民粹主义与民族主义相互渗透，世界何去何从令人深思。2017 年，习近平主席在联合国日内瓦总部提出“世界怎么了？我们怎么办？”的时代之问。作为驻英大使，我还经常思考，在当前形势下，中英两国如何开展合作，应对全球挑战？今天我愿围绕上述三个问题，与大家分享几点看法。

关于第一个问题“世界怎么了”，我认为，世界正面临三大挑战。

一是发展挑战。当前，世界经济下行压力加大，不确定不稳定因素增加。个别国家挑起和升级贸易摩擦，严重损害世界经济。国际货币基金组织将 2019 年世界经济增长预期降至 3.2%，为 2008 年全球金融危机以来的最低

* 在英国“亚洲之家”的主旨演讲。2019 年 9 月 26 日，亚洲之家。

水平。世界贸易组织预计 2019 年国际贸易仅增长 2.6%，远低于世界经济增长预期。新一轮科技革命加快推进，在提高经济效率的同时也拉大了资本、科技和劳动力报酬的差距，扩大了“数字化鸿沟”。对很多家庭而言，拥有温暖住房、充足食物、稳定工作仍是一种奢望。解决全球发展赤字问题依然任重道远。

二是治理挑战。过去一个世纪，我们历经两次世界大战的伤痛和冷战的阴云，才换来“二战”后相对稳定的国际体系。和平来之不易，秩序值得珍惜。但环顾当今世界，稳定和确定性成为“稀缺产品”。保护主义、霸凌行径不断抬头，严重冲击国际规则和多边机制，侵蚀国际社会信任与合作。现行国际秩序和治理体系不尽完美，新兴市场国家和发展中国家代表权和发言权不足，代表性和包容性不够，亟须改革完善，但怎么改、改成什么样需要各国商量着办。解决全球治理赤字依然步履维艰。

三是安全挑战。当今世界并不太平。地区冲突和局部战争持续不断，恐怖主义、极端主义依然猖獗，热点问题此起彼伏。根据斯德哥尔摩国际和平研究所的数据，2018 年世界军费支出总额增至 18 220 亿美元，同比增加 2.6%，达到冷战后最高水平。同时，各种非传统安全威胁接踵而至，气候变化、网络安全、难移民危机等不仅与我们的日常生活息息相关，也影响全球和地区局势稳定，更关乎人类的命运和未来。解决世界和平赤字依然是人类共同面临的难题。

关于第二个问题“我们怎么办”，中国给出的答案非常明确，那就是中国始终做全球发展的贡献者、国际秩序的维护者和世界和平的建设者。

一是中国为全球经济提供信心和动力。再过几天，就是新中国成立 70 周年。70 年来，中国从“一穷二白”跃升为世界第二大经济体。自 2006 年以来，中国对世界经济增长的贡献率保持在 30% 左右，成为世界经济增长第一引擎。2019 年上半年，中国经济同比增长 6.3%，处于合理区间，同世界主要经济体相比增速居领先地位。中国对外贸易和吸引外资继续保持增长，2019 年 1—8 月中国进出口总额约 2.95 万亿美元，同比增长 3.6%；中国新设立外商投资企业 27 704 家，实际使用外资约 892.6 亿美元，同比增长 6.9%。

中国深化改革、扩大开放的决心和信心更加坚定。中国坚定推进共建“一带一路”，已同166个国家和国际组织签署了共建“一带一路”合作协议，“一带一路”已成为全球最受欢迎的公共产品和规模最大的合作平台。从深化增值税改革、个税改革等减税降费政策，到不断加大知识产权保护力度、加快制定《外商投资法》实施细则，中国正持续改善和优化营商环境。从出台新版外商投资准入负面清单，到深圳建设中国特色社会主义先行示范区、上海启动自贸区临港新片区建设，再到山东、江苏、广西、河北、云南、黑龙江6省区的6个新设自由贸易试验区正式揭牌，中国对外开放的大门越来越大。中国有近14亿人口，9亿劳动力，4亿多中等收入人群，1亿多户市场主体，1.7亿受过高等教育和拥有技能的人才资源。无论外部风云如何变幻，我们坚信，中国经济发展韧性十足、潜力巨大，长期向好。中国将保持定力办好自己的事，继续将自身发展融入世界，并以自身发展促进世界发展，更好地造福各国人民。

二是中国为国际秩序提供稳定和正义。中国是联合国的创始成员国，是战后国际秩序的开创者、受益者和捍卫者。我们坚定维护以联合国为核心的国际体系、以国际法为基础的国际秩序，维护以世界贸易组织为核心的多边贸易体制。中国积极参与全球治理体系改革和建设，加入了世界几乎所有重要政府间国际组织，签署了300多项国际公约。中国曾被挡在联合国大门之外长达22年，但我们从未动摇对多边主义的信念；中国“复关”和“入世”谈判历时15年，尽管付出了代价，但我们全面履行入世承诺，矢志不渝地融入国际秩序和多边机制。中国已成为联合国常规预算第二大出资国，贡献份额达12%。作为最大的发展中国家，中国在国际上始终主持公道、捍卫公平正义，维护发展中国家共同利益，支持发展中国家扩大国际话语权和影响力。

近年来，中国日益走近世界舞台的中央，国际社会对中国关注度呈指数型上升。有人认为中国会推翻现有国际秩序“另起炉灶”，甚至还祭出“新冷战”“修昔底德陷阱”，这完全是“莫须有”的误解和担忧。中国坚持共商共建共享的全球治理观，反对赢者通吃、国强必霸的旧逻辑。中国不寻求挑战或取代谁，而是走对话而不对抗、结伴而不结盟的国与国交往新路。近两年，中美关系遇到不少困难，责任不在中方。我们始终认为，今天的中美关系完全不同于冷战时期的美苏关系。所谓“中美脱钩论”不符合时代潮流，也不符合两国利益交融的现实。中方无意与美方冲突对抗，将推进以协调、合作、稳定为基调的中美关系。

三是中国为世界和平提供担当和智慧。中国坚定不移走和平发展道路，以自身发展促进世界和平，同时倡导世界各国共同走和平发展道路。70年来，中国没有主动挑起过任何一场战争和冲突。中国实行防御性国防政策，是核大国中唯一承诺不首先使用核武器的国家。在联合国安理会五常国中，中国国防费占国内生产总值比重、人均国防费均为最低，人均国防费仅为美国的1/18、英国的1/9。中国是联合国维和行动第二大出资国和安理会五常国中派遣维和军事人员最多的国家，累计派出3.9万人次军警官兵参与维和行动；中国军舰连续10年在亚丁湾、索马里海域执行护航，先后保护了6 000多艘船舶安全。

中国倡导共同、综合、合作、可持续的新安全观，为维护世界和平贡献中国智慧。中国以负责任态度参与地区热点问题政治解决进程，致力于维护和执行伊朗核问题全面协议，维护朝鲜半岛和平稳定和对话缓和势头。中国为国际社会共同应对非传统安全威胁做出积极贡献。以应对气候变化问题为例，中国坚定支持气候变化《巴黎协定》，倡导绿色发展，至2017年中国已提前3年实现单位国内生产总值碳排放量比2005年下降40%~45%的承诺。过去10年间，中国是全球可再生能源领域的最大投资国。中国还出资200亿元人民币建立“中国气候变化南南合作基金”，用于支持其他发展中国家应对气候变化。

关于第三个问题“中英应如何合作应对挑战”，我认为双方合作互利共赢，大有可为。

2019年是中英建立代办级外交关系65周年。65年来，从建立代办级外交关系到升格为大使级外交关系，从实现香港顺利回归到建立面向21世纪的全球全面战略伙伴关系，中英关系历经风雨，取得丰硕成果。2018年双边贸易额首次超过800亿美元大关。2019年6月，第十次中英经济财金对话取得69项成果，其中，“沪伦通”开了中国与境外资本市场互联互通的先河。上个月，中英合资的恒安标准人寿成为首家在中国获准筹建养老险公司的合资寿险公司。英国还是吸引中国留学生最多、开办孔子学院最多、开展校际合作最广泛的欧洲国家。目前在英留学的中国学生近20万人，每年中英人员往来约200万人次。在脱欧背景下，“全球化英国”将为中英关系带来新的机遇。本月初，在我为庆祝中华人民共和国成立70周年举行招待会之际，约翰逊首相发来贺词，表示在英即将脱欧之际，中英关系非常重要，他对两国加强经贸合作抱有很高期待。

面对世界三大挑战，我认为，中英应加强三方面合作。

一是推动建设开放型世界经济。中英在经济发展模式、产业结构、科技创新等方面优势互补，在支持自由贸易、倡导多边主义方面共识突出。两国在贸易投资、金融服务等领域合作基础良好，在大数据、人工智能等新兴领域合作潜力巨大。今年，中英签署了第三方市场合作协议，“一带一路”合作将日益成为引领中英合作的新亮点和新增长点。此外，双方应以实际行动践行开放合作理念，为两国企业投资兴业提供公平、公正、透明和非歧视的营商环境，共同引领新一轮经济全球化。

二是推动全球治理体系改革。中英都致力于维护多边体系。在新形势下，双方可进一步拓展全球视野和国际协作，推进全球治理体系改革，共同为世界和平、稳定、发展与繁荣做出新贡献。特别是面对当前保护主义和单边主义逆风，双方应展现大国责任和历史担当，积极维护以世贸组织为核心的多边贸易体制，同时推动对世贸组织进行必要改革，增强其权威性和有效性。

三是促进世界持久和平和普遍安全。中英都是联合国安理会常任理事国和二十国集团等国际组织重要成员，双方可在应对气候变化、生物多样性、网络安全等方面加强合作，在伊朗核等国际和地区热点问题上保持密切沟通，不断为世界和平和地区稳定做出新贡献。

中英在加强合作的同时，还应妥善处理分歧。中英两国社会制度、文化传统和发展阶段不同，双方在一些问题上存在分歧很正常。重要的是相互尊重和理解，相互尊重主权和领土完整，尊重彼此核心利益和重大关切，不做损害对方核心利益的事情。只有这样，双方才能妥善处理分歧，以建设性的方式管控和化解分歧，使两国关系始终沿着正确的方向发展。

女士们、先生们，

英语谚语讲，“危急时刻更应并肩前行”（A common danger causes common action）。面对世界变局和乱局，中英作为具有重要国际影响力的大国，应当站在对历史负责、为人类担当的高度，同舟共济、共迎挑战，解答好“时代之问”，为构建人类命运共同体、为建设一个更加美好的世界贡献智慧和力量。

谢谢！

下面我愿回答大家的提问。

The Questions of Our Times Call for a Joint Response*

Lord Green,

Your Excellencies,

Members of Asia House,

Distinguished Guests,

Ladies and Gentlemen,

Good morning!

Thank you, Lord Green, for your kind introduction.

I am not a stranger here at Asia House. It has always been a pleasure to come here to share my views on major issues of common interest. And every visit to Asia House gives me new inspirations and new thoughts.

The world is undergoing profound changes unseen in a century. Changes are punctuated by chaos. Boundaries between populism and nationalism are blurred. Amid surging anti-globalisation and rising unilateralism, globalisation and multilateralism suffer backlashes. These developments are raising questions about where the world is going.

Just as President Xi Jinping asked in his speech at the UN Office in Geneva in 2017, "What has happened to the world? How should we respond?"

For me, as Chinese Ambassador to the UK, I have another important question before me, that is, how to enhance China-UK cooperation in responding to global challenges.

Today I would like to share with you my views on these three questions.

---

* Keynote Speech at Asia House. 26 September 2019.

The first question: What has happened to the world?

In my view, the world is facing three main challenges.

The first challenge is the development deficit.

The world economy is under mounting downward pressure and showing further uncertainties and instabilities. On top of that, the escalating trade friction triggered by a certain country is dealing a severe blow.

IMF has downgraded the outlook for world economic growth to 3.2%, the lowest since the outbreak of the financial crisis in 2008. WTO prediction for this year's trade growth is only 2.6%, even lower than the outlook for world economic growth.

It is true that the new round of scientific and technological revolution has resulted in higher economic efficiency. But it has also widened the gap between returns on capital, technology and labour, and it has exacerbated the "digital divide." For many families, the basic necessities of life, such as food, shelter and jobs, are still out of reach.

Cutting the global development deficit remains a daunting task.

The second challenge is the global governance deficit.

In the past century, mankind suffered the scourges of two world wars and endured the dark clouds of the Cold War before establishing a relatively stable international system. Peace has not come easy. It is all the more important that the current international order be cherished.

However, stability and certainty have become "scare commodities" today. Surging protectionism and bullying behaviours are dealing a heavy blow on international rules and multilateral mechanisms, and undermining the trust and cooperation between countries of the world.

The current international order and governance system are not perfect. They need to be more representative and inclusive in order to give more representation and greater voices to emerging economies and developing countries. This is a serious global governance deficit. Reform and improvement are badly needed to bring down this deficit. Every country must be involved in the decision-making process of such reform, including how it should be carried out and what will be the goals.

Cutting the global governance deficit remains a thorny issue.

The third challenge is peace deficit.

With incessant regional conflicts and wars, rampant terrorism and extremism, and surging hot-spot issues, the world is far from a peaceful and tranquil place.

According to the Stockholm International Peace Research Institute, the overall global military expenditure was $1,822 billion in 2018, which was an increase of 2.6% over the previous year and the highest since the end of the Cold War.

Moreover, non-traditional threats to security are mounting. Climate change, cyber security and the refugee crisis not only have an impact on our daily life and on regional and global stability. They also have a bearing on the destiny and future of all mankind.

So, cutting the peace deficit also remains a challenging work for all.

Now let me turn to the second question: How should we respond to these challenges?

Here is China's clear-cut answer: China will always be a contributor to global development, an upholder of international order and a defender of world peace.

First, China provides confidence and impetus for world economy.

In a few days, China will celebrate the 70th anniversary of the founding of the People's Republic. In the past 70 years, China has grown from an impoverished country to the second largest economy in the world.

Since 2006, China has contributed around 30% of growth globally. It is now the world's most important economic powerhouse.

China remains one of the fastest growing major economies in the world. In the first half of this year, China's economy grew by 6.3% year on year, which is well within the anticipated range.

Foreign trade and foreign investment in China have kept increasing. From January to August, import and export reached $2.95 trillion, increasing by 3.6% year on year. There were 27,704 newly-set-up foreign businesses, and the actual paid-in foreign investment totaled about $89.26 billion, up by 6.9% year on year.

China remains determined and confident in deepening reform and opening its market wider to the world.

China has promoted the building of the Belt and Road Initiative (BRI). It has signed agreements on BRI cooperation with 166 countries and international organisations. BRI is now the most popular public goods and largest cooperation platform in the world.

China is improving its business environment by:

- deepening reforms on individual income tax and VAT,
- cutting tax and lower fees,
- stepping up IPR protection,
- and formulating the supporting regulations of the Foreign Investment Law.

China is also taking new measures to open wider to the world, including:

- adopting a new negative list for foreign investment,
- establishing the Shenzhen pilot demonstration area of socialism with Chinese characteristics,
- building the new Lingang area of the Shanghai free trade zone,
- and setting up six free trade pilot zones in Shandong, Jiangsu, Guangxi, Hebei, Yunnan and Heilongjiang.

China has:

- a population of close to 1.4 billion,
- labour forces of 900 million,
- middle-income earners of more than 400 million,
- market entities of more than 100 million,
- and a well-educated and skilled talent pool of 170 million people.

No matter how things may change in the world, China has confidence in the resilience, the potential and the prospects of its economy. China will focus firmly on managing its own affairs well. At the same time, China will continue to integrate with the world, promote world development through its own development, and deliver more benefits to the people of all countries.

Second, China contributes to the stability and justice of the international order.

China is one of the founding members of the United Nations. It is a creator, beneficiary and defender of the international order established after the Second World War. China remains firm in upholding the international system with the UN as its core, the international order based on international law, and the multilateral trade system with the WTO as its core.

China has taken an active part in the reform and development of the global governance system. It has joined almost all the major international intergovernmental organisations and signed more than 300 international conventions.

China had been shut out of the UN for 22 years but never wavered in its belief in multilateralism. China had spent 15 years in negotiations to resume its contracting party status to the General Agreement on Tariffs and Trade and to join the WTO. Despite all the difficulties and prices, China has lived up to its WTO commitments fully, and integrated steadfastly with the international order and multilateral mechanisms. China is now the second largest contributor to the UN regular budget, accounting for 12% of the total amount.

As the largest developing country, China upholds justice and fairness in the world, safeguards the common interests of all developing countries, and supports the efforts of other developing countries to raise their voices and increase their influence in the world.

In recent years, as China approaches centre stage in world affairs, the interest in China from the rest of the world has increased exponentially. There are worries that China will challenge the current world order and "reinvent the wheel." There are also talks about a "new Cold War" between China and the US, and predictions that China will fall into the "Thucydides's Trap." But these are all needless worries due to misunderstandings.

In our view, global governance should follow the principle of extensive consultation, joint contribution and shared benefits. China opposes the outdated logic that "winner takes it all" or "strength leads to hegemony." China is not aimed at challenging or replacing any country. It is committed to a new path of state-to-state relations that values dialogue above confrontation, partnership above alliance.

China should not be blamed for the difficulties in China-US relations in the past two years. We believe that China-US relationship is completely different from the US-Soviet Union relationship during the Cold War. The so-called "decoupling" is not in line with the trend of the times. Nor does it tally with the fact that the interests of the two countries are deeply intertwined. China does not want conflicts or confrontations with the US. China will continue to pursue a China-US relationship that is based on coordination, cooperation and stability.

Third, China shoulders its responsibility for and contributes its wisdom to world peace.

China is committed to the path of peaceful development, and promotes world peace through its development. At the same time, China advocates that all countries should follow the path of peaceful development.

Over the past 70 years, China has never launched a single war or conflict. China follows a defense policy that is defensive in nature. It is the only nuclear power in the world to have promised no first use of nuclear weapons.

Of the five permanent members of the UN Security Council, China has the lowest level of military expenditure both as percentage of GDP and in per capita terms. Its per capita military spending is only one eighteenth of the US and one ninth of the UK.

China is also the second largest contributor to the UN peacekeeping budget and the largest contributor of peacekeeping personnel among the P5. Some 39,000 Chinese peacekeepers are serving in peacekeeping missions all over the world. In the Gulf of Aden and off the coast of Somalia, Chinese navy has carried out escort missions for ten consecutive years and ensured the safe passage of more than 6,000 ships.

China advocates a new concept of common, comprehensive, cooperative and sustainable security. This is a concept that embodies China's wisdom. Following this concept, China has engaged in the political settlement for regional hotspot issues in a responsible manner. On the Iran nuclear issue, China upholds and implements the Joint Comprehensive Plan of Action. On issue of the Korean Peninsula, China upholds peace and stability by promoting the momentum for dialogue and the easing of tension.

China has also made positive contribution to the international efforts in addressing non-traditional threats to security. Take climate change for example:

- China firmly supports the Paris Agreement on climate change and calls for green development. By 2017, it had fulfilled its promise of cutting carbon emissions per unit of GDP by 40%~45% percent compared with 2005. This means target met three years in advance.
- China has also been the world's largest investor in renewable energy in the past ten years.

- Moreover, China has set up a South-South Climate Cooperation Fund and injected 20 billion RMB yuan to help other developing countries tackle climate change.

Now I would like to turn to the third question: What should we do to enhance China-UK cooperation in responding to global challenges?

China-UK cooperation is mutually beneficial and enjoys promising prospects.

This year marks the 65th anniversary of China-UK diplomatic relationship at the chargé d'affaires level. In the past 65 years, from chargé d'affaires level to ambassadorial diplomatic relationship, from the smooth handover of Hong Kong to establishing the global comprehensive strategic partnership for the 21st century, China-UK relationship has achieved remarkable progress despite wind and rain.

In 2018, our bilateral trade exceeded $80 billion for the first time. At the tenth China-UK Economic and Financial Dialogue concluded last June, 69 outcomes were achieved, including the Shanghai-London Stock Connect, which for the first time connects the Chinese and a foreign capital market. Last month, Heng An Standard Life, a joint venture between Chinese and British companies, became the first enterprise of its kind to receive permission to establish a pension insurance company in China.

The UK has a larger Chinese student community, more Confucius Institutes, and more extensive cooperation with Chinese universities and schools than any other countries in Europe. There are close to 200,000 Chinese students here in Britain and two million mutual visits between our two countries every year.

Against the backdrop of Brexit, a global Britain will create new opportunities for China-UK relations. Early this month, Prime Minister Johnson sent a message of congratulations to the reception I hosted in celebration of the 70th anniversary of the founding of the People's Republic of China. He said that China-UK relationship will continue to be important as the UK prepares to leave the EU, and that he wants to be ambitious with greater trade and investment between our countries.

In responding to the three global challenges, China and the UK should join hands in the following three aspects:

First, promote openness in the world economy.

China and the UK have complementary strength in development model, industrial structure, and science, technology and innovation. We have consensus on supporting free trade and advocating multilateralism. We already have a sound basis for cooperation in the areas of trade, investment and financial services. And we enjoy enormous potential for cooperation in emerging areas such as big data and artificial intelligence.

Earlier this year, our two countries signed an agreement on cooperation in third markets. This will enable the two countries to work together on the Belt and Road Initiative and create new highlights and growth points in their cooperation.

Going forward, China and the UK should take concrete actions to enhance openness in their cooperation. We should foster a fair, just, transparent and non-discriminatory business environment for the companies of our two countries to make investment and set up businesses. And we could work together to lead a new round of economic globalisation.

Second, promote reform in the global governance system.

Both our two countries are committed to upholding the multilateral system. Under the new circumstances, our two countries should adopt a global vision, enhance coordination on international affairs, and advance the reform in the global governance system. We should jointly make new contribution to world peace, stability, development and prosperity.

In particular, China and the UK should stand up against the headwind of protectionism and unilateralism. This is the time for us to demonstrate our courage and shoulder historical responsibilities. We should uphold the multilateral trade system with the WTO as its core, and at the same time promote necessary reform in the WTO to improve its authority and effectiveness.

Third, promote lasting peace and universal security in the world.

As permanent members of the UN Security Council and important member states of the G20, China and the UK should build closer partnership in climate change, bio-diversity and cyber security. We should also keep close communication on regional and international hotspots such as the Iran nuclear issue, and contribute our part to peace in the world and stability in the relevant region.

While enhancing cooperation, China and the UK should also handle our differences in a proper manner.

Our two countries differ in social system, cultural heritage and development stage. It is natural that we do not always see eye to eye. The key is to:

- respect and understand each other,
- respect each other's sovereignty and territorial integrity,
- respect each other's core interests and major concerns,
- and refrain from doing anything that will undermine each other's core interests.

This is the only way to ensure that our two countries manage, control and settle differences in a constructive manner. This is the only way to keep China-UK relations in the right direction.

Ladies and Gentlemen,

Let me quote a British saying to wind up my speech, that is, "A common danger causes common action."

In face of the changes and chaos in the world, China and the UK, as major countries of global influence, should shoulder our responsibilities for the history and for all mankind.

It is important that we pull in the same direction, come to each other's aid in times of difficulties, and address challenges hand in hand. We have the responsibility to answer the questions of our times and contribute our wisdom and strength to building a community with a shared future for mankind and making our world a better and more beautiful place.

Thank you!

Now I would like to take your questions.

同舟共济，共克时艰，构建人类命运共同体*

尊敬的皇家国际事务研究所主席奥尼尔勋爵，

女士们、先生们：

大家上午好！

很高兴再次做客皇家国际事务研究所。我出使英国10年来，曾多次到皇研所演讲，每次都有新启迪、新收获。

今天，奥尼尔主席希望我介绍一下中国外交和2020年外交议程。我想从当前大家最关心的新冠肺炎疫情谈起，从中国的抗疫斗争来思考和解读构建人类命运共同体，这一当今中国外交的基本理念，也是习近平外交思想的核心要义。

这次新冠肺炎疫情传播速度之快、感染范围之广、防控难度之大，对中国和世界都是一次重大挑战。疫情发生以来，中国政府始终把人民群众生命安全和身体健康放在第一位。在习近平主席坚强领导下，中国举国上下万众一心、众志成城，采取了最全面、最严格、最彻底的防控措施，全面动员、全面部署、全面行动，打响了一场抗疫人民战争。世界卫生组织高度赞赏中国为抗疫付出的努力，认为中国树立了应对疫情的“新标杆”。

中国的疫情防控工作既是对本国人民的生命安全和身体健康负责，也是在为全球共同卫生事业做贡献。中方在国内采取远超世卫组织建议和《国际卫生条例》要求的防控措施，始终本着公开、透明、负责任的态度，开展疫

---

* 在英国皇家国际事务研究所的主旨演讲。2020年3月2日，英国皇家国际事务研究所。

情防控国际合作，共同维护和提升全球公共卫生安全。世卫组织负责人积极评价中国的抗疫工作，称中国强有力的举措不仅是在保护中国人民，也是在保护世界人民，为全球疫情防控赢得了时间。

经过艰苦努力，中国疫情防控举措取得积极成效，治愈率持续提升，死亡率保持在较低水平。我坚信，有中国共产党的坚强领导，有中国特色社会主义制度的显著优势，有强大的动员能力和今非昔比的综合实力，有全体中国人民的团结奋斗，我们一定能够战胜这场疫情。不久前，习近平主席再次主持召开会议，就统筹推进疫情防控和经济社会发展工作做出全面部署。中国在做好疫情防控的同时，正努力把疫情带来的经济社会影响降至最低，继续为世界经济发展提供有力支撑。

女士们、先生们，

面对疫情，挑战是共同的，责任是共同的。这场抗疫斗争再次证明，世界各国命运相连、休戚与共，人类社会是一个“你中有我、我中有你”的命运共同体。习近平主席提出的构建人类命运共同体理念，超越了各国社会制度、历史文化和发展阶段的差异，彰显了人类共同的价值追求，顺应了历史潮流，直面当今世界最重要最紧迫的问题，为世界的发展、人类的未来指明了正确方向。面对这场疫情，人类命运共同体理念进一步彰显了强大的正能量和感召力。

维护人类健康福祉，需要秉持人类命运共同体理念。疫情没有国界，是人类面临的共同挑战，任何一个国家都不可能置身于全球公共卫生安全之外，需要同心协力、携手抗击。秉持人类命运共同体理念，守望相助、患难与共，筑成抗击疫情的“铜墙铁壁”，就一定能同心合力打败病毒，赢得抗击疫情的最终胜利。

实现世界长治久安，需要践行人类命运共同体理念。当今世界正处于百年未有之大变局，国际形势正发生深刻复杂变化，人类社会再次面临和平还是战争、发展还是停滞、对话还是对抗、包容还是隔阂等重大抉择。秉持人类命运共同体理念，同舟共济、共迎挑战，将人类前途命运掌握在自己手中，共同建设更加和平、安全、美好的世界，反映了世界人民的普遍愿望和共同心声。

捍卫国际公平正义，需要坚持人类命运共同体理念。虽然人类已经进入21世纪第三个十年，但个别国家仍固守冷战思维，醉心霸权主义和强权政治，奉行单边主义，随意践踏他国主权。个别国家政客和媒体攻击别国发展道路，煽动意识形态对立，散播“亚洲病夫”等种族歧视谬论。这些“政治病毒”如同自然界病毒，是人类社会的公敌。秉持人类命运共同体理念，以正义压倒邪恶、真理战胜谎言、包容取缔歧视，是国际社会的共同责任。

面对上述形势和挑战，我们应该怎样建设人类命运共同体？我认为，可从以下四个方面入手。

一是坚持同舟共济，而不是同舟共“挤”，维护世界安全。中国坚定与世界各国共同奋战，全力筑牢控制疫情蔓延的防线，付出巨大努力和牺牲，得到国际社会的积极肯定和广泛支持。面对各种传统和非传统安全挑战，大国要有大国的担当，不应搞本国优先、相互对抗拆台，而应身体力行，为世界注入正能量。中国坚持积极倡导共同、综合、合作、可持续的新安全观，反对冷战思维和强权政治，与各国共谋和平与安全。近代中国饱受战乱之苦，深知和平来之不易。中国坚定不移走和平发展道路，希望其他国家也要走和平发展道路。各国都走和平发展道路，国与国才能和平相处，各国才能共同发展。新中国成立70多年来，中国没有主动挑起过任何一场战争和冲突。中国发展是要不断超越自己，不是要威胁谁、挑战谁、取代谁。中国越发展，维护世界安全的力量就越强，对世界和平的贡献也就越大。

二是坚持互利共赢，而不是你输我赢，促进共同发展。不少朋友关心疫情对中国经济的影响，我想强调的是，疫情确实给中国经济发展带来了负面影响，但这是短期的、暂时的。中国经济有着强劲的韧性和足够的“免疫力”，长期向好的基本面没有也不会改变。经济全球化发展的势头也不会发生根本改变，让世界经济的大海退回到一个一个孤立的小湖泊、小河流是不可能的。越是面对困难和挑战，我们越要坚持以开放促合作、以合作促发展。有人鼓噪对中国搞“脱钩”和“科技封锁”，这是自我封闭、自我设限、自我倒退。改革开放40多年来，开放已成为当代中国最鲜明的标识。中国对外开放的大门将越开越大。2020 年 1 月 1 日起，中国正式实施《外商投资法》，将为各国拓展对华合作提供更广阔市场和更大商机。我们也希望各国坚持开放合作，为包括华为在内的中国企业提供公平、开放、非歧视的营商环境。

三是坚持多边主义，而不是单边主义，维护国际秩序。中国是最大发展中国家，也是第一个在《联合国宪章》上签字的联合国创始会员国。中国坚定维护以联合国为核心的国际体系，以国际法为基础的国际准则，以世贸组织为基石的多边贸易体制，成为维护多边主义的中流砥柱，这与个别国家大搞单边主义和“退群”形成鲜明对比。疫情让人们再次认识到，坚持多边主义、加强全球治理、增进国际协调是当务之急。单边主义、以邻为壑换不来独善其身，最终损害的注定是本国利益和各国共同利益。在抗击疫情的战斗中，中国始终秉持人类命运共同体理念，本着公开透明的态度，坚定支持世卫组织发挥引领作用，与国际社会共同抗疫，为完善全球卫生治理做出积极贡献。

四是坚持互尊互鉴，而不是傲慢隔阂，共促人类文明。我从事外交工作已经 46 年，出使非洲、美洲、亚洲和欧洲多个国家，不同国家的文化文明都给我留下了深刻印象，使我看到不同的文明各有千秋，也各有不足。正是这种文明的差异和文明的多样性使我们这个世界丰富多彩。正如习近平主席所说：“文明因交流而多彩。文明因互鉴而丰富。文明交流互鉴是推动人类文明进步和世界和平发展的重要动力。”然而，近来西方有些人借疫情重拾“文明冲突”论调，对中国抗疫举措和发展模式说三道四，这不仅反映了他们的傲慢与偏见，也说明了他们的无知与愚昧。历史和现实告诉我们，解决人类面临的共同挑战，需要从不同的文明中寻求智慧、汲取营养。中华文明绵延五千多年，秘诀就在于兼收并蓄、和谐共生。面对疫情，中国特色社会主义制度充分展现了集中力量办大事的优势。我们将继续推进国家治理体系和治理能力现代化，积极完善重大疫情防控体制机制，健全国家公共卫生应急管理体制，也愿意学习借鉴其他国家公共卫生的有益经验。我们呼吁各国尊重世界文明多样性，摆脱东西方的划分，超越南北方的差异，坚决反对文明冲突，反对种族歧视，真正把我们赖以生存的地球家园打造成人类命运共同体。

2020 年是中国发展进程中具有里程碑意义的一年。我们将全面建成小康社会，彻底消除绝对贫困，实现第一个百年奋斗目标。2020 年 11 月，我们将举办第三届中国国际进口博览会，共同分享中国发展红利。2020 年是中欧建交 45 周年，双方将举办中国－中东欧国家领导人峰会等重大活动，共同推动中欧关系迈上新台阶。2020 年是联合国成立 75 周年，我们将继续深入参与全球治理，为解决各种全球性问题贡献更多中国智慧和中国力量。2020 年中英将分别举办《生物多样性公约》第十五次缔约方会议（COP15）和《联合国气候变化框架公约》第二十六次缔约方会议（COP26），这两场会议*将为中英双方加强应对气候变化、环境保护、野生动植物保护等方面的合作提供宝贵机遇和重要平台。

2020 年也是习近平主席访英开启中英关系“黄金时代”五周年。不久前，习近平主席与约翰逊首相通电话，为两国关系发展指明了方向。在构建人类命运共同体方面，中英是天然合作伙伴。两国同为联合国安理会常任理事国，都倡导多边主义、支持自由贸易，都是东西方文明具有代表性的国家，都肩负着促进世界和平与发展的重要使命。双方应在构建人类命运共同体上承担更多责任，展现更多作为。

一是凝聚理念共识。双方应坚定维护多边主义和自由贸易，反对单边主义和保护主义，坚持互利共赢合作导向，在相互尊重基础上照顾彼此核心利益和重大关切，树立新型国际关系和东西方大国交往的典范。

二是强化国际协作。双方要加强在重大国际和地区事务中的沟通协调，共同应对全球性挑战，为国际社会提供更多稳定性。双方可就 COP15 和 COP26 加强相互沟通和支持，推动应对气候变化国际合作，引领全球绿色和可持续发展。

三是深化务实合作。双方应加强优势互补，不断拓展人工智能、清洁能源、数字经济、金融科技等领域的合作，深化“一带一路”第三方市场合

---

* 这两场会议均因疫情分别推迟到 2021 年 10 月和 11 月举行。

作，为促进两国和世界繁荣发展做出更多积极努力。双方还要加强公共卫生合作，加快疫苗、新药研发，共同维护世界公共卫生安全。

中国文字中“危机”一词充满智慧和哲理。它是由“危”和“机”两个字组成的，即“危中有机”“危可化机”。不久前，我在BBC“安德鲁·马尔”访谈节目中问马尔先生是否懂中文，他说你能看出我不懂。我向他介绍了“危机”一词，他听得很认真。我并不是教他中文，而是向他介绍中国的哲理。由此我想到丘吉尔也有一句类似的名言：“克服困难就是赢得机遇。”（Difficulties mastered are opportunities won.）我想丘吉尔也一定不懂中文，尽管他是语言大师。可见，中西方文明有许多相近和相通之处。我们应当记住这些至理名言。历史只会眷顾坚定者、奋进者、搏击者，而不会等待犹豫者、懈怠者、畏难者。让我们携起手来，提振信心、共克时艰、化危为机、深化合作，推动中英关系“黄金时代”行稳致远，为构建人类命运共同体，为建设一个持久和平、共同繁荣、更加美好的世界做出贡献！

谢谢！

现在我愿回答各位的问题。

Pull in the Same Direction and Build a Community with a Shared Future for Mankind*

Lord O'Neil,

Ladies and Gentlemen,

Good morning!

It is a real delight to join you again at Chatham House. In my ten years as Chinese Ambassador to the UK, I have spoken at Chatham House several times. Every time I leave with new thoughts and new inspirations.

Lord O'Neill asked me to talk about China's foreign policy and International Agenda for 2020. I would like to start with how China is responding to Covid-19. This is not only because it is a topical issue which you all must be following closely.

More importantly, the way we are handling this virus outbreak, I think, could help people understand China's vision of building a community with a shared future for mankind. This is the basic concept underpinning China's foreign policy. It is also at the very centre of Xi Jinping Thought on Diplomacy.

The outbreak of Covid-19 has been a major challenge to both China and the world in terms of the speed of its spread, the scope of its impact and the difficulty to contain it.

In combating this disease, the Chinese government has regarded the safety and health of the Chinese people as the top priority. Under the strong leadership of President Xi Jinping, all the Chinese people have been standing united. The most comprehensive, strict and thorough measures have been adopted, deployed and strengthened across the country. The whole nation has been mobilised to fight a "people's war" against the

* Keynote Speech at the Chatham House. 2 March 2020.

virus.

WHO has spoken highly of China's effort. In its words, China "is setting a new standard for outbreak response."

By taking these measures, China is living up to its responsibility of safeguarding the safety and health of the Chinese people. It is also contributing to global public health. We have done more than what we are asked to do by the WHO and under the International Health Regulations.

China has also engaged in international cooperation in an open, transparent and responsible manner, in order to safeguard and improve global public health at this critical moment. The leader of WHO has emphasised that China's measures are not only protecting its own people, but also protecting the people in the whole world, and that China has bought time for the rest of the world.

Thanks to our persistent work, the prevention and control measures are showing positive effects. The cure rate has kept rising and the mortality rate is maintained at a relatively low level.

China has the strong leadership of the Communist Party of China, the advantage of socialism with Chinese characteristics, unparalleled mobilisation capability and unprecedented comprehensive national strength, and the solidarity of the Chinese people. I am confident that we will win this battle against the virus.

A few days ago, President Xi Jinping called a meeting to map out coordinated plans for epidemic response as well as social and economic development. While still focusing on containing the virus, China is also doing its best to minimise the economic impact, so that China will continue to be a powerhouse for global growth.

Covid-19 is posing a challenge for all. So is tackling it a responsibility for all. This battle against the virus once again shows that countries of the world are invariably associated with one another, sharing weal and woe.

In other words, human society is a community with a shared future. This concept proposed by President Xi Jinping transcends the differences of social system, history, culture and development stage. It embodies the common values of mankind, it reflects the trend of the times, and it answers the most important and urgent questions facing the world, that is, where should the world be heading and where does the future of mankind lie?

The ongoing battle against Covid-19 is living proof of how much we all belong to a community with a shared future for mankind and how urgently we all need to come together to build it.

To safeguard the health and wellbeing of mankind, we need this spirit of community.

Virus knows no borders. It is the common challenge facing all mankind. To safeguard global public health, countries must join hands and stand shoulder to shoulder. If we come to each other's aid in this time of difficulty and fight for our shared future, we can build an "impregnable fortress" and win the battle against the virus.

To realise sustained stability and security in the world, we need this spirit of community.

The world is undergoing profound changes unseen in a century. While the international landscape is undergoing profound and complex changes, mankind has once again come to a crossroads where we must make choices and answer these questions:

- Do we want peace or war?
- Should we move forward or backward?
- Is it better to engage in dialogue or confrontation?
- Is now a century for inclusiveness or estrangement?

Our shared future lies in our own hands. The right choice is to pull in the same direction and address challenges together in the spirit of a community with a shared future. If we choose wisely, we will embrace a peaceful, safe and beautiful world. Such a future is the common aspiration of all people in the world.

To uphold fairness and justice in the world, we need this spirit of community.

The world is entering the third decade of the 21st century. Yet, there are some people who still dream of resurrecting the Cold War, worship hegemony and power politics, clamour for unilateralism, and trample on other countries' sovereignty. Some politicians and media have attacked the development paths of other countries, fanned ideological confrontation, and made such racist remarks as the "Sick Man of East Asia."

Just like Covid-19, these "political viruses" are the common enemy of mankind. It is therefore the common responsibility of the international community, in the interests of a shared future, to ensure that justice overcomes evil, truth conquers lies, and inclusiveness prevails over discrimination.

Amid the current situation and in face of the challenges in the world, what shall we do to build a community with a shared future for mankind? I think we should make the following four efforts:

First, to safeguard international security, we should pull in the same direction instead of undercutting each other.

Covid-19 is posing a threat to global public health security. China has worked with all countries in the world and made tremendous efforts and sacrifice to check the spread of the virus. This has won extensive recognition and support from the international community.

In face of the various traditional and non-traditional challenges to security, major countries have upon them special responsibilities. They must resist the temptation to look inward or confront and undercut each other. They should take up their due responsibilities, make concrete efforts and inject positive energy into the global response to challenges.

China advocates a new concept of common, comprehensive, cooperative and sustainable security. We oppose the Cold War approach and power politics. We stand ready to work with other countries to pursue peace and security.

Having experienced untold sufferings of wars in modern times, China knows all too well that peace never comes easy. Therefore, China remains committed to the path of peaceful development, and hopes that other countries will do the same. If peaceful development becomes a global consensus, harmonious coexistence and common development can be achieved for all.

China has not started a single war or conflict over the past 70 years since the founding of new China. We strive to become a better version of ourselves. We do not want to threaten, challenge or replace anyone. As China grows stronger, it will make greater contribution to international security and world peace.

Second, to promote common development, we should engage in win-win cooperation rather than indulging in a game of "you lose, I win."

I know many of you might be concerned about the impact of the epidemic on

China's economy. I want to stress that any negative impact is short-term and temporary. This is because China's economy is highly resilient. Its "immune system" is robust. The fundamentals that sustain long-term growth have not changed and will not change.

At the same time, the momentum of economic globalisation cannot be reversed. Countries have become so interdependent economically that it is impossible to divide the vast ocean of global economy into ponds and puddles.

In face of the difficulties and challenges, it is all the more important that we deepen cooperation through opening-up and promote development through cooperation. The clamours for "decoupling" and "scientific and technological blockade" against China would only land the advocate in self-imposed isolation, restriction and backpedaling.

Opening-up has been the most salient signature of China since this policy was adopted more than 40 years ago. Going forward, China will continue to open its market wider to the world. With China's Foreign Investment Law going into effect on January 1st, foreign businesses will have greater access to Chinese market and more opportunities for closer cooperation with their Chinese partners.

It is our hope that countries of the world will all remain committed to open cooperation and fostering a fair, open and non-discriminatory environment for Chinese companies, including but not limited to Huawei.

Third, to safeguard the international order, we should uphold multilateralism and oppose unilateralism.

China is the biggest developing country in the world. It is one of the founding members of the United Nations and was the first country to put its signature on the UN Charter.

China upholds the international system with the UN at its core, champions the norms governing state-to-state relations based on international law, and defends the multilateral system with the WTO as its cornerstone. As a staunch supporter of multilateralism, China's action is a world of difference from the trumpeter of unilateralism who has withdrawn from a number of international organisations and treaties.

The outbreak of Covid-19 reminds us once again that upholding multilateralism, improving global governance and enhancing international coordination are order of the day. Going it alone or following a "beggar-thy-neighbour" policy saves no one from trouble. Instead, such an approach would only undermine the interests of both oneself and the rest of the world.

In the battle against Covid-19, China has acted in the spirit of a community with a shared future. We have been open and transparent. We have supported the leadership of WHO, stood shoulder to shoulder with the international community, and made positive contribution to improving global governance in public health.

Fourth, to advance the civilisation of mankind, we should respect and learn from each other rather than boost arrogance and build walls.

I have been a diplomat for 46 years, having worked in Africa, North America, Asia and Europe. All these years, I have been deeply impressed by the rich variety of cultures and civilisations of different countries. Each civilisation has its unique strength. It is the differences and diversity of civilisations that make our world a colourful place.

As President Xi Jinping said, "Civilisations have become richer and more colorful with exchanges and mutual learning. Such exchanges and mutual learning form an important drive for human progress and global peace and development."

In recent days, however, some people once again resort to the cliché of "clash of civilisations" and made irresponsible remarks on China's response to Covid-19 and development model. This not only reflects their arrogance and prejudice but also betrayed their ignorance.

From repeated lessons of history and from our own experience we have found it to be all too obvious that to address the common challenges to mankind, we should draw on the wisdom and absorb the nutrients of different civilisations. The secret to the continuity of the Chinese civilisation, which has gone uninterrupted for more than 5,000 years, lies in our inclusiveness and our pursuit for harmonious coexistence with other civilisations. In responding to public health crisis, the system of socialism with Chinese characteristics is showing strength in uniting all sectors and pooling all resources.

Going forward, we will continue to modernise China's system and governance capability, improve the system and mechanisms for major epidemics response, and strengthen the national public health emergency management system. We are also willing to learn from other countries' experience in safeguarding public health.

We advocate respect for diversity of civilisations. The world does not need a line drawn between the East and the West, and should bridge the gap between the South and the North. The cliché of clash of civilisations and the actions of racial discrimination are out of tune with the times. All the countries of the world should cherish our common home on Earth and take concrete actions to contribute to building a community with a shared future for mankind.

The year 2020 is a milestone in China's development. In this year, we will achieve the first centenary goal, namely to complete the building of a moderately prosperous society and eliminate absolute poverty.

In November, China will host the third CIIE, China International Import Expo, to share with the world the benefits of China's development.

This year marks the 45th anniversary of the establishment of diplomatic relations between China and the EU. The two sides will hold a number of important events, including the Summit of China and Central and Eastern European Countries, and work together to take China-EU relationship to the next level.

This year is also the 75th anniversary of the founding of the UN. China will continue to engage deeply in global governance and contribute more wisdom and strength to the settlement of global issues.

Later this year, China will host COP15 to the Convention on Biological Diversity and the UK will host COP26 to the United Nations Framework Convention on Climate Change. These two conferences will provide invaluable opportunities and important platforms for closer cooperation between China and the UK in climate change, environmental protection and wildlife conservation. (The conferences were postponed to October and November 2021 respectively due to the pandemic.)

The year 2020 also marks the fifth anniversary of China-UK Golden Era launched by President Xi Jinping's state visit to the UK in 2015. A few days ago, President Xi and Prime Minister Johnson had a telephone conversation. This conversation charted the course for the development of China-UK relations.

China and the UK are natural partners in building a community with a shared future for mankind. Both are permanent members of the UN Security Council. Both champion multilateralism and support free trade. And both are great civilisations and regard it as their mission to promote world peace and development. It is important that the two countries take up more responsibilities and make more efforts in building a community with a shared future for mankind.

First, China and the UK should build up consensus, especially on safeguarding multilateralism and free trade, opposing unilateralism and protectionism, and promoting win-win cooperation. It is important that our two countries accommodate each other's core interests and major concerns on the basis of mutual respect.

In doing so, the two countries will be able to form a new type of state-to-state relations and will set an example for relationship between major Eastern and Western countries.

Second, China and the UK should enhance international coordination.

This means our two countries should enhance communication and coordination on major international and regional issues, and work together to address global challenges. Together our two countries could provide more stability to the international community.

The upcoming COP15 and COP26 will be good opportunities for our two countries to enhance communication and mutual support, promote international cooperation in addressing climate change, and take the lead in green and sustainable development.

Third, China and the UK should deepen cooperation.

The respective strengths of China and the UK create opportunities for our two countries to expand cooperation on artificial intelligence, clean energy, digital economy and FinTech. We could also deepen the Belt and Road cooperation in third markets. Closer cooperation will enable us to make greater contribution to the prosperity and development of our two countries and beyond.

In meeting the current challenges from Covid-19, China and the UK should enhance cooperation to accelerate the development of vaccine and new medicines and treatment. It is important that we work together to safeguard global public health.

The Chinese word for "crisis" reflects the wisdom and philosophical thinking of the Chinese people. It is the combination of two words, crisis and opportunities. The Chinese people always believe there are opportunities in crisis, and we always try our best to turn crisis into opportunities.

Earlier this month when I was on BBC's *Andrew Marr Show*, I asked Mr. Marr if he speaks Chinese. He answered, "I speak no Chinese, as you may have noticed." So, I explained the Chinese word "crisis" to him, and he listened attentively. I wasn't really trying to teach him Chinese language. I was using this word to explain the philosophy of the Chinese people.

Winston Churchill once said, "Difficulties mastered are opportunities won." Churchill is a great master of language, but I don't think he spoke Chinese. But his words certainly show that there are many similarities between the Chinese and Western civilisations. We should keep these wise words in mind.

History looks kindly on those with resolve, with drive and ambition, and with plenty of guts; it won't wait for the hesitant, the apathetic, or those who shy away from challenges.

Let's have more confidence in our capability to overcome the difficulties and work together to turn crisis into opportunities. Together we can ensure the steady and sustained development of China-UK Golden Era. Together we can promote the building of a community with a shared future for mankind. Together we can make our world a better place with lasting peace and common prosperity.

Thank you!

Now, I will open the floor for questions.

第五章

中国国防

针对西方社会对中国的国防建设和军力增长存在许多误解，我利用各种机会介绍中国的国防政策。我先后两次到英军最高学府——英国国防大学联合指挥与参谋学院发表演讲。这里素称是英军培养中高级联合作战指挥军官的摇篮，同时也为 50 多个国家培训校级军官，在世界各国军校中享有较高声誉。第一次演讲的题目是《〈孙子兵法〉与中国的外交国防政策》。我以《孙子兵法》的思想为主线，深入阐述中国外交与国防政策；以“上兵伐谋，其次伐交，其次伐兵”，说明今天的中国继承了先贤的和平思想，奉行独立自主的和平外交政策和防御性国防政策，致力于和平解决国际争端，主张世界各国携手努力，保障各国共同安全与福祉，维护世界和平与稳定。

第二次演讲的题目是《“中国梦”引领中国安全观与国防建设》。我以“中国梦”为主线，说明“中国梦”就是实现国家富强、民族振兴、人民幸福，实现中华民族伟大复兴。“中国梦”不是要国强必霸，穷兵黩武、复仇雪耻，也不是要垄断能源资源、控制全球市场。“中国梦”是和平梦，中国人民希望和平，反对战争，今天中国的发展成就，是在和平条件下通过辛勤劳动创造的。“中国梦”是发展梦，让 13 亿多中国人都过上好日子，还需要付出长期、艰苦的努力。“中国梦”是合作梦，中国坚持对外开放，愿与世界各国开展互利合作。“中国梦”是共赢梦，中国不仅致力于自身发展，也愿随着自身国力增长，为世界做出更大贡献。“中国梦”与世界各国人民的梦想高度一致，中国的安全与世界和平稳定息息相关，中国的国防建设不对任何国家构成威胁，中国走和平发展道路也需要其他国家一道相向而行。

两次演讲吸引了来自近 50 个国家 700 多名中高级军官，学院中心礼堂座无虚席。摩尔斯代理校长兼院长在致答词中说：“刘大使不仅做了精彩的演讲，更回答了不少‘尖锐’问题，这样的交流有助于英军和各国学员更好地理解中国的发展道路和安全与国防政策，减少误解和误判，希望今后能听到更多像这样的来自中国的声音。”

《孙子兵法》与中国的外交国防政策 *

尊敬的英国国防大学联合指挥与参谋学院院长洛克空军少将，

女士们、先生们，

未来的将军们：

我很高兴应洛克院长的邀请访问英国国防大学联合指挥与参谋学院这座将军的摇篮。

我在英国许多大学发表过演讲，包括牛津、剑桥、帝国理工等。今天还是第一次在英国军事院校作演讲。洛克院长为今天的演讲出了好几个题目，包括中国的外交、国防政策和中欧、中英关系。

既然是在军事院校演讲，我不妨从中国古代的一部兵书谈起，这就是著名的《孙子兵法》。《孙子兵法》已有 2 500 年历史，被译成许多种语言，流传到世界各地，仅英文译本就有 17 种之多。虽然作为冷兵器时代的一部兵书，《孙子兵法》有些内容已经远离当今时代，但其许多战略、战术思想并未随历史褪色，而仍熠熠生辉。美国西点军校将之列为必读经典。英国著名军事历史学家和军事理论家利德尔·哈特（Sir B. H. Liddell-Hart）深入研究过《孙子兵法》，认为《孙子兵法》远未过时，并在为塞缪尔·格里菲思（Samuel Griffith）的《孙子兵法》英译本作序时感叹道："《孙子兵法》将我 20 多部著作所涉及的战略和战术原则几乎包罗无遗。"

我发现，《孙子兵法》对今天中国外交、国防政策的形成亦有深刻影响。

---

* 在英国国防大学联合指挥与参谋学院的演讲。2012 年 2 月 9 日，英国国防大学。

《孙子兵法》开宗明义第一句话就是："兵者，国之大事，死生之地，存亡之道，不可不察也。"孙子还认为："故上兵伐谋，其次伐交，其次伐兵，其下攻城。"可见，《孙子兵法》尽管是一部兵书，但其指导思想是"慎战"和"不战"。这与中国古代其他先哲的观点如出一辙，如老子和孟子都认为："兵者，凶器也。"这也就不难理解90年前为什么英国著名哲学家、思想家罗素在其著作《中国问题》中指出："中国历史上虽然征战连绵，但中国人天性是喜好和平的。"

《孙子兵法》及中国古代的这些和平、不战思想，是今天中国和平发展道路的滥觞。

今天的中国，立足中国国情，顺应时代潮流，坚持独立自主的和平外交政策，将维护世界和平、促进共同发展作为中国外交政策的宗旨。中国倡导互信、互利、平等、协作的新安全观，秉持积极有为的国际责任观，奉行睦邻友好的地区合作观，主张世界各国一道建立持久和平、共同繁荣的和谐世界。中国绝不搞侵略扩张，永远不争霸、不称霸，始终做维护世界和地区和平稳定的坚定力量，中国绝不走历史上"国强必霸"的老路。

今天的中国，坚定支持联合国在维护世界和平与安全中的核心地位，致力于和平解决国际争端和热点问题。中国是唯一公开承诺不首先使用核武器、不对无核武器国家和无核武器区使用或威胁使用核武器的核武器国家。中国累计向联合国30项维和行动派出各类人员约2.1万人次，是派出维和人员最多的联合国安理会常任理事国。中国积极参与反恐、防扩散领域国际合作，向索马里海域派遣海军护航编队。中国在朝核、伊朗核等热点问题上坚持劝和促谈，推动形成朝核问题六方会谈机制，发挥了建设性作用。中国同12个陆地邻国解决了历史遗留的边界问题，坚持通过对话谈判处理同邻国领土和海洋权益争端，提出"搁置争议、共同开发"的主张，尽最大努力维护南海、东海及周边和平稳定。

不久前，我在接受BBC《新闻之夜》节目采访时，主持人杰里米·帕克斯曼问我："美国为了推行民主不惜发动战争。中国想推行什么？"我当时就回答说："中国致力于构建和谐世界。我们主张国与国相互尊重、相互包容，而不是把自己的价值观和社会制度强加给别人。我们主张世界各国携手努力，保障各国共同的安全与福祉，维护世界和平与稳定。我们坚决反对在国际事务中诉诸武力。”这就是中国的和平外交政策。

与中国的和平外交政策相一致，今天中国奉行的是防御性国防战略。《孙子兵法》是一部兵书，是战争的艺术，那么战争的最高境界是什么？孙子认为是“百战百胜，非善之善者也；不战而屈人之兵，善之善者也”。孙子也提出：“非危不战”，“无恃其不来，恃吾有以待之；无恃其不攻，恃吾有所不可攻也”。

只有建立强大的国防，才能有效维护国家主权安全和发展利益；只有具备制胜的力量，才能有效地遏制战争，这是古今中外历史告诉我们的真理。中国有广阔的领土和辽阔的海洋，面对错综复杂的国际战略格局和中国安全环境，面对世界新军事变革方兴未艾的发展态势，能否化解多元和复杂的非传统安全挑战，能否有效应对暴力恐怖势力、民族分裂势力和宗教极端势力的威胁，能否打赢未来可能发生的高技术战争，成为中华民族能否实现伟大复兴的关键。

中国的国防建设不针对、不威胁任何国家，中国不会也无意同任何国家搞军备竞赛。中国的国防建设从来没有超越捍卫国家安全的需要，中国国防开支也是合理适度的。根据伦敦国际战略研究所的报告，中国的军费在世界各国中处于较低水平，2010 年中国军费占 GDP 的 1.3%，不仅远低于美国、英国、俄罗斯等传统军事强国，也低于印度、巴西等新兴国家。如果从人均军费看，中国则更低，仅有美国的 1/38，英国的 1/20。

《孙子兵法》从根本上主张不战、慎战，但并不惧战、畏战。同样，我们讲积极防御，并不是软弱可欺，而是后发制人。后发即“人不犯我、我不犯人”，制人则是“人若犯我、我必犯人”。中国积极防御军事战略的立足点，是有效遏制和防止战争，同时也是时刻准备应对战争和打赢战争。以敢战能战来达到“不战而屈人之兵”，以敢于“亮剑”而全力争取战争胜利，这是孙子兵法的精髓，也是当代中国的军魂。

女士们、先生们，

在当今世界，中欧关系是很重要的双边关系。中国是世界上最大的发展中国家，欧洲是世界上最大的发达国家集合体，中欧之间没有地缘政治争端，没有根本利害冲突。近几十年来，合作一直是双边关系的主流。中欧现在互为最大经贸合作伙伴。欧盟是中国第一大出口市场，中国是欧盟第二大出口市场，欧盟还是中国第一投资目的地和最大技术引进来源地。

中英关系的发展总体上与中欧关系步调保持一致。中英高层互访密切频繁，经贸合作亮点频现，人文交流热度频升。2012 年是中英建立大使级外交关系 40 周年，两国将举行一系列纪念庆祝活动。特别值得指出的是，中英两军关系近年来也走上快速发展轨道。2011 年，英军陆、海、空军参谋长相继访华。中英防务战略磋商和两国高级退役将领交流得到机制化。

如何进一步发展中欧、中英关系？我仍想借用《孙子兵法》及中国古人的一些智慧。

《孙子兵法》里有一句名言："知己知彼，百战不殆。"《孙子兵法》总共只有 6 074 个字，其中"知"字是出现频率最多的一个字，共出现了 79 次。今天，中欧关系及中英关系是合作伙伴关系，不是竞争对手关系，要发展和深化这种伙伴关系，就要不断加深了解，增强信任，化解疑虑，消除担忧。我想在此引用你们的一位前辈的观点，他就是曾任英军陆军野战部队司令的拉姆中将。2012 年，他作为英国退役将军代表团团长访问了中国，回来后在《泰晤士报》上发表了一篇文章，他认为，"欧洲和西方不能制造新的敌人，不能妖魔化中国，对话有益彼此了解，驱除担忧"。

中国古语说："尺有所短，寸有所长；物有所不足，智有所不明。"中欧、中英处在不同的发展阶段，面临着不同的发展挑战，彼此经济互补性强，合作利益大，双方应当充分拓展合作空间，挖掘合作潜力，努力实现互利共赢。

中欧、中英的历史文化、社会制度和价值观念不同，双方在一些问题上存在分歧是正常的。如何对待这些不同？如何处理这些分歧？我们不赞成将自己的制度视为普世模式，到处推销；不赞成将自己的价值观视为唯一正确标准，强加于人；也不赞成冷战思维，搞意识形态对抗。我们主张双方相互尊重，正视不同，平等相待；坦诚对话，求同存异，增进互信；相互借鉴，取长补短，互利共赢。

《孙子兵法》里还有一个著名的故事，讲的是中国古时候吴国人与越国人不和，当他们同船渡河时，遇到大风，他们相互救援就像人的左右手一样。这个故事成了一句成语——“同舟共济”。

在世界多极化、经济全球化、社会信息化深入发展的时代，世界是一个“地球村”。恐怖主义、大规模杀伤性武器扩散、自然灾害、气候变化、公共卫生、金融风险以及能源资源、粮食和水资源安全，是全球性问题和人类面临的共同挑战；同时，中欧利益相互依存、利益交融，实际上形成了你中有我、我中有你的命运共同体，也就是说欧洲和中国同在一条船上。中欧必须同舟共济、携手合作，努力实现可持续和包容性发展。

女士们、先生们，

今天中国的外交和国防政策，是历史积淀、时代发展和博采众长的产物，显然一部《孙子兵法》不足以概括全部，但我相信，认识《孙子兵法》这部古老的兵书，了解中国思想文化的源头，能为理解今天中国的和平发展道路增添一条途径，能为打消对中国的不必要担忧增加一些决心，能为积极开展与中国的交流合作增强一些动力。这就是我今天演讲的主旨所在。

谢谢！

下面我愿回答各位的提问。

Sun Tzu's Wisdom Behind China's Diplomacy and Defense Policy *

Air Vice-Marshal Ray Lock,

Ladies and Gentlemen,

Commanders of the Future,

It's my great pleasure to visit the Joint Services Command and Staff College.

I was delighted to accept the invitation of Air Vice-Marshal Ray Lock to give this talk.

I've visited and spoken at many British universities, such as Oxford, Cambridge and Imperial College. But today is unique in the sense that this is my first speech to a military college.

I am impressed to know that your college has won a reputation as the cradle of military leaders for Britain.

I feel privileged to speak and propose to touch on three themes:

- China's diplomacy.
- China's defense policy.
- And China's relations with Britain and Europe.

We need to take a step back to understand China's foreign and defense policy. Since this is a military college, let's trace the origin of Chinese thinking on war and peace.

The key is an ancient Chinese book.

---

* Speech at the UK Joint Services Command and Staff College. Defense Academy of the UK, 9 February 2012.

Sometime it is called *Military Principles* but the more popular translation is *The Art of War*.

This is a classical Chinese military treatise written 2,500 years ago. The book was authored by a high-ranking general called Sun Tzu.

The book has since been translated into many languages and read and studied around the world. It is said there are 17 English versions.

You might ask what relevance such an ancient book has in the high technology world of today. Some arguments in *The Art of War* do seem to be out of touch in the modern world.

But with careful study you will find that many of its strategies, tactics and thoughts are highly relevant today. The book still offers a central text of military thought for defense communities. I know that the book has been adopted as a must-read by West Point and many other military academies.

The prominent British military historian and theorist Sir Basil Henry Liddell-Hart was a student of *The Art of War*. He argued the book was far from outdated.

In his foreword for Samuel Griffith's English translation of the book, he wrote:

"It was time they went back to Sun Tzu, since in that one short book was embodied almost as much about the fundamentals of strategy and tactics as I had covered in more than twenty books."

For China, the importance of *The Art of War* has spread far beyond military studies. The book has deep influence in framing China's foreign policy and its approach to security and defense.

The opening line of *The Art of War* is:

"*The Art of War* is of vital importance to the State. It is a matter of life and death, a road either to safety or to ruin. Hence it is a subject of inquiry, which can on no account be neglected."

Sun Tzu continued:

"Thus the highest form of generalship is to balk the enemy's plan. The next best is to prevent the junction of the enemy's forces. The next in order is to attack the enemy's army in the field. And the worst policy of all is to besiege walled cities."

The Art of War stands out from other military theory books. The reason is the stress on the cautious use of force and to avoid war.

Sun Tzu is not alone in this view.

Many Chinese philosophers around his time also cautioned against war. Both Lao Tzu and Mencius warned war and conflict carry big dangers.

There have also been thinkers outside China that support this approach. The famous British philosopher, Bertrand Russell, also observed the consistent commitment to peace of China. 90 years ago, Russell wrote in his book *The Problem of China* that:

"Although there have been many wars in China, the natural outlook of the Chinese is very pacifistic."

This legacy explains China's choice of a peaceful path to development today. These are the key facts about our foreign and defense policies:

- China's commitment to an independent, peaceful foreign policy is based upon its national conditions. This reflects the needs of our time.
- At the heart of our policy is to build a peaceful world that provides shared prosperity for all.
- China calls for mutual trust, mutual benefit, equality and cooperation to build a peaceful world.
- China actively assumes its fair share of global responsibilities and seeks to shape a friendly neighbourhood.
- We want to work with all countries and contribute to a harmonious world of lasting peace and common prosperity.
- China does not believe in expansion or hegemony.
- Instead, we have always been a staunch force for world peace and regional stability.
- China will not repeat the errors of history, whereby "power leads to hegemony." That approach has plunged the world into disaster and conflict.
- China supports the centrality of the United Nations in matters affecting world peace and security.
- China is committed to addressing international disputes and related crisis in a peaceful manner.
- China is the only country that has publicly undertaken not to be the first to use nuclear weapons. In addition China will not use, or threaten to use, nuclear

weapons against non-nuclear countries or nuclear-free zones.

- China is the largest contributor to peacekeeping operations within the UN Security Council. We have sent 21,000 peacekeepers to 30 UN missions.
- China plays an active role in international counter-terrorism and non-proliferation. Currently, our naval vessels are performing escort missions in the waters off Somalia.
- China encourages peace talks on the North Korean nuclear issue. We are the host and a constructive participant in the Six-Party talks.
- The same approach applies to the Iranian nuclear issue and other critical conflicts.
- China has peacefully addressed its long-standing boundary issues with 12 of its neighbours on land. We are determined to find negotiated solutions to territorial and maritime disputes with neighbouring countries.
- China is guided by the principle of "shelving disputes and joint development." We will do everything we can to keep the South China Sea, the East China Sea and our entire neighbourhood peaceful and stable.

Recently, I spoke about the peaceful, responsible role of China in world affairs. This was on BBC Newsnight. Jeremy Paxman asked me:

"The United States will go to war to promote democracy. What do you try to promote?"

I responded:

"We are promoting a harmonious world. We believe the world will be more peaceful and prosperous if all countries respect each other, rather than imposing their own ideas and systems onto others. We believe mutual respect, mutual accommodation and working together for the common good, common security is in the interest of peace and stability of the world. So we are strongly opposed to any military solutions."

This is what China's peaceful foreign policy is all about.

Consistent with this foreign policy guideline, China's military posture is defensive in nature.

Let me explain our thinking by returning to *The Art of War* and ask this question:

"If war is an art, then what is the highest level of victory?"

Sun Tzu gives this answer:

"To fight and conquer in all your battles is not supreme excellence; supreme excellence consists in breaking the enemy's resistance without fighting."

To stress the war as the last resort for self-protection, Sun Tzu continues:

"Fight not unless the position is critical."

Essentially Sun Tzu laid out a strategy of proactive defense where he writes:

"*The Art of War* teaches us to rely not on the likelihood of the enemy's not coming, but on our own readiness to receive him; not on the chance of his not attacking, but rather on the fact that we have made our position unassailable."

Only a strong and credible force of defense can effectively protect national sovereignty and development interests.

Only such a force can effectively deter any attempt for war. This is what the pattern of world history has taught us.

China has a huge landmass and vast waters under its jurisdiction.

We face a complex international strategic landscape and security environment. In addition a new revolution in military affairs is gaining momentum worldwide.

Going forward, the critical challenges for China are threefold:

- Whether or not China can defeat diverse and complex non-conventional security challenges?
- Whether or not China can effectively deal with threats from violent terrorism, ethnic separatism and religious extremism?
- And whether or not China can win a high-tech war in the future?

The answers to these three questions determine whether China's national rejuvenation is possible.

What I want to stress are these points:

- China's defense modernisation doesn't target or threaten anyone.
- China has no interest or intention to engage in any arms race.
- China's defense building never exceeds the need for national security.
- And China's defense spending has always been reasonable and proportionate to the challenges we face.

These are key comparative facts about military spending:

- According to a report of the International Institute for Strategic Studies, China's military budget is relatively low compared to other major powers.
- Our spending was only 1.3 percent of China's GDP in 2010.
- This figure is lower than that of America, Britain, Russia.
- Also the 1.3 percent of GDP is lower than some emerging countries such as India and Brazil.
- At a per head level, China's defense spending is even lower. We are only 1/38 of America and 1/20 of Britain.

In essence, *The Art of War* talks about avoiding war and going to war with caution. But this prudent approach does not mean fear or cowardice.

It is crucial that leaders around the world understand our defense strategy. They should never mistake the principles of *The Art of War* as a display of weakness and vulnerability.

China is not to launch preemptive strikes. But in case we are threatened or under attack, there should be no doubt that China will take robust action to protect its interests.

The thrust of Chinese defense strategy is very clear. China has the deterrence and wisdom to win without fighting. But if needed, China has the courage and capability to win through fighting.

This is the essence of *The Art of War* and the soul of China's military strategy today.

Ladies and Gentlemen,

I would also address the issue of China's relations with Britain and Europe.

In today's world, the China-Europe relationship carries much weight. China is the world's largest developing country and Europe is by far the largest bloc of developed countries. We have no geopolitical tension or fundamental conflicting interests between us.

For decades, cooperation has been the defining feature of our relationship. Today, we are each other's number one trading partner. To be specific, the EU is China's largest export market, largest investment destination and the biggest technology supplier of China. And China is the EU's second largest export market.

Turning to the relations between China and Britain.

China-UK relations are also growing fast. This is a partnership marked by mutual goodwill, close high-level engagements, strong commercial ties and fast developing people-to-people exchanges.

This year, our two countries will co-host a range of celebrations to mark 40 years of full diplomatic relations.

In the context of this strengthening relationship, one particular area of good progress is our military-to-military ties.

Last year, Britain's Chief of General Staff, Chief of Naval Staff and Chief of the Air Staff all paid visits to China.

China-UK defense strategic consultation and a structured dialogue between Chinese and British retired senior military officers have been put in place.

In this final part of my talk today I would like to pose the following question:

"Going forward, how to strengthen China's relations with Britain and Europe?"

Let me borrow some wisdom from *The Art of War* and China's ancient sages.

The Art of War famously remarked:

"If you know your counterparts and know yourself, you will have nothing to fear."

What merits much attention is that the book's original Chinese text has 6,074 characters.

Within these characters the word "know" appears 79 times. That is more than any other character.

Today, Europe and Britain are China's partners, not adversaries. For our partnership to strengthen and widen, we need to know each other better. We need greater trust to disarm suspicions and concerns. Let me quote what one veteran British general said of China.

Lieutenant-General Sir Graeme Lamb is the former Commander Field Army. Last year he led a delegation of British veteran generals to China.

In *The Times*, upon his return, he wrote these words:

"We should talk to China, not demonise it. … The danger lies in making a new enemy. …When it comes to relations with the Chinese, …it's good to talk. That applies to both sides. …Knowledge dispels fear."

We Chinese have an old saying:

"Everything has its merits and demerits. And wisdom has its limits."

The fact that China is at a different stage of development from Britain and Europe means we face different sets of challenges.

This also means we have much to gain from this strong economic complementarity and from cooperation.

Greater effort must be made to widen the scope of cooperation and to tap into the rich potentials to build a win-win future.

For this to happen, our different histories, cultures, social systems and values shouldn't become barriers. The question is how we should handle differences and diversity.

Some people see their own system as universal and try to export it throughout the world. They see their own values as the only right standard, to which the whole world should be held up.

This is not what we would support. We are not in favour of imposing one's own views on others, nor do we support the Cold War style ideological confrontation.

We believe in facing up to differences squarely, with respect and a shared commitment to seek common ground. Only in this way can we achieve win-win and both succeed through good-faith mutual learning.

Talking of solidarity and cooperation, there's another well-known story arising from *The Art of War*. The story is about Warring Kingdoms. The people from the Wu Kingdom and those from the Yue Kingdom did not like each other. But when paddling across the river during a storm, they would cooperate as the right hand does with the left.

From this story came a Chinese idiom:

"Those sailing across the river in one boat should help each other."

In a multipolar world our society has become a global village. The driving forces of new technologies have shaped that globalisation.

In this globalised world collaboration is the only solution to common challenges. Global challenges are with us daily, such as:

- Terrorism.
- WMD proliferation.
- Natural disasters.
- Climate change.
- Public health.

- Financial risks.
- Energy and resource scarcity.
- Food and water safety.

All these are challenges on a global scale and threaten all of us.

China and Europe are today interlinked and interdependent and have a shared destiny.

China and Europe must show solidarity and work together to achieve sustainable and inclusive development.

Ladies and Gentlemen,

China's diplomacy and thinking on defense have deep roots in Chinese history. I have described how the ancient principles are highly relevant to the challenges of our time. China strengthens its approach by also absorbing the best ideas from other countries.

The Art of War certainly cannot capture all facets of China's conduct of diplomacy and defense policy. But it's my belief that this book provides a good beginning to understanding Chinese thinking and culture.

I hope you will be inspired to study China more with the support of *The Art of War*. I believe if you follow this path you will grasp the value of China's choice of peaceful development. This is also the road to dispel unfounded misgivings and add momentum for dialogue and cooperation.

As future military leaders from this prestigious college you have big responsibilities. As China rises, you will find my country more relevant within those responsibilities. So, I hope my thoughts today will inspire you to study China deeply.

In this way you can maximise the prospect of building a peaceful and harmonious world.

That is surely a shared goal of mutual interest for all our people.

Thank you!

Now, I will be glad to take your questions.

“中国梦”引领中国安全观与国防建设*

尊敬的詹姆斯·摩尔斯代理校长兼院长，

女士们、先生们：

很高兴时隔两年再次来到英国国防大学联合指挥与参谋学院。2012 年 2 月，我曾以《〈孙子兵法〉与中国的外交国防政策》为题在这里向你们的学长发表演讲，至今记忆犹新。

两年前讲的《孙子兵法》是中国古人的智慧，今天我想讲讲当代中国人的智慧。我认为，最能反映当代中国人智慧的是一个最具有时代特色的词，这就是“中国梦”。

要理解什么是“中国梦”，首先要理解什么是“中国”。中国国家主席习近平 1 个多月前访欧时在布鲁日欧洲学院发表的演讲中指出，中国是一个有着悠久历史的国家，一个经历了深重苦难的国家，一个实行中国特色社会主义制度的国家，一个世界上最大的发展中国家和正在发生深刻变革的国家。我认为这高度概括了中国的国家特点，中国就是这么一个古老与现代交融，发展与改革并存，背负苦难记忆，矢志民族复兴，坚定走自己发展道路的发展中大国。

理解了什么是“中国”，也就容易理解什么是“中国梦”。“中国梦”就是中国的未来发展目标，其基本内涵就是国家富强、民族振兴、人民幸福，实现中华民族的伟大复兴。“中国梦”是中国在历经千难万苦，走上发展正

---

* 在英国国防大学联合指挥与参谋学院的演讲。2014 年 5 月 20 日，英国国防大学。

途后的必然追求和不懈目标。

“中国梦”不是一个国家要国强必霸，独步天下；不是一个国家要穷兵黩武，复仇雪耻；不是一个国家要垄断能源、资源，控制全球市场；不是一个国家要独享经济好处，不顾别人死活。“中国梦”的天生属性是和平、发展、合作、共赢。

“中国梦”首先是和平梦。和平是人民的永恒期望，它犹如空气和阳光，受益而不觉，失之则难存。自近代以来被侵略、被奴役的历史记忆，让中国人尤其珍惜今天的生活，希望和平、反对战争。中国今天的发展成就，更是在和平条件下参与国际分工合作，通过人民辛勤劳动创造出来的。

“中国梦”是发展梦。没有发展，不可能实现持久和平。最近世界银行一份技术性报告称中国经济规模2014年可能超过美国，成为世界第一大经济体。国际上媒体很关注，但是中国自己很淡定，因为我们对自己的国情和国际地位有清醒的认识。中国还有2亿人生活在世界银行的贫困线标准以下，还有7 400多万困难群众靠低保生活，还有约1亿人生活在城市中的棚户区和城中村，还有几亿农村劳动力需要转移就业和落户城镇。让13亿多中国人都过上好日子，还有很长的路要走，我们需要付出长期的、扎扎实实的努力。

“中国梦”是开放合作梦。中国坚持对外开放，愿与世界各国开展互利合作。中国现在是全球128个国家最大的贸易伙伴。2013年，中国进出口总额突破4万亿美元，成为世界第一大贸易国，其中从世界各国进口了1.95万亿美元的产品。中国吸引外国直接投资近1 200亿美元，对外直接投资超过1 000亿美元。

“中国梦”是共赢梦。中国不仅致力于自身发展和造福本国人民，也愿意随着自身国力的增长，为世界做出更大贡献。十多年前，英国一位有远见的政治家说了这么一句话：“中国的发展是英国的机遇。”如果说十多年前很多人对这句话还有疑问，那么在今天则是不争的事实。因为大家都看到了实实在在的互利共赢：英国对华出口连续4年保持两位数增长，过去5年翻了一番还多；中国在英投资过去两年达130亿美元，超过此前30年的总和；英国企业在华设立的子公司、英国银行在华设立的分行越来越多。中英间的合作既促进了中国的持续发展，也带动英国走出低谷并迎来强劲增长。

不久前，中国国务院总理李克强访问了非洲，提出要推进中非产业合作、金融合作、减贫合作、生态环保合作、人文交流合作、和平安全合作六大工程，打造中非合作的升级版。中非之间的关系也是共赢的一个生动例子：中国发展好了，非洲有机遇；非洲发展起来了，中国也会受益；中国和非洲都发展进步了，世界会变得更美好。

“中国梦”是我们的追求，是我们的理想；实现“中国梦”不会一帆风顺，需要做出不懈的努力，需要应对各种各样的挑战。这些挑战有经济方面的，有安全方面的；有来自内部的，也有来自外部的。当前，来自内外安全方面的挑战尤为突出。

比如，境内外民族分裂势力、宗教极端势力和暴力恐怖势力这“三股势力”对中国国家安全构成了严重威胁。本月初，中国的学术机构发表了首份国家安全蓝皮书，指出在国际恐怖活动呈反弹之势的大背景下，中国的恐怖活动再次呈高发状态，且呈现出地域扩大的趋势。2013 年中国境内共发生暴恐案 10 起。2014 年以来，中国境内又接连发生了一系列严重的暴恐案件，其手段之残忍令人发指。

从外部看，世界和地区局势令人担忧。从北非，到中东，再到乌克兰，一些国家出现了动荡。东亚本该是风平浪静的地方，但某个国家要修改“和平宪法”，推翻战后国际秩序；还有的国家仗着有后台，有恃无恐，在领土主权问题上不断惹是生非，制造事端，破坏地区稳定和平。

此外，国际关系中还存在一种宿命论，认为新兴大国必然会挑战守成大国并与之发生冲突，这就是所谓的“修昔底德陷阱”。中国不相信“修昔底德陷阱”，不认为今天的国际关系是一种“零和游戏”，但有的国家总拿中国说事，制造所谓“中国威胁论”，到处拉帮结派，围堵中国，中国的安全环境一下子被搞得很复杂。

针对影响中国稳定和安全的这些内外因素，中国的安全观也在不断发展和演进。

过去十多年来，中国一贯积极倡导和践行互信、互利、平等、协作的新安全观。互信，是指超越意识形态和社会制度差异，摒弃冷战思维和强权政治心态，互不猜疑，互不敌视。互利，是指相互尊重安全利益，在实现自身安全的同时，为对方安全创造条件，实现共同安全。平等，是指国家不论大小、强弱、贫富，都应相互尊重，平等相待，互不干涉内政，推动国际关系民主化。协作，是指以和平谈判方式解决争端，就共同关心的安全问题进行广泛深入合作，消除战争和冲突的隐患。

中国还主张发展以“不冲突、不对抗、相互尊重、合作共赢”为特征的“新型大国关系”。在人们回顾100年前爆发的第一次世界大战和75年前爆发的第二次世界大战之际，我们有理由相信，人类在21世纪有足够的智慧不再重蹈历史覆辙，新兴大国与守成大国间可以合作解开“安全困境”，共同走和平发展道路。

最近，中国组建了国家安全委员会，提出了国家总体安全观，即以人民安全为宗旨，以政治安全为根本，以经济安全为基础，以军事、文化、社会安全为保障，以促进国际安全为依托，走出一条中国特色国家安全道路。为此，中国将既重视外部安全，又重视内部安全，对内求发展、求变革、求稳定、建设平安中国，对外求和平、求合作、求共赢、建设和谐世界；既重视国土安全，又重视国民安全；既重视传统安全，又重视非传统安全；既重视发展问题，又重视安全问题；既重视自身安全，又重视共同安全，打造命运共同体。

今天在上海开幕的亚信第四次峰会上，中国作为会议轮值主席和东道主，将在“新安全观”和“总体安全观”的基础上，推动树立“亚洲新安全观”，倡导共同安全、综合安全、合作安全和可持续安全，积极探讨建立符合地区安全实际、满足各方需要的亚洲安全与合作新架构。

女士们、先生们，

“中国梦”照亮了中国前进的方向，中国的安全观是确保“中国梦”实现的重要指南，而中国的国防建设是实现“中国梦”和贯彻中国安全观的强有力保障。

在座的各位都是军人，大概没有哪个军人会反对建设强大的国防。当然，由于各国资源禀赋、安全环境和国际地位不同，“强大”总是相对的，以满足需要为前提。中国的国防建设也是本着同样的理念。2013 年发表的《2013 年中国国防》白皮书就指出，中国要建设与中国国际地位相称、与国家安全和发展利益相适应的巩固国防和强大军队。我认为，中国的国防建设有四个基本点。

第一，中国国防力量的发展，立足于维护自身领土主权和发展利益。中国有 960 万平方公里的陆地领土，2.2 万多公里的陆上边界、1.8 万多公里的大陆海岸线和 1.4 万多公里的岛屿海岸线，是世界上邻国较多、陆地边界较长的国家之一。中国需要强大的国防力量，守护好我们的领土、领空和领海。我们不能让近代中国惨遭外敌入侵、战祸绵延不断的历史重演。同时，随着中国经济逐步融入世界经济体系，海外能源资源、海上战略通道以及海外公民、法人的安全问题日益突出。中国需要强大的国防力量，来开展海上护航、撤离海外侨民、应急救援等海外行动，维护中国的海外利益。

第二，中国国防力量的发展，始终保持在合理适度的水平。现在外界比较关注中国的军费。比如，2014 年初伦敦国际战略研究所的《2014 军力平衡报告》和简氏防务集团的报告，都认为中国的国防预算保持高增长势头，2013 年中国国防支出居世界第二，仅次于美国，并且预测中国军费开支可能会在 2030—2040 年赶上美国。但是，这些报告忽视了一个基本事实，中国经济规模是美国的 56%，国防费用只有 1/4 不到。

根据瑞典斯德哥尔摩国际和平研究所（SIPRI）2014 年 4 月发表的报告，2013 年各国军费支出占 GDP 的比重，美国是 3.8%，俄罗斯是 4.1%，英国是 2.3%，世界平均水平是 2.4%，而中国只有 2%，低于世界平均水平。同样，在世界各大国中，中国人均军费支出也是最低的，仅为美国的 1/22，英国的 1/9，日本的 1/5。中国奉行防御性国防政策，我们没有海外军事基地，除了维和人员和执行护航任务的海军编队，没有在海外部署一兵一卒。

第三，中国国防力量的发展，日趋开放透明。1998 年以来，中国已发表了 8 版国防白皮书。去年发表的白皮书首次公开了陆军 18 个集团军的番号、陆军机动作战力量人数、海空军人数和战略导弹部队导弹型号。前不久，美国国防部长哈格尔首次访华的第一天，就登上了中国第一艘航空母舰辽宁号进行参观。

几个月前，位于南京的解放军理工大学举办了第五届陆军国际学员周活动，来自桑赫斯特皇家军事学院的两位学员贾森·约翰逊和理查德·列文首次代表英国军校参加。BBC 派出记者全程跟踪采访了这一活动并在近期播出，片名叫《中国的新模范军》，时长 30 分钟。这是外国媒体首次进入中国军事院校跟踪拍摄，也是中国持续推动国防透明化、加强国际交流的一个缩影。

第四，中国国防力量的发展，为国际与地区的和平稳定做出了积极贡献。中国是联合国安理会五常国中派遣维和军事人员最多的国家，1990 年以来已累计向 20 多次维和任务派出超过 2.5 万名维和人员；是联合国 115 个维和出兵国中派出工兵、运输和医疗等保障分队最多的国家；是缴纳维和摊款最多的发展中国家。2002 年以来，中国军队已执行国际紧急人道主义援助任务 36 次，向 27 个受灾国运送总价值超过 1.2 亿英镑的救援物资。2008 年底以来，中国已派出 17 批 45 艘舰船、1 万余名官兵赴亚丁湾、索马里海域执行护航任务。中国积极参与叙利亚化武转运护航任务，迄今已完成十余批次。中国出动了 7 艘军舰、3 架军机参与搜救马航 MH370 航班。正如习近平主席所说，中国这头“东方睡狮”醒了，但它没有让世界发抖，因为它是和平的、可亲和文明的狮子。

两年前，我在这里讲过，中国以“不战而屈人之兵”为善之善者，我们主张通过协商和对话妥善管控与邻国的分歧，解决争议。我们从不惹事，但在事关中国主权和领土完整的重大原则问题上，我们绝不惧事、怕事，我们坚决采取一切必要措施捍卫中国的正当合法权益。所以我也奉劝一些国家，不要误判形势，不要低估了中国的决心和意志，也不要低估了中国的力量和能力。

女士们、先生们，

英国著名战略思想家富勒曾经如此评价他的前辈克劳塞维茨：“在克劳塞维茨所有一切的盲点中，最盲目的一点即为他从未认清战争的真正目的是和平而不是胜利；所以，和平才是政策的根本理想，而胜利则只是企图实现此种理想时所使用的一种手段。”在我们今天看来，以战促和并非必须，但和平的确是我们矢志不渝的理想。无论是“中国梦”、中国安全观还是中国国防建设，和平都是其要义和宗旨。而且我们相信，“中国梦”与世界各国人民的梦想高度一致，中国的安全与世界的和平稳定息息相关，中国的国防军事建设并不对其他国家构成威胁，中国走和平发展道路也需要其他国家一道相向而行。

今天，我很高兴再次向来自英国和世界各国的军事指挥官介绍“中国梦”、中国的发展理念和安全观念，我也欢迎大家有机会到中国参观访问、军事交流，去实地造访中国的军校、军营和军舰，与你们的中国同行一起学习、训练和演习，通过访问减少误解，通过沟通增进互信，通过交流理解什么是“中国梦”。

谢谢。

现在，我愿回答各位的提问。

China's Security Outlook and National Defense in the Context of the "Chinese Dream" *

Commandant Rear Admiral James Morse,

Ladies and Gentlemen,

It is my pleasure to come back to the Joint Services Command and Staff College.

In February 2012, you most kindly invited me to give a talk here.

In that talk, I discussed "Sun Tzu's Wisdom Behind China's Diplomacy and Defense Policy."

I drew inspiration from the wisdom of ancient Chinese civilisation.

Today, I wish to discuss contemporary Chinese vision, and one specific topic stands out more than the others.

It is the concept of the "Chinese Dream."

To understand the "Chinese Dream," one has to understand China first.

Chinese President Xi Jinping has made it much clearer and easier for us. In his speech at the College of Europe in Bruges early last month, President Xi gave a five-point summary of China. He said China is:

- a country of time-honoured civilisation;
- a country having gone through many hardships;
- a socialist country with Chinese characteristics;
- the world's biggest developing country;

---

* Speech at the UK Joint Services Command and Staff College. Defense Academy of the UK, 20 May 2014.

- and a country undergoing profound changes.

This portrayal of China may be very concise, but it is very precise.

- China is the largest developing country.
- It is where heritage meets dynamism.
- In the past three decades China has been working very hard to deliver reform and development.
- With memories of all the hardships behind us but never forgotten, China is committed to its chosen path towards national rejuvenation.

Bearing those factors in mind, it is quite easy to understand the "Chinese Dream."

It is all about where China pictures itself in the future.

It is fundamentally about prosperity and renewal of China as a nation and better lives for every Chinese.

To get where the Chinese people are today, China has gone through more than its share of trials and tribulations.

To be where the Chinese people want to be in the future, China has to be unwavering in the pursuit of its commitment.

Having said that, it is also important to understand what the "Chinese Dream" is not:

- It is not a Chinese version of "Manifest Destiny."
- It is not a Chinese edition of "Pax Britannica."
- It is not a military ambition to seek revenge on past injustices.
- It is not a plan to lock in resources, markets or benefiting at other's expense.

The "Chinese Dream," being none of those, is born with peace, development, cooperation and mutual benefit written into its DNA.

The "Chinese Dream" is a concept with peace as its foundations. It is a conviction, which is much like air and sunshine, fundamentally existential but too often taken for granted.

For the Chinese people, traumatic memories from foreign invasion and occupation make us value our peace and development today all the more. It is why China is such a champion of peace and opponent of war.

Peace enables international cooperation and makes it possible for hard work to pay. That is how China has come this far during the past three decades.

The "Chinese Dream" is one of development, the lack of which makes lasting peace untenable.

Recently there was a technical report published by the World Bank. It forecasts China's economy will surpass that of the US as soon as this year in PPP terms.

The prediction has hit headlines on many front pages and opinion columns. But we in China are relaxed about the prognosis. The reason is that China, of all countries, understands best where it is, both in the domestic agenda and on the world stage.

Let me give you a set of figures to illustrate the realities:

- 200 million people in China are still living under the World Bank poverty line.
- 74 million live on subsistence allowance.
- 100 million live in poor housing in the cities and several times of that total of people are coming to the cities to work and build for themselves the life of their dreams.
- To get where China wants to be, to build a better life for 1.3 billion Chinese, there is still a long way to go. There is no corner to cut.

The "Chinese Dream" is one of openness and cooperation:

- China is the top trading partner of 128 countries around the globe.
- And China's foreign trade last year exceeded 4 trillion US dollars, making it the world's largest trading nation.

Also last year:

- China bought 1.95 trillion-dollars worth of goods from overseas.
- Foreigners invested almost 120 billion dollars in China.
- Chinese invested over 100 billion dollars overseas.

The "Chinese Dream" is one of mutual benefit for all humanity.

The gains of China's development go far beyond its borders. This is both a fact and an intended result.

Over a decade ago, a British politician said, "China's development is Britain's opportunity." If it was still a vision with a question mark back then, it is already an accepted truth today.

These facts portray the mutual benefit rising from the advance of positive Sino-UK relations:

- For 4 straight years, British exports to China have grown by double digits.
- Britain sells over twice as much to China now than it did 5 years ago.
- Chinese investment in the UK is taking off. In the last 2 years alone, Chinese companies invested 13 billion dollars in this country. That's more than the sum total of the 3 previous decades.
- British companies and banks are expanding their presence in China too.
- The benefit of all these developments goes both ways. It has sustained China's continued development and helped the UK build momentum towards robust growth.

The mutual benefit has a global reach. Earlier this month Premier Li Keqiang visited Africa, where he put forward a vision to upgrade cooperation in 6 major areas. These include:

- Industries.
- Financial services.
- Poverty alleviation.
- Environmental protection.
- People-to-people exchanges.
- And peace and security.

Africa provides another example of mutual benefit. China's development is Africa's opportunity and vice versa. Both are doing well, and the world is a better place.

This vision and quest of China will not be all plain sailing. Hard work is a must, but that alone is not nearly enough.

It does not take an expert to tell that there is bound to be many challenges ahead:

- It could be the economy.
- It could be security.
- It could come from within or from without.

As we meet today, security concerns both domestic and overseas are posing serious challenges.

One major threat to China's national security comes from ethnic separatists, religious extremists and terrorists inside and outside the country. According to China's first National Security Blue Book published recently, terrorist activities in China are rising in the context of their global resurgence.

In 2013, there were 10 terrorist attacks in China, in more regions than previously was the case. Since early this year, there have been a number of gruesome attacks claiming innocent lives.

The bigger picture in the world is not any rosier.

There are upheavals in North Africa, in the Middle East and in Ukraine. East Asia, too, has its share of problems.

You will be very familiar with the international order established in 1945 after the war against fascism. The 70-year-consensus is being put at risk by proposed constitutional change in some country. Some others, feeling they have their "backs covered," are manufacturing troubles at the cost of regional peace and stability.

As if that's not enough, the "determinist" fallacy of collision between emerging and established powers muddies the water even more. This is the so-called "Thucydides's Trap" that I have discussed on other occasions. But the subject keeps coming back.

China is determined not to be swayed by such "determinism."

China does not see the world from a zero-sum game perspective.

But some nations do. Some seem deadly serious about ganging up to put China in the dock and accusing China of being a challenge and a threat. This approach serves no purpose. The cost is making international relations many more times complicated than needed.

China's security outlook keeps evolving in these contexts.

For more than a decade, China has been a strong champion of a new security outlook. This has at its very core mutual trust, mutual benefit, equality and coordination:

- Mutual trust comes from transcending the differences in ideology and social systems. It requires retiring the out-dated attitudes about of the Cold War and realpolitik. There is no place for suspicion or hostility in a relationship worthy of mutual trust.
- Mutual benefit demands, for a start, mutual respect of other parties' security interests. Building on that, all parties need to create enabling conditions for others' security while working for that of their own.
- Equality is the rule irrespective of differences in size, strength or prosperity. For greater democracy in international relations, every country deserves respect, equality and non-interference in its domestic affairs from others. In turn, this approach has to be reciprocated.
- Coordination is the way forward to neutralise risks of wars and conflicts. This is achieved by resolving differences through peaceful negotiations and working closely together on security issues of common interest.

In addition to the more general principles on security, China also champions a new type of relationship between major countries. It features no conflict, no confrontation, mutual respect and mutual benefit.

In the last century there was the tragedy of the two catastrophic world wars. The first started 100 years ago and the second started 75 years ago. Memories of these devastations should have given humanity enough reason and wisdom to avoid the follies of the past.

Countries, emerging or established, should draw on these lessons of the past madness. All nations should work out a solution to the security dilemma for common peace and development.

Recently, China launched a new National Security Commission and proposed a new holistic approach to national security.

This new Chinese approach encompasses many aspects of security, including security of the people, of the political system, the economy, defense, culture, society and international environment.

There is focus on security both in and outside China:

- Domestically, China aims for development, reform, stability and security.
- Internationally, China strives for peace, cooperation, mutual benefit and a harmonious world.

There is focus on security in both territorial and human dimensions, on issues both traditional and non-traditional.

China values both development and security, and while working on its own security, China cares about that for all.

The Chinese people see their own security in the shared destiny of humanity.

The Fourth Conference on Interaction and Confidence Building Measures in Asia—or CICA—opens today in Shanghai. China is the chair country and host. In that role China is building on the new outlook and holistic approach to security.

China is promoting a new Asian security outlook that is common, comprehensive, cooperative and sustainable.

Efforts will be made to explore the establishment of a new security and cooperation architecture for Asia that is tailored to regional reality and needs.

Ladies and Gentlemen,

The "Chinese Dream" illustrates China's way ahead. This is guided, in no small measure, by China's security outlooks, and secured by our national defense.

I make an assumption that no men or women in uniform like you disapproves of strong national defense! Given the diverse conditions of countries in terms of resources, security environment and place in the world, there are many shades of strength. But it starts with meeting basic security needs.

It is the same in China's case.

China's defense white paper published last year stated that the country is committed to building a solid defense and strong military befitting China's international standing, national security and development needs.

I would like to offer four observations on that.

First, China's growing defense capabilities is meant for safeguarding its own sovereignty, territorial integrity and development interests.

- China has a landmass of 9.6 million square kilometres. There are over 22,000 kilometres of land border, which is among the longest in the world.
- China has over 18,000 kilometres of mainland coastline and more than 14,000 kilometres of island coastline.
- China has more neighbours than any other country in the world.

A strong national defense is necessary if we are to defend our territorial land, airspace and sea. In the past two hundred years China was invaded many times. China will never again tolerate foreign invasion forced upon its territory.

As China's outreach increases, the need grows by the day to protect its overseas assets, maritime passages and safety of Chinese citizens and corporations abroad.

China needs to have the capabilities to protect its legitimate interests, and to deliver maritime convoy, overseas evacuations and disaster relief.

My second observation is, the growth of our defense capabilities is modest and proportionate.

Take for example the defense budget, which is reported by the IISS and Jane's publications as growing robustly, being second only to the United States in 2013 and likely overtaking the US between 2030 and 2040.

- But even a distant second doesn't do China justice. Our economy last year was 56% of the US in size while our defense spending was less than one quarter of that of the US.
- According to the April report by SIPRI (Stockholm International Peace Research Institute), defense spending accounts for 3.8% of GDP in the US, 4.1% in Russia and 2.3% in the UK. The world average is 2.4%, and China spends only a modest 2%.
- In per capita terms, a Chinese citizen only spends 1/22 of his American

counterpart on defense. To put it in more relevant perspective, a British citizen spends 9 times and a Japanese 5 times more than a Chinese.

- And there's more to it than that. China's defense policy is literally defensive in nature. China has no military base beyond its borders. China deploys no forces overseas except peacekeepers and naval escort convoys off the coast of Somalia.

My third observation is, the Chinese military is increasingly open and transparent.

Since 1998, China has published eight Defense White Papers. The latest one, issued last year, disclosed these facts for the first time:

- Designations of 18 field armies.
- The total numbers of personnel of the Chinese army, navy and air force.
- And models of China's strategic missiles.

The US Defense Secretary, Chuck Hagel, visited China in April. On the very first day of his visit he got on China's very first aircraft carrier.

A few months ago, the PLA University of Science and Technology in Nanjing organised its 5th international cadets week. Among the participants there were two officers just graduated from RMA Sandhurst, Jason Johnston and Richard Levin.

They had the company of a BBC crew who covered the week-long event. This was the first filming by foreign media in a Chinese military academy. The 30-minute long programme, called "China's New Model Army," was recently broadcast by the BBC. This is yet more evidence showing China's growing openness and outreach of defense cooperation.

My fourth observation is, growing Chinese defense capabilities contributes to international and regional peace and stability.

Consider these facts:

- China is the largest contributor of peacekeepers among the UN P5. China has sent over 25,000 peacekeepers to more than 20 UN missions since 1990.
- China is the largest contributor of peace-keeping engineers, transport and medical staff among all 115 troop contributors.

- China is the biggest financial contributor to UN peacekeeping missions among all developing countries.
- Since 2002, the Chinese military has conducted 36 international emergency relief missions, having delivered 120 million pounds worth of relief supplies to 27 countries.
- Since late 2008, China has deployed over 10,000 men and women in uniform, 45 naval vessels in 17 escort convoy formations in the Gulf of Aden and off the coast of Somalia.
- China has been instrumental in convoy operations to destroy Syria's chemical weapons. Two Chinese frigates have completed over a dozen convoy operations since late last year.
- After the MH370 incident, China sent 7 naval vessels and 3 military aircraft in search operations.

President Xi Jinping has recently said,

"The lion of China has already awakened, but this is a peaceful, pleasant and civilised lion."

Let me also quote Sun Tzu again:

"Supreme excellence consists in breaking the enemy's resistance without fighting."

China will always stand for consultation and dialogue in managing differences with its neighbours.

But on matters of major principle concerning our sovereignty and territorial integrity, appeasement is not an option.

China will not provoke, but you can bank on preparedness to defend what is rightfully China's interest.

My advice to some countries is:

- Do not misjudge the situation.
- Do not underestimate China's resolve and capabilities.

Ladies and Gentlemen,

Major General J.F.C. Fuller, the British strategist, once made these comments:

"...of all Clausewitz's blind spots, the blindest was that he never grasped that the true aim of war is peace and not victory; therefore that peace should be the ruling idea of policy, and victory only the means to its achievement."

Peace is indeed China's ruling idea of policy, and victory in war is not a necessary means to such end. At the heart of the "Chinese Dream" you find peace. That is the core characteristic of China's security outlook and defense policy.

China is convinced that its dream and the dreams of other countries and peoples go hand in hand.

China's security and world peace and stability are one and the same.

China's growing capabilities is not a threat to others and China needs all on board for that future of peace and development.

To wrap up, it is my great pleasure to discuss the "Chinese Dream," China's approach to development and security with military commanders from the UK and beyond. I hope you'll visit China some day soon.

There can be great mutual value for you visiting Chinese military academies, barracks and naval ships. By studying, training and even exercising together with your Chinese counterparts, trust will grow to reduce mistrust.

Through a visit to China you will find for yourself what the "Chinese Dream" is and what it means to you.

Thank you.

Now, I will open the floor for questions.

2016 年 5 月 17 日

在英国巴斯皇家文学科学院发表主旨演讲：《中国发展给世界带来的机遇》。

2017 年 1 月 29 日

在伦敦特拉法加广场春节庆典活动上发表讲话：《文明交流互鉴是推动人类社会进步的动力》。

2017 年 3 月 29 日

在庆祝中英建立大使级外交关系 45 周年招待会上发表讲话：《携手并肩，抓住机遇，共创中英关系美好未来》。

2017 年 9 月 6 日

在英国诺丁汉大学荣誉法学博士授予仪式上发表主旨演讲：《凝聚智慧，共建世界和平与繁荣》。

2017年11月7日

在英国工商界党的十九大精神宣介会上发表主旨演讲：《把握新时代，抓住新机遇，开创新未来》。

2017年11月21日

在英国议会发表主旨演讲宣介党的十九大精神：《引领中国发展新时代，开启中英合作新征程》。

2018 年 4 月 11 日

在“新时代中国”国际研讨会开幕式上发表演讲：《读懂新时代中国，构建人类命运共同体》。

2018 年 4 月 11 日

在《习近平谈治国理政》第二卷多语种图书首发式上发表讲话：《领悟中国智慧，感知世界情怀》。

2018年5月8日

在彭博欧洲总部发表主旨演讲：《更加开放的中国，更加美丽的春天》。

2018年9月10日

在英国议会发表主旨演讲：《共享“一带一路”合作机遇，共创中英关系美好未来》。

2018年12月6日

在英国基尔世界事务论坛发表主旨演讲：《改革促进中国发展，开放推动世界进步》。

2018年12月11日

在驻英国使馆纪念改革开放40周年主题活动上发表主旨演讲：《纪念改革开放伟业，共谱合作共赢新篇》。

2019 年 1 月 8 日

在英国牛津剑桥俱乐部发表主旨演讲:《坚持和平发展，推进合作共赢》。

2019 年 4 月 9 日

在习近平外交思想主题座谈会上发表主旨演讲：《感知东方智慧，读懂中国未来》。

2020 年 3 月 2 日

在英国皇家国际事务研究所发表主旨演讲：《同舟共济，共克时艰，构建人类命运共同体》，并与该所主席奥尼尔男爵对话，回答听众提问。

第六章

改革开放

中国的改革开放在西方一直是一个热议的话题，同时也存在不少误区。有的用西方的标准评价中国的改革；有的抱怨中国的开放力度不够；有的认为中国只搞经济改革，不搞政治改革；还有的认为改革开放失去动力；更有的担心改革开放的未来。我在英国高校、智库、媒体宣介党的十八大 、十九大精神时，一个重点内容就是全面、深入地介绍中国的改革开放。在改革开放 40 周年之际，我到英国基尔世界事务论坛发表演讲。这是欧洲规模最大的研讨国际问题的公共论坛。当天可容纳 400 多人的演讲大厅座无虚席，由于来宾数量远超预期，主办方只好临时增加不少移动座椅，但仍无法满足需求，最后只好在大厅外增设一个视频分会场。由此可见西方公众对中国改革开放的兴趣。我围绕改革开放给中国带来了什么变化、中国为什么会发生这样的变化、中国的变化将给世界带来什么这三个问题，深入浅出地介绍了中国 40 年来坚定不移走改革开放道路的原因和成果，用具体的数字和鲜活的事例，说明中国始终是世界经济的建设者、世界和平的守护者、世界秩序的捍卫者，表示中国将一如既往地与各国人民携手，共同为构建人类命运共同体贡献力量。

在剑桥大学，我针对西方有些人认为，中国只搞经济改革，不搞政治改革，指出这是对中国全面改革的一种误解。事实上，中国的经济体制改革每推进一步，政治体制改革也深化一步。人民代表大会制度、中国共产党领导的多党合作和政治协商制度不断巩固完善；民主法制建设不断加强；人权事业不断发展，我们将尊重和保障人权写入宪法，努力维护社会公平正义，促进人的全面发展。

在驻英国使馆纪念改革开放 40 周年主题活动上我发表演讲指出，中国的改革开放只有进行时，没有完成时。随着中国综合国力逐步增强，国际上有些人关注下一步改革开放将把中国引向何方。我明确地告诉大家，中国绝不走国强必霸的老路，相反，我们将始终坚持和平发展，坚持合作共赢，共同促进世界和平、发展与繁荣。

成功的道路，全面的发展*

尊敬的剑桥大学校长博里塞维奇爵士，

老师们，同学们：

很高兴应博里塞维奇校长的邀请访问剑桥大学并作演讲。

这是我出使英国后第一次来到剑桥，但我对剑桥丝毫没有陌生感。

虽然我到英国后先去了牛津，但我知道“牛津出首相、剑桥出诺贝尔奖”这句佳话，知道剑桥大学校友获得了88个诺贝尔奖，相当于英国所获诺奖的总和，在世界所有大学中保持最高纪录。

我最早认识剑桥，是因为徐志摩先生在这里留下了《再别康桥》这样的千古绝唱，也是因为李约瑟博士在这里写就了鸿篇巨制《中国科学技术史》。

我第一次走进“剑桥”，是29年前我在美国塔夫茨大学弗莱彻学院读书的时候。当时弗莱彻学院由塔夫茨大学和哈佛大学共同管理，两院校图书馆使用统一索引，我经常去位于“剑桥”的哈佛大学图书馆查阅资料。

今天，我走进“正宗”的剑桥，这既是一次工作性质的访问，推动剑桥大学与中国的教育合作，也是一次个人的精神寻旅，品味剑桥800年的文化积淀。当然，我也愿就大家关心的中国话题，与你们交流讨论。

上周，根据中日两国的最新GDP统计数字，中国正式超过日本成了世界第二大经济体。世界上各大媒体都将此作为热点新闻进行报道。世界再次聚焦中国，围绕中国问题的讨论一直方兴未艾，现在再次升温。我总结了一

---

* 在英国剑桥大学的演讲。2011年2月22日，英国剑桥大学。

下人们热议的几个问题：一是中国成为世界第二大经济体说明了什么；二是中国是否很快会成为世界第一；三是中国能否持续高速发展；四是中国发展对世界意味什么。

今天，我想就这些问题谈谈我的看法。

首先，中国成为世界第二大经济体说明了什么？我认为，它说明了中国发展道路的成功。

中国为什么会取得如此成功？中国成功的经验是什么？

中国成功靠走适合自己国情的道路。一个13亿多人口的大国，一个有五千年文明历史的古国，该走什么样的道路才能发展，教科书上没有现成的答案，历史上也没有可以参考的先例。但中国人民在中国共产党坚强领导下，“摸着石头过河”，牢牢把握自己的国情，不断探索实践，开拓创新，借鉴吸取世界各国有益经验，实现了天翻地覆的变化。

中国成功靠“改革开放”。开放，不仅是经济上的对外开放，从封闭半封闭到全方位、多层次、宽领域对外开放，更是思想头脑的解放、社会的自由宽松、政府的公开透明。改革，不仅是改革经济制度，将高度集中的计划经济体制改革为充满生机和活力的社会主义市场经济体制，也是政治、社会、文化的全面改革和建设。

西方有些人认为，中国只搞经济改革，不搞政治改革。这是对中国全面改革的一种误解。事实上，30多年来，中国的经济体制改革每推进一步，政治体制改革也深化一步。人民代表大会制度、中国共产党领导的多党合作和政治协商制度，在中国政治生活中的地位越来越高，作用越来越大。30多年来，中国民主法制建设不断加强，坚持依法治国，几千年形成的人治社会正在向法治社会转变。30多年来，中国人权事业有了大发展，我们将尊重和保障人权写入了宪法，依法保障全体社会成员平等参与、平等发展的权利，同时加强国际人权合作。

历史上，中国并非没有尝试过西方式的民主，但都并未给中国带来繁荣和富强。今天，我们找到了一条适合自己发展的道路，建立了有中国特色的民主制度，我们有什么理由动摇？有什么理由折腾？

第二个问题，中国是否已在“坐二望一”，很快就会超过美国？

回答这个问题前，我们不妨看以下几对关键词。

一是“总量”和“人均”。尽管中国经济总量成了世界第二，2010年达到5.8万亿美元，但人均GDP只有4 300美元，仍排在世界百位左右，与中等发达国家相距甚远，仅占英国的1/9，美国的1/10。

二是“沿海”与“内地”，以及“城市”与“农村”。中国的沿海地区很发达，城市很繁荣，但是中国西部经济仍很落后，而且中国的城镇化率仅有46%，城乡居民收入比高达3.23∶1。我曾在中国较贫困的省份之一甘肃担任两年省长助理，对此深有感触。甘肃地处大西北，自然条件恶劣，沙漠化对当地人民的生存构成了严峻挑战，经济发展困难很大。许多农村的孩子没有电脑，更从来没有上过互联网。很多孩子在完成国家九年义务阶段教育后，由于经济原因不得不中止学业。

三是“制造”与“创造”。中国是制造业大国，但很多产品只有加工、封装等劳动力密集型环节在中国完成，研发设计、关键部件和市场营销都在国外，中国处在国际产业链的末端。中国出口商品中90%是贴牌生产，每部手机售价的20%、计算机售价的30%、数控机床售价的20%~40%，都要支付给国外专利持有者。从“中国制造”到“中国创造”还有很长的路要走。

四是“粗放”与“集约”。有数据显示，中国单位GDP的能耗是国际水平的三四倍，是英国的八倍。中国消耗了全球46%的钢铁、16%的能源、52%的水泥，但仅创造了全球8%左右的GDP。中国经济发展效率还有待大幅提升，需要从“粗放型”向“集约型”发展。

因此，中国经济总量虽然已居世界第二，但是人均水平和GDP质量还远没有达到发达国家的水平。我们不是“谦虚”，也不是“虚伪”，更不是想逃避“责任”，而是中国仍然是一个不折不扣的发展中国家。集中精力搞建设，一心一意谋发展，是我们长期的优先任务。我们不追求“虚名”，要的是实实在在的国强和民富。

第三个问题，中国已经高速行进了30多年，今后还能持续快速发展吗？

回答是肯定的。中国还处在工业化中期阶段和城镇化加速上升阶段，中国仍需要大量的基础设施投资，需要在未来20年安置3亿多人口，将其从农村迁移到城市，需要满足人民消费结构从温饱向小康升级换代的需求，需要实现西部地区向东部地区的发展水平看齐，因此中国经济并不缺乏动力，仍有很大的发展空间，我们有充分理由保持乐观。

中国2010年年底制定了“十二五”规划，即将在下月交由全国人民代表大会审议，这将是未来5年中国发展的重要蓝图。

我们要对中国经济结构进行战略性调整。我们将努力扩大内需，促进经济增长向依靠消费、投资、出口协调拉动转变。我们将加强农业，提升制造业核心竞争力，发展战略性新兴产业，加快发展服务业，促进经济增长向依靠第一、第二、第三产业协同带动转变。我们将统筹城乡发展，促进区域良性互动、协调发展。

我们要积极推进科技进步和创新，加快建设创新型国家。正如邓小平先生曾经指出的，科技是第一生产力。中国今后的发展必须向主要依靠科技进步、劳动者素质提高、管理创新转变。

我们要更好地保障和改善民生。发展经济，归根结底是为了人民的幸福。我们将完善保障和改善民生的制度安排，把促进就业放在优先位置，推进基本公共服务均等化，加大收入分配调节力度，使发展成果惠及全体人民。

我们要建设资源节约型、环境友好型社会。中国人均GDP要向西方国家看齐，但人均能源消费绝不能赶超发达国家，因为我们生活的地球实在承受不起。我们不能走西方国家工业化的老路。我们要节约能源，降低温室气体排放强度，发展循环经济，推广低碳技术，积极应对气候变化，促进经济社会发展与人口资源环境相协调，走可持续发展之路。

第四个问题，中国发展了，对世界意味着什么？是福还是祸？是机遇还是威胁？

我们不妨看三点。

一是中国给世界和平带来威胁了吗？中国奉行独立自主的和平外交政策，庄严地向世界承诺永远不称霸，永远不搞扩张；主张不干涉别国内部事务和谈判解决国际争端；倡导互信、互利、平等、协作的新安全观。中国是联合国安理会常任理事国中派出维和人员最多的国家，累计参与 24 项联合国维和行动，派出上万名维和人员；中国向索马里海域派出护航舰队，与多国舰队一道打击海盗，维护国际水域的安全；中国大力倡导朝核问题六方会谈，努力维护半岛和地区的和平稳定。无论是从中国的外交思想，还是外交行动来看，中国都是世界和平的维护者、稳定的促进者。

二是中国给世界经济带来威胁了吗？金融危机以来，中国为全球经济增长提供了重要支撑。2010 年发达国家经济仍步履维艰，在全球有效需求不足的情况下，中国扮演着向全球输出总需求的重要角色。欧盟 2010 年对华出口增长 31.9%，英国则增长 42%。2010 年中国经济继续保持两位数增长，对世界经济增长的贡献率达到 20%。今后 10 年，中国将继续奉行互利共赢的开放战略，市场对外开放程度将进一步提高，在国际贸易中的比重会不断上升，从国际市场的进口仍会迅速增加。这些对世界各国来说，只会是巨大的发展机遇。

三是中国对现行国际体系构成威胁了吗？中国作为一个负责任的大国，是国际体系的参与者、建设者和贡献者。我们与发达国家和新兴经济体就促进世界经济金融治理广泛开展合作，共同倡导加强 G20 机制；我们加强与发展中国家的传统友谊，帮助经济开发和实现减贫，过去两年里中国向其他发展中国家的贷款已经超过了世界银行；我们支持、倡导并践行多边主义，推动国际关系民主化，积极参与区域合作进程，努力促进国际体系更加有效地应对气候变化、能源和资源、粮食安全、恐怖主义等全球性挑战。

总之，中国的发展对世界是福不是祸，是机遇不是威胁。世界对中国不应感到担忧，更不应感到恐惧。美国前总统富兰克林·罗斯福说得好：“我们唯一恐惧的就是恐惧本身。”

老师们、同学们，

800 多年来，剑桥大学秉承“此地乃启蒙之所和智慧之源”（拉丁语：Hinc lucem et pocula sacra）的校训，努力探索世界，不断追求真理。半个多世纪前，李约瑟博士以其睿智打开了中国古代科技的历史宝库，重拾了伟大的中华文明。今天，当你们放眼中国，你们会发现中国正在走一条前人没有走过的道路，中国的实践可能超出了人们以往的知识积累。面对今天的中国这一丰富的宝藏，我衷心地期望剑桥大学的学子们遵循你们的校训，不断探索，大力挖掘，成为英国乃至世界范围内研究当代中国的领军者。

谢谢。

下面我愿回答大家的提问。

The Road to Success and Comprehensive Development*

Vice Chancellor Sir Leszek Borysiewicz,

Faculty members,

Students,

It is my great pleasure and privilege to visit Cambridge at the invitation of the Vice Chancellor and to speak at the Judge Business School.

This is my first visit to Cambridge as Chinese Ambassador to the UK. Yet Cambridge is no stranger to me. I heard a saying: "If you want to meet prime ministers, go to Oxford; but for Nobel Prize winners, go to Cambridge." Cambridge alumni won 88 Nobel Prizes, as many as the prizes won by Britain as a country, ranking first in all the universities around the world.

I first got to know Cambridge from Chinese poet Xu Zhimo who wrote his best-known poem *Farewell to Cambridge*, and later from Dr. Joseph Needham who wrote and edited the epic series *Science and Civilisation in China*.

My first visit to a place called Cambridge was 29 years ago when I was a student at the Fletcher School of Law and Diplomacy, which was then jointly administered by Tufts and Harvard. As Fletcher and Harvard shared the same library call number, I went to the Harvard Cambridge Library quite often.

Today I have finally come to the real Cambridge, both on a personal journey to fulfill a long-cherished dream of seeing Cambridge and experiencing its 800-year heritage

* Speech at the University of Cambridge. 22 February 2011.

and on an official visit to discuss educational cooperation and to talk about China.

Last week one of the headline news was that China has officially overtaken Japan as the world's second largest economy. This has put China in the limelight once again and stoked an ongoing discussion about China. Many questions were asked:

- What does China being the second largest economy tell us?
- How soon is China going to be number one?
- Will China be able to sustain such rapid growth?
- What does China's development mean to the world?

The list can go on and on. But these are the most asked questions. Let me share my thoughts about these questions.

First question: What does it tell us that China rolls in at number two? I think it tells the successful story of China's development.

The secret to China's success is simple and open. That is: China has found a development model well suited to its national conditions. How should we go about developing a country with 1.3 billion people and a history of five thousand years? Neither textbooks nor history has given us the ready answer. Under the strong leadership of the Communist Party of China, the country managed to "cross the river by feeling for the stones" as Mr. Deng Xiaoping termed it. We explored our way forward in a pioneering spirit by combining the useful experiences of other countries with the unique circumstances of China.

China's success also lies in its commitment to reform and opening-up. Opening-up means embracing the global economy at every level and in every area. But it is much more than that. It also means freeing your mind, fostering a more open and diverse society. It means nurturing a culture of open and transparent government. Reform is about transforming the planned economy to a vibrant socialist market economy. It is also about making comprehensive progress in political, social and cultural spheres.

Some people in the West believe that China has carried out reform only in economic sector, not in political system. This is a misunderstanding of China's comprehensive reform. During the past three decades, political reform has come with economic reform every step of the way, and political progress has been achieved hand in hand with economic growth. We have seen a growing role of the National People's Congress and multi-party political consultation under the leadership of the Communist Party. Democratic decision making and the legal system has been strengthened. The millennium-old pattern of "rule by man" is giving way to "rule of law." We have also seen significant progress in human rights. The promotion and protection of human rights has been written into the Chinese Constitution. All the citizens enjoy the rights protected by law to equal participation and development. We have also strengthened international cooperation on human rights.

It was not for lack of trying that Western-style democracy did not bring China the prosperity and strength it had wanted so badly in its modern history. Now that we have found our own road to success and Chinese style democracy, why should we waver or give it up?

Second question, how soon is China going to overtake the US? Before we answer this question, let's look at some key words:

Aggregates and *per capita*. China's economic aggregates stood at 5.8 trillion US dollars in 2010, ranking second in the world. But its per capita GDP was merely 4,300 US dollars, lower than about 100 other countries, only one ninth of the UK, and one tenth of the US.

Coastal and *inland*, *urban* and *rural*. We have in China both rich cities in the coastal regions and under developed poor regions in the west of the country. The urbanisation rate is only 46%, and the urban/rural income ratio is as high as 3.23 to 1. I served for two years as Assistant Governor in one of the poorest provinces in northwest China—Gansu. Gansu suffers from tough natural conditions. Desertification threatens the livelihood of the local people and economic development is a huge challenge. Many of the children in the countryside do not have access to computers or the Internet. Many boys and girls have to drop out of school because their families cannot afford their continued education.

Made in China and *created in China*. For all its manufacturing strength, China is still at the lower end of the value chain. In many cases only the labour-intensive parts of production such as processing and packaging are done in China. R&D, design, key components and marketing are done elsewhere. 90% of China's export commodities are OEM products. 20% of the retail value of every mobile phone, 30% of that of computers and 20%~40% of that of Computer Numerical Control machine tools go to foreign patent owners. There is still a long way to go from "Made in China" to "created in China."

Energy-intensive and *energy-efficient*. Statistics show that China's energy intensity is 3 to 4 times that of the international average and 8 times that of the UK. China consumes 46% of the world's iron and steel, 16% of energy, 52% of cement, and only produces 8% of the world's GDP. China still has a lot to do to raise the quality and efficiency of its economic growth.

Although China is now the number two economy in the world, we still lag far behind developed countries in per capita income and quality of GDP. China is still a developing country, not because we are modest or hypocritical, or we wish to escape from our responsibilities. Development will remain a top priority for China for a long time to come.

Third question: Can China sustain its fast growth after three decades?

The answer is positive. China is still in the course of rapid industrialisation and urbanisation. This is a phase when massive infrastructure investment is needed. 300 million people are expected to move from the countryside to the cities in the next 20 years. The Chinese people need to upgrade their consumption pattern, and the western regions need to catch up with their eastern counterparts. So, driving force is never lacking for the Chinese economy, and there is plenty of potential to be tapped. We have reasons to be optimistic about the future.

The National People's Congress will review China's 12th Five-Year Plan at its annual session next month. This is an important blueprint for China's development in the next 5 years.

We will carry out strategic economic restructuring to expand domestic demand and promote balanced growth driven by consumption, investment and exports. We will strengthen agriculture, increase the competitiveness of manufacturing, and give priority to emerging industries and the services sector. The aim is to seek a balanced and coordinated development between urban and rural areas and between China's eastern and western regions.

We will promote scientific and technological progress and innovation. We will speed up efforts to turn China into an innovation-driven country. As Mr. Deng

Xiaoping pointed out, "There is no other productive force more important than science and technology." Our future development must rely on scientific and technological progress, a higher quality labour force and innovative management.

We will continue to improve the lives of our people. Economic development is aimed at serving people's interests. We will improve social security, increase job creation, promote equal access to public services and balance income distribution. This will ensure that the benefits of development will be shared by all.

We will build an energy-efficient and environment-friendly society. We need to catch up with developed countries in terms of per capita GDP, but not per capita energy consumption, as this would be unsustainable for our planet. China cannot follow the traditional Western way of industrialisation. We must raise energy efficiency, reduce emission intensity, develop a circular economy, extensively apply low-carbon technologies and actively address climate change. We must promote sustainable development, achieving an appropriate balance between economic, social progress and population, resources and the environment.

The fourth and last question: What does China's development mean to the world, a blessing or catastrophe, opportunities or threats? This question can be answered in three aspects:

Is China a threat to world peace? China follows an independent foreign policy of peace. We solemnly pledged to the world that hegemony or expansion is never an option for China; China stands for non-interference in others' internal affairs and negotiated solutions to international disputes. China believes that security should be based on mutual trust, mutual benefit, equality and coordination. China is the largest contributor of peacekeepers amongst the UN P5, having sent ten thousand peacekeepers to 24 UN missions. It has sent escort ships to the waters off the Somali coast and worked with the navies of other countries to combat piracy and improve safety in international waters. It has actively worked to facilitate the Six-Party Talks to uphold peace and the stability on the Korean Peninsula and in Northeast Asia. China is in every way an upholder of peace and a facilitator of stability.

Is China a threat to the world economy? China has been a crucial support for global growth since the start of the financial crisis. It drove global demand at a time when developed countries were in economic difficulties. This was reflected in the 31.9%

increase of EU exports and the 42% increase of UK exports to China last year. China maintained a double-digit growth last year, and contributed 20% of global economic growth. China will continue to pursue a strategy of win-win opening-up over the next decade. Its market will open wider, its share in international trade will increase, and its imports will rise. These will no doubt create enormous opportunities for countries around the world.

Is China a threat to the international system? China has been participating in and contributing to the current international system as a responsible major player. It has entered into extensive cooperation with its partners in developed and emerging economies on the reform of global economic and financial governance, and jointly advocated a greater role of the G20. It has strengthened traditional friendships with other developing countries and helped them develop their economies and reduce poverty. The loans it has provided to other developing countries in the past two years have surpassed those of the World Bank. It supports and practices multilateralism, and stands for greater democracy in international relations. This can be seen by its active participation in regional cooperation, along with the support it gives to tackling global challenges such as climate change, energy, resources, food security and terrorism.

China's development is a blessing, not a catastrophe to the world. It means opportunities, not threats. It is not to be worried about, still less feared. As Franklin Roosevelt put it, "the only thing we have to fear is fear itself."

Faculty members and students,

Over the past 8 centuries, the University of Cambridge has stayed true to its motto "From here, light and sacred draughts" (*Hinc lucem et pocula sacra*) in its tireless pursuit of the world's truth and knowledge. More than half a century ago, Dr. Joseph Needham uncovered the treasures of China's ancient science and civilisation. Today when you look at China, you will realise that it is embarking on a journey no country has ever made. This goes beyond the knowledge of human beings and offers enormous opportunities. I therefore encourage you to follow Cambridge's motto to renew your efforts in tapping the rich resources China has to offer and lead the UK and the world in studying and understanding today's China.

Thank you.

Now, I would like to take questions from you.

创新是中国发展的关键*

尊敬的奥尼恩斯校长，

老师们、同学们：

英国人常说“Last but not least”（最后但也同样重要），这正好可以用来形容我今天访问帝国理工学院。因为，在英国“G5”精英大学中，帝国理工学院是我最后到访的一所，而帝国理工学院无论是实力，还是知名度，显然不逊于其他四所中的任何一所（牛津、剑桥、伦敦政治经济学院和伦敦大学学院）。

我今天演讲的主题是中国的创新，这是奥尼恩斯校长给我出的题目。其实这也是我一直在思考的课题，可以说我们不谋而合。就我而言，这个题目的由来还要追溯到 2011 年初我访问剑桥大学的时候。我参观了著名的李约瑟研究所，当时该所研究人员提到了李约瑟先生在著述《中国科学技术史》时发现的一个难题——“李约瑟之谜”，即古代中国科技成果遥遥领先于其他文明，而为何在明清以来的近代，中国科技水平远远落在了西方后面？据我所知，这个谜团目前并没有标准、统一的答案，各种解答林林总总，可谓见仁见智。

“李约瑟之谜”是关于近代中国的问题，事实上，关于当代中国，同样也有一个谜，这也是我在各种场合经常被问到的一个问题：当代中国飞速发展，其成功的秘诀是什么？对这个问题的回答也有很多不同说法。

---

* 在英国帝国理工学院的演讲。2012 年 1 月 18 日，英国帝国理工学院。

今天，我想谈一下我对这两个问题的思考，并尝试给出我的一个解答：创新。无论近代中国的落后，还是当代中国的进步，都可归结为有无创新。

近代中国的落后，是由于明清实行闭关锁国政策，以天朝自居，故步自封；是由于自给自足、靠天吃饭的小农经济；是由于腐朽的科举制度迫使知识分子皓首穷经，却无经世济用之学；是由于列强入侵，造成人民流离失所，国家切肤之痛。而正是种种内外因素的综合作用，扼杀了中国制度创新和科技创新的动力，束缚了创新思想和创新精神，破坏了创新条件和环境。因而，近代中国举步不前。当西方工业革命方兴未艾、科技突飞猛进时，中国的停滞守旧就意味着衰弱落后。

那么当代中国又是如何重拾创新脚步，从而实现中国的繁荣复兴的？中国近 30 年的发展脉络给了最好的诠释。

第一，中国准确把握时代主题，顺应人民愿望，做出了改革开放的历史性决策。我们改革不适应生产力发展的政策和体制，结束长期对外封闭的状况，实行“引进来，走出去”。我们“摸着石头过河”，边摸索实践，边总结推广。改革开放既是政策创新，也是制度创新，更是思想创新，为中国的现代化建设注入了强大活力，改变了中国的面貌。

第二，中国确立社会主义市场经济体制，突破只有资本主义才能搞市场经济的认识误区，从而发挥了市场在国民经济资源配置中的基础性作用，极大地解放了生产力。这一体制创新促使中国短期内迅速建立了全国统一开放的市场体系和日臻熟练的宏观调控体系，使中国经济在短短 30 多年内从世界第 15 位跃升为第 2 位。

第三，中国2001年加入世界贸易组织，创新对外经济合作方式，在更大范围、更高水平上参与国际经济合作和竞争，大力发展开放型经济，推动中国和世界的关系发生了深刻变化。10年来，我们不断降低进口产品关税税率，取消所有不符合世界贸易组织规则的进口配额、许可证等非关税措施，全面放开对外贸易经营权，扩大外资市场准入。10 年来，中国货物贸易额的全球排名由第六位上升到第二位；累计吸收外商直接投资居发展中国家首位；对外直接投资年均增长 40% 以上，2010 年居世界第五位；中国每年平均进口

7 500 亿美元的商品，为贸易伙伴创造了大量就业岗位和投资机会。

第四，中国积极推进政治体制改革，不断创新国家管理方式。我们不照搬西方国家的三权分立制度，而是根据自己的国情，不断完善人民代表大会制度和中国共产党领导的多党合作及政治协商制度，努力发展中国特色的民主制度。我们不断加强法制建设，制定了 200 多部法律。各级干部的录用选拔引进了公开招考、差额选举、竞争上岗、任前公示和民主测评等制度，努力做到选贤任能，广纳人才。我们积极将网络和微博纳入社会管理的新方式，政府更加贴近民众。我们提出了“生存权和发展权是首要的基本人权”的重要观点，将尊重和保障人权写入中国的根本大法——宪法，制定了以促进人权为主题的国家行动计划。

第五，中国提出了“科学技术是第一生产力”，制定了“科教兴国”战略，树立了建设“创新型国家”的目标。中国的科技投入持续大幅增长，占国内生产总值的比例目前超过了 1.5%，形成了比较完备的科技基础条件和学科布局。中国建立和完善了科技奖励制度和知识产权制度，出台了一大批激励自主创新的政策措施。中国发明专利授权量已上升到世界第 3 位，国际科学论文总量居世界第 2 位，被引用量居世界第 8 位。中国在高温超导、纳米科技、量子通信、生命科学等领域取得了具有世界先进水平的创新成果，超级杂交水稻、汉字激光照排、高性能计算机、第三代移动通信等许多重大关键产业技术取得了重要突破。中国的基础工业、制造业和新兴产业的技术创新水平显著提高，高技术产业已经成为国民经济持续增长的新动力。中国将科技创新大量运用在推动节能减排、服务北京奥运和上海世博、支撑三峡工程和青藏铁路等重大的工程和活动中。中国成功实施载人航天和探月工程，为人类和平利用太空做出了新的贡献。

第六，中国走新型的发展道路——和平发展道路，既通过维护世界和平发展自己，又通过自身发展维护世界和平。中国 20 世纪 50 年代在世界上首倡“和平共处五项原则”。改革开放后，中国先后提出“和平与发展是世界的主题”、建立“国际政治经济新秩序”和构建“和谐世界”主张，奉行互利共赢的开放战略，倡导互信、互利、平等、协作的新安全观。

老师们、同学们，

中国经过改革开放33年来的创新式发展，已经取得了非凡的成就。但面对未来，中国犹如逆水行舟——不进则退，我们没有任何理由懈怠，没有任何理由停滞，必须披荆斩棘，勇往直前，必须与时俱进，不断开拓创新。

第一，中国将继续推进制度创新。我们将不失时机地继续推进经济、政治、社会体制改革创新，不断解放和发展社会生产力，坚决破除一切妨碍科学发展的思想观念和体制机制弊端；我们将继续健全民主制度，丰富民主形式，拓宽民主渠道；我们将贯彻以人为本、执政为民原则，加强和创新社会管理，特别是加快推进以保障和改善民生为重点的社会建设，促进社会和谐稳定。

第二，中国将全力推进经济创新。我们将积极应对发展中存在的不平衡、不协调和不可持续的问题，加快推进经济发展方式改变和经济结构调整，改变经济增长主要由出口和投资拉动的局面，着力扩大国内需求，着力促进产业结构优化升级。2.0版的中国经济，应当再也不需要用出口8亿件衬衫换一架空客A380。

第三，中国将大力加强科技创新。我们将争取到2020年全社会研究开发投入占GDP的比重提高到2.5%以上，科技进步贡献率达到60%以上，国际科学论文被引用量进入世界前5位。我们将力争在信息、生物、材料和航天领域的前沿技术达到世界先进水平，能源开发、节能技术和清洁能源技术取得突破，在重点行业和重点城市建立循环经济的技术发展模式。我们将努力培养一批具有世界水平的科学家和研究团队，建成若干世界一流的科研院所和大学以及具有国际竞争力的企业研究开发机构，形成比较完善的国家创新体系，努力推动“中国制造”向“中国创造”转变。

第四，中国将积极推动文化创新。现在英美正在热映一部电影《铁娘子》（*Iron Lady*），这里我愿引用这位铁娘子的一句话：“只出口电视机而不是思想观念的国家，不可能成为超级大国。”当今世界，文化越来越成为综合国力竞争的重要因素，中国必须以高度的文化自觉和文化自信，着眼于提高民族素质和塑造高尚人格，以更大力度推进文化改革发展，不断进行文化创造。我们将在弘扬中华优秀传统文化的基础上，包容、借鉴和吸收其他民族先进文化成果，形成与中国国际地位相对称的文化软实力，提高中华文化对外影响力，努力创造出中华文化的新魅力和新辉煌。

第五，中国将坚持不懈致力于外交创新。我们将继续探索和平发展道路，打破“国强必霸”的大国崛起传统模式，超越曾把人类一次次拖入对抗和战乱的老路。我们将以命运共同体的新视角，以同舟共济、合作共赢的新理念，寻求多元文明交流互鉴的新局面，寻求各国应对多样化挑战的新方式，寻求世界实现包容性发展的新途径，不断赋予和平发展道路新内涵和新实践。

老师们、同学们，

创新是一个民族进步的灵魂，是一个国家兴旺发达的动力。一个没有创新能力的民族，难以屹立于世界先进民族之林。回顾中国近几百年来的落后与进步、衰弱与复兴，更证明了这条颠扑不破的宝贵历史经验。

最后，借用帝国理工学院的校训：“知识是帝国的光彩和守护者。”（Scientia imperii decus et tutamen.）我想说：“创新是中国的光彩和守护者。”

谢谢。

现在，我愿回答老师和同学们的问题。

Innovation: China's Path to Success*

Sir Keith O'Nions,

Teachers and Students,

People in Britain often say "last but not least."

I like this way of saying that you may be last—but you are just as important as any other on a list.

My visit to Imperial College London today is right to be described this way.

Imperial College London is the last G5 elite universities in Britain I have visited.

But your university matches any of the other four—Oxford, Cambridge, LSE and UCL. Your reputation, strengths and innovations are much admired worldwide.

Sir Keith O'Nions has most kindly invited me to speak about China's innovation.

I am very glad to respond to this request. I have been reflecting a great deal on the issue of innovation. I was able to do this in my postings around the world. As Ambassador in Britain, I am privileged to see many parts of the UK and so I continue to compare innovation in UK, China and around the world.

In the UK last year one visit made a particular impact. This was at Cambridge University and its famous centre of Sinology, the Needham Research Institute. It was there that my discussion with the research fellows touched upon what is known as the "Needham Question."

In his series of books called *Science and Civilisation in China*, Dr. Needham compared human progress in China and the rest of the world. There is a broad consensus inside China and worldwide about his conclusions. These were that for

---

* Speech at the Imperial College London. 18 January 2012.

most of the past two millennia China had led the world in scientific and technological innovation. The "Needham Question" asks why China stopped innovating around three hundred years ago.

In other word, how did China lose all the advantage it had gained? Needham lists many fields in which China led the world. The most famous inventions that China gave the world were paper, printing, gunpowder and the magnetic compass. European countries grasped these inventions and greatly improved them. The consequence was that European countries rapidly overtook China in scientific and technological prowess.

On the "Needham Question" there is no agreed answer amongst scholars both inside China and worldwide. Different conclusions may capture different facets of the truth.

The "Needham Question" is about what happened to China centuries ago. However, there is another question related to modern China I would like to introduce to you.

What I am always being asked is this:

"What's the secret behind China's decades of fast growth?"

Naturally, there have been many explanations.

Today, I will give you my answer to the two questions — the "Needham Question" and "Fast Growth in China."

My answer is clear and simple.

It is all about innovation.

This is the keyword to explain China's baffling decline and its rapid rise today.

From mid-14th century to the mid-20th century, China's economic decline was not by accident. A range of factors combined to make it happen.

In the Ming and Qing dynasties China had a closed-door policy. This created an illusion inside China about the country's economic superiority. It led to conceit among its rulers. It blinded them to the fast and deep changes elsewhere in the world. They were unaware of the innovation driving the economies of Europe and later the USA.

Economic historians have estimated that by 1840 China still accounted for a third of global GDP. But the speed of the industrial revolution in the rest of the world was leaving China further and further behind. China's entrenched and self-reliant economy strangled market forces, trade, and crucially innovation. It brought the country to a virtual standstill.

In China the out-of-date feudal civil service examination forced intellectuals to be preoccupied with past literature. It positively discouraged developing insights necessary to meet challenges of their time.

The invasion of European powers drove China to the brink of collapse.

The result was utter disaster for China.

China failed to develop a can-do spirit. Chinese people lost the drive for institutional and scientific innovation. Even worse, this happened when the industrial and technology revolution began to gather greater and greater momentum elsewhere in the world. China's stagnation sped up its decline in relation to rising western powers.

If China lost itself in the dawning of this new world, then how did it manage to find a path toward rebirth and prosperity?

The immediate past thirty years of development gives a clear answer. It is not surprising that innovation is the theme that runs through the answer!

There are six points I want to make.

First, China's reform and opening-up policies were ground-breaking in the history of the world.

The policies responded to the needs of the time and people's aspirations. But how was this done? The answer was some very innovative thinking and actions:

- China reversed old policies and constructed new mechanisms to propel productivity gains.
- China reopened the door to the world after decades of disengagement.
- China encouraged two-way flow of capital, technology and human resources with the world.
- And China took the reform forward step by step like "crossing the river by feeling for the stones."

The reform and opening-up was a policy and institutional innovation. It brought enormous changes to the way Chinese people think. It infused strong vitality into China's modernisation drive and transformed the nation.

Second, China built up a socialist market economy.

Chinese people ditched the dogma that the market economy is the preserve of capitalism. This gave market forces a central role in resource allocation. The result was dramatic as it unlocked immense productive potential.

The ground-breaking step led to the creation of a single market nationwide over a short period of time. It was also a starting point toward a sophisticated macroeconomic policy framework.

All these explain China's breathtaking economic rise in the past thirty years or so. The period saw the Chinese economy jump from the 15th place on global GDP rankings to become the world's number two.

Third, joining the WTO in 2001 redefined China's role in the world economy.

China promoted international economic cooperation in new ways. It means that China is more deeply and widely involved in international economic cooperation and competition.

The statistics show how China has helped drive global trade and prosperity.

Ten years on, China has slashed the import tariff rate. China has cancelled all the WTO-inconsistent non-tariff measures such as import quota and certificates. China has liberalised international trading rights and widened market access for foreign investors.

The past ten years showed a rapid rise of China's trade value from the sixth place to the second spot in the world.

On the FDI inflow China tops the table among developing countries. Meanwhile, it has grown to be the world's fifth largest investor country, with an outbound investment growing over 40 percent every year.

China imports an annual 750 billion US dollars of goods. This has generated a huge number of jobs and investment opportunities for its trading partners.

Fourth, China is moving forward with innovation in its political reform.

China is exploring new approaches to run the country. Instead of copying the so-called "western political system," China is developing its own style of democracy. This is tailored to its own national circumstances.

These are some of the innovations:

- China is improving the people's congress system and the multi-party cooperation and political consultation led by the Communist Party of China.
- The legal system is being strengthened with over 200 laws made.
- Officials are appointed on principles of meritocracy.

- Effective mechanisms have been set up to deliver transparency and accountability. These include open examination, competitive election, and seeking public comments with regular assessment.
- We are using the Internet and micro blogs to enrich public interaction. The aim is to bring the government closer to the people.
- We believe in the centrality of the right to survival and the right to development in human rights.
- In China, "respect and protect human rights" has been written into the constitution and a national human rights action plan has been adopted.

Fifth, China's development has been guided by the vision that "science and technology are the primary productive forces."

We have unveiled a strategy of national rejuvenation through science and education. There is a deep commitment to turn China into an innovative society.

The Chinese budget for science and technology continues to rise quickly. It now reaches over 1.5 percent of GDP.

China has built a strong foundation and comprehensive disciplinary structure for scientific research.

In turn, China has also improved research rewards and an intellectual property protection regime. A wide set of incentives have been put in place to encourage innovation.

The number of invention patent grants in China has risen to number two in the world. Furthermore, we produce the second highest number of scientific research papers, with a reference amount ranking eighth globally.

The results of these policies can already be seen. China has world-leading research outcomes in high-temperature super-conductivity, nanotechnology, quantum teleportation and life sciences.

China also achieved breakthroughs in a broad range of major industries, including super hybrid rice, Chinese character laser typesetting, high-performance computer and third generation mobile communication.

China's primary, manufacturing and emerging industries are gaining a stronger innovation capacity. Its high-tech sector is providing new momentum to sustain economic growth.

The Chinese are employing technology innovations in major energy-saving and emission-cutting projects. The best examples include the Beijing Olympic Games, Shanghai World Expo, Three Gorges Project and Qinghai-Tibet railway.

In space technology, our successful manned space missions and lunar probe project have made new contribution for mankind to use space peacefully.

Sixth, China has committed to a path of peaceful development.

Chinese people are deeply aware that preserving a peaceful world and achieving development in China are mutually reinforcing.

China initiated the Five Principles of Peaceful Coexistence in the 1950s. After the reform and opening-up started, China went further. The Chinese government defined peace and development as the theme of the world and called for a new political and economic order.

Today, China's ambition is to achieve world harmony. To do so, my country will continue with these values that are of benefit for all the wide world:

- The opening-up strategy.
- Building mutual trust.
- Shared benefits.
- Equality and coordination as essential elements to build a secure world.

Teachers and students,

China's 33 years of reform and opening-up is an endeavour unprecedented in the history of the world.

At its core is a story about innovation and its consequent huge success.

History also shows that success can produce complacency.

Complacency can also be the enemy of innovation.

So, China must not slacken its innovation efforts or stand still. Instead, China needs to move on with an even stronger will to innovate.

We will advance institutional innovation.

China's economic, political and social reform will continue.

The government of China has a constant recognition of the need to innovate to unleash the productive potential, free people's minds and fix institutional weaknesses.

China will strengthen its democratic institutions and widen the forms and channels of participation in democracy.

"Put people first" will remain the overarching governance principle. The central mission will be to support and improve people's lives and promote social harmony and stability.

China will push forward economic innovation.

China will tackle those unbalanced, uncoordinated and unsustainable elements in the economy.

To do so, the focus is to shift to a domestic demand-led growth away from export and public investment.

China will restructure its economy and move our industries up the value chain.

A Chinese "economy 2.0" means we don't need to sell 800 million shirts to buy an Airbus A380 anymore.

China will strengthen scientific innovation.

Chinese R&D to GDP ratio will rise to above 2.5 percent.

Technology will contribute to over 60 percent of economic growth. China will be among the top five countries whose academic papers are most frequently referenced.

China will invest more to develop frontier technologies in information, bioscience, material engineering and space.

A sustainable development strategy is key. So, China will seek more progress in new energy development, energy-efficient technologies and clean energy.

These goals require China to produce more outstanding scientists and researchers. It means building top-rate research institutes, high quality universities and globally competitive R&D centres.

To move from "made in China" to "created in China," China will build a full-fledged national innovation system.

China will push forward cultural innovation.

One recent box office hit in Britain and America is the film *Iron Lady*.

Let me quote what Prime Minister Margaret Thatcher, the Iron Lady, said of culture: a country that exports televisions—but not ideas—has no hope of becoming a superpower.

In today's world, culture has increasingly become a weighty component of national power.

China will further enhance its cultural identity with greater confidence. So how will this be done?

China will build on the Chinese cultural heritage and absorb the best of other civilisations. In this way the Chinese people will build up a new culture and a cultural influence that fits well with China's global profile.

The mission is to expand China's cultural influence worldwide. In turn this will secure deeper cross-cultural mutual respect and understanding about Chinese culture.

China will continue its diplomatic innovation.

China will further explore the path toward peaceful development. It will lead by example to break the cycle of power and hegemony. This approach embraced by previous rising powers drew mankind into constant confrontation and conflict.

What China calls for is a spirit of solidarity and a sense of common purpose within the world community.

China supports intercultural dialogues and exchanges. They represent the best chance for building a global partnership to tackle the diverse challenges the world faces.

It will not only buttress China's peaceful development, but also make common development possible for all.

Teachers and Students,

China has a history of rising—falling—and rising again, over the past two millennia.

The decline and rejuvenation of China over the past centuries provide the best proof of the argument for innovation.

I believe that innovation is the soul and spirit of national progress.

Innovation is the driver of a thriving society.

A nation without innovative power can't secure a solid footing in the world.

The motto of the Imperial College London is "Scientia imperii decus et tutamen" (knowledge is the adornment and protection of the empire).

Let me borrow your motto to give my conclusion about China's success.

Innovation is the adornment and protection of China.

Thank you!

Now, I will be glad to take your questions.

全面深化改革是中国发展的强大动力*

尊敬的英国改革俱乐部政治委员会主席里德教授，

女士们、先生们：

很高兴来到具有悠久历史的英国改革俱乐部作演讲。

早在我到英国工作以前，甚至可以说在我青年求学时代，我就知道伦敦有一个绅士俱乐部——“改革俱乐部”。因为在凡尔纳的小说《八十天环游地球》中，书中的主人公斐利亚·福克先生就是改革俱乐部的会员，著名的打赌就发生在这里，环游的起点和终点也是这里。当然，我相信现在改革俱乐部再也不允许打赌了；即使不搭乘飞机，环游地球再也不需要 80 天了。我也知道现在改革俱乐部再也不仅限绅士参加，而是接受女性会员，正如今天在座的有很多女士。

改革俱乐部因《1832 年改革法案》而成立。据说即使到了如今，俱乐部会员仍要宣誓支持该改革法案，你们仍有一个专门称呼——“改革者”。所以，今天来到改革俱乐部，在改革派的中心与“改革者”交流，我很容易就想到了一个演讲主题：改革。

“改革”这个词在过去 35 年里，与中国牢牢地联系在一起。1978 年，中国共产党举行了十一届三中全会，拉开了中华大地的改革序幕。35 年来，中国实行改革开放政策，扫除了影响发展社会生产力的许多障碍，中国跃升为世界第二大经济体，成为世界经济增长的引擎之一。可以说，改革改变了中

* 在英国改革俱乐部的演讲。2013 年 11 月 20 日，英国改革俱乐部。

国，改革富强了中国。

35 年过去了，我们解决了国家发展中的一系列旧问题，同时也遇到了一些新问题。如何破解发展中面临的难题，化解来自各方面的风险挑战，推动经济社会持续健康发展？中国给予了明确回答，这就是坚定改革信心，以更大的政治勇气和智慧、更有力的措施和办法继续推进改革事业。就在上周，中国共产党召开了十八届三中全会，这次会议可以说是举世瞩目，因为它为中国全面深化改革作了一次总部署。

现在大家都在分析解读党的十八届三中全会及其制定的改革总体方案的具体含义。我认为可以用三个以 D 开头的英语单词，进行“3-D”即立体式解读。

第一，决心（Determination）。会议表明中国决心以促进社会公平正义、增进人民福祉为出发点，进一步解放思想，坚决破除各方面的体制机制弊端。几天前《金融时报》一篇报道的标题就是《北京显示释放市场力量的决心》。十八届三中全会释放的信号就是中国准备冲破思想观念的障碍，突破利益固化的樊篱，使一切劳动、知识、技术、管理、资本的活力竞相迸发，使一切创造社会财富的源泉充分涌流，使发展成果更多、更公平地惠及全体人民。

第二，设计（Design），而且突出顶层设计。邓小平先生在改革开放之初，曾这样形象地描述中国的改革：“摸着石头过河。”因为中国的改革是一项前无古人的事业，既无前人的实践经验可资借鉴，又无现成的理论指导，所以只有自己去试、去闯，去探索成功的道路。而现在，中国的改革已进入深水区，一项改革措施如果触及利益格局，就会引发矛盾和阻力，现实情况就要求中央来进行顶层设计，总揽全局，整体谋划，协调各方。因此，十八届三中全会明确提出要加强顶层设计和“摸着石头过河”相结合，提高改革决策科学性，广泛凝聚共识，形成改革合力。这次新设立的中央全面深化改革领导小组，就是一个改革的总指挥部，它负责改革总体设计、统筹协调、整体推进、督促落实，就是要确保改革的系统性、整体性和协同性，就是要使各项改革举措在政策取向上相互配合、在实施过程中相互促进、在实际成效上相得益彰。

第三，部署（Deployment）。这次会议对全面深化改革作了系统部署，也明确了重点。系统部署就是强调坚持和完善基本经济制度，加快完善现代市场体系，加快转变政府职能，深化财税体制改革，健全城乡发展一体化体制机制，构建开放型经济新体制，加强社会主义民主政治制度建设，推进法治中国建设，强化权力运行制约和监督体系，推进文化体制机制创新，推进社会事业改革创新，创新社会治理体制，加快生态文明制度建设，深化国防和军队改革。其中，经济体制改革是全面深化改革的重点，核心问题是处理好政府与市场的关系，使市场在资源配置中起决定性作用和更好发挥政府的作用。这样的总体部署就构成了改革的整体推进和重点突破相互促进。

此次会议是全面深化改革的一次总动员、总部署，同时确定了改革的15个领域里的55个重大改革任务和300多条重大改革措施。比如，要求建立公平开放透明的市场规则，实行统一的市场准入制度，探索对外商投资实行准入前国民待遇加负面清单的管理模式；放宽投资准入，统一内外资法律法规，推进金融、教育、文化、医疗等服务业领域有序开放，放开建筑会计、会计审计、商贸物流、电子商务等服务业领域外资准入限制，进一步放开一般制造业等；确保依法独立公正行使审判权、检察权，保证国家法律统一正确实施；完善人权司法保障制度，重申国家尊重和保障人权，明确废止劳动教养制度，健全社区矫正制度。全面深化改革不仅有明确具体的任务，而且有明确的时间表，这就是到2020年完成各项改革任务，在重要领域和关键环节改革上取得决定性成果，改革进程是可检查、可评估的。

可以说，十八届三中全会吹响了中国新一轮改革的“集结号”。正如《经济学人》一篇文章的标题所评述的：“中国为今后改革铺平了道路。”如果说，过去35年的改革使中国摆脱了贫穷落后的状态，那么，今天中国的“二次改革”就将实现中华民族伟大复兴，实现13亿中国人民的“中国梦”。

各位“改革者”，

改革不可能一蹴而就，也不可能一劳永逸，这一情况不仅发生在中国，也发生在英国。从英国历史上看，我演讲开始提到的《1832年改革法案》，它适应于工业革命给英国社会带来的变化，扩大了选民的基础，标志着英国现代议会制度真正开始建立。但它在历史上只是被称为“第一次议会改革”，此后还经历了1867年、1884年和1918年三次重大议会改革。直到今天，英国议会还在不断演变中，比如近几年英国新设立了上院议长，也曾对下院议员的投票选举方法进行公投，现在还在讨论是否要改革上院议员的产生办法，废除世袭改为竞选。所以改革总是处于不断进行中，制度需要不断自我完善。

中国全面深化改革，不但将为中国的发展进步提供强大的动力，而且将给中英合作带来更多机遇。改革确定了完善现代市场体系、构建开放型经济新体制、推进法治中国建设目标，意味着中国将建立更加公平的市场竞争、更加开放的服务业、更加便捷的投资手续、更加严格的知识产权保护、更加良好的法制环境；也意味着中国的企业和个人将成为对外投资主体，发挥自身优势并以创新方式到境外开展绿地投资、并购投资、证券投资和联合投资等。改革确立了促进城乡发展一体化目标，意味着中国的市场将持续甚至成倍扩大，消费潜力得到进一步释放。改革确立了提高文化开放水平目标，意味着中国将加大对外文化交流，加大吸收借鉴优秀文化成果，引进人才、技术和经营管理经验。所有这些将有力地促进中英在经贸、金融和文化等领域的交流与合作。

就在下月初，卡梅伦首相将访问中国，他还将率领庞大的企业家代表团。此次访华正值中共十八届三中全会召开不久，我相信改革将是中英两国领导人会晤的一大主题，双方将充分介绍各自改革思路与经验，深入探讨改革给双边关系带来的新机遇，共同设计规划两国未来合作的新蓝图。

女士们、先生们，

在历史上，《1832 年改革法案》的通过经历了艰难曲折，但其意义彪炳史册，所以它又被称为“伟大的议会法案”。今天，中国的全面深化改革同样需要攻坚克难，但正惟其艰难、因其复杂，这一新的改革事业注定将是伟大的，必将产生重大而深远的影响，开辟中国发展的全新时代。同样，进一步发展中英关系也需要做出不懈努力，排除各种障碍，但只要中英双方做到相互尊重、平等相待、求同存异、互利共赢，我们也必将开辟中英新型大国关系之路，将两国关系提升到新水平、新高度。

谢谢。

下面我愿回答大家的提问。

Comprehensively Deepening Reform Provides a New Driving Force for China's Development*

Chairman Brian Holden-Reid,

Ladies and Gentlemen,

It is a pleasure and honor for me to speak at your time-honored Reform Club.

I knew about the Reform Club long before I became the Chinese Ambassador in London. When I was a young student, I read about a gentlemen's club in London by the name of the Reform Club. The French writer Jules Verne was responsible for that.

I was intrigued by the hero in his book *Around the World in Eighty Days*. As you will know well Mr. Phileas Fogg was a member of the Reform Club and this is where his famous gamble took place. The beginning and the end of his journey were both here in your Club.

Of course, I am sure gambling is no longer allowed here nowadays. Nor does it take 80 days to travel around the world, by air or not. And the membership is no longer limited to gentlemen, either. You do have female members now, as I can see many ladies here.

The Reform Club was founded following the passage of the Reform Act 1832. I am told that even today membership still requires a pledge of support to this Act. You are called "Reformers."

So, when I am here at the "centre of Reformists" to address a group of reformers, I

---

* Speech at the Reform Club. 20 November 2013.

have naturally and inevitably chosen reform as the theme of my speech.

No talk about China in the past 35 years can go without the word of "reform."

The Third Plenum of the 11th Central Committee of the Communist Party of China in 1978 unveiled a massive reform programme across China.

Over the past 35 years, the reform and opening-up policy has transformed China:

- The policy removed numerous constraints throttling productivity.
- The policy catapulted China to the position of the second largest economy in the world.
- The policy turned China into one of the engines of global economic growth.

It is an understatement to say that reform has changed China and enriched China.

Thirty-five years on, we have resolved a host of old problems facing China. At the same time, we have a raft of new problems before us:

- How to crack the problems arising in the course of development?
- How to avert risks of various kinds?
- How to promote sustainable economic and social development?

China's answer is an explicit one. This is to have greater confidence in reform. It means we will continue to push forward reform with greater political courage and wisdom as well as more powerful measures.

Just last week another Third Plenum was held in Beijing. This was the Third Plenum of the 18th CPC Central Committee. This meeting attracted world-wide attention as it drew up a master plan for comprehensively deepening China's reform.

There have been much interpretation and deciphering of this Plenum and the reform plan it has set out. I suggest we take a 3-D reading. That is to do a three-dimensional analysis with three English words that begin with capital D. These are:

- Determination.
- Design.
- And Deployment.

First, determination. This plenum sent out a clear message. China is determined to free up fixed mindsets and overcome institutional drawbacks. The aim is to promote social fairness and improve people's welfare. As one headline in the *Financial Times* said, "Beijing Signals Determination to Unleash Market Forces."

The signals from this Third Plenum indicate that China is prepared to discard outdated ideas and shatter the grip of vested interests. The aim is for all labor, knowledge, technology, management and capital to play an active role:

- China wants to fully tap into the potential of all sources of social wealth.
- China wants every Chinese to get a fair share of the fruits of development.

Second, design, particularly top-down design.

In the early days of China's reform, Mr. Deng Xiaoping used a metaphor that has become very famous. He described China's reform endeavor as: "crossing the river by feeling the stones."

Mr. Deng Xiaoping had every reason to make that remark because China's reform was a brand-new enterprise:

- There was no experience to learn from.
- There were no guiding theories to follow.
- China had no choice but explore by itself and face whatever outcome.

Now, China's reform has entered the "deep water." Any reform measure that threatens vested interests will meet complaints and resistance. This makes top-down design from the central government highly necessary. Reality calls for comprehensive planning and coordination among different agencies by the central leadership.

As a result, the Third Plenum made a clear statement on combining top-down design and "crossing the river by feeling the stones." The Third Plenum stressed:

- optimising decision-making;
- building broad consensus;
- and forming a synergy in reform.

The newly founded Central Taskforce on Deepening Reform is in effect a "headquarters of reform":

- It is tasked with overall planning, coordination, monitoring implementation of reform measures and achieving synchronised progress.
- It will ensure that reforms across China take place in a systematic, universal and balanced way.
- It will guarantee reform measures are aligned in policy objective, enhance each other in enforcement and complement each other in results.

The third dimension is deployment.

The Third Plenum both made systematic deployments and identified priority areas for deepening reform. The deployments are aimed to:

- Stick to and further improve China's basic economic system.
- Build a modern market economy at a faster pace.
- Transform government functions.
- Deepen the reform of fiscal and taxation system.
- Achieve balanced development in rural and urban areas.
- Build an open economy.
- Advance socialist democracy.
- Strengthen socialist political institutional building.
- Enforce rule of law.
- Apply stricter control and oversight on the exercise of power.
- Innovate institutions for cultural development.
- Renovate social programmes.
- Introduce new models for social management.
- Better protect the eco-environment.
- And deepen reform of national defense and the armed forces.

A key area among all these is economic reform. The kernel of this issue is to have a proper relationship between the government and the market. Such a relationship should allow the market to play a decisive role in allocating resources, yet at the same time enable the government to play a more effective supervisory role.

As I said, this Third Plenum was both sweeping and specific. It is a rally and general mobilisation for deepening reform. Meanwhile, it specified 300 measures to achieve 55 reform tasks in 15 sectors. Let me give you some examples:

- Formulate fair, open and transparent market rules.
- Adopt a uniform market access regime.
- Experiment with a pre-establishment national treatment and negative list approach towards foreign investment.
- Increase access for foreign investment.
- Harmonise laws and regulations governing both domestic and foreign investments.
- Orderly open up financial, educational, cultural and healthcare sectors.
- Relax restrictions on foreign investment in such services sectors as construction, accounting, auditing, logistics and e-commerce.
- Further open up the manufacturing sector.
- Ensure lawfulness, independence and impartiality of judicial and prosecutorial authorities.
- Ensure universal and exact enforcement of national laws.
- Improve the system for legal protection of human rights.
- Reaffirm that the state respects and protects human rights.
- Abolish the system of reeducation through labour.
- And improve the community correction system.

The master plan for comprehensively deepening reform delivers two factors:

- It spells out the specific tasks.
- It also sets out a timetable.

This gives a schedule to accomplish all reform tasks and achieve conclusive results in key areas by 2020. This means the reform process will be both measured and evaluated.

It is fair to say that this Third Plenum has sounded the clarion call for a new wave of reform in China.

As the title of an article in last week's *The Economist* magazine says:

"China paves the way for reform."

The reform in the past thirty-five years has lifted China out of poverty and backwardness. Now, the second round of reform from this Third Plenum will realise the great revitalisation of the Chinese nation. The reforms will make true for China's 1.3 billion people—the "Chinese Dream."

Dear Reformers,

Reform cannot be accomplished at one stroke. Nor can it be done once and for all. It is the case in China. So, it is here in Britain.

If we look back through British history, and take as an example the Reform Act 1832 that was the catalyst to create your Club. The Reform Act 1832 responded to the great changes in British society brought about by industrialisation and an enlarged electorate. It marked the birth of a genuine modern parliamentary system in Britain.

But, do not forget that the Reform Act 1832 is also known as the first reform act. Later Britain went through three major parliamentary reforms respectively in 1867, 1884 and 1918.

Even today, the British parliament is still evolving. For example, you have in recent years created the position of Lord Speaker. Nowadays, you are still debating on how one should become a peer and the possibility of replacing heredity positions with elections.

So, reform is an ongoing process. Institutions need constant updating.

The sweeping reform in China will powerfully drive China's development. Moreover, these reforms will bring new and greater opportunities for China-UK cooperation.

The reform has set the targets to build a modern and open market economy as well as strengthen rule of law. This means that China will provide a more level playing field:

- There will be a further opening-up of the services sector.
- There will be a streamlining of the procedures for foreign investment.

- There will be stricter enforcement of IP protection.
- And there will be a more predictable legal environment.

It also means that Chinese companies and individuals will be actively engaged in overseas investment. They will give full play to their advantages. They will invest in creative ways such as green land investment, mergers and acquisitions, buying securities and bonds and setting up joint ventures.

The Third Plenum has set out the goal of achieving balanced and synchronised development in rural and urban areas. This means the Chinese market will multiply. Consumption potential will be unbridled. That offers immense openings for UK enterprises.

The reform has also aimed to promote cultural development. This means China will broaden international cultural exchanges, draw on the finest culture of foreign countries, import talent, technologies and expertise. All in all, these reforms will greatly boost China-UK exchanges and cooperation in economic, finance and cultural sectors.

Early next month, Prime Minister David Cameron will visit China. He will bring with him business leaders from every sector, large and small. This visit takes place soon after the Third Plenum and all the reforms that have emerged from it.

I am sure reform will feature prominently in the talks between the leaders of our two countries.

It is certain that the two sides will update each other on their respective views and experience of reform.

There will be in-depth discussions on the new openings brought about by reform in both China and the UK.

It is the moment to jointly draw up a blueprint for the future of China-UK cooperation.

Ladies and Gentlemen,

The passage of the Reform Act 1832 was not easy. Yet it is the difficulties that have earned it a worthy mention in the history books. It is rightly called the Great Reform Act.

Today, China's reform is also confronted with enormous difficulties. But the greatness of this cause comes from its difficulty and complexity. Once accomplished, it will have far-reaching influence and usher in a brand-new era in China.

Likewise, we need to make relentless efforts and overcome various kinds of obstacles to further advance China-UK relations. I am confident we can positively advance if we follow these principles:

- We must respect each other.
- We need to treat each other as equals.
- We should seek common ground while putting aside differences.
- And we have to work together for win-win outcomes.

With these principles we will be able to find a path for China and the UK to forge a new type of relationship between big countries.

We will be able to take China-UK relations to a new level.

Thank you!

Now, I will open the floor for questions.

改革促进中国发展，开放推动世界进步 *

尊敬的基尔世界事务论坛主席博因顿先生，

尊敬的基尔大学校长麦克米兰教授，

女士们，先生们：

大家晚上好！

感谢基尔世界事务论坛的盛情邀请和基尔大学的热情接待。博因顿主席告诉我，我是第一个在基尔世界事务论坛发表演讲的中国大使，我对于创下这项新纪录倍感荣幸。

博因顿主席希望我介绍一下中国的改革开放及对世界的影响。这个话题可谓恰逢其时。2018 年恰好是中国改革开放 40 周年。40 年前，中国开启了改革开放的伟大历史征程。40 年来，从解放思想到锐意改革，从与世界接轨到深度融入世界，中国人民用勤劳和智慧书写了人类发展史上的奇迹。正如习近平主席所说："改革开放这场中国的第二次革命，不仅深刻改变了中国，也深刻影响了世界。"

孔子说："四十而不惑。"所谓"不惑"，就是对事物发展变化有了清晰了解，对自身选择不再疑惑。今天，我想结合中国的改革开放谈三个问题，帮助大家更好地了解中国的发展变化及中国对世界的影响。

第一个问题，改革开放给中国带来了什么变化？我认为改革开放给中国带来的变化是巨大的、深刻的、历史性的。

---

* 在英国基尔世界事务论坛上的主旨演讲。2018 年 12 月 6 日，英国基尔大学。

第一，中国经济实现了划时代的腾飞。40 年前，中国 GDP 总量仅为 1 750 亿美元，居世界第 10 位，占世界经济的比重只有 2%。今天，中国 GDP 总量达 12 万亿美元，按不变价计算增长了 33.5 倍，占世界经济 15% 左右。中国已成为世界第二大经济体、第一大工业国、第一大货物贸易国、第一大外汇储备国，220 多种产品产量居世界第一。40 年来，中国国内生产总值年均增长约 9.5%，创造了“二战”后一个国家 GDP 增长持续时间最长、增长率最高的世界纪录。

目前，中国经济由高速增长转向高质量发展。中国在载人航天、探月工程、超级计算、北斗导航、量子通信等高技术领域取得重大突破，在高铁、移动通信、核电等领域处于世界先进水平。以高铁为例，中国形成了世界上速度最快的铁路系统。每天早上 8 点，就有 1 700 多列高铁在中国版图上穿梭，平均每 84 秒就有一辆高铁驶过最繁忙的上海站。上个月我回国述职，乘坐了从北京至南京的高铁，1 000 多公里仅需 4 个小时。上周，我乘火车去苏格兰鹰谷开会，不到 600 公里的路走了整整 6 个小时。现在，英国朋友问我，英国什么时候会有中国式的高铁？我说，希望这一天不会太遥远。

尤其值得一提的是，中国新产业、新业态、新模式不断涌现。中国数字经济蓬勃发展，移动支付用户已经超过 5 亿，正引领全球支付体系迈入新时代。每年 11 月 11 日，中国有一个类似“黑色星期五”的网购狂欢节。今年“双 11”当天，网购成交量超过 2 000 亿元人民币，相当于中英年度贸易额的 1/3。

第二，中国人民生活发生了天翻地覆的变化。40 年来，中国人民生活从短缺走向充裕、从贫困走向全面小康，提前完成联合国“千年发展目标”“可持续发展议程”的减贫要求。中国绝对贫困人口从 7.7 亿减少至 3 000 多万，累计减贫 7.4 亿人，占同期全球减贫人口总数 70% 以上。中国已建成分别覆盖超过 9 亿人和 13 亿人的基本养老保险和医疗保险体系，实现了九年制义务教育全面免费，织就了世界上最大的社会保障网络。居民收入持续较快增长，连续多年“跑赢”同期国内生产总值的增速。

中国已经形成规模为 4 亿多的世界上最大中等收入群体，这一数字已超过美国总人口，消费能力和消费需求大幅提升。举例而言，20 世纪 70 年代，中国老百姓的家庭消费水平是百元级的，即“三转一响一咔嚓”——手表、缝纫机、自行车，收音机和照相机；到了 80 年代，家庭消费水平升级为千元级的，即“三机一箱”——电视机、洗衣机、录放机和电冰箱；到了 90 年代，家庭消费水平是万元级的，即“两电一调”——电脑、电话和空调。进入 21 世纪，中国老百姓家庭消费水平晋升为十万元到百万元级的，消费水平以汽车、住房和旅游为代表。

第三，中国与世界的关系发生了历史性的变化。40 年来，中国坚持打开国门搞建设，成功实现从封闭半封闭到全方位开放的伟大转折。从“引进来”到“走出去”，从加入世界贸易组织到共建“一带一路”，中国连续多年对世界经济增长的贡献率超过 30%，已成为世界经济增长的稳定器和动力源。中国提出构建人类命运共同体、建立新型国际关系等理念，其中构建人类命运共同体理念已经被写入联合国和二十国集团等文件，为人类和平与发展事业做出了自己的贡献。

当前，越来越多的中国人走出国门，从事商贸、投资、求学、旅游等活动。2017 年中国在境外设立企业超过 3 万家，在海外的劳务人员约 100 万，留学生约 137 万。2017 年全年，中国公民出境旅游人数超过 1.3 亿人次，同比增长 7%。上个月，我们在上海成功举办了首届中国国际进口博览会，这是迄今世界上第一个以进口为主题的国家级展会。172 个国家、地区和国际组织参会，3 600 多家企业参展，意向成交额达 578.3 亿美元。英国是博览会主宾国之一，安德鲁王子和福克斯国际贸易大臣率 50 多家英国企业参会，双方签署了约 20 亿英镑的合作协议。

同时也应看到，中国仍是世界上最大的发展中国家，人口多、底子薄、人均水平低，发展不充分、不平衡、不可持续等问题仍很突出。目前，中国人均国内生产总值排在世界第 71 位，人类发展指数全球位列第 91 位。中国还有 3 000 多万贫困人口、8 000 多万残疾人，需要照顾的老年人口超过 2 亿，每年需要解决的就业人口就达 1 500 万。我曾在中国较贫穷省份之一甘肃省担任省长助理，深知中国发展挑战巨大、任务艰巨。作为一个拥有 13 亿多人口的大国，中国的前进道路仍然充满困难和挑战。但有中国共产党的领导，有13亿多人民的勤劳和智慧，我们有信心、有能力攻坚克难，开创更加美好的未来。

第二个问题，中国为什么会发生这样的变化？我认为原因主要有三个。

一是中国始终坚持走自己的路。一个国家的道路走得对不对、好不好，要用事实来说话，要看这个国家发展得怎么样、老百姓日子过得怎么样。中国的发展成就充分证明，中国选择了一条适合本国国情的发展道路。历史上，中国曾经尝试过不少外来制度，但都水土不服，无法生根。最后在中国共产党的领导下，逐步探索并形成了中国特色社会主义道路，中国才实现从站起来、富起来到强起来的伟大飞跃。新时代中国特色社会主义道路是中国人民选择的、最适合中国的道路。

中国特色社会主义道路是在改革开放的实践中形成和发展起来的，它不仅改变了中国的面貌，也拓展了发展中国家走向现代化的途径，为解决人类问题贡献了中国智慧和中国方案，表明通向现代化的道路不止一条，只要找准正确方向、驰而不息，“条条大路通富强”。

二是中国始终以开放包容的姿态拥抱世界。“海纳百川，有容乃大。”世界上有200多个国家和地区，有不同文化、种族、宗教和社会制度。在全球化时代，任何国家都不能关起门来搞建设，要开放就需要包容。包容就是要尊重各国自主选择社会制度和发展道路的权利，把世界多样性转化为发展活力和动力；包容就是要推动不同文明取长补短、交融互鉴，把文化差异性转化为推动人类社会进步、维护世界和平的纽带。

当今世界正经历新一轮大发展、大变革、大调整。随着世界多极化、经济全球化、社会信息化深入发展，世界上不同制度、不同文化、不同发展阶段的国家相互紧密依存、利益深度交融，达到人类历史上前所未有的广度和深度，已逐步形成利益共同体、责任共同体和命运共同体。冷战思维、零和博弈已经不合时宜，本国优先、独善其身只能四处碰壁，开放包容、和平合作才是唯一正确选择。

三是中国始终秉持合作共赢的精神发展与其他国家的合作。合作共赢是中华文化的精神内核。改革开放 40 年，中国走向世界、融入世界的方式始终是通过合作共赢实现的。中国始终认为，在考虑自身利益、做好自己的事的同时，不能损害其他国家利益，必须同舟共济，努力加强政策协调，减少负面外溢效应，让世界各国实现联动增长，在普惠中追求共赢。

2018 年是习近平主席提出“一带一路”倡议 5 周年。“一带一路”建设秉持共商共建共享的原则，它源于中国，惠及世界，已成为世界各国合作共赢的平台。5 年来,“一带一路”建设从理念转化为行动，从愿景转变为现实，从“写意画”走向“工笔画”。截至 2018 年 9 月，中国已与 140 多个国家和国际组织签署合作文件。中欧班列累计开行数量突破 1 万列，到达欧洲 15 个国家 43 个城市，2017 年初义乌—伦敦班列顺利实现首次往返。中国与沿线国家货物贸易累计超过 5 万亿美元，与 13 个沿线国家签署或升级了 5 个自贸协定，成为 25 个沿线国家最大的贸易伙伴。中国对“一带一路”沿线国家投资超过 860 多亿美元，其中在沿线国家建立 82 个经贸开发区，吸引 6 000 个项目，创造 24 万多个工作岗位，给当地创造税收几十亿美元。2019 年，中国还将举办第二届“一带一路”国际合作高峰论坛，我们欢迎英国各界朋友积极参与。

第三个问题，中国的变化将给世界带来什么？我认为，中国将在世界上发挥三个作用。

首先，中国是世界经济的建设者。多年来，中国一直是世界经济增长的主要引擎之一。1997 年亚洲金融危机肆虐之时，中国坚持人民币不贬值，宁愿自己承受压力，支持周边邻国渡过难关。2008 年国际金融危机席卷全球，中国经济保持强劲增长，成为稳定世界经济的压舱石，并为之后的复苏做出了不可替代的贡献。预计未来 15 年，中国进口商品和服务将分别超过 30 万亿美元和 10 万亿美元。

作为最大的发展中国家，中国是发展中国家的真诚朋友和密切伙伴。中国通过分享经验、提供援助、培训人员等各种方式支持其他发展中国家加快脱贫。中国迄今已向 160 多个国家和国际组织提供了近 4 000 亿元人民币发展援助。中国的对外援助坚持不附加任何政治条件，尊重受援国的需要，助力提升各国的自主和可持续发展能力，受到了发展中国家的广泛欢迎。2018年9月，中非合作论坛北京峰会成功召开，达成一系列重要成果，进一步凝聚了中非合作论坛框架下55方、26亿人民团结合作的意愿和共识。会上，中国为下阶段中非务实合作提出了产业促进、设施联通、贸易便利、绿色发展、能力建设、健康卫生、人文交流、和平安全“八大行动”，决定再向非洲提供600亿美元支持，同时免除部分非洲国家债务。

其次，中国是世界和平的守护者。作为联合国安理会常任理事国，中国肩负着维护世界和平的特殊责任。在世界战火纷飞的每一个角落，都有中国维和人员的身影。中国已经是联合国维和行动第二大出资国和安理会五常国中派遣维和军事人员最多的国家。已累计派出3.7万人次军警官兵参与维和行动，有21位中国军人和警察在联合国维和行动中献出了宝贵生命。中国军舰连续10年在亚丁湾、索马里海域执行护航，先后保护了6 000多艘船舶的安全，其中也包括英国商船。中国已组建完毕8 000人规模的维和待命部队及常备维和警队。此外，中国在非洲部署了首支直升机分队，为联合国及有关国家维和人员开展多项培训。

中国参与了当今几乎所有国际和地区热点问题的解决进程，在朝核、伊朗核、缅甸、阿富汗、叙利亚、南苏丹、反恐等问题解决进程中贡献中国智慧，提出中国方案，发挥着建设性作用。在朝鲜半岛核问题上，中国始终坚持实现半岛无核化、维护半岛和平稳定、通过对话解决问题，积极推动美朝接触和南北关系缓和，发挥了不可替代的重要作用。

最后，中国是世界秩序的捍卫者。当今世界正处于重要十字路口，国际规则受到冲击，多边机制面临挑战，国际局势充满不稳定和不确定性。坚持多边主义、自由贸易，还是听任单边主义、保护主义肆虐蔓延？这是关系到各国的未来发展，关系到人类前途命运的关键问题。中国始终认为，在国与国交往中，存在差异和出现分歧在所难免，关键是要在相互尊重的基础上，按照公认的国际规则，以务实和建设性方式管控和化解分歧。因此，我们积极维护以联合国为核心的多边体制，反对任何一方按照自己的意愿随意取舍或选择规则。

中国始终积极融入现行国际体系，参与了当今世界几乎所有重要政府间国际组织，签署了300多项国际公约，在全球治理体系中发挥着越来越重要的作用。中国加入世界贸易组织的谈判历时15年，尽管付出了代价，但我们履行了所有承诺，坚持融入世界经济体系。中国愿在维护多边贸易体制核心价值、保障发展中成员发展利益、遵循协商一致决策机制的基础上，与英国及其他国家一道，共同推进世贸组织改革。

大家都很关心当前的中美贸易摩擦。在不久前二十国集团领导人峰会上，中美两国元首成功会晤并达成共识，同意停止加征新的关税，并指示两国经济团队加紧磋商，朝着取消所有加征关税的方向，达成互利双赢的具体协议。这是一个积极进展。中美作为两个大国，合则两利、斗则双输。我想强调的是，有些人根据几百年来大国兴衰的历史，认定国强必霸，认为中国今后也会称霸，甚至会挑战和取代美国在世界上的领导地位。这是一个重大战略误读和误判。中国坚持走的是和平发展道路，坚持一条有别于其他大国崛起的发展道路。中国既不会去成为谁，也不会去挑战谁，更不会去取代谁。单边主义、保护主义最终只能是“搬起石头砸自己的脚”。中国始终主张通过平等对话与协商，按照规则和共识予以妥善解决。中国的立场，不仅是在维护自身正当权益，也是在维护自由贸易体系，维护国际规则秩序，维护世界经济复苏的前景，维护世界各国的共同利益。

女士们，先生们，朋友们，

“万物并育而不相害，道并行而不相悖”，这是中国对世界的理解。中国是一本厚重的书，这本书里没有对外侵略，没有奴役他国，没有国强必霸，有的是“改变自己，影响世界”的中国逻辑，有的是“兼容并蓄，开放包容”的中国智慧，有的是“平等协商，劝和促谈”的中国方案。希望今天我的演讲能作为大家今后阅读中国这本书的一个序章。我期待大家不断增进对中国的了解和认知，希望中英两国人民与世界人民携手努力，共同为构建人类命运共同体贡献力量！

谢谢大家！

下面我愿回答大家的提问。

Reform Advances Development in China and Opening up Promotes Progress in the World*

Chairman Bill Boynton,

Vice-Chancellor Trevor Mcmillan,

Ladies and Gentlemen,

Good evening!

Let me begin by extending my thanks to Keele World Affairs for your kind invitation and to Keele University for your warm hospitality.

Chairman Boynton told me that I am the first Chinese Ambassador to speak at Keele World Affairs Meeting. I regard it as a great honour.

I am asked by Chairman Boynton to talk about China's reform and opening-up, and its influence on the world. I think this is a timely topic as this year marks the 40th anniversary of China's reform and opening-up.

Forty years since China embarked on this great and historic journey, we have liberated our minds and carried out courageous reform; we have reached out to the world and become an integral part of the globalisation process. With diligence and wisdom, the Chinese people have created a miracle in the history of human development.

Just as President Xi Jinping said, "Reform and opening-up, which is China's second revolution, has not only profoundly changed the country but also greatly influenced the whole world."

Confucius said, "At forty, one has no doubts." After forty years of reform and

---

* Speech at the Keele World Affairs Meeting. Keele University, 6 December 2018.

opening-up, China has no doubts about its choice forty years ago.

Today, in the context of reform and opening-up, I would like to share with you my views on three questions. I hope what I am going to say will provide you with a better understanding of China's development and its influence on the world.

The first question is: How is China changed by reform and opening-up? In my opinion, the changes are enormous, profound and historic.

First, China's economy has grown by epoch-making leaps and bounds.

Forty years ago, China was the tenth largest economy, with a GDP of $175 billion and accounting for 2% of the world's total.

Over the past forty years, China has maintained an average annual growth rate of 9.5%. This is the world's highest GDP growth rate for the longest time since the Second World War.

Today, China's GDP stands at $12 trillion, increasing 33.5 times in real terms and accounting for 15% of the world's total. It is the world's second largest economy with the biggest foreign exchange reserves. It is also the biggest industrial country, largest trader in goods and top producer of more than 220 products.

Today, China is shifting from high-speed growth to high-quality growth. We have achieved major breakthroughs in manned space programme, lunar exploration, supercomputer, satellite navigation, quantum communications and other hi-tech fields. In areas such as high-speed rail, mobile telecommunications and nuclear energy, China is also a leader in the world.

Take high-speed rail for example. China has built the world's fastest railway network. Every day at eight o'clock in the morning, there are more than 1,700 express trains running across China. On average, one express train passes through Shanghai Railway Station, the busiest in China, every 84 seconds.

While on home leave in China last month, I took an express train from Beijing to Nanjing more than 1,000 kilometres away. It took me only four hours. Last week, I traveled from London to Gleneagle of Scotland less than 600 kilometres away, and spent six hours on the train. My British friends asked me, when will the UK have a high-speed rail network like China's. I said, I hope it won't be long.

Another good example is the booming new industries and business models. With more than 500 million people using mobile payment, the digital economy is thriving in China. China is leading the new era of global payment system. On November 11th, China's equivalent of "Black Friday," online shopping topped 200 billion RMB yuan in a single day. This is one third of the annual trade between China and the UK.

Second, reform and opening-up have changed the life of the Chinese people beyond recognition.

The past 40 years have seen shortage replaced by affluence and poverty replaced by moderate prosperity.

In poverty reduction, China has hit the targets set by the Millennium Development Goals and the 2030 Agenda for Sustainable Development of the UN ahead of schedule. China's population in absolute poverty has dropped from 770 million to a little over 30 million. This means 740 million people have been lifted out of poverty. That accounts for more than 70% of the concurrent world total.

In social security, China has built the world's largest network, with a basic pension insurance system covering more than 900 million people and a basic health insurance system covering 1.3 billion. On top of that, we have put in place a nine-year free and compulsory education system.

In household income, the increase has been faster than GDP growth for many years. Today, China has the world's largest middle-income population, that is, more than 400 million. This is larger than the entire population of the United States.

Consumer needs and spending power have kept growing.

- In the 1970s, the main "dream items" of Chinese households were the watch, sewing machine, bicycle, radio and camera. The average costs were a few hundred RMB yuan.
- In the 1980s, the "dream items" changed to the TV set, washing machine, tape recorder and refrigerator. The average costs rose to a few thousand.
- In the 1990s, computer, telephone and air conditioner became the new "dream items," each costing more than ten thousand RMB yuan.
- Today, the "dream items" for the 21st century Chinese households are house, car and holiday. The average spending ranges from hundreds of thousands to several million RMB yuan.

Third, reform and opening-up have transformed China's relations with the world.

For 40 years, China has stayed committed to opening up the country to the outside world. The once closed and semi-closed country became one that opens up on all fronts.

From embracing foreign businesses at home to exploring access to the world, from becoming a WTO member to proposing the Belt and Road Initiative, China has played the role of world economic stabiliser and powerhouse. China's contribution to global growth has been more than 30% for many years in a run.

China has also contributed to world peace and development by proposing to build a community with a shared future for mankind and a new type of international relations. The former has been endorsed in documents of the UN and the G20.

Today, more and more Chinese are trading, investing, studying or holidaying abroad. As of 2017, there were more than 30,000 Chinese companies, about one million Chinese contract workers and 1.37 million Chinese students all over the world. Chinese tourists made more than 130 million overseas trips in 2017, which was 7% more than the previous year.

Last month, the first China International Import Expo was successfully held in Shanghai. This was the first-ever national-level Expo dedicated solely to import. Delegations from 172 countries, regional economies and international organisations gathered in Shanghai, more than 3,600 companies took part in the Expo and $57.83 billion worth of deals of intended purchases were signed.

The UK was a country of honour at the Expo, where more than 50 British companies led by The Duke of York and Secretary of State for International Trade Liam Fox signed about £2 billion of deals with Chinese companies.

However, despite the tremendous progress, China remains the world's largest developing country. Our population is large. Our economic foundation remains weak. In terms of per capita GDP, we are a long way behind many other countries in the world. On the whole, we still face the bottlenecks of insufficient, imbalanced and unsustainable development. Let me give you some numbers.

- China ranks the 71st in the world in per capita GDP and the 91st in human development index.

- There are still 30 million Chinese living in poverty.
- More than 80 million people with disabilities.
- Over 200 million pensioners in need of care.
- And about 15 million new workforce in need of a job every year.

I once served as Assistant Governor of Gansu, one of the least developed provinces in China. I know from personal experience the severe challenges China has to face and the daunting tasks China has to shoulder. As a big country with more than 1.3 billion people, China is bound to encounter numerous difficulties and challenges on its way ahead. But under the leadership of the Communist Party of China and with the diligence and wisdom of 1.3 billion Chinese people, we have the confidence and capability to overcome difficulties and create a beautiful future.

The second question I wish to discuss with you is: Why is China able to achieve these changes? I think there are three reasons.

First, China has been following a path of its own choice.

How do you judge whether a country has taken the right path, or the one that suits? I think you have to prove with concrete facts whether this path is leading to better development and higher standard of living. China's achievements are strong proof that China has chosen a development path that suits its national conditions.

Historically, China experimented with many foreign governance systems. But these could not settle in or take root. After trial and error, the Communist Party of China led the nation onto the path of socialism with Chinese characteristics. Years of hard efforts along this path have enabled China to gain independence, grow prosperous and become strong.

Socialism with Chinese characteristics in the new era is the choice of the Chinese people. It is gradually defined in the process of reform and opening-up. It is the most suitable path for China.

- It has led China to a profound transformation.
- It is an effective way to development and modernisation.
- It represents China's wisdom and solution in addressing the problems of human society.

- And it shows that there could be many roads leading to prosperity. Countries only have to find the right direction and stick to it.

The second reason is that China has embraced the world with open arms.

"The ocean is vast because it admits all rivers." The world is composed of more than 200 countries and regions. They are different in culture, race, religious belief and social system. Globalisation is a way of life that no one can escape from. No country can achieve development behind closed doors.

But openness requires one to be inclusive. Being inclusive is about respecting other countries' rights to choose their own social systems and development paths independently. It is about turning diversity into dynamism.

Being inclusive is also about encouraging mutual learning between different civilisations, so that the different strengths of diverse cultures could be channeled into promoting social development and safeguarding world peace.

The world is undergoing a new round of profound development, transformation and adjustment. Increasing multi-polarity, economic globalisation and IT application have drawn countries of the world closer. Despite their differences in social system, culture and development stage, countries are more interdependent and their interests are more deeply integrated to an extent and depth unprecedented in human history. This has turned the world into a community with shared interests, shared responsibilities and a shared future.

In the dynamics of this community,

- Cold war and zero-sum game mentality is outdated.
- "Put one's own country first" and "mind one's own business" do not work.
- Being open and inclusive, and pursuing peace and cooperation are the only right choice.

The third reason is that China has engaged in win-win cooperation with other countries.

Win-win cooperation is at the centre of the Chinese culture. It is through win-win cooperation that China, in its 40 years of reform and opening-up, reached out to and deepened its integration with the world.

Countries have their own interests to take care of and goals to pursue. But these should not be done at the expense of other countries. In a world of interconnected development, countries are all in the same boat and need to lend a hand to each other, enhance policy coordination and strive for win-win results.

The Belt and Road Initiative is aimed at enhancing connectivity.

It has been five years since President Xi Jinping proposed the Belt and Road Initiative. This Chinese Initiative has delivered benefits to the whole world over the past five years. It follows the principles of extensive consultation, joint contribution and shared benefits, and serves as a platform for win-win cooperation between all countries in the world.

In the past five years, the BRI has been translated from an idea to actions, from a vision to reality. To borrow a terminology of traditional Chinese painting, the sketching of BRI is now completed with "freehand brushwork" and it is time to attend to the details with "fine brushwork."

- By last September, China had signed cooperation agreements with more than 140 countries and international organisations.
- More than 10,000 China Railway Express freight trains have travelled between China and 43 cities in 15 European countries. Early last year, a China Railway Express train made its first-round trip between China's Yiwu and London.
- Trade in goods between China and countries along the BRI routes has exceeded $5 trillion. China has signed or upgraded five trade agreements with 13 countries and is now the largest trading partner of 25 countries along the routes.
- China has also invested more than $86 billion and helped establish 82 economic and trade cooperation zones in countries along the BRI routes. These zones now host 6,000 projects which have created more than 240,000 jobs and contributed billions of dollars in tax to the local community.

Next year, China will host the second Belt and Road Forum for International Cooperation. It is open to British friends from all walks of life.

Now let me come to my third and last question: What do the changes in China mean to the world? I believe that China will play an important role in the world in the following three aspects:

First, China is a contributor to world economy.

Over the years, China has been a key engine driving world economic growth.

- In 1997, when the financial crisis hit Asia, China's currency came under enormous downward pressure. But China stood firm, kept the RMB stable and help its neighbours tide over the difficulties.
- In 2008, when the financial crisis engulfed the world, China maintained robust growth. It served as a ballast stone for the world economy, and made indispensable contribution to the economic recovery afterwards.
- In the coming 15 years, China plans to import more than $30 trillion of goods and more than $10 trillion of services.

As the world's largest developing country, China is a sincere friend and close partner of other developing countries. Through experience sharing, aid and personnel training, China has supported other developing countries in their fight against poverty.

As of today, China has provided nearly 400 billion RMB yuan in development aid to more than 160 countries and international organisations. In doing so, China did not attach any political strings and always attends to the needs of recipient countries and aims to improve their capability of independent and sustainable development. This is why Chinese assistance is always warmly received by the developing countries.

Last September, the Forum on China-Africa Cooperation held a successful Summit in Beijing. Fifty-four countries and the AU Commission participated in the Summit, representing 2.6 billion African people. The Summit saw the signing of important outcomes and the consolidation of African aspiration and consensus for unity and cooperation. It rolled out eight major initiatives on industrial promotion, infrastructure connectivity, trade facilitation, green development, capacity building, health care, people-to-people exchange, and peace and security. China also pledged $60 billion in support of African development and canceled the debts of some African countries.

Second, China is a defender of world peace.

As a permanent member of the UN Security Council, China shoulders and has fulfilled the special responsibilities of safeguarding world peace. Wherever war rages, Chinese peacekeepers stand in harm's way.

- China is the second largest contributor to the UN peacekeeping budget and the largest contributor of peacekeeping personnel among the UN P5.
- China has sent a total of 37,000 Chinese military and police officers to various UN missions and 21 brave Chinese soldiers gave their lives for the lofty cause of peacekeeping.
- China has set up an 8,000 strong peacekeeping standby force and a standby peacekeeping police force.
- In the Gulf of Aden and off the coast of Somalia, China has carried out escort missions for ten consecutive years, ensuring the safe passage of more than 6,000 ships, including those from the UK.
- In Africa, China has deployed the first helicopter unit and provided a number of personnel training courses for the UN and relevant countries.

China has been a partner in the international response to almost all regional and hotspot issues. From the Korean Peninsula to Iran, from Myanmar, Afghanistan to Syria and South Sudan, and in the fight against terrorism, China has contributed its wisdom, proposed its solutions and played a constructive role.

On the Korean Peninsula nuclear issue, in particular, China has played an indispensable role. We stay committed to denuclearisation of the Peninsula, to peace and stability on the Peninsula, and to addressing problems through dialogues. China has also facilitated contacts between the US and the DPRK and the ease of tensions between the North and the South.

Third, China will be an upholder of world order.

The world is standing at an important crossroads. The international rules are under attack, the multilateral system is facing challenges, and the international landscape is strewn with instabilities and uncertainties.

Shall we uphold multilateralism and free trade, or allow unilateralism and protectionism to spread? This is a critical question that bears on the development of all countries and the future of mankind.

China always believes that in state-to-state relations, it is natural that countries have different opinions. It is crucial that we manage, control and address these differences on the basis of mutual respect, in accordance with the universally-accepted international rules, and in a practical and constructive manner.

Therefore, we should uphold the multilateral system with the UN as its core and oppose cherry-picking international rules according to one's own will.

China has been active in integrating with the existing international system. China has taken part in almost all the important intergovernmental organisations in the world and signed more than 300 international conventions. It is playing an increasingly important role in the global governance system.

The negotiations on China's accession to the WTO lasted 15 years. Despite all the cost, China has fulfilled all pledges and remained firm in being a part of the world economic system.

China stands ready to work with the UK and other countries to advance the reform in the WTO on the basis of upholding the core values of the multilateral trade regime, protecting the interests of developing members and following the principle of consultation and consensus.

I know many of you have been following closely the trade frictions between China and the US. Several days ago, President Xi Jinping and President Trump had a successful meeting during the G20 Summit. They reached consensus on not imposing new additional tariffs. They also agreed to instruct the economic teams of the two sides to step up negotiations toward the removal of all additional tariffs and a concrete agreement leading to win-win results.

This is a positive development. China and the US are both major countries. Cooperation will benefit both countries while confrontation serves the interests of neither side.

Some people seem to believe that the history of the rise and fall of big countries will repeat itself and that a country with increasing strength will surely seek hegemony. Along this logic, they conclude that China will seek hegemony in the future and even challenge or replace the leading role of the US in the world. This is a major strategic misunderstanding and misjudgment concerning China.

I wish to reiterate that China is committed to the path of peaceful development. This development path is different from previous emerging powers. China will not take the role of other country, or challenge or still less replace any country.

In state-to-state relations, unilateralism and protectionism will backfire. Anyone going down this path is “lifting a stone only to drop it on one’s own feet.”

Differences do exist between countries. The proper way to address them is equal-footed dialogue and consultation according to rules and based on consensus. This is China’s position. By taking this position, China not only safeguards its own legitimate rights and interests but also upholds the free trade system, defends the international rules and order, protects the prospects of world economic recovery and advances the common interests of all countries in the world.

Ladies and Gentlemen,

Dear Friends,

We have a saying in an ancient Chinese classic which goes like this:

“All living creatures grow together without harming each other; all roads run parallel without interfering with one another.”

This represents China’s view of the world.

If we compare China to a book, this is not one about invading or enslaving other countries. It is not about strength leading to hegemony.

- This is a book about China’s logic, which says “be your better self and influence those around you.”
- This is a book about China’s wisdom, which champions inclusiveness and openness.
- This is a book about China’s solution, which advocates equal-footed consultation and peace talks.

I hope my speech will serve as a preface to this book.

I hope you will open this book, read it and gain a better understanding of China.

And I hope the people of our two countries will join hands with people all over the world to build a community with a shared future for mankind!

Thank you!

Now, I will be glad to take your questions.

纪念改革开放伟业，共谱合作共赢新篇*

尊敬的英国四十八家集团俱乐部主席佩里先生，

尊敬的英国社会科学院院士、英国社会学学会前会长阿尔布劳教授，

尊敬的英国中国商会会长耿金海先生，

尊敬的各位议员，

女士们、先生们：

欢迎大家出席今天的活动，与我们一道纪念中国改革开放40年伟大历程，共同展望中国与世界携手同行的新征程。借此机会，我谨向长期支持中国改革开放事业、长期致力于中英友好合作的各界人士，表示衷心感谢！

40年前，在邓小平先生倡导下，以中共十一届三中全会为标志，中国开启了改革开放的历史征程。40年来，中国人民众志成城、不懈奋斗，谱写了国家和民族发展的壮丽史诗。40年筚路蓝缕,40年砥砺奋进,40年春风化雨，这段波澜壮阔的历程给了我们许多启示。我认为，其中四条弥足珍贵。

第一，天道酬勤，自强不息。一分耕耘一分收获。40年来，中国人民生活从贫困走向小康，人均可支配收入增长22.8倍，贫困人口减少7.4亿。今天参加我们活动的来自中国贵州偏远山区的苗族绣娘，就是中国贫困人口脱贫致富的缩影。她们不但摘掉了贫困帽子，而且从深山走出国门、走向世界，向世人展示中国少数民族文化的魅力。40年来，中国国内生产总值年均

---

* 在中国驻英国使馆纪念改革开放40周年主题活动上的主旨演讲。2018年12月11日，伦敦西敏市中央礼堂。

增长约9.5%，总量达12万亿美元，增长33.5倍，占世界经济比重从40年前的2%，增至今天的15%。中国已成为世界第二大经济体、第一大工业国、第一大货物贸易国、第一大外汇储备国。这些成绩不是谁的恩赐和施舍，而是中国人民驰而不息、含辛茹苦干出来的。因此，观察中国的改革开放，既要看到中国人民得到了什么收获，又要看中国人民付出了什么辛劳。

第二，与时偕行，革故鼎新。变革创新是推动人类社会向前发展的根本动力。40年来，中国坚持解放思想、实事求是，实现解放思想与改革开放相互激荡、观念创新与实践探索相互促进，极大地激发了人民的积极性、主动性和创造性。40年来，中国以敢闯敢干的勇气和自我革新的担当，不断完善中国特色社会主义制度，不断革除阻碍发展的各方面体制机制弊端，实现了从“赶上时代”到“引领时代”的伟大跨越。因此，观察中国的改革开放，既要看到思想引领的巨大作用，又要看到实干担当的时代精神。

第三，海纳百川，有容乃大。开放带来进步，封闭必然落后。40年来，中国既强调独立自主、自力更生又注重对外开放、合作共赢。从创建深圳特区到加入世界贸易组织，从沿海沿边开放到西部大开发，从自由贸易试验区到“一带一路”建设，中国勇于到世界市场的汪洋大海中经风雨、见世面。40年来，中国从大规模“引进来”到大踏步“走出去”，以开放包容的姿态加强同世界各国的互容、互鉴、互通，成功实现从封闭半封闭到全方位开放的伟大转折。因此，观察改革开放，既要看到打开国门搞建设的明智抉择，又要看到虚心学习其他民族和国家优秀文明成果的大国胸襟。

第四，立己达人，兼善天下。改革开放是中国和世界共同发展进步的伟大历程。40年来，中国在对外开放中始终展现大国担当，为应对亚洲金融危机和国际金融危机做出重大贡献，对世界经济的贡献率连年超过30%，成为世界经济增长的稳定器和动力源。40年来，中国在对外合作中坚持重信守诺、计利当计天下利，累计吸引外资超过2万亿美元，已经成为120多个国家和地区的最大贸易伙伴。上个月在上海举办的首届中国国际进口博览会，进一步显示了中国扩大开放的诚意和决心。因此，观察改革开放，既要看到中国自身发展取得的长足进步，又要看到中国为世界做出的突出贡献。

女士们、先生们，

中国的改革开放只有进行时，没有完成时。同时，随着中国综合国力逐步增强，国际社会很多人都高度关注下一步改革开放将把中国引向何方，将给世界带来什么影响。我可以明确地告诉大家，中国绝不走国强必霸的老路。相反，我们将始终坚持和平发展，坚持合作共赢，共同促进世界和平、发展与繁荣。我们不仅是这样说的，也是这样做的。

第一，提出顺应潮流的重大理念。在全球化时代，国际社会要风雨同舟，不要各自为营；要患难与共，不要以邻为壑。为此，中国提出构建相互尊重、公平正义、合作共赢的新型国际关系，构建持久和平、普遍安全、共同繁荣、开放包容、清洁美丽的人类命运共同体，推动全球治理体系变革朝着更加公平合理的方向发展。这些重大理念聚焦维护世界和平、促进共同发展的时代主题，强调坚持多边主义，倡导国际公平正义，为人类发展进步开辟了一条康庄大道。

第二，搭建开放融通的国际平台。“一带一路”是一个开放包容的国际合作平台，得到各方积极响应和热情参与。5 年来，中国已同 140 多个国家和国际组织签署了共建“一带一路”合作协议，对“一带一路”沿线国家投资超过 860 多亿美元，其中在沿线国家建立 82 个经贸开发区，吸引 6 000 个项目，创造 24 万多个工作岗位。中国将于 2019 年举办第二届“一带一路”国际合作高峰论坛，欢迎各国各界人士积极参与。相信在大家共同努力下，“一带一路”一定能不断落地生根、开花结果。

第三，拓展平等互惠的合作机遇。2018 年以来，中方宣布了一系列扩大开放重大举措，包括继续深化市场化改革、保护产权和知识产权、鼓励公平竞争、主动扩大进口。未来 15 年，中国预计将进口 24 万亿美元商品，吸引 2 万亿美元境外直接投资，对外投资达到 2 万亿美元，出境旅游超过 20 亿人次。未来中国将不断提升发展的内外联动性，在实现自身发展的同时，更多惠及世界其他国家和人民。

第四，展现勇于负责的大国担当。作为大国，意味着对地区及世界和平与发展肩负更大责任。面对当今世界不稳定、不确定因素突出等挑战，中国将始终把为人类做出新的更大贡献作为自己的使命，坚定维护开放型世界经济和多边贸易体制，反对保护主义、单边主义；将积极参与全球治理，支持扩大发展中国家在国际事务中的代表性和发言权；将坚持走和平发展道路，发展全球伙伴关系，让世界更加和平安宁，让人类生活更加幸福美好。

女士们、先生们，

伟大的事业需要伟大的实践。中国改革开放40年取得的成就得到包括英国在内的国际社会的大力支持和广泛参与。40年来，中英关系取得跨越式发展，已成为中国与世界深度融合的一个缩影。展望未来，中国进一步深化改革开放与英国打造“全球化英国”相互契合，这将为两国各领域合作提供更加广阔的空间和更多历史性机遇。在新的历史时期，如何更好抓住机遇、深化中英合作，是中英各界人士需要认真思考的课题。我有以下三点想分享。

一要以理性心态看待彼此发展。双方应始终以长远和战略眼光，视彼此发展为机遇而非挑战或威胁，不做损害对方核心利益和破坏双方战略互信的事。只有尊重彼此核心利益和重大关切，尊重彼此国家主权和领土完整，才能确保两国关系始终沿着正确的轨道前行。只有着眼大局、妥善处理分歧、增进战略互信，中英关系的大厦才能更加坚实雄伟。

二要以伙伴精神促进务实合作。双方应加强战略对接和政策协调，深化传统优势领域合作，拓展新产业新业态合作，充分挖掘经贸、金融、能源、科技、人文等领域的合作潜力，切实将双方互补优势与发展机遇转化为合作成果。英国愿做“一带一路”建设的“天然合作伙伴”，两国应抓住明年第二届“一带一路”国际合作高峰论坛机遇，拓宽和把握“一带一路”合作广度和深度，打造中英务实合作新亮点。

三要以开放视野应对全球挑战。中英同为联合国、二十国集团、世贸组织等重要成员，对世界和平与发展负有特殊责任，双方应旗帜鲜明反对保护主义，共同构建开放型世界经济。在推进全球治理改革时，要倡导以规则为基础加强全球治理，反对实用主义和双重标准。在推进贸易和投资、知识产权保护、数字经济合作的同时，要坚持为各国营造共同的发展机遇和空间，为世界经济增长提供强劲动力和稳定环境。

女士们、先生们，

习近平主席指出："21世纪是合作的世纪。心胸有多宽，合作舞台就有多广。"抚今追昔，我们相信，中华民族伟大复兴的"中国梦"必将在改革开放新的征程中得以实现。展望未来，我们将与包括英国在内的各国一道，以改革创新的精神，以攻坚克难的勇气，抓住合作机遇，分享发展红利，共同为构建人类命运共同体贡献力量！

谢谢！

Great Cause, Great Achievements and Great Future*

Chairman Stephen Perry,

Professor Martin Albrow,

Chairman Geng Jinhai,

Lords and MPs,

Ladies and Gentlemen,

A very warm welcome to all of you!

It is a real pleasure to have so many friends with us today to mark the 40th anniversary of China's reform and opening-up, and to look forward to a new journey where China joins hand with the rest of the world to march forward.

Please allow me to take this opportunity to express my sincere thanks to people from all walks of life who have supported China's cause of reform and opening-up and committed themselves to enhancing friendly cooperation between China and the UK!

Forty years ago, Deng Xiaoping initiated China's reform and opening-up. The third Plenary Session of the 11th Central Committee of the Communist Party of China held in December 1978 marked the beginning of this historic journey.

These 40 years have been a glorious chapter in the history of China. It is written with the pioneering, relentless and united efforts and the unswerving dedication of the Chinese people.

The past 40 years have many lessons for us. I think the following four are most

---

* Keynote Speech at the Commemorative Event of the 40th Anniversary of China's Reform and Opening-up. Central Hall Westminster, London, 11 December 2018.

valuable.

The first thing we have learnt is that fortune favours the brave and hard working.

No pain, no gain. The people of China have made persistent and painful efforts over the past 40 years.

As a result of these efforts, poverty is being gradually replaced by moderate prosperity, per capita disposable income has risen by 22.8 times, and 740 million people have been lifted out of poverty.

Today we have with us a seamstress of the Miao ethnic group from the remote mountainous areas of Guizhou Province. She is a best illustration of China's achievements in poverty reduction and better life for the people. She and her fellow seamstresses have not only said goodbye to poverty but also traveled all the way from their remote mountain home to show the world the charm of China's ethnic culture.

As a result of the persistent efforts, China's GDP has been growing at an average annual rate of 9.5% and increasing by 33.5 times. It now stands at $12 trillion.

As a result of these efforts, China now accounts for 15% of the world GDP, compared to 2% forty years ago. It is the world's second largest economy, biggest industrial country and largest trader in goods with the biggest foreign exchange reserve.

These achievements are not a handout from others. They are the results of 40 years of hard efforts by the Chinese people. Therefore, when we assess the achievements of reform and opening-up, we must not only look at how much the Chinese people have gained. It is also important to recognise the hard efforts they have made.

The second lesson is that we must follow the trend of the times and keep reforming the old and embracing the new.

Reform and innovation are the fundamental forces driving human society forward.

In the past 40 years, we have liberated our minds and sought truth from facts. Liberation of the mind has led to reform and opening-up, and the reform and opening-up has in turn further emancipated the mind. This has been a mutually reinforcing interaction between innovative ideas and trials and errors. In the process, the enthusiasm, initiative and creativeness of individuals have been greatly stimulated.

In the past 40 years, with undaunted courage and responsibility for self-perfection, we have kept improving socialism with Chinese characteristics and removing institutional and systemic obstacles hindering our development. These 40 years have seen China catching up and joining those in the forefront of the times.

So, when we observe China's reform and opening-up, we must see it as the success of visionary ideas and concrete actions that are mutually reinforcing.

The third lesson is, to borrow a Chinese motto, "The ocean is vast because it admits all rivers."

Openness brings progress and isolation leads to backwardness.

In the past 40 years, China emphasised independent development as well as open and win-win cooperation. From establishing the Shenzhen Special Economic Zone to acceding to the WTO, from opening the coastal and border areas to developing the western inland region, from setting up pilot free trade zones to advancing the Belt and Road Initiative, China has taken brave steps into the world market.

In the past 40 years, China has welcomed foreign businesses with open arms and vigorously explored access to the world. We have enhanced mutual learning and connectivity with other countries in the world with an open and inclusive attitude. The once closed and semi-closed country became one that opens up on all fronts.

When we look at China's opening-up, we must not only see it as a wise decision for China's economic development. It is also important to recognise China's inclusive attitude towards the civilisations of other nations and countries.

Let me quote Confucius to explain the fourth lesson we have learned from reform and opening-up. That is, "To establish ourselves, we should help others establish themselves and deliver benefits to the whole world."

Reform and opening-up is a great journey. On this journey, China and the rest of the world have achieved progress hand in hand.

In the past 40 years, China has always shouldered its responsibility as a big country.

- It has played an important role in tackling the Asian financial crisis of 1997 and international financial crisis of 2008.
- Its contribution to global growth has been more than 30% for many years in a row.
- It has been a stabiliser and powerhouse of world economy.

In the past 40 years, China has always honoured its promises in its cooperation with other countries and acted in the interest of the world. Foreign companies have invested over $2 trillion in China, and China has become the largest trading partner of more than 120 countries and regions. The first-ever China International Import Expo held in Shanghai last month is yet another demonstration of China's sincerity and resolve to open its market wider to the world.

So, when we assess the achievements of reform and opening-up, we must not only look at China's domestic development but also its enormous contribution to the world.

Ladies and Gentlemen,

Reform and opening-up is an on-going process. China will not stop its steps. And China's comprehensive national strength will continue to grow. Many people in the world may wonder:

- How will reform and opening-up change China in the future?
- And what will these changes mean to the world?

My answer is definite and clear: China will never seek hegemony as it grows stronger. Instead, China will remain committed to peaceful development, win-win cooperation and world peace, development and prosperity.

This is not rhetoric. China has taken concrete actions to live up to its words.

First, China has shared its visions with the world that reflect the trend of our times.

In a globalised world, countries are all in the same boat and need to come to each other's assistance instead of only minding one's own business. They need to share weal and woe instead of pursuing interests at the expense of their neighbours.

It is in this spirit that China has proposed:

- to foster a new type of international relations featuring mutual respect, fairness, justice and win-win cooperation;
- to build an open, inclusive, clean and beautiful community with a shared future for mankind, a future of lasting peace, universal security and common prosperity;
- and to develop a fair and more reasonable global governance system.

These visions are in line with the trend of safeguarding world peace and promoting common development. They highlight multilateralism, advocate fairness and justice in the world, and point to a future of greater human progress.

Second, China has built an international platform for open cooperation and connectivity.

China has proposed the Belt and Road Initiative. In the past five years, this Initiative has received warm response and enthusiastic participation.

- China has signed cooperation agreements on the BRI with more than 140 countries and international organisations.
- It has invested more than $86 billion in countries along the BRI routes.
- And it has established in these countries 82 economic and trade development zones, which host 6,000 projects and has created more than 240,000 jobs.

Next year, China will host the second Belt and Road Forum for International Cooperation. We welcome people from all walks of life in the world to participate in the Forum.

I am confident that with the concerted efforts of all parties, the BRI will take root in more countries and bear more fruits.

Third, China has created more opportunities for equal-footed and mutually-beneficial cooperation.

Since the beginning of this year, China has announced a number of important measures of further opening-up, including:

- deepening market-oriented reform,
- protecting property rights and IPR,
- encouraging fair competition,
- and expanding import.

In the coming 15 years, China plans to import $24 trillion of goods, open up a 2-trillion-dollar market to foreign investors and invest $2 trillion overseas. Chinese tourists will make more than 2 billion overseas visits.

Going forward, China will continue to deepen its integration with the world in order to achieve better development at home and at the same time share the benefits of its own development with other countries.

Fourth, China has displayed the courage to shoulder its responsibilities as a big country.

In a world with increasing instabilities and uncertainties, China will continue to do what a big country should do, namely shoulder more responsibilities for regional and world peace and development.

- China will continue to make new and greater contribution to mankind, uphold the open world economy and multilateral trade regime, and oppose protectionism and unilateralism.
- China will take an active part in global governance, and support the developing countries in having a greater representation and bigger say in international affairs.
- At the same time, China will remain committed to peaceful development at home and forge partnerships around the world. World peace and better life for the people are always our top priorities.

Ladies and Gentlemen,

A great cause calls for great actions. Over the past 40 years, the international community, including the UK, have given their support for China's reform and opening-up and taken an active part in it. Their actions have been instrumental in the success of this great cause. The China-UK relationship, after 40 years of leaps-and-bounds, is a best illustration of China's deep integration with the world.

Going forward, China plans to deepen reform and open its market wider to the world. This matches well with the UK's goal of building a "global Britain." Such synergy will open up broader space and create more opportunities for the cooperation between our two countries in various areas. How to seize these opportunities and deepen China-UK cooperation is an important issue to be addressed by people from all walks of life in both countries. In my opinion, we should do the following.

First, China and the UK should view each other's development with a rational attitude.

Our two countries should always look at our bilateral relations from a long-term and strategic perspective. We should see each other's development as opportunities rather than challenges or threats. We should refrain from undermining each other's core interests or our strategic mutual trust.

The only way to keep our bilateral relations on the right track is to respect each other's core interests, major concerns, sovereignty and territorial integrity. We must bear the larger picture in mind, address differences properly and enhance political trust so as to ensure that this edifice of China-UK relations stands tall and firm.

Second, China and the UK should promote business cooperation in the spirit of partnership.

Our two countries should match our development strategies and enhance policy coordination. While deepening cooperation in traditional areas, we need to explore opportunities in new industries and new models. We should tap the potential in our cooperation in the areas of economy, trade, financial services, energy, science, technology, culture and people-to-people exchanges and translate our complementary advantages and development opportunities into concrete outcomes.

In Belt and Road cooperation, the UK is a "natural partner" of China, to quote Chancellor Philip Hammond who attended the Belt and Road Forum for International Cooperation as the personal envoy of the Prime Minister. The second Forum scheduled for next year will offer a great opportunity. Our two countries should seize this opportunity to expand and deepen our cooperation on the BRI and achieve new highlights in the business cooperation between our two countries.

Third, China and the UK should address global challenges with an open mind.

As important members of the UN, G20 and WTO, China and the UK shoulder special responsibilities for world peace and development. It is important that our two countries stand against protectionism and work together to build an open world economy.

In promoting reforms of the global governance system, we should strengthen rule-based global governance and oppose expediency and double standard. While promoting trade, investment, IPR protection and cooperation on digital economy, we should create more opportunities and space for the common development of all countries in order to provide strong impetus and a stable environment for world economic growth.

Ladies and Gentlemen,

President Xi Jinping said, "The 21st century is a century for cooperation. The stage for cooperation will be as broad as the mind."

Looking back at our success over the past 40 years, we are convinced that the "Chinese Dream" of national rejuvenation will come true as we press ahead on the new journey of reform and opening-up.

Going forward, we will continue to advance in the spirit of reform and innovation, and with the courage to overcome all the difficulties ahead. And we are ready to join hands with the UK and other countries to seize the opportunities of cooperation and share development benefits. Working together, we can build a community with a shared future for mankind!

Thank you!

第七章

中国机遇

关于中国的发展对世界意味着什么，西方社会始终争论不休。其观点大体可分为三类：一是认为中国的发展是机遇；二是认为是挑战；三是认为是威胁。对于这三种观点，我的基本做法只有一个，即从正面介绍中国的发展，阐述中国对世界的机遇。用中国发展前景"光明论"提振信心，用与中国合作"机遇论"澄清"中国挑战论"，驳斥"中国威胁论"。我在英国巴斯皇家文学科学院发表演讲，重点谈两个问题：一是怎么看中国的发展；二是中国的发展对世界意味着什么。我从四个方面说明中国经济不会出现"硬着陆"，前景会更加光明；从五个方面阐述中国的发展对世界、对英国的机遇。一是中国通过自身发展促进世界经济共同发展；二是中国构建全方位对外开放格局给世界带来新机遇；三是中国积极推进国际发展合作事业；四是中国旗帜鲜明地展现大国责任和担当；五是中国的发展给英国带来更多新机遇。

在法国巴黎银行举办的"全球市场大会"上，我发表题为《共享中国机遇，共创美好未来》的主旨演讲。我围绕如何看待中国经济前景、如何抓住中国机遇，与各国企业家和金融家分享看法。我指出中国经济"四大亮点"：一是增长稳，二是质量高，三是潜力大，四是贡献多。开放的中国将给欧洲和英国带来"三大机遇"：一是开放合作的机遇，二是开放创新的机遇，三是开放共享的机遇。

在彭博研讨会上我发表题为《坚持开放、合作、协商，为世界增添"中国信心"》的主旨演讲。我提出三个问题：国际社会是选择"开放"还是"封闭"；中国如何在实现自身发展的同时带动其他国家发展；中美能否避免"修昔底德陷阱"，避免"贸易战"殃及世界经济。我通过回答这三个问题，诠释提振世界经济、促进各国共同发展的"中国信心"。我强调，世界好，中国才会好；中国好，世界才会更好。中国愿以更大的开放分享发展机遇，以更好的合作推进互利共赢，以更多的协商谋求共同发展，为世界增添"中国信心"。

中国发展给世界带来的机遇*

尊敬的巴斯皇家文学科学院主席史蒂夫·沃顿博士，

尊敬的巴斯市长威廉·桑德里议员，

尊敬的巴斯大学校长布雷克韦尔教授，

尊敬的巴斯斯巴大学副校长萨默尔斯教授，

尊敬的霍莱特议员先生，

老师们、同学们，

女士们、先生们，

很高兴应邀访问美丽的历史文化名城巴斯。巴斯被誉为英国漂亮典雅的城市之一，早在 1987 年就列入世界文化遗产名录。同时，我感到很荣幸能够在著名的巴斯皇家文学科学院发表演讲。

长期以来，巴斯皇家文学科学院、巴斯大学、巴斯斯巴大学等著名院校在专业教育、学术研究等方面取得了丰硕成果，不仅培养了一大批各领域顶尖人才，还为促进英国与中国之间的教育交流合作做出突出贡献。巴斯大学是新中国成立后较早接受中国学生的英国大学之一。早在 20 世纪 70 年代，一批中国青年学生来巴斯大学进修，他们中的许多人学成回国，成为各自领域的领军人物，为中国的现代化建设做出卓越贡献。目前，仍有许多来自中国的学子慕名前来求学。今天在座的就有不少他们的代表。他们象征着中国的未来，也象征着中英关系的未来。我祝你们在巴斯生活、学习顺利，祝你

* 在英国巴斯皇家文学科学院的演讲。2016 年 5 月 17 日，英国巴斯皇家文学科学院。

们早日学成，为国家建设添砖加瓦，为中英关系发展增光添彩。

巴斯皇家文学科学院举办的国际事务系列讲座，把主题确定为“我们眼中的世界事务”，反映出贵院放眼全球的广阔视野。今天的首场讲座聚焦中国，也充分体现了贵院对中国以及中英关系的高度重视。

今天，我想利用这个机会，重点谈两点：一是怎么看中国的发展；二是中国的发展对世界意味着什么。

首先，怎么看中国的发展？当前人们最关心的是中国的经济是否会出现“硬着陆”。我刚刚从中国述职归来，在国内的所见所闻使我对当前中国经济的总体情况有深切感受。我可以明确地告诉大家，中国经济长期向好的基本面没有改变。在可预见的将来，中国经济不会出现“硬着陆”，前景会更加光明。我对中国经济充满信心主要有四方面原因。

第一，中国经济持续增长，增速处于合理区间。2015 年，在世界经济增长放缓大背景下，中国经济增速达到 6.9%。虽然首次低于 7%，但这一增速是在中国 GDP 总量已高达 10 万亿美元的基数上取得的，现在的 6.9% 相当于 5 年前的 10%，而现在的增量相当于一个中等国家全年的 GDP。同时，这一增速在世界主要经济体中仍位居前列，绝对增量居全球第一。从近期经济指标看，中国 2016 年第一季度 GDP 增速达到 6.7%，经济实现平稳开局。国际社会不少经济专家认为，中国经济正在进入回暖通道。国际货币基金组织 2016 年 4 月发布的《世界经济展望》春季报告中，将 2016 年和 2017 年中国经济的增长预期均比 1 月调高 0.2 个百分点，充分体现了该组织对中国经济稳中向好态势的坚定信心。

第二，中国经济结构正在发生重大积极变化。中国经济增长比过去有所放缓，相当程度上是中国主动进行结构调整的结果。因此，准确把握中国经济走势，不仅要看增速，更要看到经济增长的结构性变化。从产业结构看，2015 年第三产业占 GDP 比重首次突破 50% 大关，比 2014 年提高 2.4 个百分点。服务业比重的提升有助于增加高收入就业机会，推动中国向高附加值产业上游迈进，意义重大。从需求结构看，2015 年消费对经济增长的贡献率超过 60%，经济增长主要靠内需拉动。从经济增长质量看，单位 GDP 能耗下降，民生指标保持稳定发展。2015 年全国城镇新增就业 1 066 万人。2016 年第一季度，服务业增幅达 7.6%，占 GDP 比重达 56.9%，比 2015 年同期提高两个百分点；居民收入增长和消费水平都超过 GDP 增速，这表明经济结构调整正稳步推进。有国际评论认为，传统经济分析方法过多关注工业领域数据，未能准确展现转型中的中国经济全貌。这一观点值得大家深入思考。

第三，中国经济具备巨大潜力和广阔增长空间。中国正处于新型工业化、信息化、城镇化、农业现代化同步发展进程中，经济韧性好、潜力足、回旋余地大。2015 年中国的城镇化率是 56.1%。与发达国家 80% 以上的城镇化率相比，中国的城镇化空间广阔，将蕴含巨大的发展需求。按照地区发展指数初步测算，西部地区比东部地区至少落后 10 年。未来中西部地区基础设施和生活水平的稳步提高，将释放出巨大的发展潜力。中国的教育优势也不可忽视。中国拥有大专学历以上的人口现已超过 1.1 亿人，将为经济发展积累巨大的人才红利。中国在适度扩大总需求的同时，着力加强供给侧结构性改革，改善了经济的供求平衡和市场预期，初步产生积极效果。近一时期，一些媒体关注中国的债务问题，事实是目前中国的财政赤字和政府债务余额均处于安全线内，远低于美、欧、日等主要经济体，为下一步宏观调控留下了空间。

第四，“十三五”规划为中国发展绘就崭新蓝图。2016 年是中国“十三五”规划的开局之年，也是全面建成小康社会决胜阶段的开局之年。2016 年 3 月，中国“两会”通过了“十三五”规划，确立了新的系统发展理念，即“创新、协调、绿色、开放、共享”五大发展理念，明确了今后 5 年中国经济社会发展的主要目标、重点任务和重大举措，标志着中国发展进入新的转型升级征程。“创新”就是把发展基点放在创新上，形成促进创新的体制架构。“协调”就是在协调发展中拓宽发展空间，在加强薄弱领域中增强发展后劲。“绿色”就是更加重视生态文明建设，继续推进节能减排，大力发展低碳经济。“开放”就是进一步完善对外开放战略布局，形成对外开放新体制。“共享”就是发展为了人民、发展依靠人民、发展成果由人民共享。“十三五”规划和“五大发展理念”，致力于破解难题，补上短板，增强动力，厚植优势，将引领中国经济未来5年乃至长远发展。随着"十三五"规划的稳步落实，全面深化改革各项举措逐步到位，中国经济将走得更好、更稳、更远。

总的来看，中国经济完全具有保持较长时间中高速增长的潜力和条件。当然，面对世界经济下行压力和国内转型升级带来的挑战，中国经济发展的过程可能不是线性的，但是趋势向好，将始终保持长期健康稳定的积极态势；短期内可能会遇到这样或那样的瓶颈和困难，也遭遇到中国股市的波动等种种问题，但我们不回避问题，也不否认困难，而是满怀信心迎接挑战，终将取得突破和成功。

女士们、先生们，

我谈了如何看待中国发展的问题。现在我来谈第二个问题：中国的发展对世界意味着什么，中国经济的光明前景将给在座各位、给英国及世界带来什么影响。引用习近平主席的话说，"当今世界，相互联系、相互依存是大潮流。随着商品、资金、信息、人才的高度流动，无论近邻还是远交，无论大国还是小国，无论发达国家还是发展中国家，正日益形成利益交融、安危与共的利益共同体和命运共同体"。今天的中国与世界、中国经济与世界经济正在深度融合。中国的发展得益于世界，也将造福于世界。因此，中国的发展对世界是机遇，对英国是机遇。这主要体现在五个方面。

第一，中国通过自身发展促进世界经济共同发展。中国经济高速发展30多年，是世界公认的经济发展动力源。特别是国际金融危机爆发以来，中国在世界经济最困难的时刻承担了拉动增长的重任。2015年，中国经济对世界经济增长的贡献率超过25%，在主要经济体中首屈一指。中国现在是世界第一大出境旅游消费国，2015年中国全年出境游人次达1.2亿，其中自由行出境人次达到8 000万、人均消费11 624元人民币，成为全球消费疲弱形势下的一大亮点。据英国旅游局统计数据，2015年前9个月到访英国的中国游客人次达21.4万，消费金额达到4.35亿英镑。在伦敦、爱丁堡、巴斯，到处可见中国游客的身影。中国已经成为世界第一大贸易国和第二大对外投资国，今后5年，中国进口商品将超过10万亿美元，对外投资将超过6 000亿美元。中国已经并将继续成为推动全球消费和扩大全球投资的生力军。可以说，把中国这样一个拥有13亿多人口的大国发展好、建设好，本身就是对世界经济发展的重要贡献。作为推动世界和平和可持续增长的重要力量，中国的发展将为全人类带来互利共赢的福音。

第二，中国构建全方位对外开放格局，为世界带来新机遇。中国对外开放的大门将进一步敞开。我们的市场将更加开放，制度将不断完善。自从30多年前在深圳启动改革开放以来，中国经历了翻天覆地的变化，开启了史无前例的工业化进程。作为中国新一轮改革开放的起点，上海自贸区为政府行政审批开出了“负面清单”“责任清单”“权力清单”三张清单，大大推动了贸易便利化。我们将有序扩大金融服务业等领域的开放，放宽市场准入，致力于为外国企业、机构、人员对华交流合作提供便利。我们正在大力推进“一带一路”倡议，旨在打造东起亚太经济圈、西系欧洲经济圈的经济带，一大批重点项目已在各国落地生根。这将成为世界经济新的增长点。“独行快，众行远。”我们将不断提高开放型经济水平，欢迎其他国家共同分享中国发展带来的机遇。

第三，中国正在尽己所能地推进国际发展合作事业。我们积极推动南南合作向更高水平、更深层次发展，为发展中国家经济增长和民生改善做出应有贡献，并推出一系列具体行动和建议。2015年，习近平主席在联合国成立70周年系列峰会期间，宣布中国将设立“南南合作援助基金”，首期提供20亿美元，用于支持发展中国家落实2030年可持续发展议程。今后10年，中国将设立总额10亿美元的中国—联合国和平与发展基金，中国还将加入新的联合国维和能力待命机制，建设维和警队和维和待命部队。未来5年，中国将向发展中国家提供“6个100”项目支持，包括100个减贫项目、100个农业合作项目、100个促贸援助项目、100个生态保护和应对气候变化项目、100所医院和诊所、100所学校和职业培训中心。未来5年，中国将向发展中国家提供12万个来华培训和15万个奖学金名额，为发展中国家培养50万名职业技术人员。中国还提出对最不发达国家投资、免除部分国家贷款债务、设立国际发展知识中心等多项惠及发展中国家的务实举措。

第四，中国正在旗帜鲜明地展现大国责任和担当。中国从世界和平与发展的大义出发，在应对全球性挑战等方面切实发挥负责任大国作用。中国与各方一道促成巴黎气候变化大会达成全面、均衡、有力度的协议，就是一个很好的例证。我们积极推动变革全球经济治理体制中不公正、不合理的安排，推动国际货币基金组织、世界银行等国际经济金融组织切实反映国际格局的变化。这种改革并不是推倒重来，也不是另起炉灶，而是创新完善。今年，中国将携手各方办好二十国集团（G20）杭州峰会，积极促进全球经济金融治理。近年来，中方还倡议创立亚投行和金砖国家新开发银行，为现有国际金融体系提供补充。我们高兴地看到，近期亚投行将与亚洲开发银行开展联合贷款合作。这充分说明亚投行与现有多边开发银行完全可以相互补充、互利共赢。今后，中国将同各方携手努力，坚定维护以《联合国宪章》宗旨和原则为核心的国际秩序和国际体系，推动构建以合作共赢为核心的新型国际关系，丰富打造人类命运共同体等主张，弘扬共商共建共享的全球治理理念。

第五，中国的发展给英国带来更多新机遇。当前，中英关系正处于历史机遇期。2015 年，习近平主席成功对英进行国事访问，两国领导人决定共同构建中英面向 21 世纪全球全面战略伙伴关系，共同开启持久、开放、共赢的“黄金时代”。这为中英加强各领域务实合作指明了方向。目前，英国是中国在欧盟内的第二大贸易伙伴，中国是英国在欧盟外的第二大贸易伙伴。2015 年中英双边贸易额 785.2 亿美元，保持总体稳定态势。中方对英非金融类直接投资额为 132 亿美元，英国已成为吸引中国投资最多的欧洲国家。英国也是中国赴欧留学人数最多的国家。目前中国赴英各类留学人员 15 万人，英国在华留学生有 6 000 余人。此外，两国还缔结了 55 对友好省市关系。

机遇不仅表现在双边合作层面，还体现在两国所具备的全球视野与世界影响，以及双方在多边舞台上开展的国际合作。作为联合国安理会常任理事国和国际上负责任的大国，中英两国应共同以创新和改革引领世界经济发展方向，共同促进国际发展合作事业，共同推进全球经济治理改革步伐和共同维护国际与地区的和平稳定。

谈到地区的和平与稳定，近来各方都很关注南海问题。不久前，我先后在《泰晤士报》和《金融时报》发表文章，阐述中国政府的立场。我想在座的各位也一定关心这个问题，因此今天也利用这个机会谈几点看法。

南海问题的实质是一些国家非法侵占中国南沙群岛部分岛礁所引发的领土问题以及海洋划界争端。自 20 世纪 70 年代以来，菲律宾、越南等国共非法侵占了中国南沙群岛 42 个岛礁，并据此主张所谓海洋权益。一些国家编出各种理由为其非法行为辩护，如声称南沙群岛是“无主地”，以所谓“先占原则”据为己有。另一些国家则试图以“地理临近”等各种理由自圆其说。菲律宾还恶人先告状，单方面提起所谓仲裁案。

事实上，早在公元前 2 世纪的汉代，中国人民就在南海航行，并在长期实践中最早发现了南海诸岛，这比巴斯公元 43 年建城的时间还早了 200 多年。中国人那时起就在南海有大规模的航海和渔业捕捞活动。

现在西方人多用 Spratly Islands 称呼中国的南沙群岛，这源于 1843 年英国船长理查德·斯普拉特利（Richard Spratly）所谓“发现”并“命名”了南沙群岛。事实是，早在 2 000 多年前，中国人就最早对南海诸岛命名了。

首先，中国最早对南海诸岛进行管辖。自 1 000 多年前的唐代以来，中国历代政府持续对南沙群岛及其附近海域行使主权管辖。对此中国有充分的历史和法理依据，国际社会也长期予以承认。

其次，中国最早对南海诸岛进行开发利用。中国人民长期以来在南海诸岛及海域从事捕捞、种植和其他生产活动。许多岛礁都曾留下中国渔民的房屋、墓地等遗迹。英国牛津大学博物馆里就收藏了有关中国南海的珍贵历史地图，充分证明中国人开发利用南海的情况。英国海军部测绘局 1868 年版《中国海指南》详细记载了仅有中国渔民在南沙群岛生产和生活的事实。

综上所述，南海诸岛根本不是所谓“无主地”。历史上，一些国家试图挑战中国对南海诸岛的主权，但都被中国政府和人民的维权行为所驳回。1933 年，法国一度侵入中国南沙群岛 9 个岛屿，中国政府就此向法方提出严正交涉，中国各界也纷纷谴责法国的侵略行径。“二战”期间日本非法侵占了南海诸岛。“二战”后，根据《开罗宣言》《波茨坦公告》，中国收复了包括南沙群岛在内的南海诸岛。1948 年，中国政府公布南海断续线，重申在南海的主权和相关权利。

“二战”后相当长时期内，并不存在所谓的南海问题。南海周边的地区也没有任何国家对中国在南沙群岛及其附近海域行使主权提出过异议。直到从20世纪70年代开始，一些南海周边国家觊觎南海的丰富自然资源，开始非法侵占南沙岛礁。

巴斯是个珍视历史、尊重历史的城市，我希望刚才关于南海历史经纬的介绍不但帮助大家了解南海问题的历史，而且有助于大家准确判断今天南海地区的形势，正确理解中国政府的立场。

多年来，中方一直保持高度克制，主张通过友好协商谈判和平解决有关争议。事实上，中菲在双边文件中早已就通过双边谈判解决南海有关争议达成了协议。中国也与东盟国家共同签署了《南海各方行为宣言》，一致同意通过友好磋商与谈判以和平方式解决问题。目前，中国和东盟国家正在就制定“南海行为准则”进行磋商。可以说，在中国和东盟国家的共同努力下，南海问题在不断朝着妥善解决的方向迈进。但菲律宾违背《联合国海洋法公约》规定和《南海各方行为宣言》精神，单方面强推仲裁的行为严重损害了这一进程，破坏了地区和平与稳定。

有人说中国不接受、不参与仲裁案违反了国际法，这种看法与事实恰恰相反。仲裁案的实质是领土和海洋划界问题。《联合国海洋法公约》诞生于1982年，领土问题并非其管辖范畴。关于海洋划界问题，中方也早已根据《联合国海洋法公约》的规定做出了排除性声明，明确排除了仲裁等第三方解决机制。英国自己也做出了类似的声明。可以说所谓的仲裁案在一开始就是非法和无效的，中国的做法正是在行使国际法赋予的合法权利，无可指责。反观菲律宾的行为，不但背信弃义，而且侵犯了《联合国海洋法公约》的权威性和完整性，这才是真正对国际法的违反和侵害。

另外，一些人关心中国的岛礁建设和南海自由航行问题，担心中国在自己主权范围内的岛礁建设会影响航行自由。我想说的是，中国岛礁建设除满足必要的国土防卫需求外，更多的是为各类民事需求服务，以更好地履行中国在海上搜救、防灾减灾、海洋科研、气象观察、生态环境保护、航行安全、渔业生产服务等方面承担的国际责任。

至于所谓的“南海航行自由”，更是一个伪命题。现在每年有十几万艘船只经过南海，从没听说哪艘船的航行受到阻碍。在中国和周边国家的共同努力下，南海航行自由从来不是问题。事实上，中国每年 70%~80% 的贸易和能源需要通过南海航线，有大量中国渔民在南海谋生。作为南海最大沿岸国，没有哪个国家比中国更关心南海地区的航行和飞越自由。中国在这片海域搞建设，既是为了自身发展需要，也是为了向地区各国提供公共产品。这些建设不但不妨碍航行自由，而且会为各国船只的通行提供便利服务和保护。英国路透社报道，一些船东认为，中国在南海的活动有利于海域的安全，中国在南海岛屿部署救援力量，会缩短营救时间，增加营救机会。

同时应当指出的是，南海的和平稳定和航行自由需要各国的共同努力。一些域外国家借“航行自由”之名，在南海炫耀武力，派遣军用舰机抵近中国南沙群岛有关岛礁邻近海、空域进行挑衅，利用自己的力量优势践踏别国主权安全和海洋权益。这些国家鼓吹的“航行自由”实质上是“横行自由”，这才是南海地区和平稳定以及真正航行自由的最大威胁。域外国家关心南海地区的形势，我们可以理解，但我们希望它们多做有利于地区和平稳定的事，而不是挑拨地区国家之间的矛盾，更不是挑衅，制造事端，威胁别国安全，破坏地区稳定。中国将继续与各国共同努力，维护南海的和平与稳定，将南海建设成为“和平之海”“友谊之海”“合作之海”。

女士们、先生们，

今天我向大家谈了怎么看中国的发展和中国的发展对世界意味着什么，希望有助于大家从更广阔的视角观察和认识世界，对你们的系列讲座“我们眼中的世界事务”能有所帮助。

巴斯皇家文学科学院与英国著名生物学家、进化论的奠基人达尔文有着很深的渊源。这位改写了现代科学进程的伟人在个人自传中写道：“我之所以能在科学上成功，最重要的一点就是对科学的热爱，坚持长期探索。”2 000 多年前，中国古代著名思想家荀子曾说：“锲而舍之，朽木不折；锲而不舍，金石可镂。”这两位先驱的话告诉我们，做任何事情要想取得成功，都需坚持不懈。所以，我们也需要坚持不懈地加强沟通，促进合作，共同开创中英关系“黄金时代”的广阔前景，为促进世界和平与发展、推动人类文明进步做出贡献！

最后，衷心祝愿巴斯市经济社会发展、对外交流合作各项事业取得更大进步，继续为增进中英友好往来与互利合作贡献力量。

谢谢！

现在我愿回答大家的提问。

China's Development Brings Opportunity to the World*

Dr. Steve Wharton,

Councillor William Sandry,

Professor Breakwell,

Professor Sammells,

Mr. Ben Howlett,

Dear teachers and students,

Ladies and Gentlemen,

It gives me real delight to visit your beautiful city. Bath deserves its reputation as one of the most lovely and elegant cities in the UK. As a result, none should be surprised that Bath was listed as a world heritage site in 1987.

I am honoured to be invited to speak here at the prestigious Bath Royal Literary and Scientific Institution.

Over the years, your Institution, the University of Bath, the Bath Spa University, and many other well-known institutions here, have made enormous achievements in education and research. You have cultivated a large number of top-class specialists in different areas. Also, from a Chinese perspective, Bath has made a remarkable contribution to the educational exchanges between China and the UK.

The University of Bath was the first one in Britain to enroll students from the People's Republic of China. Many of the young Chinese students who studied here

* Speech at Bath Royal Literary and Scientific Institution. Bath Royal Literary and Scientific Institution, 17 May 2016.

in the 1970s are now leaders in their respective areas back in China. They have made tremendous contribution to China's development.

Today, Bath retains its attraction to young students from China seeking further education. I am very pleased to see many of them here this evening. Perhaps I can share these thoughts with them:

- You are the future of China.
- You also represent the future of the China-UK relationship.
- I hope you like it here and do well in your studies.
- Your achievements here can make your country proud of you.
- And, in turn, you can utilise the knowledge and experience gained to promote positive China-UK relations.

Today's event is one of the Institution's World Affairs Lecture series.

The theme of these lectures, *World Affairs: Through Our Eyes*, is a reflection of the global vision of the Institution. I thank you for focusing on China in this very first lecture of the series. This certainly underscores the importance that you attach to China-UK relations.

In my speech today, I will try to answer two questions:

- First, how should we look at China's development?
- Second, what does China's development mean to the world?

Let me start by answering the first question.

The most frequently asked question nowadays is whether China's economy will have a "hard landing." I have just returned from my annual leave and official consultations in China. I would like to share with you an authoritative analysis of China's overall economic performance. I can tell you with complete confidence that the fundamentals of China's economy remain strong and positive in the long run. There are bright prospects overlooked by those foreign observers who predict a "hard landing." Here are four reasons for my optimism.

First, economic figures show that China has maintained a reasonable growth rate.

Amid worldwide slowdown in 2015, China continued to grow at 6.9%. Though this was for the first time below 7%, that growth, nonetheless, represents an added amount that is equivalent to 10% growth five years ago, given the fact that overall GDP now stands at ten trillion US dollars.

The increment is almost the size of the annual GDP of a medium-sized country. Compared with other major economies, China is definitely in the lead in growth rate and at the top in absolute increment.

In the first quarter of this year, China's GDP grew at 6.7%. This suggests a steady start to 2016. Most economists around the world believe that China's economy is turning for the better. In its *World Economic Outlook* published in April, the IMF raised its forecast for China's growth in both 2016 and 2017 by 0.2%. This is a clear sign of confidence in the long-term, steady growth of China's economy.

My second reason for optimism is that China's economic structure is undergoing major and positive changes.

The current moderate growth, to a large extend, is the result of China's proactive structural adjustments. So, to have an accurate understanding of China's economic performance, one needs to look at not only the speed of growth, but also, how growth spreads out sectorwise.

In terms of industrial structure, the service sector, for the first time in history, made up more than half of China's total GDP in 2015. This was 2.4 percentage points higher than that of 2014. The advance of the service sector is highly significant as it is a core driver of China rising up the value-added economic chain. In addition, the service sector growth is a path that creates a high level of well-paid jobs.

In terms of demand, last year consumption contributed over 60% of China's total growth. Domestic demand became the major driver of growth.

In terms of the quality of growth, energy intensity per unit of GDP continued to decrease and livelihood-related indicators remained stable. A total of 10.66 million new urban jobs were created in 2015.

This momentum continued in the first quarter of 2016. Most significantly, the service sector expanded by 7.6% and continued to have a higher share in the GDP at 56.9%. This was two percentage points higher than the same period last year. Both individual income and consumption have increased faster than GDP.

These positive trends are all evidence of steady progress of structural adjustments.

Recent studies suggest that the conventional way of economic analysis, with too much focus on industrial statistics, usually fails to reflect the true picture of China's economy in transition. This view deserves some attention.

My third positive point is that China's economy has huge potential and much space for further growth.

China is undergoing a new type of industrialisation, IT application, urbanisation and agricultural modernisation. In this process, China's economy will build up its resilience, display its potential and open up space for growth.

China's urbanisation rate in 2015 was 56.1%. That is quite low compared with the advanced economies, where urbanisation is usually above 80%. What this means is urbanisation in China will provide ample space and demand for growth.

Another growth potential lies in the regional development gap. China's western provinces are at least ten years behind their eastern peers in terms of development. The demand for better infrastructure and higher quality of life in China's western provinces will release tremendous development potential.

Then we should look at the advantages in Chinese education. China has the advantage of well-educated work force. In China, over 110 million people have an associate degree or above. This is a huge pool of talent which will sustain further development in China.

While moderately expanding overall demand, the government is also focusing on supply side reform. The reform, which improves supply-demand relations and market expectations, has produced initial effects.

A few words about the debt issue in China which recently caught media attention. China's deficit and government debt is secure and much lower than that of the US, Europe and Japan. This leaves enough room for further macro-regulation.

My fourth point regarding optimism is that China has mapped out a new blueprint for development in next five years. This is known as the 13th Five-Year Plan.

2016 is the opening year of the 13th Five-Year Plan. It also marks the beginning of a crucial stage leading up to the building of what Chinese people call, "a moderately prosperous society."

The Plan rolls out major goals, tasks and measures for the economic and social development in the next five years. It marks the beginning of a new journey towards economic transition and upgrading. The highlights of the Plan are five development concepts. They are innovation, balanced growth, green economy, opening-up and inclusive development.

- Innovation will become a new growth driver and will need an economic system and structure that is more innovation-friendly.
- Balanced growth will strengthen the weak links and open up more spaces for growth.
- Green economy prioritises environmental protection and the pursuit of a low-carbon economy. This means more emphasis on energy conservation and emission reduction.
- Opening-up means China will continue to improve its opening-up layout and upgrade its opening-up structure.
- Inclusive development means development is always for the people, of the people and shared by the people.

The 13th Five-Year Plan and the five development concepts aim to address existing challenges, make up for weak links, empower the engine of growth and consolidate comparative strengths. The ideas and concepts will guide China's economic development in the next five years and beyond. With the implementation of the Plan and related reform measures, China's economy will continue to grow with steady progress.

These are key points about the bigger picture going forward:

- China has the potential and capability to sustain medium-to-high growth in the long run.
- The long-term, overall trend is positive.
- However, the downward pressure of the global economy, and the economic transition and upgrading inside China, means that China's growth will not be all plain sailing.
- From time to time, challenges and difficulties will occur, including stock market fluctuations.

- But China will not hide from problems or deny them.
- China has the confidence to face up to the challenges and prevail.

Ladies and Gentlemen,

Let me turn to the second question.

What does China's development mean to the world? That is, how will it affect you, the UK and the world? Let me first of all quote President Xi Jinping. He said in a speech during his state visit to the UK last year:

"In today's world, interaction and interdependence is the general trend. With cross-border flows of goods, capital, information and people, regardless of distance, size and level of development, countries are increasingly finding themselves in a community of common interests and shared future, based on intertwined interests and common challenges."

Today, China has deeply integrated itself into the world. This means that the Chinese economy is very much part of the global economy. The outcome of this historical change is very positive for all humanity. For Chinese people China's development has benefited from such integration. For the world people China's development is delivering benefits.

So, my answer to the question is, China's development means opportunity to the world. It means opportunity to the UK. There are five reasons why I believe so.

First, China's development is a contribution to the common development of the world.

After more than 30 years of high-speed growth, China is now widely recognised as a powerhouse of the world economy. In particular, in times of global economic crisis, China has taken decisive actions to power up growth. This has had a major positive impact when the world economy was facing severe challenges. For example, in 2015, China led the major economies and contributed over 25% of global growth.

China is now the biggest country of origin in terms of overseas tourism. Last year, Chinese tourists made more than 120 million outbound trips, including 80 million self-arranged trips. This means benefit for many economies as Chinese tourist spending per trip per person was over 1,000 pounds or 11,624 RMB yuan. This trend is especially notable at a time when the global consumption was sluggish.

According to VisitBritain, in the first nine months of last year, Chinese tourists made

214,000 trips to the UK. These Chinese visitors spent a total of 435 million pounds. Chinese tourists are no strangers in London, Edinburgh, and of course, here in Bath.

China is now the world's biggest trading nation and second largest investor in nations outside of China. In the next five years, China will import more than 10 trillion US dollars in goods and make over 600 billion US dollars in overseas investment.

All these facts demonstrate how China has become a major driving force for global consumption and investment. In addition, this role will remain unchanged in the years to come. Let me put it this way. The development and progress of a country with 1.3 billion people is in itself a huge contribution to the world. It is a major force for good to deliver peaceful and sustainable global growth. This is a mutual benefit for all humanity.

Let me now turn to the second benefit. China's newly introduced opening-up measures will bring new opportunities to the world.

This means that China will keep its door open, further liberalise its market and improve rules and institutions.

You will recall that the first round of reform and opening-up started in Shenzhen over three decades ago. The eventual impact across China was profound. That saw the industrialisation of China that is unmatched in human history in terms of scale and speed.

The establishment of the Shanghai Free Trade Zone marked the beginning of a new round of opening-up in China. To streamline government administrative approval and to delegate power, the Shanghai FTZ introduced three lists:

- The "negative list."
- The "accountability list."
- And the "power list."

These three lists have greatly promoted trade facilitation.

With the financial services sector, China will open up its market and increase access in an orderly fashion. This will facilitate foreign enterprises, institutions and individuals in their businesses and cooperation in China.

China has also introduced the Belt and Road Initiative. This is a vision of an economic belt that extends from the Asia-Pacific region in the east to Europe in the west. Projects are already underway in many countries along this belt. This will create a new growth point for the world economy.

There is a saying:

"If you want to walk fast, walk alone; if you want to walk far, walk together."

China will continue to build an open economy. China is ready to share the opportunities of its development with the world.

The third benefit is that China is doing its best to advance international cooperation on development.

China is committed to higher-level and deeper South-South Cooperation. We have worked to help with the economic growth and life improvement in fellow developing countries through a number of proposals and concrete actions.

During the UN meetings for commemorating the 70th anniversary of its founding last year, President Xi Jinping announced China's decision to establish a fund to support South-South Cooperation. The initial pledge of two billion US dollars will be used to support the implementation of the 2030 Agenda for Sustainable Development.

In the next decade, China will establish a China-UN Peace and Development Fund with one billion US dollars. China will also join the new UN Peacekeeping Capability Readiness System. Through this China will create peacekeeping forces consisting of a police unit and emergency standby teams.

In the next five years, China will carry out in other developing countries the initiative known as "Six 100s." This will include:

- 100 poverty reduction programs.
- 100 agricultural cooperation projects.
- 100 trade promotion and aid programs.
- 100 environmental protection and climate change programs.
- 100 hospitals and clinics.
- And 100 schools and vocational training centers.

In the next five years, China will support the developing world with further practical help:

- 120,000 training opportunities.

- 150,000 scholarships.
- And help train 500,000 technicians.

Other initiatives include:

- Increasing investment in the least developed countries.
- Cancelling some of the debt of designated nations.
- And setting up an international development knowledge centre.

The fourth benefit is that China as a big country is doing its bit and taking up its responsibilities.

China is committed to world peace and development. In the face of global challenges, China has been a consistent and responsible player. The Chinese government has taken concrete steps to tackle the shared world difficulties. One example is the comprehensive, balanced, and ambitious agreement at the Paris Climate Change Conference. China worked very hard with other countries to enable the conclusion of the agreement.

China has also actively pushed for reforms of global economic governance. The aim is that the IMF, World Bank and other international economic and financial institutions will truly reflect the changes in the global architecture. Such reforms do not mean to abolish the existing system and "reinventing the wheel." They are meant to improve the management of the global economy through innovative approaches. This year, China will host the G20 Summit in the city of Hangzhou. China hopes to join hands with all other parties to work for better global economic and financial governance at the summit.

In this same spirit of mutual cooperation China has made other initiatives, for example, the establishment of the Asian Infrastructure Investment Bank (AIIB) and the New Development Bank with other BRICS nations.

The thinking behind these new banks is that they will serve to compliment, rather than replace, the existing global financial system. The recent decision of AIIB to undertake a joint loan with the Asian Development Bank is welcome news. It certainly shows that it is fully possible for the AIIB and other existing multilateral development banks to pool their respective strengthens and engage in win-win cooperation.

Going forward, China will continue to work with other countries:

- To firmly uphold the international order and system underpinned by the purposes and principles of the UN Charter.
- To build a new type of international relations featuring win-win cooperation with other countries.
- To enrich the idea of community of common future for all mankind.
- And to spread the idea of global governance that is widely consulted, jointly built and shared by all.

The fifth benefit is that China's development will bring more opportunities to the UK.

There is now a historic window of opportunity for China-UK relationship. Last year, Chinese President Xi Jinping paid a successful state visit to the UK. Leaders of both our countries made a number of agreements:

- To jointly build the global comprehensive strategic partnership for the 21st century.
- And open up the Golden Era for enduring, open and win-win relationship between China and the UK.

This state visit has charted the course for stronger and result-oriented cooperation between China and the UK.

At present, Britain is China's second largest trading partner in the EU while China is Britain's second largest trading partner outside the EU. Last year our bilateral trade volume was a steady 78.52 billion US dollars. Chinese non-financial, direct investment in the UK totaled 13.2 billion US dollars. This has made the UK the top destination for Chinese investment in Europe.

The UK also tops the list in many other areas. It is the largest recipient of Chinese students. Now about 150,000 Chinese students are studying in the Britain. The number of British students in China is about 6,000. There are also 55 twin city relationships between our two countries.

Opportunities for cooperation exist, not only in bilateral fields, but also in global affairs given the global vision and influence of both countries.

- Both China and the UK are key players and responsible partners in world affairs.
- Both are permanent members of the UN Security Council.

These positions and responsibilities provide a powerful platform for collaboration for China and UK in the global arena. Both nations can:

- Work together on innovation and reforms in order to provide the right leadership to world economic development.
- Join hands to deliver progress in international development cooperation.
- Pull together on reforms of the global economic governance.
- And make concerted efforts to safeguard international and regional peace and stability.

Talking about regional peace and stability, there is one issue that caught the world's attention recently. This is the South China Sea.

Not long ago, I wrote articles for *The Times* and the *Financial Times* respectively to expound on the Chinese government's position.

I would like to use this opportunity to go a bit deeper into this topic as I believe it must be of interest to many of you here this evening.

The South China Sea issue, at its very heart, is about disputes over territorial sovereignty and maritime delimitation. The issues arise from the illegal occupation of part of China's Nansha Islands.

The Philippines, Vietnam and others have since 1970s illegally occupied a total of 42 islands and reefs in Nansha, based on which they made their "maritime claims."

Some of the countries attempt to get away with illegal occupation by referring to Nansha Islands as "Terra Nullius" and claiming "prior possession." Others try to invoke "geographical proximity" as justification. The Philippines went even further as to initiate a so-called "arbitration."

Let me share with you some historical facts. As early as 200 BC, during the Han Dynasty, the Chinese were the first to discover the islands and reefs in the South China

Sea. That was almost 200 years before the city of Bath was built, which was in 43 AD. Back then, Chinese were recorded to have large-scale seafaring and fishing activities in the South China Sea.

Today, Nansha of the South China Sea is called *Spratly Islands* in the western countries. The reason for the name difference comes from a Richard Spratly a British sea captain. Spratly thought it was he who had "discovered" and "named" the islands in 1843. But actually, the Chinese had named the Nansha Islands about 2,000 years before he did.

China is also the first to conduct administration in the South China Sea. The Tang Dynasty was established in China between AD 617 and AD 907 and, ever since then, successive Chinese governments have maintained administration over Nansha and the waters around them. This means that China's sovereignty claims are built on strong historical and legal evidence, which the international community have long recognised.

China is also the first country to develop and live on the islands in the South China Sea. For centuries, the Chinese have been engaged in fishing, planting and other activities on the islands and in the nearby waters. The remains of this continuous habitation can be seen through archaeological evidence. For example, piles of building foundations, wells, temples, tombs, can be seen and found on many of the islands.

The world-famous Ashmolean Museum in Oxford has a collection of maps of the South China Sea. These clearly testify about these early activities by the Chinese. The fact that only Chinese lived on the Nansha islands is recorded clearly in the book called *The China Sea Pilot* published by the British Navy in 1868.

This extensive historical evidence points to the fact that the islands and reefs in the South China are not "Terra Nullius."

Historical records also have shown that attempts to challenge China's sovereignty over South China Sea islands encountered continual resistance from the Chinese government:

- In 1933, France invaded nine islands in Nansha.
- The then Chinese government lodged solemn representations to the French authority and the general public in China denounced the invasion.
- During World War II, the islands in the South China Sea were illegally occupied by Japan.

- After the war, China restored sovereignty of the Nansha Islands in accordance with the Cairo Declaration and the Potsdam Proclamation.
- In 1948, the Chinese government announced the "dotted lines" to reassert China's sovereignty and related rights and interests in the South China Sea.

For decades after World War II the South China Sea has never been an issue. There was no challenge on China's sovereignty over the Nansha Islands and the waters around it by any country around the South China Sea. But during the 1970s some countries try to lay claim on the natural resources in the South China Sea. It was then that some nations began to occupy illegally some of the islands.

Here in Bath, you value and respect history because history matters and history helps one understand the present. In this spirit of dialogue, I hope that my briefing will have succeeded with three goals:

- Inform you about the past.
- Help you gain an accurate understanding of the situation today.
- And, be accurately briefed about the position of the Chinese government.

Over the years, China has all along exercised a high-level of self-restraint. China has always stood for solving disputes peacefully through friendly consultations and negotiations between countries in the region.

Take the case of relations between China and the Philippines. China and the Philippines have long since reached an agreement on a bilateral approach to the South China Sea disputes. The Declaration on the Conduct of Parties in the South China Sea was signed between China and ASEAN (the Association of South East Asian Nations) where China and the Philippines are both members. In that Declaration on the Conduct of Parties in the South China Sea there is an explicit commitment to friendly consultations and negotiation for a peaceful resolution. At present, China and ASEAN countries are having talks on formulating the "Code of Conduct" in the South China Sea. Such joint efforts between China and ASEAN are paving the way for the appropriate settlement of the issue.

However, the Philippines decided not to abide by the spirit of the Declaration on the

Conduct of Parties in the South China Sea which they signed. Instead, the Philippines chose to the route of arbitration unilaterally through the Permanent Court of Arbitration in the Netherlands. This action by the Philippines has seriously damaged and undermined regional peace and stability. China has consistently and repeatedly stated that it rejects and does not accept the arbitration claim by the Philippines.

Related to this so-called arbitration are repeated assertions in the foreign media outside China. These claim that China is not obeying the established and agreed maritime laws governing the oceans and seas of the world.

Is China violating the international law as some has claimed? Absolutely not and quite the opposite.

The so-called arbitration is illegal and invalid from the very beginning because it is in essence about territorial sovereignty and maritime delimitation.

The United Nations Convention on the Law of the Sea (UNCLOS) does not have jurisdiction over issues related to sovereignty.

As for maritime delimitation, China made a declaration years ago in accordance with the UNCLOS to exclude disputes on maritime delimitation from compulsory arbitration or any third-party mechanism. Over 30 other countries, including the UK, have made similar declarations.

That is why the arbitration case brought by the Philippines against China is illegal and invalid. In reaction to that arbitration what China did is simply exercising its legitimate rights empowered by the international law. The behaviour of China, in terms of international law, is beyond reproach.

What really does damage to international law is the act of the Philippines in going against its early commitment. This action is undermining the authority and integrity of the UNCLOS.

Another frequently asked question is about current activity on islands in the South China Seas that are the sovereign property of China: Will China's development of, and construction on these islands affect the freedom of navigation in the South China Sea? The answer to this question is very clear: Certainly not.

Apart from minimum defense facilities, the construction on China's own islands is primarily civilian in purpose. They will enable China to better fulfill its international obligations, including maritime search and rescue, disaster relief and prevention, maritime scientific research, meteorological observation, eco-environmental protection, navigation safety, and fishing services.

As for the "concerns over freedom of navigation," this is completely a false argument. Every year more than 100,000 vessels pass through the South China Sea. None of them has been ever run into any problem with freedom of navigation thanks to the joint efforts of China and other countries in this region.

In fact, no country cares about freedom of navigation and over-flight in the South China Sea more than China. This is why: China is the biggest littoral state in the South China Sea. Every year 70%~80% of China's trade and energy supply pass through the South China Sea. A large number of Chinese fishermen make a living in the South China Sea.

China's construction in the South China Sea is not just for the development of its own islands. Better infrastructure on these islands also provides public benefits to countries in the region. Instead of affecting the freedom of navigation, these facilities will offer services and protection to ships passing by. According to Reuters interview with some ship owners throughout Asian countries, China's building efforts in the South China Sea are good for maritime safety and security, as the rescue capability deployed on the islands can provide immediate help and increase chances of survival.

Peace and stability are of great importance as well as the freedom of navigation in the South China Sea. To achieve that, all must work together. But if "freedom of navigation" became an excuse to flex military muscles, this poses a serious threat to peace in the region. Actions of certain countries to send military jets and warships on close-in reconnaissance in the nearby waters and air space of China's islands and reefs is a dangerous provocation to China and its sovereign rights. China cannot be expected to ignore a direct challenge to the sovereignty, security and maritime rights of its own legitimate territory. Such military action on the pretext of "freedom of navigation" is in reality a license to bully. That would be the biggest threat to the real freedom of navigation and the peace and stability in the South China Sea.

It is understandable that some countries outside the region pay close attention to the South China Sea. China positively encourages these countries to speak up and do things that are in favour of peace and stability in the region. What China finds intolerable is actions that sow discord among countries in the region, or actions triggering troubles. China is opposed to any behavior that threatens others and undermines stability. Given all those points, I can assure you that China will continue to work with all parties to safeguard the peace and stability of the South China Sea. China seeks to build it into a sea of peace, a sea of friendship and a sea of cooperation.

Ladies and Gentlemen,

Today, I have talked about China's development and what it means to the world. I hope that my speech has offered a fresh perspective in seeing "World Affairs through our eyes."

As I know, your Institute has a proud record of links with the renowned British scientist, Charles Darwin, who has truly changed the course of modern science. Let me quote what he wrote in his biography. He said,

"...My success as a man of science... has been determined... by complex and diversified mental qualities and conditions. Of these, the most important have been—the love of science—unbounded patience in long reflecting over any subject—industry in observing and collecting facts..."

The great Chinese thinker Xun Zi, who lived around 2,000 years ago, had this to say with similar sentiments:

"Giving up halfway cannot even have rotten wood cut apart; with unremitting efforts, metals and stones are able to be shaped well."

The two giants of human endeavour, Charles Darwin and Xun Zi have told us about one truth—the importance of perseverance. That is crucial factor if any success is to be secured.

Perseverance is what we need in strengthening our communication.

Perseverance is needed in promoting stronger cooperation, in creating brighter prospects for the Golden Era of China-UK relations.

And perseverance is essential in making contribution to world peace, development, and the advancement of human civilisation.

In conclusion, I wish the City of Bath greater success in economic and social development.

I look to the continued contribution from Bath to the friendly interaction and win-win cooperation between China and the UK.

Thank you.

Now, I will open the floor for questions.

坚持开放、合作、协商，为世界增添“中国信心”*

尊敬的彭博欧洲总部主席考特齐亚兹先生，

尊敬的英国财政部经济国务大臣格伦先生，

尊敬的各位来宾，

女士们，先生们：

下午好！

很高兴再次到访彭博社。当前，全球经济风险上升，不稳定、不确定性因素增多，世界各国都在探寻应对之策。彭博社在此时举办“探索新丝绸之路”研讨会可谓恰逢其时。我认为，世界经济现在最需要的就是两个字——“信心”。

今天我想通过回答三个问题，诠释提振世界经济、促进各国共同发展的“中国信心”。

第一个问题：随着单边主义、保护主义不断抬头，国际社会是选择“开放”，还是选择“封闭”？中国的答案很明确，即坚持扩大开放，为推动世界经济强劲增长提供信心。

一是扩大开放的决心不变。对外开放是中国的基本国策，不是一时一事的权宜之计，而是基于自身经济高质量发展的自觉行动，是基于经济全球化时代潮流的必然选择。在刚刚结束不久的二十国集团大阪峰会上，习近平主席再次向世界宣布了中国将进一步开放市场、主动扩大进口、持续改善营商

---

* 在彭博研讨会上的主旨演讲。2019 年 7 月 10 日，伦敦彭博欧洲总部。

环境、全面实施平等待遇、大力推动经贸谈判等五大举措。中国以实际行动再次证明了扩大开放的坚定决心和大国担当，赢得了国际社会好评。

二是扩大开放的步伐不乱。一个时期以来，某个西方大国固守“本国优先”，大搞“贸易霸凌”，全球产业格局和贸易形势受到严重冲击。面对这些外部压力，中国没有屈服，也不会自乱阵脚，将继续把推动“一带一路”建设作为对外开放合作的管总规划，使“一带一路”造福更多国家和人民。在成功落实首届“一带一路”国际合作高峰论坛达成的5大类279项成果基础上，2019年4月中国再次成功举办第二届“一带一路”国际合作高峰论坛，与会各方达成了总计6大类283项合作成果，项目合作协议总额高达640多亿美元，共建“一带一路”正式迈入高质量发展新阶段。

三是扩大开放的势头不减。中国认为，经济全球化是不可逆转的大趋势，融入世界经济是不容改变的大方向，因此扩大开放不管遇到多少困难和挫折都不会动摇。目前中国制造业已基本放开，现代服务业准入限制持续减少，金融业开放步伐明显加快、开放水平明显提升。下一步中国将加快市场开放，扩大外商准入。原来规定的2021年取消证券、期货、寿险外资股比限制提前至2020年；2019年版外资准入负面清单条目由原来的48条措施减至40条。2018年中国支付的外国专利许可费和技术使用费超过300亿美元，较10年前增长近4倍。下一步中国将加大知识产权保护力度，争取年内完成《外商投资法》配套法规，继续完善对外开放法律体系，打造开放透明、公平竞争的营商环境。近年来中国多次自主降税，贸易加权平均税率只有5.2%，低于绝大多数发展中国家，接近发达国家平均水平。下一步中国将继续自主降低关税总水平，扩大进口，办好第二届中国国际进口博览会，使中国“市场红利”让更多国家受益。

第二个问题：近年来经济全球化深入发展，但发展赤字依然存在，中国如何在实现自身发展的同时带动其他国家发展？中国的答案很明确，即坚持合作共赢，为实现世界经济包容平衡增长提供信心。

以国际金融领域合作为例，在大数据、区块链等新技术推动下，金融科技、普惠金融、绿色金融等新领域快速发展，国际金融市场发展面临新机遇和新挑战。在此背景下，中英分别作为新兴金融大国和传统金融强国，双方加强金融合作，将给双边和国际投资者带来巨大机遇。

一是投资机遇。2019 年 4 月 1 日，中国债券被纳入彭博巴克莱全球综合指数，这是中国债券市场开放的又一重大成果，体现了中国在全球金融市场上的地位不断提升，也反映出国际投资者对中国市场的信心。上个月，第十次中英经济财金对话在伦敦成功举行，取得了 69 项成果，“沪伦通”是其中亮点之一。“沪伦通”正式启动，标志着中英分别作为世界第二大和第三大资本市场真正实现互联互通，拓宽了中英双向跨境投融资渠道。中英还将继续就债券市场互联安排开展可行性研究，为两国和国际投资者带来更多投资机遇。

二是绿色机遇。2018 年，中国绿色债券发行额突破 300 亿美元，同比增长 33%。上个星期（7 月 2 日），英国举行了第三届绿色金融峰会，格伦大臣在会上发布了英国《绿色金融战略》。事实上，中英在绿色金融领域一直互为主要合作伙伴。2018 年 6 月，中国工商银行伦敦分行发行了 15.8 亿美元的等值绿色债券，成为伦敦证券交易所历史上规模最大的绿色债券。目前，双方成立了中英绿色金融工作组，设立了中英绿色金融中心，发布了《“一带一路”绿色投资原则》。中英还欢迎两国金融机构开展合作，在英国和其他市场发行离岸绿色资产支持证券。未来中英还将创建由私营部门推动的投资平台，支持和投资英国绿色技术公司，以促进其在中国等新兴市场的开发应用，努力在绿色金融产品创新、标准制定、风险监管等领域发挥更大引领作用。

三是平台机遇。伦敦金融城是世界领先的全球金融中心，也是中国金融服务合作的重要伙伴。伦敦是全世界最大的人民币离岸交易市场。截至 2019 年 2 月，共有 113 只人民币债券在伦交所上市，总规模超过 300 亿元人民币。上个月我出席了中信银行伦敦分行开业仪式，这是第 8 家在伦敦设立分行的中资银行。可以说，这不仅是中资银行国际化发展的又一“里程碑”，也是对金融城光明前景的“信任票”。我相信，未来伦敦金融城将继续在人民币国际化、地方金融合作、第三方市场合作等领域发挥重要平台作用。

第三个问题：近来中美关系广受各方关注，贸易磋商动向牵动各国神经，两国能否避免“修昔底德陷阱”，避免“贸易战”殃及世界经济？中国的答案很明确，即坚持对话协商，为维护世界经济稳定提供信心。

中方始终坚持通过对话磋商解决经贸争端。不久前中美两国元首在二十国集团大阪峰会期间举行会晤，双方同意在平等和相互尊重的基础上重启经贸磋商。英国工商界十分关注中美元首达成的共识能否落到实处，英国媒体也不停地问我中美经贸磋商的前景。我手上虽然没有预测未来的“水晶球”，但我认为把握好四点非常重要。

一是正确看待彼此定位。中美建交40年来的历史经验表明，两国合则两利、斗则俱伤。因此，双方要视彼此为伙伴而非对手。中国的发展根本上是为了满足中国人民对美好生活的向往，而不是挑战谁或取代谁。中国决不会重蹈“国强必霸”的覆辙，将坚持走和平发展道路。

二是理性看待相互竞争。在经济全球化时代，合作与竞争是国际关系的正常现象。只要心胸足够大，视野足够广，世界就足够大，容得下各国共同发展繁荣。如果我们一味放大竞争，就会挤压合作空间。只有摒弃你输我赢的零和思维，才能在深化合作中形成良性竞争，携手实现互利共赢。

三是勇于体现大国担当。作为大国，意味着对地区和世界和平与发展肩负着更大责任，而不是“颐指气使”的更大权力。中国坚持捍卫自身合法利益就是一种大国担当。我们呼吁其他国家，特别是大国能以负责任的态度，相向而行，共同维护以规则为基础的多边贸易体制。

四是携手捍卫共同利益。一个和平稳定的国际环境符合中美两国和国际社会的共同利益。在这场没有硝烟的“贸易战”中，无人能置身事外。各国投资者也都是单边主义、保护主义和贸易霸凌的受害者。我希望在座的工商界人士不做“沉默的大多数”，而做开放自由理念的践行者、多边贸易秩序的维护者、经济金融合作的促进者，以实际行动为世界经济发展注入更多信心、更多正能量。

女士们，先生们，

“独行快，众行远。”世界好，中国才会好；中国好，世界才会更好。中国愿以更大的开放分享发展机遇，以更好的合作推进互利共赢，以更多的协商谋求共同发展，为世界增添“中国信心”。希望中英两国企业家发扬伙伴精神，同舟共济，共克时艰，坚持开放、合作、协商，共同开创世界美好未来！

最后，预祝本次研讨会取得圆满成功！

谢谢！

China Stays Committed to Openness, Cooperation and Consultation, and Brings Confidence to the World*

Chairman Constantin Cotzias,

Economic Secretary John Glen,

Distinguished Guests,

Ladies and Gentlemen,

Good afternoon!

It is a real delight to join you again at Bloomberg.

The Bloomberg Forum on "Navigate the New Silk Road" could not have been timelier, as countries of the world explore ways to tackle the rising risks, instabilities and uncertainties in the world economy. In my opinion, what the world economy needs most now is "confidence."

Today, I would like to explain what China is doing to boost confidence and promote common progress by answering the following three questions.

The first question is: in face of rising unilateralism and protectionism, should countries of the world choose openness or isolation?

China's answer is clear: we remain committed to further opening-up. This commitment boosts confidence in robust economic growth.

First, China has demonstrated firm resolve to open its door wider to the world.

---

* Keynote Speech at the Navigate the New Silk Road Forum. Bloomberg European Headquarters, 10 July 2019.

Opening-up is a basic national policy of China. It is not a matter of expediency, but a natural choice. It is for the purpose of realising high-quality economic growth, and it is in line with the trend of globalisation.

At the G20 Summit in Osaka last month, President Xi announced five important measures. They are:

- Open up the Chinese market wider.
- Expand imports.
- Improve the business environment.
- Equal treatment for all foreign investment.
- Advance trade talks.

These concrete measures reaffirm China's resolve and courage in opening its door wider to the world. It is met with enthusiastic response from the international community.

Second, China has taken firm steps to open its door wider to the world.

When a certain big Western country insisted on putting itself first and adopted bullying trade policies, the global industrial landscape and trade situation came under severe stress.

China has not succumbed to outside pressures. Nor will it stop the steps of opening-up. China will continue to advance the Belt and Road Initiative as the master plan for its opening-up. And in this process, China will strive to make sure that more countries and people will benefit from BRI.

At the first Belt and Road Forum for International Cooperation two years ago, 279 outcomes covering five areas were reached and all have been implemented. Last April, the second Forum was successfully held, where 283 outcomes covering six areas were reached, and more than 65 billion dollars of deals on cooperation projects were signed. The second Forum marked the beginning of a new stage for high-quality BRI development.

Third, China has kept up the momentum of opening-up wider to the world.

Economic globalisation is an irreversible trend. Greater integration into the world economy is the major direction that cannot be changed. Therefore, no matter how many difficulties or setbacks China encounters, it will not waver in opening its door wider to the world.

As we speak, China's manufacturing sector is basically open. It is gradually lifting restrictions on access to the modern services sector. And it is opening up the financial sector with accelerated pace and at a higher level. Going forward, China will continue to quicken its steps to increase market access for foreign investment. Taking for example foreign ownership caps in joint venture firms in sectors such as securities, future and life insurance, China has brought forward the deadline for lifting the caps from 2021 to 2020. At the same time, China has also cut short the 2019 edition of the negative list on foreign investment, reducing the 48 items on the list to 40.

In 2018, China paid more than 30 billion dollars in patent fees and royalties to overseas license holders or rights owners. That's nearly four times more than ten years ago. Going forward, China will take further steps to foster an open, transparent and fair business environment. These steps include:

- strengthen IPR protection,
- strive to complete the supporting regulations of the Foreign Investment Law by the end of this year,
- and continue to improve the legal system for opening-up.

In recent years, China has taken the initiative to cut tariffs many times. Its trade-weighted average tariff only stands at 5.2%. This is lower than the majority of the developing countries, and close to the average level of developed countries. Going forward, China will continue to take the initiative to cut overall tariffs and expand imports. Later this year, China will host the second China International Import Expo. This will be an opportunity to share China's market with more countries.

Now let me turn to the second question: despite deepening economic globalisation, development gaps between different countries still exist. What can China do to continue serving as a growth engine for the world while pursuing development at home?

Again, China's answer to this question is clear: we remain committed to win-win cooperation. This commitment will boost the confidence in the inclusive and balanced economic growth in the world.

Take the international financial cooperation for example.

Driven by big data, blockchain and other new technologies, FinTech, inclusive finance and green finance are developing rapidly. This has brought new opportunities and new challenges to the international financial market.

Against this backdrop, financial cooperation between our two countries—one with newly-acquired financial strength and the other a traditional financial power—will create enormous opportunities for investors from both countries and the world as a whole.

First, the opportunity for investment.

On April 1st this year, Chinese bonds were included in the Bloomberg Barclays Global Aggregate Index. I think this is an important success of the ever more open Chinese bond market. It shows China's growing role in the global financial market. It also reflects the confidence of global investors in the Chinese market.

Last month, the tenth China-UK Economic and Financial Dialogue was successfully held in London. Of the 69 outcomes reached at the EFD, the Shanghai-London Stock Connect is a highlight. Its official launch marks the realisation of real connectivity between China and the UK as the world's second and third largest capital market respectively. It also expands the channel for two-way, cross-border investment and financing between China and the UK.

China and the UK will continue to conduct feasibility studies on the arrangement for connectivity between the bond markets, so as to create more opportunities for investors from both our two countries and the world.

Second, the opportunity for green development.

In 2018, China issued over 30 billion dollars of green bond, achieving 33% increase year on year. Last week, the UK hosted the third Green Finance Summit. At the summit, Economic Secretary Glen announced the Green Finance Strategy.

In fact, China and the UK have been major partners in green finance. In June 2018, the London Branch of the Industrial and Commercial Bank of China issued green bond worth 1.58 billion dollars. This was the largest ever green bond listing on the London Stock Exchange.

China and the UK have also set up the Green Finance Taskforce, launched the Green Finance Centre, and issued the Green Investment Principles for Belt and Road

Development.

Our two countries welcome the collaboration between Chinese and UK financial institutions on the issuance of offshore green asset-backed securities in the UK and other markets. Both sides will create investment platforms driven by the private sector to support and invest in UK green technology firms to scale-up in new markets, including China. We will also do more and try to take up the lead in product innovation, standard setting, risk supervision and management in green finance.

Third, the opportunity of platforms.

The City of London is a leading global financial centre, and an important partner of China in financial services.

First of all, London is the world's largest offshore RMB market. By last February, a total of 113 RMB-denominated bonds had been listed on the London Stock Exchange. The total value is more than 30 billion RMB yuan.

Second, many Chinese banks have made London their home. Last month, I attended the opening ceremony of China CITIC Bank London Branch. It was the eighth Chinese bank to set up a branch in London. This was not only a new milestone in the efforts of Chinese banks to explore the global market, but also a "vote of confidence" for the future of the City of London.

I am confident that going forward, the City of London will continue to serve as an important platform for RMB internationalisation, for subnational financial cooperation between China and the UK, and for the two countries' cooperation in third markets.

Now let me turn to the third question of my speech. It is about the China-US relations and trade talks, which has caught the world's attention. How can the two countries avoid the "Thucydides's Trap" and a "trade war" that could do so much harm to the world economy?

Once again, China's answer to this question is clear: we remain committed to dialogue and consultation. This commitment will boost confidence in the ability of the world economy to remain stable.

China has been committed to addressing trade frictions through dialogue and consultation. Not long ago, the Chinese and US Presidents met during the G20 Summit in Osaka. The two sides agreed to restart the trade talks on the basis of equality and mutual respect.

The UK business community has followed the event closely and is eager to know whether the agreement will be delivered. And British media kept sounding me out about the prospect of China-US trade talks.

I do not have a crystal ball, but I think the following four points are very important for the future of China-US relations.

First, China and the US should have a right understanding of each other's goal.

Forty years of China-US diplomatic relationship show that the two countries stand to gain from cooperation, and lose from confrontation. Therefore, it is important the two sides see each other as partners rather than rivals.

For China, the ultimate goal of development is to meet the aspiration of the Chinese people for a better life. It is not China's goal to challenge or replace anyone. China will not go down the beaten path of Western powers and let its development be led to hegemony. Instead, China will remain committed to the path of peaceful development.

Second, China and the US should view their competition in a sensible manner.

In an age of economic globalisation, both cooperation and competition are part of a normal relationship between countries. With a broad mind and a broad horizon, it would not be hard to see that the world is big enough for all countries to achieve common development and prosperity.

If we over-exaggerate competition, we could run the risk of missing the opportunities. The right thing to do is to renounce the zero-sum mentality of "you lose, I win." Only by doing so can we engage in a healthy competition and at the same time deepen cooperation for win-win results.

Third, China and the US should shoulder due responsibilities as big countries.

Big countries have big responsibilities for regional and world peace and development, but not big power to be bossy.

By safeguarding its legitimate interests in trade talks, China has shouldered its responsibility for global economy and trade. We call on other countries, especially big countries, to act in a responsible manner, head towards the same direction and uphold the rule-based multilateral trade system.

Fourth, China and the US should join hands to safeguard the common interests of the world.

A peaceful and stable international environment serves the common interests of

China, of the US and of the international community. No one can stay aloof from this "trade war."

Investors are easy victim of unilateralism, protectionism and bullying trade policies. The business community should not be the "silent majority." I hope you will stand up in support of open and free trade, uphold the multilateral trade order, and promote economic and financial cooperation. I hope you will take concrete action to put confidence and positive energy back into the world economic growth.

Ladies and Gentlemen,

As a saying goes,

"If you want to go fast, walk alone; If you want to go farther, walk together."

China will develop better in a better world; and the world will be a better place with a better China.

China stands ready to share its development opportunities through further opening-up. China will promote win-win results through better cooperation. China will pursue common development through consultation. China will work hard to bring back confidence in the world economy.

I hope the business leaders of our two countries will carry forward the spirit of openness, cooperation, consultation and partnership. In that spirit, I hope and believe you will work together to overcome all difficulties and build a better future for our world!

In conclusion, I wish this Forum success!

Thank you!

共享中国机遇，共创美好未来*

尊敬的法国巴黎银行企业及机构银行主席帕皮亚斯先生，

尊敬的法国巴黎银行英国区主席弗斯特拉滕女士，

女士们，先生们：

大家下午好！

很高兴应邀出席法国巴黎银行（BNP Paribas）举办的“2019 年全球市场大会”。此次大会聚焦全球金融市场，探寻未来发展机遇，具有重要的现实意义。

大会举办方希望我谈一谈中国经济。我愿围绕如何看待中国经济前景、如何抓住中国机遇，与大家分享几点看法。

首先，我来谈谈如何看待中国经济发展前景。

当今世界正处于百年未有之大变局。我们是选择开放还是封闭，选择合作还是对抗，选择共赢还是零和，攸关世界经济未来发展方向。当前，贸易保护主义上升，世界经济面临的不确定、不稳定因素增多。国际货币基金组织预计，2019 年世界经济增速将仅为 3%，为 2008 年国际金融危机以来最低。作为全球第二大经济体，中国经济这艘大船经受住了风浪考验，保持了总体平稳和长期向好的发展态势。我认为，中国经济有“四大亮点”。

一是增长稳。改革开放 40 年来，中国经济持续快速发展，年均增速高

---

* 在法国巴黎银行“2019 年全球市场大会”上的主旨演讲。2019 年 11 月 14 日，伦敦圣潘克拉斯万丽酒店。

达 9.4%。2019 年前三季度，中国国内生产总值约为 10 万亿美元，同比增长 6.2%，增速在全球主要经济体中位居前列；中国城镇新增就业人口将近 1 100 万，居民人均可支配收入实际增长 6.1%，经济增长给人民带来实实在在的利益和稳稳满满的获得感；中国实际使用外资超过 1 000 亿美元，同比增长 6.5%，每天有超过 100 家外资企业在中国诞生。

二是质量高。中国经济“含金量”更足。内需成为拉动经济增长的主要动力，2019 年前三季度中国最终消费对经济增长的贡献率达到 60.5%；经济增长创造就业能力更强，据测算，目前中国国内生产总值每增长 1 个百分点，大约可以拉动新增就业岗位 206 万个，比十年前高出一倍。中国经济“绿色”更足。习近平主席强调，绿水青山就是金山银山。中国绿色发展取得显著成就，中国 2018 年碳排放强度比 2005 年下降 45.8%，单位国内生产总值能耗过去 5 年累计下降 20.3%，煤炭消费比重历史性降至不足 60%。中国已成为全球最大的可再生能源投资国。

三是潜力大。习近平主席曾说，“中国经济是一片大海，而不是一个小池塘”。中国有近 14 亿人口，9 亿劳动力，1.7 亿受过高等教育和拥有技能的人才资源，超过 4 亿中等收入群体，1 亿多个市场主体，拥有无与伦比的市场规模、人才优势和发展活力。目前中国研发投入规模全球第二，2018 年科技进步贡献率达到 58.5%。上个月，世界银行发表《2020 营商环境报告》，中国营商环境排名由第 46 位大幅上升到第 31 位，提升了 15 位。

四是贡献多。中国经济不仅造福中国人民，也造福世界。新中国成立 70 年来，中国人民生活水平不断提高，人均国内生产总值按不变价计算增长 70 倍，人均预期寿命从 35 岁提升至 77 岁，累计 7 亿多人摆脱贫困，占全球减贫人口的 70% 以上。中国对世界经济增长的贡献率连续 13 年居世界第一，保持在 30% 左右，超过美、欧、日总和。中国提出“一带一路”倡议 6 年多来，累计向沿线国家投资超过 1 000 亿美元，为东道国创造税收 40.9 亿美元、就业岗位 36.7 万个。中国主动向世界开放市场，首创举办中国国际进口博览会。三天前刚刚闭幕的第二届中国国际进口博览会，累计意向成交 711.3 亿美元，比首届增长 23%。未来 15 年，中国进口商品和服务将分别超过 30 万亿美元和 10 万亿美元。

其次，我谈一谈中国经济发展将给中英、中欧合作带来什么机遇。

两周前，中共十九届四中全会成功召开，做出了关于坚持和完善中国特色社会主义制度、推进国家治理体系和治理能力现代化若干重大问题的决定，其中包括很多深化改革、扩大开放的重要举措。九天前，习近平主席在第二届中国国际进口博览会开幕式上发表重要讲话，全文 24 次提到“开放”，传递出的突出信息就是中国开放的大门只会越来越大，各国应共建开放合作、开放创新、开放共享的世界经济。

展望未来，中国将继续坚定不移地走中国特色社会主义道路，继续为世界和平、发展、繁荣、进步做出贡献。中国将坚持以开放促改革、促发展、促创新，推进更高水平的对外开放。我认为，“开放”是中国经济未来发展的鲜明主题词，“开放的中国”将给英国和欧洲带来“三大机遇”。

一是开放合作的机遇。面对经贸摩擦和矛盾，协商、合作才是正道。中英、中欧在维护多边主义、支持全球化等方面理念相通、利益相同，应共同维护多边贸易体制，反对保护主义，推动建设开放型世界经济。中国将进一步扩大市场开放，更加重视进口的作用，不断完善市场化、法治化、国际化的营商环境。《外商投资法》将于 2020 年 1 月 1 日起生效。中国金融业开放进程将进一步加快，包括全面取消在华外资银行、证券公司、基金管理公司等金融机构业务范围限制，扩大投资入股外资银行和外资保险机构的股东范围，允许外国保险集团公司投资设立保险类机构等，这些都将为中英、中欧金融合作提供新机遇和新空间。中国不断扩大对外开放，同时也希望其他国家秉持开放合作态度，为中国企业，包括华为这样的优秀企业，在当地投资兴业提供公平竞争和非歧视的投资环境，实现互利共赢。

二是开放创新的机遇。新一轮科技革命和产业变革的浪潮奔腾而至，将对人类生产模式、生活方式产生深刻影响。中英、中欧在科技创新上互有优势，要共同把握数字化、网络化、智能化等发展机遇，以更加开放的姿态激励创新，探索新的增长动能。新技术正在深刻改变金融业态，中英、中欧金融科技创新活跃，市场需求广阔，发展势头强劲，双方可以在区块链、普惠金融、绿色金融等领域加大创新合作力度，提升金融服务的广度、深度和质量，为双方经贸合作不断注入新动力。

三是开放共享的机遇。习近平主席指出，要“推动经济全球化朝着更加开放、包容、普惠、平衡、共赢的方向发展”。“一带一路”倡议已成为广受欢迎的国际公共产品和规模巨大的国际合作平台，也是推动经济全球化的新引擎。中国秉持共商共建共享原则，推动共建“一带一路”高质量发展。目前，中国已同137个国家和30个国际组织签署197份共建“一带一路”合作文件。中英、中欧可依托“一带一路”平台，在银行业、投融资、保险业、资产管理等领域加强合作，还可在第三方市场合作方面联手打造更多亮点，推动当地经济发展，促进民生改善，实现优势互补、互利共赢，更好地造福世界各国人民。一周前，中国在巴黎成功发行40亿欧元主权债券，昨天在伦敦证交所上市。这是中国15年以来第一次发行欧元主权债券，也是迄今为止中国政府单次发行最大规模的外币主权债券。这充分体现了中国对欧洲金融市场的重视，向国际市场特别是欧洲投资者传递了中国全方位高水平开放的信息，将进一步推动中欧深化金融合作，共享发展机遇。

女士们、先生们，

当前世界经济既面临机遇，也面临挑战。香港地区作为国际金融中心，是英国、法国及国际金融机构布局中国市场的重要基地。但近一段时期，香港地区接连不断的大规模违法暴力行径，已经将香港地区推到了极为危险的境地。特别是最近几日持续升级的暴力行径，极大地破坏了香港地区社会秩序与法治。暴徒的行为天理不容，我们对此予以最强烈的谴责。我们绝不能任由暴力在香港地区肆虐，坚决支持特区政府、香港警方和司法机关坚守法治原则，果断采取一切必要手段，强力遏制打击各种违法暴力行为和恐怖主义行径，尽快止暴制乱、恢复秩序，还香港地区以安定，还民众以安宁。我们希望包括英国、法国在内的国际社会能够认清香港地区事态本质，坚决谴责和反对暴力行径，多做有利于香港地区繁荣稳定的事情而非相反。我希望，英国、法国及欧洲金融界和工商界对香港地区保持信心，也希望得到你们的理解和支持，共同支持香港地区重现东方明珠的光彩。

中国有句古语，“明者因时而变，知者随事而制”。英国有句名言，“一个明智的人总是能抓住机遇，把它变成美好的未来”（A wise person always seizes the opportunity and turns it into a better future）。法国也有句格言，“抓住机遇，顺势前行”（il faut savoir profiter du vent arriere tant qu’il souffle dans la voile; you have to know how to take advantage of the backwind as long as it blows in the sail）。中国始终从战略高度重视发展中英、中欧关系。一个更加开放、更有活力、更具担当的中国，必将给包括英国、法国等在内的欧洲国家以及世界各国带来更多机遇。我希望，在座工商界朋友们记住我们先哲的名言，坚定信心，抓住机遇，加强合作，为中英、中欧关系发展打造更多积极成果，为世界经济发展开创更加美好的未来。

谢谢！

现在我愿回答大家的提问。

Share the Opportunities of China and Join Hands to Create a Better Future *

Mr. Alain Papiasse,

Mrs. Anne Verstraeten,

Ladies and Gentlemen,

Good afternoon!

It is a real delight to join you at the Global Markets Conference 2019 held by BNP Paribas. This Conference is highly timely as it focuses on the global financial market and explore opportunities for future development.

I was asked by the Conference to talk about China's economy. So, I would like to share with you my thoughts about China's economic prospect and how to seize the opportunities that China has to offer.

First, how shall we view China's economic prospect?

The world is now undergoing profound changes unseen in a century. What choice we make between openness and isolation, between cooperation and confrontation, between win-win and zero-sum games will determine the direction of world economic development.

Due to the surging protectionism and rising uncertainties and instabilities in the world economy, the IMF forecast for growth this year is only 3%, the lowest since the international financial crisis in 2008.

Against this backdrop, China's economy, the world's second largest, has withstood

---

* Keynote Speech at the Global Markets Conference 2019 Held by BNP Paribas. St. Pancras Renaissance Hotel, London, 14 November 2019.

the test of storms and maintained a steadily growing momentum. In my opinion, there are four highlights in China's economy.

The first highlight is steady growth.

China's economy has enjoyed rapid growth at an average rate of 9.4% for 40 years since the beginning of reform and opening-up. In the first three quarters of this year,

- China's GDP reached about 10 trillion dollars, increasing by 6.2% year on year. That was one of the fastest among major economies in the world.
- Close to 11 million jobs were created, and average disposable income increased by 6.1% in real terms. Economic growth has brought tangible benefits and given our people a strong sense of achievement.
- Paid-in foreign investment exceeded 100 billion dollars, increasing by 6.5% year on year. On average, more than 100 foreign-owned companies are opened in China every day.

The second highlight is high quality.

The quality of China's economic growth has been improved.

- Domestic demand has become the primary driving force for economic growth. In the first three quarters of this year, final consumption contributed 60.5% of economic growth.
- Economic growth generates more jobs. It is estimated that every one percentage point of GDP growth creates about 2.06 million new jobs. That is twice the figure ten years ago.

China's economic growth has also been greener. President Xi Jinping said, "Clear waters and green mountains are as valuable as mountains of gold and silver." China has achieved remarkable success in green development.

- In 2018, China's carbon intensity dropped by 45.8% compared with 2005.
- Energy consumption per capita GDP has been brought down by 20.3% in the past five years.

- The use of coal has been cut down to an unprecedented level of less than 60% of overall energy consumption.
- China is now the world's largest investor in renewable energy.

The third highlight is huge potential.

President Xi Jinping said, "The Chinese economy is not a pond, but an ocean."

China has:

- close to 1.4 billion people,
- 900 million workforce,
- 170 million well-educated and skilled talent pool,
- more than 400 million middle-income earners,
- and more than 100 million market entities.

These mean a huge market, a high-quality talent pool and tremendous vitality.

China ranks second in the world in terms of R&D expenditure. In 2018, scientific and technological progress contributed 58.5% of economic growth. According to the World Bank's Doing Business 2020 report released last month, China's "ease of doing business" ranking has risen from 46 to 31.

The fourth highlight is great contribution.

China's economy has benefited people from both China and beyond.

In the past 70 years since the founding of the People's Republic of China,

- Chinese people's living standard has kept improving.
- Per capita GDP has grown by 70 times in real terms.
- Average life expectancy has increased from 35 to 77.
- More than 700 million people have been lifted out of poverty, which accounts for more than 70% of the global poverty reduction.

At the same time,

- China has contributed about 30% of world economic growth, ranking first for 13 years in a row and more than the US, the EU and Japan combined.

- In the past six years since the Belt and Road Initiative was proposed, China has invested more than 100 billion dollars in countries along the routes, added 4.09 billion dollars to the tax revenue of host countries, and created 367,000 jobs for local communities.
- China has taken the initiative to open its market to the world by way of but not limited to the China International Import Expo (CIIE). At the second CIIE concluded three days ago, 71.13 billion dollars worth of purchasing deals were initialed. That was 23% more than the deals signed during the first CIIE a year ago.
- In the next 15 years, China is expected to import more than 30 trillion dollars of goods and more than 10 trillion dollars of services.

Now I would like to talk about the opportunities that China's growth will create for China-UK and China-EU cooperation.

Two weeks ago, the fourth plenary session of the 19th Central Committee of the Communist Party of China was successfully held. The session adopted the decision on major issues concerning upholding and improving the system of socialism with Chinese characteristics and advancing the modernisation of China's system and capacity for governance. This decision rolls out a number of important measures for deeper reform and further opening-up.

At the opening ceremony of the second CIIE nine days ago, President Xi Jinping delivered an important speech. Opening-up was mentioned 24 times in his speech, which sent a loud and clear message that China will open its door wider to the world. It also calls on all the countries to work together and build an open world economy through cooperation, with innovation and for mutual benefit.

Going forward, China will remain committed to the path of socialism with Chinese characteristics, and continue to contribute to world peace, development, prosperity and progress. China will also promote reform, development and innovation through a higher level of opening-up.

I would say that opening-up is the key word for China's economic development in the future. An open China will create three important opportunities for the UK and the EU.

The first opportunity comes from open cooperation.

Consultation and cooperation are the right way to address frictions and differences over trade. China, the UK and the EU have the same belief and common interests in safeguarding multilateralism and supporting globalisation. It is important that we join hands to uphold the multilateral trade system, oppose protectionism, and promote the building of an open world economy.

China will open its market wider, put more emphasis on import, and foster a market-oriented and law-based business environment that is in line with international practice. The Foreign Investment Law will come into force on 1st January 2020. The opening-up of the financial sector will be accelerated.

- China will abolish completely the business scope restrictions on foreign financial institutions in China such as banks, securities firms and fund management companies.
- China will remove the limits on investment and shareholding in foreign banks and insurance institutions.
- And China will allow foreign insurance groups to set up insurance institutions.

All these will create new opportunities and open new space for China-UK and China-EU financial cooperation.

As China continues to open its market wider, we hope that other countries will, likewise, adopt an open attitude on cooperation, and foster a fair and non-discriminatory environment for Chinese companies, such as Huawei, to do business there. This will contribute to win-win results.

The second opportunity arises from innovation.

The surging waves of a new round of scientific and technological revolution and industrial transformation will have a deep impact on the production models and life style of mankind.

China, the UK and the EU have respective advantages in science, technology and innovation. We should work together to seize the opportunities brought by the wide application of digital technology, Internet and smart technology. We should embrace innovation with a more open attitude and explore new driving forces for growth.

New technologies are also bringing deeper changes to the financial sector. China, the UK and the EU are active in FinTech innovation. We all have a huge market and a strong growth momentum in this area. We could enhance cooperation on innovation in blockchain, inclusive finance and green finance. This could improve the scope, depth and quality of our financial services, and boost our cooperation on economy and trade.

The third opportunity comes from shared development.

President Xi Jinping said that we should work to ensure a more open, inclusive, balanced and win-win globalisation. To this end, China proposed the Belt and Road Initiative (BRI). It has now become a popular public good for the world and a huge platform for international cooperation. It has also given a new impetus to economic globalisation.

In building BRI, China follows the principles of extensive consultation, joint contribution and shared benefit. It is now pursuing high-quality BRI development. As we speak, China has signed 197 documents on jointly building BRI with 137 countries and 30 international organisations.

China, the UK and the EU could enhance cooperation on BRI in the areas of banking, investment, financing, insurance and asset management. We could also work together to promote cooperation on projects in third markets, so as to promote the economic growth and improve people's life in host countries. This could enable us to match our comparative strengths, achieve win-win results, and deliver more benefits to the people of all the countries in the world.

A week ago, the Chinese government issued 4-billion-Euro-denominated sovereign bond in Paris. I am glad it was listed on the London Stock Exchange yesterday.

This is the first issue of Euro-denominated Chinese sovereign bond in 15 years. It is also the largest-ever single issue of foreign-currency-denominated sovereign bond by the Chinese government.

This reflects the importance China attaches to the European financial market. It sends a clear message to the international market, especially to European investors, that China will open up at a higher level on all fronts. And China will continue to deepen financial cooperation and share development opportunities with the EU.

Ladies and Gentlemen,

The world economy is facing opportunities as well as challenges. Hong Kong, as an international financial centre, is an important base from where many British, French and international financial institutions go on to explore the Chinese market. However, the incessant large-scale illegal violent activities over recent months have pushed Hong Kong into an extremely dangerous situation. In particular, the recent escalation of violence has dealt a severe blow to the public order and rule of law in this city.

The acts of the rioters are absolutely intolerable and deserve the strongest condemnation. Such violence should not be allowed to continue. The Government of the Hong Kong Special Administrative Region, the Hong Kong police and judicial institutions should be given strong and complete support in upholding rule of law, and taking all necessary, decisive and forceful measures to curb and combat all types of illegal, violent and terrorist activities. We firmly support them in ending violence and restoring order as soon as possible so as to restore stability in Hong Kong and tranquility for the people.

It is our hope that the international community, including the UK, France and the EU, will have a clear understanding of the nature of the current situation in Hong Kong, firmly condemn and oppose violence, and do more things that are conducive to the prosperity and stability in Hong Kong.

I hope that the financial and business community in the UK, France and other European countries will have confidence in Hong Kong. I hope, with your understanding and support, Hong Kong, this oriental pearl, will once again shine brightly.

Ladies and Gentlemen,

China always approaches China-UK and China-EU relations from the strategic perspective and attaches great importance to these relations.

China will be more open.

China will continue to grow vigorously.

China is a responsible member of the international community.

China will create more opportunities for all the countries in the world, including the UK, France and other European countries.

An adage in China goes, "A wise man changes as time and event change." British people often say, "A wise person always seizes the opportunity and turns it into a better future." I learnt there is a similar saying in France, which goes, "You have to know how to take advantage of the backwind as long as it blows in the sail." (*Il faut savoir profiter du vent arriere tant qu'il souffle dans la voile.*)

The wise men of all our countries have taught us to seize the opportunities. So, I hope the business leaders present today will follow this advice, shore up confidence and enhance cooperation. I am sure you will work for more productive China-UK and China-EU relations, and create a better future for the development of the world economy.

Thank you!

Now, I would like to take your questions.

后 记

我离任回国后，一些党政机关、高校、智库请我作报告，谈“讲好中国故事”的经验和体会。我总结了“五种意识”和“十种能力”。

一是增强政治意识。要深刻认识“讲好中国故事”关系到为实现中华民族伟大复兴营造有利的外部舆论环境。习近平总书记说，我们党带领人民经过不懈奋斗，基本解决了“挨打”“挨饿”问题，但“挨骂”问题还没有得到根本解决。解决了“挨打”问题，使中国人民站起来；解决了“挨饿”问题，使中国人民富起来；还没有根本解决“挨骂”问题，说明我们国家仍处于由富转强、将强未强时期。要实现中华民族从站起来、富起来到强起来的伟大飞跃，必须解决“挨骂”问题。换句话说，解决“挨骂”问题将伴随从站起来、富起来到强起来的全过程。这充分说明解决“挨骂”问题的长期性和艰巨性，也说明“讲好中国故事”的重要性和必要性。

二是增强责任意识。习近平总书记说，各级领导干部要主动去做国际传播工作，主要负责人既要亲自抓，也要亲自做。使英 11 年，我始终牢记使命在身、责任在肩，把“讲好中国故事”作为自己第一责任。面对挑衅攻击，毫不畏惧，挺身而出。第一时间发声，揭穿谣言，澄清事实，说明真相，批驳谬论，维护国家形象和尊严。

三是增强主人翁意识。讲中国故事，不只是领导的事，也不只是外交官的事，而是每一个中国人的事。每个中国人到了国外，不论你做什么，旅游、经商、留学，都是中国的形象代言人，外国民众期待从你那了解中国的情况，听到中国的故事。遇到抹黑中国的情况，每个中国人都有义不容辞的责任站出来说话，维护国家的尊严。出使英国期间，我除了要求使馆外交官外，还鼓励中国企业家、留学生、学者、记者多与英国民众交流，讲中国的故事，讲家乡的变化，使英国民众了解一个真实、立体、全面的中国。

四是增强斗争意识。习近平总书记指出，中华民族伟大复兴不是轻轻松松、敲锣打鼓就能实现的，实现伟大梦想必须进行伟大斗争。在百年变局和世纪疫情叠加的背景下，国际舆论斗争更加尖锐复杂。个别西方国家对我们实施全面打压、遏制，捏造各种谎言抹黑我们，妖魔化、污名化的手法无所不用其极。我们必须针锋相对地进行斗争，维护国家的利益和尊严。

五是增强大局意识。胸怀国内国外两个大局，学深悟透党中央大政方针，特别是习近平新时代中国特色社会主义思想和习近平外交思想，把握国内改革发展大局和外交工作全局，这是“讲好中国故事”的前提。

增强“五种意识”，还要提高“十种能力”，即政治判断能力、公共外交能力、调研能力、交友能力、利用外国主流媒体能力、备战能力、沟通能力、应变能力、外语能力、学习能力。

本书收录了我使英 11 年发表 700 次演讲中的 35 篇，这期间中国和世界都发生了很大变化。由于演讲时间跨度长，现在读起来会感到有些故事时过境迁，有些认识有待提高，这正说明“讲好中国故事”是一个不断深化和发展的过程，“五种意识”和“十种能力”也有一个不断增强和提高的过程，说明“讲好中国故事”只有进行时，没有完成时。

在此，我要感谢陈雯、王起、曾嵘、冯家亮、王小晶等同志，他们参与了本书的审核、校对、联络等工作。我还要感谢中信出版集团董事长王斌、灰犀牛分社总编黄静和她的团队，他们为本书的出版付出了大量心血，其敬业精神给我留下深刻印象。

最后，我要特别感谢为本书写推荐语的英国朋友。他们中有前内阁大臣、议员，有著名企业家、金融家、科学家，有知名学者、大学教授，有公爵、男爵、勋爵。从他们的评语中，我感受到他们对中英关系的支持和对中英合作的期盼，更感到“讲好中国故事”的意义和影响。可以说，他们的推荐语是对“讲好中国故事”最好的诠释。

2022 年立冬